HENRY JAMES AND REVISION

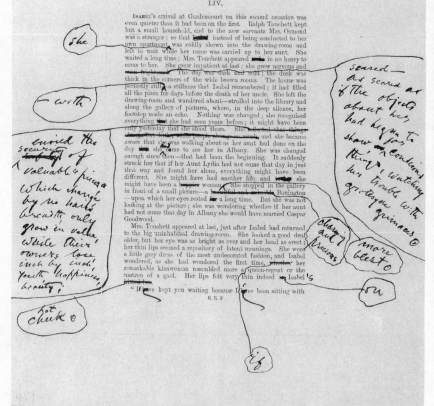

A sheet showing James's 1906 manuscript revision of *The Portrait of a Lady*, using pasted-up pages from the 1882 Macmillan one-volume edition. The passage and its revisions are discussed on p. 224.

HENRY JAMES
AND REVISION

The New York Edition

PHILIP HORNE

CLARENDON PRESS · OXFORD
1990

Oxford University Press, Walton Street, Oxford OX2 6DP

Oxford New York Toronto
Delhi Bombay Calcutta Madras Karachi
Petaling Jaya Singapore Hong Kong Tokyo
Nairobi Dar es Salaam Cape Town
Melbourne Auckland
and associated companies in
Berlin Ibadan

Oxford is a trade mark of Oxford University Press

Published in the United States
by Oxford University Press, New York

British Library Cataloguing in Publication Data

Horne, Philip
Henry James and revision: the New York edition.
1. Fiction in English. American writers. James, Henry
1843–1916
I. Title
813.4

ISBN 0–19–812871–1

Library of Congress Cataloging in Publication Data

Horne, Philip.
Henry James and revision: the New York edition/Philip Horne.
p. cm.
Includes bibliographical references.
1. James, Henry, 1843–1916—Technique. 2. James, Henry,
1843–1916—Criticism, Textual. 3. Editing—History—20th century.
I. Title.
PS2127.T4H67 1990 813'.4—dc20 90-34110
ISBN 0–19–812871–1

Typeset by Butler & Tanner Ltd, Frome
Printed and bound in
Great Britain by Bookcraft Ltd
Midsomer Norton, Bath

Preface

The opening three chapters are introductory. The first is biographical: an account of the New York Edition and its troubled history. The second is more general, dealing with the predicament of the reviser—the writer caught between the fear of not finishing and the fear of spoiling. The third examines the conditions on which James can feel confident about revising, and the connections between his writing about revision in the Prefaces and his literary practices elsewhere.

The fourth, fifth, and sixth chapters deal with the revision of major novels. That on *Roderick Hudson* discusses the continuities between the beginning and the later phase of James's career, and carries on the concerns from the third chapter about the conditions which are necessary to successful creative activity. That on *The American* attends to the detail of James's practice in revising and compares it with his descriptions of the process in the Prefaces. That on *The Portrait of a Lady* considers the novel's transitional status, and reflects on Isabel Archer as a revision of Minny Temple.

The seventh, eighth, and ninth chapters find their subjects in novellas—works whose comparative brevity allows their revisions to be treated more comprehensively. In each case the chapter discusses the relation between the revisions and the handling of point of view, and the way in which they suggest the story is to be read. *Daisy Miller* and *The Aspern Papers* both recount the failure of a male hero to understand a situation and a woman: the focus of these chapters is on the specific effects compassed by the third-person narration of the former and the first-person narration of the latter. *The Lesson of the Master* is treated as a variation on *Roderick Hudson*, a meditation on the risk to life that for James is involved in an artistic career.

The final chapter tells of what may be called the end of James's personal relationship with language—his old age and death.

An appendix provides a chronology of the period during which James was concerned with the New York Edition, bringing together mostly unpublished material from a number of sources to suggest the scale and context of his activity as a reviser.

The book has a generally chronological movement, and much of it has a biographical aspect, in that it is devoted to eliciting James's feelings about his life as a writer and the life of his writing. Katherine McClellan's 1905 photograph of James in Northampton, Massachusetts, which appears on the cover, shows him curiously inspecting his own pen as he holds it, already in motion, over the page. It could stand as an emblem for this book, which itself looks closely at the movements of James's pen.

Acknowledgements

Over the long period it has taken for this book to be completed I have incurred debts of gratitude to many individuals and institutions. I am glad to be able to express my thanks, for help, advice, hospitality, encouragement, and support, to the following, several of whom have read and commented on portions of it: Judith Aronson, Rodney Dennis, Howard Erskine-Hill, Pat and Lux Feininger, Tamara Follini, Philip Gaskell, Jean and Richard Gooder, Eric Griffiths, Judith Hawley, Julian Hoppit and Karin Horowitz, Pico Iyer, Dan Jacobson, Robert Jones, Danny Karlin, Siobhan Kilfeather, Jonathan Lear and Cynthia Farrar, Karl Miller, Alastair Morgan, S. Gorley Putt, Neil Rennie, Bernard Richards, David and Katy Ricks, Peter Robinson and Rosemary Laxton, David Sexton, Adam Strevens, Peter Swaab, Lindsey Traub, David Trotter, Keith Walker, and Henry Woudhuysen. The research on which much of it is based could not have been undertaken without initial support from the Department of Education and Science, then an Allen scholarship from Cambridge University and a Research Fellowship at Christ's College, Cambridge. I have also been greatly assisted by research grants from Jesus College, Cambridge, Christ's College, Cambridge, the British Academy, and University College London. I am grateful too for the helpfulness and courtesy of staff at the Bancroft Library at Berkeley, the Beinecke Library at Yale, the Bodleian Library, the British Library, the Cambridge University Library, the Firestone Library at Princeton, the Houghton Library in Harvard, the Huntington Library in Pasadena, and the New York Public Library (Berg Collection). I owe acknowledgements for permissions to the Bancroft Library, University of California, Berkeley; to the Beinecke Library, Yale University; to the Henry W. and Albert A. Berg Collection in the New York Public Library; to the Firestone Library, Princeton University; to the Houghton Library, Harvard University; to Charles Scribner and Sons for permission to use material in the Scribner archive at Princeton; to the library of Smith College, Northampton, Massachusetts, for permission to use the photograph of James by Katherine McClellan reproduced on the cover; to the Houghton Library, for permission to reproduce as the frontispiece a page of the manuscript revision of *The Portrait of a Lady*; and above all to Alexander James, who has kindly granted permission for much unpublished copyright material to be quoted. Part of Chapter 6 appeared in an article in the *Journal of American Studies*, to which I am grateful for permission to reprint it here. I have special debts to my thesis supervisor, Adrian Poole; to Sylvia Sylvester, the Fellows' Secretary at Christ's College, Cambridge; to Kim Scott Walwyn, my patient editor; and to Christopher Ricks. The book is dedicated to my parents.

P. H.
University College London

Contents

Note on Texts and Abbreviations

There is much quotation in this book, and for economy of reference abbreviations are used for the works most cited. The distinction between short story, novella, and novel is nebulous in James's case, and may mislead: I therefore give the titles of all James's fictions in italic, with the single exception of inverted commas for 'The Middle Years', the story of 1893, to distinguish it from the posthumous volume of autobiography with the same name. I refer to certain early texts of works by their dates (e.g. *1882*) to distinguish them from the revised texts of the New York Edition (*NYE*); in the case where several early texts date from the same year (1883) the context makes clear which is meant.

We know from surviving manuscripts in the Houghton Library which text and edition James revised from for the *NYE* of *The American* and *The Portrait of a Lady*; printed pages from each book are pasted on to larger sheets and the margins filled with alternative readings in his handwriting. For *Roderick Hudson* he seems likely to have used not the 1876 or 1879 editions, but, as with *The American*, the Macmillan Collected Edition of 1883. He thanked his agent Pinker for 'the admirable pasting-up job' done on *Roderick Hudson* as well as *The American*; which strengthens the likelihood that the same edition was used for both. When I collated sample sections of the 1879 (revised from 1876) London edition of *Roderick Hudson* with the 1883 Collected Edition—which is very similar—21 of the 1883 readings were reproduced in the *NYE*, as against 6 of those from the 1879 text. Since the variants are often matters of punctuation, to which James gave scrupulous care in revising for the *NYE*, this cannot be taken as clear evidence, but I have treated it as suggesting the probable early text he used, and accordingly given references to *1883*.

With *Daisy Miller*, collating 71 pages of the text of the 1879 first edition against the 1883 Collected Edition produced yet more doubtful results. In 9 places where there were variant readings the *NYE* introduced quite new material. Otherwise, it followed *1883* in 12 places and *1879* in 5—which again suggests *1883* as James's copy-text, but not very decisively.

As a later work, *The Aspern Papers* seems most likely to have been revised from its first book edition in two volumes of 1888; and *The Lesson of the Master* from that in one volume of 1892. I have given references to these editions.

I have come across at a late stage one other extant set of manuscript revisions, not dealt with in this book: James's rough pencilled marginal jottings in a two-volume copy of *The Tragic Muse*, most of which are incorporated verbatim into the NYE. The book is in the Beinecke Library at Yale (*2a/J233/890d); it is an 1892 impression of the 1890 Houghton, Mifflin and Co. American first edition (A34).

Biblical references are to the Authorized Version, Shakespeare references to the 1987 Oxford edition by Stanley Wells and Gary Taylor.

The numbers in brackets in the following list are those in Leon Edel and Dan H. Laurence, *A Bibliography of Henry James* (The Soho Bibliographies, viii), 3rd edn., revised with the assistance of James Rambeau, Oxford, 1982.

AS   Henry James, *The American Scene*, London, 1907 (A63a).
Autobiog. Henry James, *Autobiography*, ed. F. W. Dupee, New York, 1956; repr. Princeton, 1983: consists of *A Small Boy and Others* (1913), *Notes of a Son and Brother* (1914) and *The Middle Years* (1917).
CHEP ii   *Œuvres Complètes de Honoré de Balzac: La Comédie Humaine: Études Philosophiques*, ii, texte révisé et annoté par Marcel Bouteron et Henri Longnon, Paris, 1925.
EH   Henry James, *English Hours*, Boston, 1905 (A62a).
GB   Henry James, *The Golden Bowl*, London, 1905 (A60b).
HJL   *Henry James Letters*, ed. Leon Edel, 4 vols., Cambridge, Mass., 1974–84 (C175).
HMS   Harvard MS of *The American* revision for the NYE, reproduced in *Henry James: 'The American': The version of 1877 revised in autograph and typescript for the New York Edition of 1907, reproduced in facsimile from the original in the Houghton Library, Harvard University*, with an introduction by Rodney G. Dennis, London, 1976 (A106).
IH   Henry James, *Italian Hours*, London, 1909 (A67a).
LC   Henry James, *Literary Criticism*, ed. Leon Edel and Mark Wilson, 2 vols., New York and Cambridge, 1984.
LHJ   *The Letters of Henry James*, ed. Percy Lubbock, 2 vols., New York, 1920 (C4b).
Nks.   *The Complete Notebooks of Henry James*, ed. Leon Edel and Lyall H. Powers, New York and Oxford, 1987.
NYE   *The New York Edition of the Novels and Tales of Henry James*, 24 vols., New York and London, 1907–9 (A64a and A64c).
Rev.   *The Reverberator*, 2 vols., London, 1888 (A31a).
THJ   *The Tales of Henry James*, ed. Maqbool Aziz, 3 vols. (5 still forthcoming), Oxford, 1973 to date.
TS   Henry James, *Transatlantic Sketches*, Boston, 1875 (A2a).
W.o.D.   Henry James, *The Wings of the Dove*, London, 1902 (A56b).

I

The New York Edition

i. An Expensive Job

On 13 October 1908 Henry James wrote to his agent James Brand Pinker that he had called on Macmillans to obtain copies of two of the works in their English issue of the New York Edition of his Novels and Tales, and had been made to pay for them. Frederick Macmillan was buying sheets from Charles Scribner and felt he must charge the author cost price. James ruefully commented that 'It all adds to my sense of literature being for me, somehow, ever only an *expensive* job.'[1] Seven days later this mild ironic surprise was followed by a severe shock: the first really clear statement from Scribners of how little money he was to make from his 'long & devoted labour'. The news, he told Pinker, was 'a bitter grief'.[2]

On 2 November he wrote with a little more cheerfulness to his cousin 'Bay', Ellen Emmet Rand, explaining his protracted failure to correspond as a consequence of the edition's 'abysmal traps to labour, to ingenuity, and, above all, to *time*'; it

> was to prove so much more exhausting and overwhelming a business than I had conceived in advance that my only way through it, I had early to recognise, was to sit tight, [and] neglect everything else ... I am just *now* only out of the wood, rather spent and sore, but the Edition a reality and an honour (though I say it who shouldn't)—only rather expensive in its multitude, with its beauty, and at its cost, alas, to chuck about much, in complimentary fashion (*HJL* iv. 499).[3]

Such mixed feelings—of being spent, but in the accomplishment of something real, and sore, but in achieving honour—suggest James's sense that the unremunerativeness of the 'business' left him having made more of a sacrifice than he had anticipated—though one he

---

[1] HJ to Pinker, 13 Oct. 1908 (Yale MS).

[2] HJ to Pinker, 20 Oct. 1908 (Yale MS) (quoted in Michael Anesko, '*Friction with the Market*', Oxford, 1986, p. 162).

[3] In fact William's widow Alice gave the *NYE* to Bay Emmet as a wedding present in 1911; HJ getting an author's discount of 25%, so that the whole set cost $36 (HJ to Alice H. James, 7 Apr. 1911, Harvard MS).

could not quite regret having made. The loss incurred financially was all the more painful in that it registered in cash terms a failure of public appreciation of the art which had gone into the edition.

In April of 1908, even before the bad news came, James was writing of the *NYE* to Frederick Macmillan (who did not until June make his proposal to take on the English issue) that it was worth doing but costly. The project 'has proved a task of the most arduous sort', he wrote, 'such as I can't but be glad of, but such as I at the same time wouldn't have had the courage to undertake had I measured all the job was to cost me'.[4] When in October the cost *had* been dismayingly measured, James's April image of oppressive cosiness—'The Edition has smothered me . . . like an enormous feather-bed'[5]—turned deadlier, evoking a beast of the jungle: 'like the convolutions of a vast smothering boa-constrictor, such voluminosities of Proof—of the Edition—to be carefully read—still keep rolling in' (*LHJ* ii. 107).

The numb gloom into which he was plunged by this shock was compounded by another: on 14 December 1908 he had to answer a letter from Scribners informing him that his volumes of tales, to which he had already composed Prefaces, were uneconomically long, and that the carefully sorted and ordered groupings would have to be 'mechanically' redistributed. At first this was just too much to bear: 'the charm is at the best considerably broken, and I don't, so to speak, much care what happens!', he began by claiming. But then his letter picks up and keeps going for pages of detail, stoically and responsibly adjusting the plan, working out how to 'furbish up something!'[6]

All this gives a context to the last sentence of the *Golden Bowl* Preface, probably written early in 1909 and certainly written under some stress,[7] where 'care' is 'nothing if not active' and 'finish' is 'nothing if not consistent' (*LC* ii. 1341). We can see his pain at the Scribners' pieces of bad news as sharpened by his knowledge that *he* has, really, none of the 'licence of disconnexion and disavowal' (*LC* ii. 1340) he there attributes to some authors, but is one of those committed, however ridden by contingencies, to active care and con-

---

[4] HJ to Macmillan, 5 Apr. 1908 (*Letters to Macmillan*, selected and edited by Simon Nowell-Smith, London, 1967, p. 173).

[5] *Letters to Macmillan*, p. 174.

[6] HJ to Scribners, 14 Dec. 1908 (Princeton TS).

[7] In a card sent to Scribners on 8 Mar. 1909 he describes the *Golden Bowl* Preface as 'written these many weeks', adding that 'I am making an alteration in it' (Princeton MS).

sistent finish. This consciousness of authorial commitment gives the edge of exasperation to his outbreak to Howells on 23 July 1909: 'What a monstrously and brutally stupid race is the avid and purblind one of Publishers, who never seem dimly to guess that authors can't to advantage be worked like ice-cream freezers or mowing-machines ...'.[8] In fact Scribners had James's (financial rather than artistic) interests at heart, as well as their own, in changing the volume arrangement. This does not diminish, however, the heroism of James's persistence with the *NYE*, at a time when royalties were so reduced. He finds himself going on at his own expense; and, courageously, hangs the expense.

Michael Anesko in his fine book on James's *Friction with the Market* gives an excellent account of the difficulties with the arrangement and preparation of the *NYE* in the context of a particularly unstable Anglo-American publishing scene. He makes a vigorous and salutary presentation, backed by painstaking research, of James's compromises in the market-place, his relative astuteness as a maker of deals. This view of James's business capacity should be seen as an emphasis which helps put his art in perspective, but it should not be allowed to reduce the primacy of his art over his commercial shrewdness for us or for him. James's art was not entirely at his own disposition for commercial use; it frequently and unpredictably required more space or more time than the market would easily afford him. The market is a necessary fact with which his art has to come to terms, and from which it has to obtain terms; James's constant effort is to reconcile the diverging insistences of these two kinds of value.

The *NYE* was certainly undertaken for money, though not only for money. In 1911 James wrote to Edith Wharton of 'my Edition, on which I had counted for the bread of my vieux jours'.[9] And on 30 January 1908, to W. E. Norris, another confrère, he devoutly wished that 'it *may* make a little money for me—the consummation sordidly aimed at'.[10] Its failure to make money, on the scale which would have been necessary to justify his long interruption of what Scribners' bad news made him call 'out-&-out "creative" work' (*HJL* iv. 498), was

---

[8] In this letter to W. D. Howells, 23 July 1909 (Harvard MS), James recommends him not to undertake Prefaces to his works: 'I found mine—of much scanter number—an almost insurmountable grind toward the end'.

[9] HJ to Edith Wharton, 20 Dec. 1911 (quoted in Millicent Bell, *Edith Wharton and Henry James: The Story of their Friendship*, London, 1966, p. 167).

[10] HJ to W. E. Norris, 30 Jan. 1908 (Lubbock TS, Harvard).

not clearly foreseen by any of the parties involved: the extraordinary complicatedness of the arrangements, between James in Rye, Pinker in London, Scribners in New York and Houghton, Mifflin in Boston (who as copyright-holders of some books insisted on printing the whole Edition), prevented this outcome from being anticipated before it so shatteringly came out. From the guilty and solicitous tone of the letters between Pinker and Scribner after the disappointment, moreover, one can surmise that as decent businessmen they felt responsible for allowing James to sink so much time and energy in an unpaying enterprise without giving him due warning of the dangers. James's letters at the crisis suggest that he may have felt subtly betrayed, pointing out that 'in the absence of special warning' he had been permitting himself to expect 'some probable fair return' (*HJL* iv. 498). It is likely that he had felt his agent and publisher would protect him from working for nothing; *his* business, with Pinker deputed to negotiate and hustle, was more purely literary. Conrad, another client, testified to Pinker's value, in a letter to James, as the INP, 'the Imperatively Necessary Pinker'.[11] In 1906, while Pinker was efficiently seeing off the mendacious Chicago publisher Herbert Stone, who had obstructively claimed indefinite rights over *In the Cage* and *What Maisie Knew*, James had written him that 'You came in—after that "Maisie" time—none too soon to save my life!'[12] James was more upset by the *NYE* disappointment because Pinker had been so reliable since May 1898: a reliability for which his ten per cent had seemed to James a fair payment.

It was a couple of years after Pinker had thus come in to save James that he received a politely enquiring telegram from E. C. Burlingame of Scribners, sent on 2 April 1900: 'Would You Care on any terms to arrange for Collected Edition Henry James | Burlingame'.[13] Pinker's reply, pencilled at the bottom, was 'Disposed Consider James'. The disposition lay dormant while *The Ambassadors*, *The Wings of the Dove*, and *The Golden Bowl* increased the size of the potential collection; then in August 1904 James sailed to his native land to gather impressions for *The American Scene*, and Pinker contacted Burlingame to revive the proposal.[14] On 14 September James wrote to Pinker from the lakeside house of his brother William at Chocorua that there

---

[11] Joseph Conrad to HJ, 20 Sept. 1907 (Harvard MS).
[12] HJ to Pinker, 27 Mar. 1906, from Reform Club (Yale MS).
[13] E. C. Burlingame (of Scribners) to Pinker, 2 Apr. 1900 (Princeton MS telegram).
[14] As Maqbool Aziz shows in *The Tales of Henry James*, vol. ii, Oxford, 1978, p. liv.

seemed no urgency about 'the matter of the Collective Edition', for which Pinker was thinking of crossing the Atlantic. 'It strikes me that the Collective Edition may perhaps be discussed better after I have been here six months than sooner' (*HJL* iv. 323). On 2 March 1905 he wrote again, just back from the South and about to head West, to the effect that his hands were full with *The American Scene* and that no other projects than the Collective Edition required Pinker's presence.[15] He was to sail home in the Cunard *Saxonia* on Independence Day 1905. On 11 May he wrote again to Pinker from New York with more keenness: 'I shall feel some regret, I think, if I shall have left the country without the question of my collective Edition having in any degree been started, or the ground sounded for it. I feel quite helpless, myself, as regards soundings, & it is moreover a question on which there is much to be said . . .'[16]

Pinker arrived in New York on or shortly after Tuesday 6 June 1905, while James was booked to be out of town lecturing at Bryn Mawr and Baltimore; but a letter was left for him by the author at the 'Cambridge' hotel so he could get started on negotiations. James had a few memoranda to convey.

Only remember, please, that my idea is a Handsome Book, distinctly, not less so than the definitive RLS, or the ditto GM; and also that I have made up my mind not to let it include absolutely *everything*. It is best, I think, that it should be selective as well as collective; I want to quietly disown a few things by not thus supremely adopting them. Likewise I cherish the idea of the *Scribners'*, preferentially; there is another firm we wot of, the idea of which I rather *don't* cherish.[17]

He returned from Philadelphia on Tuesday 13 June. His agent evidently had a busy and a tricky time.[18] On 25 June 1905 James wrote from

---

[15] HJ to Pinker, 2 Mar. 1905, from Cambridge, Mass. (Yale TS).

[16] HJ to Pinker, 11 May 1905, from New York (Yale MS).

[17] HJ to Pinker, 6 June 1905, from New York (Yale TS; 'rather' is an afterthought in MS, as is the underlining of '*don't*'). The other firm is pretty certainly Harper's; the Stevenson and Meredith editions had been brought out by Scribners (whose Kipling was a model he mentioned more often).

[18] He tried to negotiate, for instance, a £100 payment from Scribners to Macmillan—not chargeable to James's royalty account—for permission to use certain of the author's works (George P. Brett of Macmillan wrote that the sum 'represents the loss to us on our ledgers up to this time on our publication of these works by Mr. James' (Macmillan (New York) to Pinker, 21 June 1905 (Princeton TS)). Some problem came up about the terms, though; on 7 Feb. 1906 Pinker was proposing to Scribners on HJ's suggestion that 'on the Macmillan novels you should pay 2½% more royalty until the extra royalty equalled the payment to Macmillans' (Princeton TS).

Cambridge, Massachusetts, to Pinker, who was by then sailing back to England, to say 'how sorry I am for the up-hill moments, in New York, that you found yourself again condemned to. You will tell me more about them, and I shall feel but the more obliged to you for having successfully dealt with them.'[19] According to James's friend Elizabeth Robins, the actress and author, who accompanied him on the voyage back to England (made, in the event, not on the *Saxonia* but on the later-torpedoed *Ivernia*), 'he did not stick very closely to his revision of "Roderick Hudson" '.[20] He was thus at least launched by early in July.

On 30 July, back in the fold at Lamb House, he sent a copious memorandum to the Scribners about the Edition, determining the title for the set:

I should particularly like to call it the New York Edition if that may pass for a general title of sufficient dignity and distinctness. My feeling about the matter is that it refers the whole enterprise explicitly to my native city—to which I have had no great opportunity of rendering that sort of homage (*HJL* iv. 368).

He mentioned at the same time that 'the revision, the re-manipulation, as I may call it, of *The American* and *Roderick Hudson* is demanding of me, I find, extreme (and very interesting) deliberation'. As yet, however, James had probably not settled into the method of revision he was to use for the *NYE*; for a week later, on 7 August, he wrote to thank Pinker 'for having the "Roderick Hudson" pages so beautifully put into condition for revision for me. This is a brilliant piece of work which will greatly help me & for which I am exceedingly obliged to you.'[21] And on 1 September 1905 he wrote to Pinker again to send 'the hearty thanks I owe you for the beautiful, beautiful last job of pasting-up work done, which has put the book into a form it is a joy for me

---

[19] HJ to Pinker, 25 June 1905, from Cambridge, Mass. (Yale TS).

[20] Elizabeth Robins, *Theatre and Friendship: Some Henry James Letters with a Commentary by Elizabeth Robins*, New York, 1932, p. 251. On 28 Mar. the following year, HJ recommended Pinker's services as an agent to Miss Robins with special reference to the *NYE*: 'he has just arranged a very complex and difficult job for me in a masterly way—the matter of a "handsome" collective (and *selective*) Edition Définitive of my writings, in the U.S. and here—a tiresome worrying business through the scatterment of my books through a number of publishers, who were all to be triumphantly dealt with. He has so dealt and made the thing possible—I couldn't have *touched* it by myself' (*Theatre and Friendship*, pp. 256–7).

[21] HJ to Pinker, 7 Aug. 1905 (Yale MS).

to work upon'.[22] The beauty James found in the pasted-up sheets of *The American*, where the original text was cut out and stuck on to larger pages, is that they afford him a margin for revision, more space into which to expand with new sense.

In the 30 July memorandum James (who was working concurrently on *The American Scene*) was promising, in the event too blithely, complete revised copy of both *Roderick Hudson* and *The American*, including their respective Prefaces, by 25 September; but administrative hitches supervened, giving him more time, and on 29 September he was writing to Pinker 'without impatience' in response to news of a Scribners delay: 'The margin for revision meanwhile accruing is very welcome to me; and welcome also, I think, the prospect of a size greater than the Kipling. Let us be as great as possible!'[23] James's exhilaration at the expected 'greatness' is clear; but the dimensions of the volumes were later among the strong reasons for their unprofitability.

While James's imagination continued to play over both his large projects, hard business was causing the Scribners to delay. Houghton, Mifflin, one of the several firms with a property in James's books, made a punitive stand on the monopolistic and commercially reactionary 'fundamental principle'[24] that 'the books of a productive author should be kept under one imprint, and that the method inaugurated by literary brokers of pitting one house against another and selling their client to the highest bidder is not one to be encouraged'.[25] They therefore insisted on themselves printing, at their Riverside Press, the *NYE* volumes of the books they held—an insistence which threatened the profitability of the whole venture for Scribners; to the extent that the New York firm wrote enquiring if they themselves wanted to undertake the publishing of the set. Any such wish they utterly disavowed, with the sanctimonious assurance that they did not want 'to be disobliging or take any dog-in-the-manger attitude'.

James himself, hard at work in Rye, was not directly bothered with these troubles, which Pinker muffled for him—though himself at a remove from the difficulties between New York and Boston. On 3 November 1905 James wrote to his niece Peggy that 'all the time I haven't been doing the American Book, I have been revising with

---

[22] HJ to Pinker, 1 Sept. 1905 (Yale TS).
[23] HJ to Pinker, 29 Sept. 1905 (Yale TS).
[24] Houghton, Mifflin and Co. to Scribners, 19 Sept. 1905 (Princeton TS).
[25] Houghton, Mifflin and Co. to Scribners, 25 Oct. 1905 (Princeton TS).

extreme minuteness three or four of my early works for the Edition
Définitive (the settlement of some of the details of which seems to be
hanging fire a little between my "agent" and my New York publishers;
not, however, in a manner to indicate, I think, a real hitch)' (*LHJ* ii.
36–7). There *was* a real hitch, though, of which Pinker only learnt
when he received a letter sent by Scribners on 31 October. His reply
on 9 November confessed to discomposure and sincerely trusted that
some compromise would be possible. 'I should be very sorry indeed
to have to go to Mr. James and tell him that the negotiations had
fallen through with yourselves, as he had settled down quite happily
to the idea that his affairs were in your good hands.'[26] Pinker had at
the same time to state that 'I do not quite understand from your letter
what the difficulty is', though he presumed it was to do with the price
Houghton, Mifflin were asking for the printing. On 10 November
Pinker wrote to Houghton, Mifflin in an attempt to clear up the
problem, and on 23 November George Mifflin wrote ingratiatingly to
Charles Scribner, who had again been in touch with him, to explain
that 'our suggestions (hardly intended for you as "conditions")' could
be adjusted, since 'it would be very unpleasant to stand in the way of
[Mr James's] securing a uniform Edition of his writings'.[27] Mifflin's
resentful attitude to 'literary brokers' surfaced again in a way which
suggests how uphill some of Pinker's moments in America must have
been. Mifflin told Scribner:

I ought to add that Mr. Garrison has refreshed my memory as to a very
informal talk I had with Mr. Pinker which I confess had gone entirely out of
my recollection. I do now remember some general words did pass between us
as to a uniform Edn. but I did not connect you in any way with it and indicated
only the general lines on which our volumes should be included. No formal
or definite understanding was ever reached.

The following day Mifflin wrote with a trace of apology to Pinker that
the 10 November letter from London had immediately caused him to
renew contact with Scribner in order to settle things: 'There has
evidently been some slight misunderstanding of detail on my part with
reference to the whole transaction.'[28] He restated the principle of

[26] Pinker to Scribners, 9 Nov. 1905 (Princeton TS).
[27] George H. Mifflin to Mr Scribner, 23 Nov. 1905 (Princeton MS). Another letter of
20 Dec. 1905 (Princeton TS) makes further attempts to justify the conduct of Houghton,
Mifflin in the matter.
[28] George H. Mifflin to Pinker, 24 Nov. 1905 (Princeton TS).

hostility to uniform editions of works scattered among different publishers—making clear it was a principle waived now only because of the involvement of James and Scribner.

On the morning of 5 December James learned from Pinker of the problem and at the same time of its solution, and at once wrote back gratefully, in a way illustrative of his reliance on Pinker's good agency.

I had rather taken for granted that some difficulty had come up between New York and Boston, but felt that I might trust you to untangle the skein, if it was to be untangled at all; and felt meanwhile quite peaceful and resigned—glad in fact not to have to think of the matter, as my actual work makes all due demand on my wits. But I feel greatly indebted to you for the patience, ingenuity and diplomacy you have, in the whole matter, I am sure, been putting at my service; so that I am really delighted with the good result you announce. May everything now go more smoothly on![29]

The next day Pinker wrote to Scribner thanking him for a just-received letter of reassurance, and suggesting that the English publication could be arranged later as a direct sale of sheets to an English publisher.

Herbert Stone of Chicago, bolder and worse than Mifflin, showed what *he* was made of as an impediment to the smooth going on of the Edition when on 30 December he lied about having purchased *In the Cage* and *What Maisie Knew* outright.[30] This took some sorting out. On 26 March 1906 Pinker explained to Scribners that the English publishers (Heinemann and Duckworth) were certain Stone 'quite understood that there was a time limit on the rights, and it is curious that he can produce no contract'.[31] In the same letter he enclosed James's signed copy of the *NYE* contract. On 27 March James wrote to Pinker that he would see Gerald Duckworth about the contractual situation, and expressed outrage: 'it's *monstrous*—the pretension of Stone that after his *whole* behaviour in the matter of "Maisie", as to serialization & book both—he had possessed himself of a perpetual property in the book. He knew, & he knows, that he was utterly shabby about it.'[32] On 28 March, having received this further assurance, Pinker confidently wrote to Scribners to go ahead; and 'as Messrs. Stone's

---

[29] HJ to Pinker, 5 Dec. 1905 (Yale TS). The 'actual work' was *The American Scene*: on 23 Nov. HJ had written to his brother William that 'I am working off my American book very steadily' (*HJL* iv. 381).

[30] Herbert S. Stone (Publishers Chicago) to Scribners, 30 Dec. 1905 (Princeton TS). He was in the process of selling his list to Messrs Fox Duffield.

[31] Pinker to Scribners, 26 Mar. 1906 (Princeton TS).

[32] HJ to Pinker, 27 Mar. 1906 (Yale MS).

rights in these volumes have lapsed, Mr. James will feel bound to take measures to prevent further exploitation of the books'.[33] Stone was thus deftly removed from the *NYE*'s path and put in his place.

Such awkwardnesses were not allowed to hold up the progress of the Edition. On 7 February 1906 Pinker, returning the draft contract for the *NYE*, assured Scribners that the revised copy for the first volume (*Roderick Hudson*) would be sent by him 'In a few days ... as Mr. James has practically completed it.'[34] On 19 February he was again hoping to send it 'very shortly, as Mr. James tells me that it is nearly ready'.[35] On 8 March he sent the first 161 pages of revised copy for the novel;[36] and on 12 March the balance of revised copy went off: 'the preface shall follow as soon as Mr. James can get it to his satisfaction.'[37] But *The American Scene* was still keeping James under pressure; when on 9 March he had enclosed to Pinker the last batch of revised copy for *Roderick Hudson*, he had said 'I will follow it with its new Preface as soon as possible, but am afraid I may, for nervousness' sake, have to do another paper for Munro [editor of the *North American Review*] before I can write it.'[38] Two months later, on 9 May, James was mentioning in a letter to Scribners that he would soon be going back from town to 'the quiet of the country—whence I shall very quickly send you the Preface of *R. H.*' (*HJL* iv. 403). In fact it was not till 17 August that James sent off the completed Preface, together with that for *The Portrait of a Lady*.[39]

The whole edition was to be characterized by such anticipations of speedier completion than professional conditions or artistic conscience allowed: the letter to Pinker of 9 March had also committed itself to the view that 'I am pleased to gather (now that I see the retouches of the American clearly exhibited) that they are required on a smaller scale than those of R. H. & therefore will take less time to do.' It was,

[33] Pinker to Scribners, 28 Mar. 1906 (Princeton TS).

[34] Pinker to Scribners, 7 Feb. 1906 (Princeton TS).

[35] Pinker to Scribners, 19 Feb. 1906 (Princeton TS).

[36] He also mentioned that Constable would be writing to Scribners to negotiate the purchase of sheets for the English issue of the *NYE* (Pinker to Scribners, 8 Mar. 1906 (Princeton TS)). Constable did write to Scribners on 14 Mar., but rather gloomily anticipating that 'the sale with us would be but small', both of de luxe and uniform editions; they offered to buy the sets only 10 or 25 at a time. The letter concludes ominously: 'You will realise that the difficulty here is that so many different people have the copyright for so many different books by this Author' (Princeton TS).

[37] Pinker to Scribners, 12 Mar. 1906 (Princeton TS).

[38] HJ to Pinker, 9 Mar. 1906 (Yale MS).

[39] HJ to Scribners, 17 Aug. 1906 (Princeton TS).

however, 15 February the following year before James sent off the Preface to New York, following the heavily revised copy with an apology and a justification. 'Please pardon my long delay—which must have been discouraging to you—over *The American*; it has all been the fruit of the intrinsic difficulty of happy & right & *intimate* revision—which defied considerations of time: the process has had to be so extremely deliberate. But it is, thank goodness, needed; the aspect of the book is essentially improved, its attraction augmented &, above all, I am now "out of the wood".'[40]

ii. *Collective and Selective*

By 9 May 1906 James had received a long letter from Scribners, written on 27 April, enclosing a specimen page, which he approved, and 'a memorandum showing the approximate number of words in each novel'.[41] James's reply declares that 'I quite adhere to my original idea as to the total number of volumes' and then that 'I regard twenty-three volumes as sufficient for the series and have no wish to transcend it' (*HJL* iv. 403).[42] James had always relished, up to a point, the prospect of a chance 'to quietly disown a few things by not thus supremely adopting them' (as he had written on 6 June 1905); he had told the disapproving Robert Herrick on 7 August 1905 that

Its *raison d'être* (the edition's) is in its being selective as well as collective, and by the mere fact of leaving out certain things (I have tried to read over *Washington Square* and I *can't*, and I fear it must go!) I exercise a control, a

[40] HJ to Scribners, 15 Feb. 1907 (Princeton MS). Since Nov. 1906 James had additionally written a couple of *Bazar* papers and his chapter of the composite novel *The Whole Family*, and had had problems finding a typist to replace his Miss Gregory; but since he usually revised in the evenings, and did other work in the mornings, this does not convict him of scanting his *NYE* commitments.

[41] Scribners to HJ, 27 Apr. 1906 (Princeton TS).

[42] Michael Anesko has pointed out that Leon Edel is misled and misleading in taking this to suggest that 'From the beginning HJ decided that he would keep his edition within the limits of twenty-three volumes' (*HJL* iv. 404 n.), since the 'original idea' is that expressed in his memorandum of 30 July 1905, which does not mention any particular number, let alone the twenty-three of Balzac's *Comédie Humaine*: 'reducing the number of volumes to an array that will not seem, for a collective edition, very formidable' (*HJL* iv. 366). James here presents this earlier policy of sifting and selecting as compatible with the Scribners 27 Apr. news that 'the total number of volumes will be 23. This is in excess of what was proposed' (Scribner's to HJ, 27 Apr. 1906 (Princeton TS); see '*Friction with the Market*', pp. 149–50). He regards 'Four Volumes for the Shorter Novels and Four for the Tales ... as quite definite', assuring Scribners 'that I am perfectly satisfied with Eight Volumes for the two classes' (*HJL* iv. 403).

discrimination, I treat certain portions of my work as unhappy accidents—
(many portions of many—of all—men's work are) (*HJL* iv. 371).

The discriminations to be made were not absolutely firm, however. On
1 November 1905 James discouraged Auguste Monod from translating
Madame de Mauves and *The Siege of London* into French, calling
them 'those primitive cases', and stating that 'In an *Edition définitive*
that I am preparing of my novels and tales, I am omitting both the
things you name'.[43] In the event both of these works were included in
what James was in the spring of 1907 to describe to Monod as 'la belle
et bonne édition définitive et collective de toutes mes fictions qui va
bientôt paraître, très revue et très triée'.[44]

  The possibility of the omission of *The Bostonians* from the *NYE*
caused some dismay on 1 February 1910 to W. D. Howells. He wrote
to James that 'I've the impression, the fear that you're not going to
put it into your collection, and I think that would be the greatest
blunder and the greatest pity'.[45] One of the reasons Howells had this
fear and impression was the uncertainty of James's words about it in
a letter of 17 August 1908, when he was already well past its chronological slot among the earlier novels, and in the middle of preparing
the Shorter Novels and Tales. He began by admitting that 'it has
racked me a little that I've had to leave out so many things that would
have helped to make for rather a more vivid completeness' (*LHJ* ii.
99)—'had to', that is, through a mere constraint of space rather than
through 'deep-seated preference and design'.

I have even, in addition, a dim vague view of reintroducing, with a good deal
of titivation and cancellation, the too-diffuse but, I somehow feel, tolerably
full and good 'Bostonians' of nearly a quarter of a century ago; that production
never having, even to my much-disciplined patience, received any sort of
justice. But it will take, doubtless, a great deal of artful re-doing—and I
haven't, now, had the courage or time for anything so formidable as touching
and retouching it. I feel at the same time how the series suffers commercially
from its having been dropped so completely out (*LHJ* ii. 100).

It still preyed on his mind near the end of his life, as is apparent from
his letter to Gosse of 25 August 1915, replying to a query about its

  [43] *Letters to A. C. Benson and Auguste Monod*, ed. E. F. Benson, London, 1930, p. 97.
  [44] *Letters to A. C. Benson and Auguste Monod*, p. 104. ('The fine definitive and
collective edition of all my fictions which is soon to appear, much revised and carefully
selected'.)
  [45] W. D. Howells to HJ, 1 Feb. 1910 (Harvard MS).

non-inclusion; the matter focused his sense of the *NYE* as 'practically a complete failure' from the business point of view, and its revision as unfairly neglected by critics. 'The immediate inclusion of the *Bostonians* was rather deprecated by my publishers', James recalled (*HJL* iv. 777): the words of the Scribners on 27 April 1906 had been, 'we think it will be better not to consider at present the including of THE BOSTONIANS. This can be taken up at any time later if it seems desirable.'

Even at this fairly early stage James was bothered by the need to be more than critically—or less than critically—exclusive. In the writing of his fiction, the artistic economy that requires an organic function for every element in a work is quite distinct from the commercial economy of the strictly contingent demands of publishers, which threaten to reduce his intentions to senseless brevity:[46] here likewise there is a difference for him between enforced and voluntary omissions. On 12 June 1906 he wrote assenting to Scribners' proposal that the eight volumes of shorter things should not exceed 120,000 words apiece. He would keep them down at whatever cost; but

> The 'cost' will be a little, I am afraid, that of some critical animadversion on certain things missed by the reader, things that might rather confidently have been looked for: or perhaps I had better say that I *should* apprehend something of that sort were there more serious or attentive criticism nowadays to reckon with. I am not without the sense that the question of a supplementary volume or two—putting quite new books aside—may have to come up in the fulness of time; and for this possibility any omitted things that are really characteristic enough to mar completeness by their absence may meanwhile wait.[47]

The failure of the *NYE* to yield commercial reward and James's 'bitter grief' at it in due course made this wait everlasting.

Early in 1908, as he began to move from the preparation of the Shorter Novels to that of the Tales, James again expressed his sense that what would be quietly disowned would count in part as a loss. On 26 February he wrote to Scribners, giving a provisional contents list:

> most of the following tales will be in it, but ... three or four of these will have, after rigid selection, to rejoin the mass, really quite considerable, of the omitted. (Four or five of my books, and a great many shorter stories come

---

[46] 'The insufferable 5000 words' of the magazine short story, for instance (HJ to Pinker, 19 Jan. 1909 (Yale MS)).
[47] HJ to Scribners, 12 June 1906 (Princeton TS).

under this head. I drop for instance, in addition to The Bostonians, The Europeans, Washington Square, 'Confidence', The Sacred Fount etc.)...[48]

Of the list of tales in the letter, six were ultimately to be omitted from the *NYE*.[49] The length limit, set by Scribner at 120,000 words and somehow mistaken by the amplifying James as 150,000 words per volume, was one restriction on his freedom to include what he wanted. On 20 July 1908 he sent off copy for Volume Fifteenth which he worked out would 'somewhat exceed the 150,000 words (the usual number) of a Volume; but I am wondering if without gross inconvenience you could now let me add, at the end of this same series,... two short things, Miss Gunton of Poughkeepsie and Fordham Castle.'[50] Naturally enough, this attempt to fit in more than had been agreed was politely refused by Scribners. The volume already made 608 pages, 28 more than any other, without the two extra stories, and the publishers pointed out that the 166,000-word *Ambassadors* had already been divided into two volumes because of its length, and for the sake of 'symmetry and its connected material advantages'.[51] The two stories ended up in another volume.

A postscript to the 20 July letter recorded the arrival of the large-paper copies of *NYE* xi (' "What Maisie Knew" and so forth') and xii (' "The Aspern Papers" etc.'). This had 'the effect of making me see with anguish that I might well have made the latter Volume a little more substantial—by the addition of two or three short things that I should have been glad to get into it, and that would have fitted there particularly; but that I was timorous about including...'. By 6 August, the temporary mislaying of a page of 'Brooksmith' prompted James to give voice again to his pangs: 'if I do have to omit "Brooksmith", it won't be, alas, the only valuable item our limits of space compel me greatly to regret!'[52] The exclusion of a work from the *NYE*, then, does not prove James wished to 'quietly disown' it.

---

[48] HJ to Scribners, 26 Feb. 1908 (Princeton TS).
[49] *A New England Winter, The Papers, The Solution, The Path of Duty, Glasses,* and *The Diary of a Man of Fifty.*
[50] HJ to Scribners, 20 July 1908 (Princeton TS).
[51] Scribners to HJ, 30 July 1908 (Princeton TS).
[52] HJ to Scribners, 6 Aug. 1908 (Princeton TS). James replied to Pinker on 24 Feb. 1907, apropos of an offer from Nelsons of a sevenpenny reprint of one of his works, that 'The one thing I *can* think of is "The Other House", which I don't put into the N.Y., & yet *should* be willing, decidedly, to present afresh. (I have been looking it over.)' (Yale MS).

iii.   The Higher Perfection

One of the last letters James wrote, on 4 October 1915 to Edward
Marsh, concerned the composition of his Preface to Rupert Brooke's
Letters from America. When done, he says, it will have to be done
over; 'as it is ever the second doing, for me, that is *the* doing' (*HJL* iv.
780). The implication is that only in the exact adjustment of nuance—
in the 'finish' of a work—does his writing finally take on its constitutive
pattern of senses, the special meaning and character which are its
raison d'être.

This idea of the second doing as '*the* doing' for James can be seen
in the protracted process of composition of *The Golden Bowl* in
1903 and 1904, just before his departure to the United States and his
undertaking of the *NYE*. Writing to Pinker on 20 May 1904, James
outlines 'the way I do it—*the* way I seem condemned to; which is to
overtreat my subject by developments and amplifications that have, in
large part, eventually to be greatly compressed, but to the prior operation of which the thing afterwards owes what is most durable in its
quality' (*LHJ* ii. 15).[53] A couple of years later James repeats even
more ruefully—for the sake of an ironic barb—this sense of being
'condemned' to the long way round, in contrast to his addressee, the
vividly simplifying Wells. He describes himself as 'I who was accursedly
born to touch nothing save to complicate it' (*HJL* iv. 421; 8 November
1906).

On 23 November 1903 in a letter to Howard Sturgis such complications make it touch and go whether the *Bowl* will be completed.
James evokes 'the humiliating difficulty I am having here over my own
stuff—in which I've come nearer to sticking fast than ever in anything'
(*HJL* iv. 294). And this in spite of his resolve not to repeat the
lengthiness of *The Wings of the Dove*, expressed in 1902 to Lucy
Clifford, whose 'discriminations' about that book he had admitted to
be just. 'I have been through them all myself and exhaustively read
the moral (of its manner, size and muchness). A special accident
operated, a series of causes conspired, to make it write itself that

---

[53] Lubbock omits part of the letter (see n. 58) which is in the Beinecke Library (Yale
TS). Theodora Bosanquet, James's secretary, confirms James's account of his method
of preparation: 'At the beginning he had no questions of compression to attend to, and
he "broke ground", as he said, by talking to himself day by day about the characters
and construction until the persons and their actions were vividly present to his inward
eye. This soliloquy was of course recorded on the typewriter' (Theodora Bosanquet,
Henry James at Work, London, 1924, p. 9).

way—but they won't, absolutely they won't, conspire again. I have got them *under*.'[54] *The Golden Bowl* has a strikingly poised middle, unlike the misplaced one of which James was to complain in *The Wings of the Dove* Preface; but its 'size and muchness' are much of a muchness with the other work's, and in 1911 he was to describe the novel to Edith Wharton as an 'interminable and formidable job,... the most arduous and thankless task I ever set myself' (*HJL* iv. 591). The 'arduousness'—felt in 1903 as 'the humiliating difficulty'—is self-inflicted, then; it is his own goal that James has to get through to, his own complex intention that he has to execute.

On 25 October 1903 James wrote to Pinker that he recalled his promise to Methuen of copy for the whole *Bowl* 'for the end of November—if humanly possible'; but that 'As the case stands—and as I fear is always inevitably the case with me I am not now as far toward completion as I should like—and being overpressed maddens me and destroys my work.'[55] He therefore adjusted the schedule, offering three-quarters of copy by the end of November, 'following them up at a quick rate with the final quarter'. The suggestion made by Methuen in response to this took James two or three days to think over, but on 1 November he wrote again to Pinker to accept 'a delay of some three or four months for the publication of *The Golden Bowl*', to August 1904, on the grounds that 'it will ease me off and contribute to the higher perfection, so to speak, of the book'.[56] They would receive the whole copy 'in some 10 or 12 weeks from now'—that is, between the middle and end of January 1904.

On 13 April 1904, two and a half months after this deadline, James wrote to his brother William that 'I have been pressing hard toward the finish of a long book, still *un*finished (but not very much, thank heaven!) which I am doing with such perfection that every inch is done over and over; which makes it come expensive in the matter of time...'.[57] 'The higher perfection, so to speak,' dictates the expensive second doings, the process of amplifications and compressions which is so costly of time and effort. The book may have been 'not very much' unfinished, but on 20 May 1904, in the letter cited above, James's response to Pinker shows him still in the relative state of

---

[54] HJ to Lucy Clifford, 8 Sept. 1902 (Lubbock TS, Harvard).
[55] HJ to Pinker, 25 Oct. 1903 (Yale TS) (the letter also appears in *HJL* iv. 285, where it is described as 'MS' and the punctuation is not quite correct).
[56] HJ to Pinker, 1 Nov. 1903 (Yale MS).
[57] HJ to William James, 13 Apr. 1904 (Harvard MS).

writing, as it were, rather than absolutely finished.

I will indeed let you have the whole of my M.S. on the very first possible day, now not far off; but I have still, absolutely, to finish, and to finish right, and Methuen's importunity does meanwhile, I confess, distress me. I have been working on the book with unremitting intensity the whole of every blessed morning since I began it, some thirteen months ago, and I am at present within but some twelve or fifteen thousand words of Finis (*LHJ* ii. 15).[58]

'Absolutely' to finish *is* 'to finish right', and this 'rightness' is determined by the material worked on rather than by the timetable of the publishers. James has to protect the processes of the study from 'being overpressed', pressed into print, through the impatience of Methuen, and goes on to make the best of a long, hard job. 'But I can only work in my own way—a deucedly good one, by the same token!—and am producing the best book, I seem to conceive, that I have ever done. I have really done it fast, for what it is, and for the way I do it . . .' Three weeks later, on 11 June, James, on the grounds that the novel was 'so all *but* finished',[59] was resisting another invitation to postpone publication; he promised the whole would be ready by 1 July. On 28 June he had 'but one more chapter of my interminable book to write'.[60] On 29 June Pinker raised, very late, the possibility of serializing the book in the United States, and the business of dividing it into instalments further delayed James's ending. On 10 July James could finally write that he was coming up to town 'to bring you safely my Part Twelfth, which is finished, praise to the Highest!'[61] On 2 August the chapters cut for serialization (which had been 'heartbreaking excisions'[62]) were restored—nothing had come of the idea—and work on the 'interminable book' came to an end, for the time being, as the compositors began *their* composition of it.

James had said after *The Wings of the Dove* partially exceeded his control that he would not suffer the same problem the next time, having got the causes of it '*under*'. While finishing the novel before that, *The Ambassadors*, he had with equal confidence predicted that he would take less time in future. He wrote to Pinker on 'June 31st' 1901, giving himself an extra day of the month, and explaining the

---

[58] Lubbock tactfully omits 'and Methuen's importunity does. . . distress me'.
[59] HJ to Pinker, 11 June 1904 (Yale MS).
[60] HJ to Pinker, 28 June 1904 (Yale TS) ('book' is an MS substitution for 'task').
[61] HJ to Pinker, 10 July 1904 (Yale TS).
[62] HJ to Pinker, 30 June 1904 (Yale TS).

non-transmission of 'finally-finished fiction': 'It has been a long, long job—and not from interruptions (of late), or disasters, for I've kept steadily and intensely at it. It's simply that the thing itself has *taken* the time—taken it with a strong and insistent hand.—This Constable one will, for intrinsic reasons, take less; besides being already well started' (*HJL* iv. 193).

The difficulties we see James struggling with here in the composition of the late novels, caught between his businesslike wish to have them done and paid for and his artistic need to keep on intensely finishing them, are difficulties which are repeated in the *NYE*—both in the events of its snag-ridden preparation and in the expansive self-determining principle imaginatively discovered in so many of his works through the process of revision. James himself wrote of the revised *American* going to Scribners 'in as perfect form as that of the Golden Bowl'.[63] Once he is launched, 'the thing itself', a quickly formed fictional entity which imposes its own conditions on his imagination, takes hold and struggles with the author's extrinsic personal and commercial constraints of space and time. For James to ascribe this primacy to 'the thing itself' is to counter the contractual claims of the market with those of a creative responsibility to the material and his calling. This is not for his own convenience: 'the thing itself' can impose 'humiliating difficulty' on its author.

There is a reward, though not a very worldly one, for this sort of exhausting dedication. On 9 September 1904 James was promising Scribners, who were about to publish *The Golden Bowl*, 'never again to write so long a novel'—chastened by his mistakes, one might think. But the seriousness of the promise is at least qualified by the assertion that follows: 'The best work of my life has, however, I think, gone into the G.B.'[64] The labour of 'doing with such perfection that every inch is done over and over', humanly costed, makes an expensive job, as James repeatedly rediscovered; and the 'perfection' attained, provisional and approximate, never is that of 'absolutely' finishing. At the provisional ending of the process, though, while James is somewhat depleted, the work is something solid: he is 'rather spent and sore, but the Edition a reality and an honour'. The 'reality' and the 'honour' are only abstractions, but they have such reality as words have and can in part take away the 'bitter grief' of a wound like the blank

---

[63] HJ to Pinker, 7 Apr. 1906 (Yale MS).
[64] HJ to Scribners, 9 Sept. 1904 (Princeton MS).

Scribners account-sheet. The 'reality' of the Edition is for James akin to that of 'the thing itself': through all the humiliating difficulties of a literary career he can always call on the sense that his work, which is his life, *has* life.

Such belief in the results of perfectionist craftsmanship does not easily transmit itself to readers, as is shown by the failure of James's royalties. And the writer's 'bitter grief' when the value of his 'best work' goes unrecognized is slow to be appeased. Not long before his death, on 25 August 1915, James wrote to Edmund Gosse of the 'extremity of labour' he had put into his revisions for the New York Edition. To bring home his sense of the neglect they had suffered, he reached for words from a poem commemorating the failure of another kind of royalty, Shelley's 'Ozymandias'. The grim joke of 'Ozymandias', one James recognizes and ruefully applies to himself, is the fate that befalls the tyrant's utterance: 'Look on my works, ye Mighty, and despair!' The monument intended to inspire awe is a 'colossal wreck' in a desert,[65] and the ruin becomes an emblem of the futility of human endeavour. James's revisions, in his hyperbolic account, do little better; his confidence in them makes no impression on the world: 'The Edition is from that point of view really a monument (like Ozymandias) which has never had the least intelligent critical justice done it—any sort of critical attention at all paid it—& the artistic problem involved in my scheme was a deep & exquisite one, & moreover was, as I hold, very effectively solved.'[66]

[65] *The Complete Poetical Works of Shelley*, edited with textual notes by Thomas Hutchinson, Oxford, 1904, p. 605.
[66] *Selected Letters of Henry James to Edmund Gosse, 1882–1915: A Literary Friendship*, ed. Rayburn S. Moore, Baton Rouge and London, 1988, p. 313.

2

Rights and Wrongs of Revision

i. *'Stopping, that's Art': Keats, Pope, Wordsworth, Tennyson*

Dogs are notorious for returning to their own vomit, and we are proverbially suspicious of those who won't leave well alone. Writers are understandably sensitive about going back to their works after any lapse of time, about interfering, meddling, tinkering, or fiddling with the product of their original impulse. It is a matter of legend that our greatest poet never blotted a line. Some notions of the creative process seem especially to preclude returns and rehandlings:

He never corrects, unless perhaps a word here or there shd occur to him as preferable to an expression he has already used—He is impatient of correcting, & says he would rather burn the piece in question & write ano^r or something else—'My judgment' (he says), is as active while I am actually writing as my imagin^n In fact all my faculties are strongly excited, & in their full play—And shall I afterwards, when my imagination is idle, & the heat in which I wrote, has gone off, sit down coldly to criticise when in Poss^{on} of only one faculty, what I have written, when almost inspired.'—This fact explains the reason of the Perfectness, fullness, richness & completion of most that comes from him—He has said, that he has often not been aware of the beauty of some thought or expr^n until after he has composed & written it down—It has then struck him with astonishm^t—& seemed rather the prod^n of another person than his own—He has wondered how he came to hit upon it.[1]

The poet is John Keats, in the account of his friend Woodhouse, giving a modestly inspirational version of his poetic procedures—which 'the Perfectness, fullness, richness and completion of most that comes from him' would generally be thought to justify. Keats himself was an intensive reviser—but at the time of first composition, not afterwards.

Keats's phrase 'sit down coldly to criticise', expressing a common qualm, cannot be allowed as doing justice to all revision that follows composition after an interval. It looks as if it presumes that the original

[1] From Richard Woodhouse's criticism of a sonnet by Keats, July (?) 1820, *The Keats Circle: Letters and Papers and More Letters and Poems of the Keats Circle*, 2nd edn., 2 vols., ed. Hyder Edward Rollins, Harvard, 1965, i. 128–9 (omitting cancelled phrases).

'heat' of composition is irretrievable: what if this is not so? If it restricts the original occasion of writing to a one-off heated burst, it implicitly scants longer works which require a longer genesis. But 'coldly' equivocates between qualifying 'sit down' and 'criticise'; so that the rhetorical question *may* only apply to *some* subsequent occasions, those 'when my imagination is idle', when Keats is 'in Poss^on of only one faculty'. Keats's sentence throws its weight against the possibility that there might be other subsequent occasions, when imagination and judgement would warmly combine again; but it does not in so many words exclude it.

Even Keats, moreover, mediating between the claims of imagination and judgement, which work together in the heat of his writing, does not put himself under a strict embargo as far as later adjustments are concerned: '*unless* perhaps a word here or there should occur to him as preferable to an expression he has already used'. The romantic moods of heat and cold suggest poetic fits of imaginative ecstasy in a way which '*almost* inspired' finally belies. What Keats describes is a state of attention, a concentration sufficiently comprehensive to combine critical perspective with local creative intensity. The mature Keats habitually brought to bear 'that craftsman's exigence which demands "a brighter word than bright, a fairer word than fair"';[2] but what if the perfectionist demands of craftsmanship have not all been met by the end of the first compositional session, a possibility even Keats's strong statement leaves open?

The difficulty for the writer is knowing when to stop. Henry James was much aware of the Romantic poets and their preoccupation with such creative predicaments, which influenced the terms in which he recognized his own problems and achievements. In the chapter he contributed in 1907 to a novel by twelve authors, *The Whole Family*, James invented a prissily self-conscious 'Married Son', Charles Edward, an artist *manqué* in bourgeois Middle America, whose ramifying first-person account of the novel's goings-on leads him to reflect, with comic extravagance, on Art.

When you paint a picture with a brush and pigments, that is on a single plane, it can stop at your gilt frame; but when you paint one with a pen and words, that is in *all* the dimensions, how are you to stop? Of course, as Lorraine [his wife] says, 'Stopping, that's art; and what are we artists like, my dear, but

---

[2] M. R. Ridley, *Keats' Craftsmanship: A Study in Poetic Development*, Oxford, 1933; repr. London, 1965, p. 13.

those drivers of trolley-cars, in New York, who, by some divine instinct, recognise in the forest of pillars and posts the white-striped columns at which they may pull up?'[3]

James's self-parodic eloquence is a comment on his own difficulties in setting limits to his reseeing of the action the contributors of earlier chapters had so short-sightedly bungled; but the passage can also remind us that 'the white-striped columns' stand at different points on each artistic journey, and that the 'divine instinct' for recognizing where to 'pull up' may be acquired through grace rather than works. It is fortunate that Woodhouse sees 'Perfectness' and 'completion' in many of Keats's poems, since otherwise the poet might simply not be 'finishing' his works, might be failing to cover all the ground.

The nature of the work being revised, and its aptness for simplification or elaboration, will affect the placing of the 'white-striped columns' and the length of the artistic journey. We could take as an exemplary case a revision made by Pope at the climactic moment of *The Rape of the Lock*, where Lord Petre cuts Arabella Fermor's hair, causing division between their families. The version of May 1712:

> He first expands the glitt'ring *Forfex* wide
> T'inclose the Lock; then joins it, to divide;
> One fatal stroke the sacred Hair does sever
> From the fair Head, for ever, and for ever!   (i. 115–18)

In the much-expanded 1714 version, Pope interposes a couple of couplets, delaying the 'fatal stroke':

> The Peer now spreads the glitt'ring *Forfex* wide,
> T'inclose the Lock; now joins it, to divide,
> Ev'n then, before the fatal Engine clos'd,
> A wretched *Sylph* too fondly interpos'd;
> Fate urg'd the Shears, and cut the *Sylph* in twain,
> (But Airy Substance soon unites again)
> The meeting Points the sacred Hair dissever
> From the fair Head, for ever and for ever!   (iii. 147–54)[4]

If the poem as a whole constitutes an interposition in the quarrel, plays on sunderings in the interests of reunion, and makes a great deal out

---

[3] *The Whole Family: A Novel by Twelve Authors*, New York, 1908 (repr. New York, 1986, introduced by Alfred Bendixen), pp. 167–8. See a review by the present writer, *London Review of Books*, 9/5 (5 Mar. 1987), 14–16.

[4] Alexander Pope, *The Rape of the Lock*, ed. Geoffrey Tillotson, London, 1941; repr. 1981, pp. 85, 53.

of a small-scale severance only to refuse it ultimate seriousness, then this revision does the same: it shows an attempt 'fondly' to avert disaster, divides the *1712* couplets only to join them again, and represents a tragic halving which we are promptly assured does no real harm. Pope's 'Airy Substance' echoes 'Ethereal substance ... | Not long divisible' from *Paradise Lost* vi. 330–1, drawing on the moment when Satan 'in half cut sheer ... first knew pain' and consciously anaesthetizing the wound. The distancing effect of a reversion from present historic to past historic tense squeezes yet more supernatural 'Machinery' into the human event, jokily turning 'first ... then' into 'now ... now ... *Ev'n then*' so that even after the apparently decisive and incisive 'divide' there is a micro-second of seeming evitability. The doubling of the singular 'One fatal stroke' into the pair of 'meeting Points', and the pluralizing of 'does sever' into the near-homophone 'dissever', carry on the play of union and disunion in the work, where the division of a hair leads to the division of houses that might have been united.

The Rape of the Lock readily accommodates such workings-in, for the premiss of the poem already in the *1712* version is that the trivial real event triggering the feud be mock-heroically elaborated, over-treated with the full apparatus of epic in order to find a literary equivalent for the disproportion and excess of the Fermor and Petre reactions. The work's form is ironically conceived, that is; further exaggeration and the interposition of more charming conceits comfortably become part of it. Even so, Geoffrey Tillotson admits, 'It may ... be argued that the poem in its *1712* form was better proportioned as a narrative, that the additions are too bulky for the slight thread of the story';[5] the two texts, separated by only two years, thus enter into a rivalry, compete for approbation according to criteria which may vary with the reader, and indeed with the author's mood.

When Henry Crabb Robinson received a copy of Wordsworth's *Poetical Works* in 1827, he wrote to Dorothy Wordsworth, wondering if William did not feel that a problem of loyalty sprang from his multiple revisions:

I have received the new edition and am indeed grateful for it ... In the work of collation I have yet been able to make but little progress But I have seen enough to rejoice both in the quantity of the new and the quality of the alterd The variations of the three editions I possess are a matter of very interesting

---

[5] *The Rape of the Lock*, pp. 18–19.

remark . . . I have sometimes thought that Mr. W: on looking over his various
readings must feel as a mother does who while caressing her youngest child,
doubts whether she is not wronging the elder that is away.[6]

Texts are like children: the one conceived when the author is youngest
becomes the eldest, and the one conceived when the author is oldest
is the youngest. 'Freshness', that much-sought quality associated with
youth, can thus be thought to belong either to the youngest (most
recent) text, or to the youngest incarnation of the author (the text
furthest back in the past). The decent, commonplace antithesis of
warm youth with cold age prizes the earliest version; but is balanced
by other decent commonplaces: that the wisdom of experience carries
more weight than the rashness of innocence and ignorance, and that
the newest products are the most up-to-date and the best for us.
Evidently the revising author will in most cases tend to caress his
latest-born, and frequently to smother and suppress all others; but
especially when works have been previously published, the elder offspring will have certain rights and very possibly existing friends outside
the family. In Wordsworth's own case, the current inclination is to
prefer the texts of the young poet—politically, theologically, and
poetically 'radical'—to those of the older, in all these respects sup-
posedly more 'Victorian'. For those subscribing to this view, the
Keatsian feeling that the poet's work is 'rather the production of
another person than his own' should have warned Wordsworth not
to tamper with his original creation; for the passage of time, the lapse
of the first creative impulse, thus makes the writer an interloper on
what are no longer his own premises.

   It might have been with this angle of attack in mind that Wordsworth
framed a defensive prefatory note to a late version of the comic poem
Benjamin the Waggoner, probably in 1836.

> This Poem was at first ~~writ~~ thrown
> off ~~from~~ under a lively impulse of feeling
> ~~in~~ during the first fortnight of the month
> of Jan^ry 180[6] and has since
> at several times been carefully revised
> and with the Author's best efforts, retouched &
> inspirited
>
>   W Wordsworth[7]

---

[6] Quoted in *'Benjamin the Waggoner' by William Wordsworth*, ed. Paul F. Betz,
Ithaca and Brighton, 1984, p. 28.
   [7] *'Benjamin the Waggoner'*, p. 145.

The revisions of phrasing here show a solicitous author making his best efforts first to suggest the carefree flow of initial composition ('thrown off under a lively impulse of feeling') and then the attention 'carefully' and redeemingly paid on subsequent occasions. The Keatsian notion of the full simultaneous play of all the faculties in the moment of composition is supplanted by a notion where first impulses seem to need later checking and regulation. Wordsworth would not accept that he has '[sat] down coldly to criticise when in Poss^on of only one faculty, what [he has] written, when almost inspired': 'retouched & inspirited' makes the physical rehandling and alteration of the substance of the poem amount also to a spiritual animation of it, as if the life it initially got from the 'lively impulse' hadn't been enough. To say 'inspirited' rather than 're-inspirited' is to make a sizeable claim about one's 'youngest child', and about one's present self, and also to put oneself in serious danger of 'wronging the elder that is away'; but such risky gestures are intimately necessary to the imaginative world of this poet, who, when seeking a striking simile for deadened perceptual fixity, could come up with the finishing of a literary work. 'Lifeless as a written book'[8] is a perturbing phrase to meet in a written book.

Ernest de Selincourt said of Wordsworth that 'It is probable that no poet ever paid more meticulous or prolonged attention to his text.'[9] Wordsworth resisted the imputation that his revisions might not be improvements, and might even constitute trespasses on property no longer his own. His resistance stemmed from a desire to make his *œuvre* a living organism or complete body of works with unbroken connection to his living self. In 1842 his 'Prelude, Prefixed to the Volume Entitled "Poems Chiefly of Early and Late Years"' charged his book to

> Go, single—yet aspiring to be joined
> With thy Forerunners that through many a year
> Have faithfully prepared each other's way.[10]

This injunction 'to be joined' refers to an intrinsically inscrutable process: who is to judge what 'joining' here really involves? The

---

[8] William Wordsworth, *The Prelude: 1799, 1805, 1850: Authoritative Texts: Context and Reception: Recent Critical Essays*, ed. Jonathan Wordsworth, M. H. Abrams, Stephen Gill, New York, 1979, 1805 text, viii. 727, p. 304.

[9] Quoted in *The Salisbury Plain Poems of William Wordsworth*, ed. Stephen Gill, Ithaca and Hassocks, 1975, p. ix.

[10] *William Wordsworth, Poems*, ed. John O. Hayden, 2 vols., Harmondsworth, 1977, ii. 874.

authority of the ageing poet, who is unlikely to be an impartial
arbiter, should perhaps not be permitted to obstruct the public's, and
posterity's, appreciation of the *shape* of his achievement in early
maturity; as Wordsworth does in his revisions and reclassifying
regroupings. Yet to deny this authority of the final text in a poet's
lifetime, especially when such care and thought have been invested in it,
is difficult to justify without taking up a superior and partly dismissive
attitude to the poet's own set of intentions.

Our difficulty about confidently accepting or rejecting his later
changes is continuous with Wordsworth's own creative anxiety about
his powers. Poets may be worried by the idea that their fame will not
outlive them, but they are also fretted by the possibility that they will
outlive their own poetic capacities. In his 'Imitations of Horace' Pope
ponders the topic:

> Years foll'wing Years, steal something ev'ry day,
> At last they steal us from our selves away;
>
>   .   .   .   .
>
> This subtle Thief of Life, this paltry Time,
> What will it leave me, if it snatch my Rhime?
> If ev'ry Wheel of that unweary'd Mill
> That turn'd ten thousand Verses, now stands still.[11]

Pope's urbane wit here makes the turns of his versification result from
the rotations of a mill-wheel, treats his creative activity as a mechanical
cranking-out of lines. For the thirty-one-year-old Wordsworth in the
opening section of the poem he later entitled 'Ode: Intimations of
Immortality from Recollections of Early Childhood', written in 1802,
the loss of a former self is viewed differently, less as a stoppage of
production than as a severance of vision:

> The things which I have seen I see them now no more.[12]

The broken statement of immediate fact, with its redundant but affecting 'them', is reseen in the completed 1804 version of the poem and
made a loss of general capacity:

---

[11] 'The Second Epistle of the Second Book of Horace Imitated by Mr Pope', *The Poems of Alexander Pope: a one-volume edition of the Twickenham text with selected annotations*, ed. John Butt, London, 1977, p. 652.
[12] *'Poems in Two Volumes', and Other Poems 1800–1807 by William Wordsworth*, ed. Jared Curtis, Ithaca, 1983, p. 361.

The things which I have seen I now can see no more.[13]

In 'Lines written a few miles above Tintern Abbey', the returning poet is 'changed, no doubt, from what I was', but seeks relief in the thought that 'other gifts | Have followed, for such loss, I would believe, | Abundant recompense'.[14] It is possible to hear in 'I *would* believe' the mildly plaintive note of a momentarily acknowledged wishfulness. Wordsworth's grand self-satisfaction in his own ambitious doings and redoings is always stalked by loss and self-doubt.

'Lifeless as a written book' in Book viii of *The Prelude* turned out to be prophetic, for on completing the poem in 1805 Wordsworth was not as pleased as he had hoped.

I had looked forward to the day as a most happy one; and I was indeed grateful to God for giving me life to complete the work, such as it is; but it was not a happy day for me; I was dejected on many accounts; when I looked back upon the performance it seemed to have a dead weight about it, the reality so far short of the expectation; it was the first long labour that I had finished, and the doubt whether I should ever live to write *The Recluse*, and the sense which I had of this poem being so far below what I seemed capable of executing, depressed me much ...[15]

We will see how such a disappointed sense of the deadness of 'a written book' afflicts James too as his works succeed each other; and how, like Wordsworth, he responds by revising—though less in the Wordsworthian mode of revision soon begun and repeatedly applied, in spite of his readjustments between magazine and book form, than in that of revision long-delayed and then intensively thoroughgoing. Wordsworth's 'doubt', at any rate, 'whether I should ever live to write *The Recluse*' (his projected great philosophical poem) was justified: the line in the 1805 *Prelude* referring to it as forthcoming—'But this is matter for another song' (xi. 184)—was as the Norton editors tell us 'not removed until Wordsworth's final revision, in 1839 or later'. The 1850 text just says, poignantly, 'But leave we this' (xii. 140).[16] Even so, by Isabella Fenwick's account the 1839 revision of the poem was moving to Wordsworth as a sign of unfailing powers: 'it seemed always on his

[13] *'Poems in Two Volumes'*, p. 271.
[14] Wordsworth and Coleridge, *Lyrical Ballads*, ed. R. L. Brett and A. R. Jones, London, 1981, pp. 115, 116.
[15] Wordsworth to Sir George Beaumont, quoted in Mary Moorman, *William Wordsworth: A Biography: The Later Years 1803–1850*, Oxford, 1968, p. 55.
[16] *The Prelude*, pp. 424, 425.

mind—quite a possession', she says; and he was eloquent on the subject of his success in revising, 'of the difficulties he has had and how he had overcome them, of the *beautiful* additions he had made, and all the why and wherefore of each alteration'. She records the sixty-eight-year-old Wordsworth's greatest emotion in this connection, the tears drawn from him by a comment from his wife Mary, who rarely paid compliments: 'Well, William, I declare you are cleverer than ever.'[17] Wordsworth's tears make a possible sly suggestion on her part, that his revisions are merely clever, feel unlikely. She may, though, be deliberately having resort to a grudging, unsatisfactory term in order to avoid the false note that would be struck by sublime praise in a familiar domestic relation.

To be not just 'cleverer than ever', but wiser, truer, righter, is the aspiration of the revising artist: to stave off the imbecility of age and beyond it the silence of the grave, through creative activity, for as long as possible. The act of writing is in the first place an attempt to re-present the past, and to save it by artistic vividness—or at least half-save it—from death and oblivion. In Book xi of the 1805 *Prelude* Wordsworth is less absolutely blind to 'the things which I have seen' than in the Ode, and opposes failing sight to the preservative powers of verse and their effect on his own spiritual well-being:

> I see by glimpses now, when age comes on
> May scarcely see at all; and I would give
> While yet we may, as far as words can give,
> A substance and a life to what I feel:
> I would enshrine the spirit of the past
> For future restoration   (xi. 337–42)[18]

Wordsworth hopes the relation between feeling and writing will be a reciprocally sustaining one: the 'future restoration' is probably of *him*, poetry as a restorative, but it may also refer to his rehandling of *it*, the poet as restorer of his poem. At any rate, writing is to be a 'substance' able to 'enshrine' a 'spirit', a unifying of the past and present selves which, at other moments of intense memory, have seemed disturbingly distinct (both clear and separate):

---

[17] Quoted in *William Wordsworth: A Biography: The Later Years 1803–1850*, p. 501.
[18] *The Prelude*, pp. 432–4. When age really comes on, with the aged Wordsworth's revision for the 1850 text, the sustaining aspiration is more qualified: 'enshrining, | Such is my hope' (xii. 284–5, p. 435).

> so wide appears
> The vacancy between me and those days,
> Which yet have such self-presence in my mind
> That sometimes when I think of them I seem
> Two consciousnesses—conscious of myself,
> And of some other being.   (ii. 28–33)[19]

This double 'self-presence' is given 'a substance and a life' in *The Prelude*, but only 'as far as words can give'. The limits of language impose melancholy limitations on the poetic registration of feelings. Revision, though, can be a second chance to push back the limits of words, represents an effort to bring at least two selves—the poet at the time of first composition and the later, wiser poet—into co-operation, so that the text of the poem becomes the medium for a living relation.

Every revision marks a more or less different vision from that in an earlier text; so it is likely that every revision will be felt progressive according to some criteria and retrograde according to others. More beautiful may be less vigorous; more intelligible less suggestive; more vivid less impartial. Wordsworth has left us some poems in puzzlingly diverse versions, where it is hard to decide which criteria to espouse; such as 'Old Man Travelling' in the 1798 *Lyrical Ballads*, which in 1800 is called by its 1798 subtitle, 'Animal Tranquillity and Decay, A Sketch'. At the end of the 1798 poem, after a carefully loaded description of his shuffling gait, the narrator asks the slow-going old man 'whither he was bound', and receives an answer in direct speech, beginning with an exclamation:

> 'Sir! I am going many miles to take
> 'A last leave of my son, a mariner,
> 'Who from a sea-fight has been brought to Falmouth,
> 'And there is dying in an hospital.'[20]

But in the 1800 edition the answer is flattened into indirect speech:

> That he was going many miles to take
> A last leave of his son, a mariner,
> Who from a sea-fight had been brought to Falmouth,
> And there was lying in an hospital.

This version removes us from the dramatizing address of 'Sir!', and

---

[19] *The Prelude*, p. 66.
[20] *Lyrical Ballads*, pp. 106–7.

ends with a daringly low-key substitution of 'lying' for 'dying' ('A last leave' is thus left to convey the moving fact by a nationally charac- teristic understatement). The marvelling report of the inexplicit poet makes the old man an object of wonder. In the 1800 version, of course, we cannot *know* that what we are getting is a simple transposition of direct speech—it could be the poet's abstract of a long monologue; and there is a point of view which would regard the 1800 version as infringing the old man's right to speak. Such a view would hardly be placated by the text of 1815 and after, which ends with the description of the old man's gait, before the narrator has even addressed him: 'He is by nature led | To peace so perfect, that the young behold | With envy, what the old man hardly feels.' The tension between 'Old *Man* Travelling' and '*Animal* Tranquillity and Decay', which can be seen at work in the 1800 shift from direct to indirect speech, leaving room for doubts about the old man's articulacy, is finally resolved—or, objectors might say, dissolved—in this reduction of the poem to its first part, where the weight falls on insensibility, on 'what the old man hardly feels'. It is a live question whether the 1815 poem evokes enough human feeling for this 'hardly' to have the proper poignancy. It can certainly be argued that the muted but not yet silenced exchange between poet and old man in 1798 and 1800 sounds as a measure of humane correction, of social reconnection, against the opening treatment of him as a mysteriously alien, only-just-human being on the verge of becoming an object in nature.

Every work makes different demands of the reviser, and every reviser inevitably approaches a work otherwise than as its original author. There may be reasonable qualms about Wordsworth's statement of principle in 1830 to Alexander Dyce: 'You know what importance I attach to following strictly the last Copy of the text of an Author.'[21] It would be equally wrong, however, to have no qualms about dis- regarding 'the last Copy of the text of an Author'.

'Wm. wrote out part of his poem and endeavoured to alter it and so made himself ill.'[22] Dorothy Wordsworth's diary for 26 January 1802 bluntly evokes some of the strain of the endeavour of revision. The same strain afflicted a later nineteenth-century poet, Alfred Tenny- son—only more severely, for Tennyson did not have Wordsworth's

[21] Quoted in *William Wordsworth, Poems*, i. 23.
[22] Quoted in Mary Moorman, *William Wordsworth: A Biography: The Early Years 1770–1803*, Oxford, 1968, p. 520.

possibly justifiable self-confidence. If Wordsworth's revisions largely constitute an assertion of the poetic authority of self (*new* self), those of Tennyson, a self-doubting individual anxious to serve as the poetic voice of his less consciously troubled nation, frequently defer to the authority of his readers and reviewers. When readers disagree with one another about a poem, and when a poet disagrees with himself about it, such revision will show the strain.

The American poet Frederick Goddard Tuckerman, who had recently visited the Tennysons, wrote on 22 February 1855 with what one imagines to be some embarrassment.

Do you remember my quoting some lines one evening from a newspaper and objecting to the rhymes 'blunder'd' and [']Hundred', thinking it should read 'blundered'? I had then seen exactly *three* lines, and knew nothing of the connexion. Judge then of my surprise at discovering the whole poem in an American paper, with your name attached.[23]

'Was there a man dismayed?' The gaffe is just about atoned for, immediately afterwards, with handsome praise.

I read it with a mixture of astonishment and delight and think it a most noble performance, the finest irregular Ode ever written upon the grandest subject. The repetitions too are wonderfully effective and I cannot help hoping that this poem will not receive any alterations. (Of course I refer to your general habit of retouching your poems and not to any remark of mine.)

But it was too late for Tuckerman to retract, and in any case other connoisseurs of rhyme had commented on the imperfection. On 8 July Tennyson wrote to Tuckerman promising him a copy of *Maud, and Other Poems*, due to be published on 28 July and containing 'The Charge of the Light Brigade'. The comments had found a sensitive, prickly target, whose apology for giving 'offence' showed he had taken it:

You will find in my little volume 'The Charge of the Light Brigade' with the 'blunder'd' that offended you and others, omitted. It is not a poem on which

---

[23] *The Letters of Alfred Lord Tennyson*, ed. Cecil Y. Lang and Edgar F. Shannon, Jr., 2 vols. to date, Oxford, 1981, 1987, ii. 108. A text of the poem with all relevant variants is to be found in *The Poems of Tennyson*, ed. Christopher Ricks, 3 vols., London, 1987, ii. 510–13; and there is a full account by Edgar Shannon and Christopher Ricks of 'the skill and tact—themselves illuminated by a major temporary lapse—with which the artist perfected his work' in ' "The Charge of the Light Brigade": The Creation of a Poem', *Studies in Bibliography*, 38 (1985), 1–44 (it is from this article that I take the text of the letters).

I pique myself but I cannot help fancying that, such as it is, I have improved it.[24]

Having thus seemed to confess by unboldly withdrawing the lines in question that *he* had 'blunder'd', Tennyson changed his mind or his 'fancy' again less than a month later in a letter to John Forster. He had learned that the soldiers in the Crimea themselves liked the version with 'blunder'd' and 'hundred', and sent what was in the controversial respects the original text to be distributed there by the Society for the Propagation of the Gospel.

The soldiers are the best critics in what pleases them. I send you a copy wh retains 'the light Brigade' & the 'blunder'd' & I declare I believe it is the best of the two & that the criticism of two or three London friends (not yours) induced me to spoil it.[25]

Here we find the poet who 'cannot help fancying that ... I have improved it' by crucial omissions (the other being of the poem's final injunction to 'Honour the Light Brigade'), engaged within a few weeks in restoring them and declaring superlatively of the resultant version 'I believe it is the best of the two' (not even just 'the better'). Tuckerman apparently wrote at the beginning of October reiterating his sense that the 1854 text of the poem, the one he had originally seen, would have been best without an alteration; for in October Tennyson wrote back to him that 'You are quite right about the Charge. I was overpersuaded to spoil it.'[26]

Overpersuasion and moderate, reasonable persuasion were not the only influences prompting Tennyson to revise. He suffered from the nervousness of the perfectionist at the prospect of publication, in a degree which led him, for *In Memoriam*, nearly to anticipate in fact the fantasy of Henry James's hero Dencombe in 'The Middle Years' of 1893, whose 'ideal would have been to publish secretly, and then, on the published text, treat himself to the terrified revise, sacrificing always a first edition and beginning for posterity and even for the collectors, poor dears, with a second'.[27] Tennyson's printing of about twenty-five copies of his 'Elegies' to Arthur Hallam in (probably) March 1850, two months before their official publication, was less 'secret' than 'private', but the few friends to whom he sent it were

[24] *The Letters of Alfred Lord Tennyson*, ii. 114.
[25] (6 Aug. 1855), *The Letters of Alfred Lord Tennyson*, ii. 117.
[26] (17 Oct. 1855), *The Letters of Alfred Lord Tennyson*, ii. 133.
[27] *Terminations*, London, 1895, p. 181.

'perfectly welcome to a copy' only 'on the condition that when the book is published, this vaunt courier of it shall be either sent back to me, or die the death by fire'.[28] This printing, known by Tennyson scholars as the 'trial edition', is partly a pre-emptive manœuvre manifesting a consciousness that, in Pope's words, 'whoever publishes, puts himself on his tryal by his country'.[29] Critical friends can have their say and perhaps save the poet from unfriendly critics, whose judgements may be fiercer. But it is also in part a mark of the perfectionist and sensitive author shy of publication because possessed by a sense of its momentousness. Many of Tennyson's poems were long arriving in print after their first composition. In 1847 he wrote to his aunt Russell on the subject of his 'Elegies', contemplating, like Wordsworth with the posthumously published and thus eerily-named *Prelude*, the possibility of never giving this major work to the world in his lifetime. 'With respect to the non-publication of those poems which you mention, it is partly occasioned by the considerations you speak of, and partly by my sense of their present imperfectness; perhaps they will not see the light till I have ceased to be. I cannot tell but I have no wish to send them out yet.'[30] Personal reticence is thus a partial motive (as with *The Prelude*); but a sense of 'present imperfectness' dictates in him this holding-off from the publicity of print, even after a gestation spanning many years.

Something similar happened with 'Tithonus', originally written as 'Tithon' in 1833 and put away. Thackeray in 1859 asked so insistently for something to help start the *Cornhill Magazine* 'that I ferreted among my old books and found this "Tithonus", written upwards of a quarter of a century ago'.[31] Like *In Memoriam*, 'Tithonus' arises out of the death of Tennyson's friend Hallam; as with Wordsworth, questions of publication and textual detail in the poetry become inextricable from the strong feelings, the hopes, ambitions, griefs, and despairs of the poet's human life. The 1833 Tithon recalls feeling the sensual glow of Aurora's dawn,

> Ay me! ay me! with what another heart,
> By thy divine embraces circumfused,

---

[28] *The Letters of Alfred Lord Tennyson*, i. 321.

[29] 'A Letter to the Publisher' in 'The Dunciad Variorum', *The Poems of Alexander Pope*, p. 319.

[30] Quoted in Hallam Tennyson, *Alfred Lord Tennyson: A Memoir*, 2 vols., London, 1897, i. 243.

[31] *The Letters of Alfred Lord Tennyson*, ii. 252.

Thy black curls burning into sunny rings ...[32]

In 1860 Tithonus, with the poignant remove of Tennyson's further 'quarter of a century', finds a more broken, divided note here:

> Ay me! ay me! with what another heart
> In days far-off, and with what other eyes
> I used to watch—if I be he that watched—
> The lucid outline forming round thee; saw
> The dim curls kindle into sunny rings; ...[33]

The revising poet's question about his own identity with the young poet 'in days far-off'—is it 'rather the production of another person than his own'?—is turned to creative account in the poem. It appears as the anguished wonder 'if I be he that watched', and enriches—that is for poor Tithonus impoverishes—the experience of Tennyson's ageing-but-immortal character. The doubt about the integrity and continuity of the authorial 'I' over time—which threatens both the success and the legitimacy of all attempts at revision—is here turned to artistic advantage in the revision of a memory of uncannily distant days.

ii. Free Handling: James

Henry James was conscious of 'the circumstance that the poets then, and the more charming ones, *have* in a number of instances, with existing matter in hand, "registered" their renewals of vision' (*LC* ii. 1334). James's 'then' refers to his extending the word 'poet' to cover all creative writers, in the passage which precedes this one in the Preface to *The Golden Bowl* (the final piece of work—bar proof-reading—he did for the New York Edition). Arguing for the significance of the developed authorial 'taste' which manifests itself in the new readings of a revised text, James has stated that the 'poet' 'feels this himself, good man—he recognises an attached importance—whenever he feels [his] consciousness bristle with the notes, as I have called them, of consenting re-perusal; as has again and again publicly befallen him, to our no small edification, on occasions within recent view' (*LC* ii. 1333). And anticipating objections to the treatment of

---

[32] *The Poems of Tennyson*, i. 622.
[33] *The Poems of Tennyson*, ii. 610–11.

the language of prose with a seriousness customarily reserved for that of poetry, James has made a forceful appeal to first principles:

It has befallen him most frequently, I recognise, when the supersessive terms of his expression have happened to be verse; but that doesn't in the least isolate his case, since it is clear to the most limited intelligence that the title we give him is the only title of *general* application and convenience for those who passionately cultivate the image of life and the art, on the whole so beneficial, of projecting it. The seer and speaker under the descent of the god is the 'poet', whatever his form ... (*LC* ii. 1333–4).

James concedes that the public 'occasions within recent view' on which 'poets' have revised their works have mostly 'happened' to involve verse. He seems likely to be thinking of Browning's great final collected edition of his works in sixteen volumes, published in 1888–9, and of the posthumous Tennyson edition of 1894, incorporating last revisions, which was the basis of the grand Eversley edition in nine volumes, issued like the New York Edition by Macmillan in 1907–8. He was certainly also aware of the collected editions of Meredith and Stevenson, and of Kipling, twenty-two years his junior—all three 'poets' in verse as well as in prose fiction.

The *Golden Bowl* Preface depicts James as having for a long time before the New York Edition shared the reluctance we find in Keats to reconsider past works: not perhaps a wish to 'burn the piece in question', but at least 'to get and to keep finished and dismissed work well behind one, and to have as little to say to it and about it as possible' (*LC* ii. 1330).[34]

This should not though be taken as meaning that James had failed, earlier in his career, to return to already published writings in order to refit them for reissue. He produced in 1883 a fourteen-volume

---

[34] The cases are not quite congruent: 'finished and dismissed' refers to *published* works, whereas Keats seems to be thinking of manuscripts. If we try to make a distinction, however, between the alterations made in a drafting process aiming towards a first printed publication, and those in the revision of a published text, we run into difficulties: not all manuscript revisions are part of a drafting process; and for some writers even publication can be part of a drafting process. Every writer's attitude to print is a mark of artistic individuality. The attempt at such a distinction is further complicated by cases, such as *The Prelude* and *In Memoriam*, where works have circulated in manuscript fair copies for a considerable length of time before they are published, thereby receiving changes over much greater spans of years than many works which are printed, published, and revised soon afterwards for a second edition. The very diversity of circumstances and attitudes, though, makes each individual's practice of revision critical evidence about his or her sense of what writing involves.

collected edition of his works, in carefully prepared texts, and in 1885 three volumes of *Stories Revived*, many of which were extensively worked over. But between *Partial Portraits* of 1888 and 1905, when he revised many early travel-pieces for collection in *English Hours*, James published no retrospective collections of this order; which is presumably what the Preface is referring to.

James shows early in his career, like Wordsworth and Tennyson, to whose works he frequently alludes, an elegiac sense of the passage of time and its effects in human lives. Rather like Tennyson, who wrote in his young manhood poems about old men preoccupied with evanescence and the long perspective, James published in 1879, at the age of thirty-six, *The Diary of a Man of Fifty*. The story could be taken as an allegory of revision, in so far as its hero is prompted vividly to recall his own bitter experience years before, in a risky love-affair from which he baled out perhaps too soon, by returning to the place where it happened and seeing a parallel situation to that ambiguous past one in the younger generation. He has a quasi-authorial decision to make: whether to permit the new affair to run what he expects to be its unhappy natural course, or to intervene with the wisdom of experience. His diary begins with a passage that revives the concerns figured by the 'two consciousnesses' in *The Prelude* or Tennyson's 'what another heart' and 'what other eyes' in 'Tithonus'. The perception of the past, like Wordsworth's of the cave, starts as 'lifeless as a written book', and then comes wonderfully back to life.

They told me I should find Italy greatly changed; and in seven and twenty years there is room for changes. But to me everything is so perfectly the same that I seem to be living my youth over again; all the forgotten impressions of that enchanting time come back to me. At the moment they were powerful enough; but they afterwards faded away. What in the world became of them? What ever becomes of such things, in the long intervals of consciousness? Where do they hide themselves away? In what unvisited cupboards and crannies of our being do they preserve themselves? They are like the lines of a letter written in sympathetic ink; hold the letter to the fire for a while and the grateful warmth brings out the invisible words. It is the warmth of this yellow sun of Florence that has been restoring the text of my own young romance; the thing has been lying before me today as a clear, fresh page (*THJ* iii. 334).[35]

---

[35] The same images and verbal patterns come up in 'The Middle Years', a story published in 1893 when James *was* fifty, when Dencombe, whose art has been his life, is reading his last book. The 'clear, fresh page' is echoed in 'the fresh pages' there

The spirit of the past has here been enshrined not in such substance as words can give, but in some 'unvisited cupboards and crannies of our being'. Even so, the old text, the early 'impression', comes in for 'future restoration'. Recovered experience is imagined as the surviving life of a book or letter—for writing is a powerful though imperfect image for the rescue of memories from oblivion—and James's ingenuity finds 'sympathetic ink' (an exact pun on one nineteenth-century name for invisible ink) to imply that the ink somehow holds and preserves the original feelings, feels *with* us. He resorts to the image of an old text being warmed into 'a fresh clear page' in order to render this 'self-presence' in his hero's mind of his long-gone youth. The year before, James had extensively revised his first novel, *Watch and Ward* of 1871, hitherto published only in the *Atlantic Monthly*, for issue in volume form.

In 1885 James wrote to Benjamin Ticknor saying that his forthcoming volume was to be called '(probably at least) "Stories Revived" (not *revised*!)'.[36] But they had been: shortly after this he belies the joke by writing of 'correcting and amending' the stories included 'with my customary deliberation'—like an *habitué* of the practice. The 'Notice' to the first volume of *Stories Revived* points out, of the earlier stories, that 'In the matter of revision ... they have been very freely handled', 'in every case minutely revised and corrected—many passages being wholly rewritten'.[37] The note struck by Wordsworth's reintroduction of *Benjamin the Waggoner* in his 1830s version as 'retouched & inspirited' is re-sounded in the writer's assurance here: 'He is confident that they have gained, not lost, freshness by the process of retouching to which they have been subjected.' One of the changes involved offers a jocular parody of the kind of 'overpersuasion' from which Tennyson had suffered. James wrote to his old friend in Cambridge, Massachusetts, Grace Norton, on 21 March 1885 to let her know that he was sending her the latest version of another of his old stories:

You shall have still one thing more: a thing (*A Most Extraordinary Case*) which I well remember Jane and you talking about to me one evening at

---

(*Terminations*, p. 170), and the 'yellow sun of Florence' which revives this freshness recurs in 'the spring sunshine on the page' (*Terminations*, p. 171). In both cases the text fades only to return: 'all the forgotten impressions of that enchanting time come back to me' comes back as 'He had forgotten what his book was about ... Everything came back to him' (*Terminations*, pp. 170–1).

[36] HJ to Ticknor, 30 Jan. 1885 (Berg MS).

[37] 'Notice', dated 'February 1885', to *Stories Revived*, 3 vols., London 1885, vol. i.

Shady Hill, a thousand years ago, and our having an immense, interminable laugh over. The heroine in it nibbled a cake, which you didn't like; and in this revision I have suppressed the cake and the nibbling, thinking of you, but with the feeling, throughout, that the lady must be hungry (*HJL* iii. 76–7).

It may have been ungenteel for Caroline Hofmann, telling the hero she loves and who loves her that she is to marry another, to eat in the *Atlantic Monthly* original:

'Don't be afraid,' said Caroline, smiling, and taking a bite from her cake (*THJ* i. 256).

But a sinister suggestion may be introduced when the story is revived in 1885:

'Don't be afraid,' said Caroline, patting her skirt softly with her whip.[38]

The domestic gesture cedes to the potentially melodramatic here, in a story James was never again to revive.

The impulse to revise stirred in James even when self-effacement might seem to be required by the nature of the task in hand—such as a translation from the French of Daudet's *Port-Tarascon* in 1890. James is to be found retouching and, most would grant, inspiriting.

Par les routes poudreuses des banlieues de Tarascon passait au grand trot le cabriolet de Tartarin, conduisant lui-même, avec le Père Baillet assis près de lui sur le devant, serrés l'un près de l'autre pour faire un rempart de leur corps au duc de Mons, enveloppé d'un voile vert et dévoré par les moustiques, qui l'assaillaient rageusement de tous côtés, en troupes bourdonnantes, altérés du sang de l'homme du Nord, s'acharnant à le boursoufler de leurs piqûres.[39]

A literal translation might read:

Through the dusty roads of the outskirts of Tarascon would speed Tartarin's coach, driven by its owner, with Father Baillet squeezed beside him on the front seat to make a rampart of their bodies for the Duc de Mons, who was wrapped in a green veil and devoured by mosquitoes that were furiously attacking him from all sides in buzzing hordes, slaked with the Northerner's blood and determined to swell him up with their stings.

Here is James's:

On the dusty roads of the neighborhood Tartarin's gig kept passing at a swinging trot. Tartarin in person and Brother Baillet, placed in front, sat as

---

[38] *Stories Revived*, iii. 260.
[39] Alphonse Daudet, *Port-Tarascon: Dernières Aventures de l'Illustre Tartarin*, Paris, 1890, p. 42.

close together as possible, to make a rampart of their bodies for the Duc de Mons, enveloped in a green veil and devoured by mosquitoes, which assailed him with rage on all sides in buzzing battalions, in spite of Tartarin and the Brother, in spite of the veil, in spite of the great whacks his Grace dealt himself. Gorged with the blood of the man of the North, they continued to apply an unrelenting sting to surfaces already completely distended.[40]

The Gallophile James keeps close touch with French idiom here in his translating: 'assailed him with rage' and 'the blood of the man of the North' may initially come across as ploddingly literal, mere transliteration. But for James the French word *rage* has absolutely different connotations from its English relatives, which his seeming literalism avoids obliterating; and the excessively grand and overblown epic sound of 'the man of the North' actually renders the mocked heroic aspirations of the pompous Southerners of Tarascon. What may surprise us more than this is the apt but gratuitous comic inflation of the mosquito attack: the introduction of the triple barricade the insects succeed in piercing ('in spite of Tartarin and the Brother, in spite of the veil, in spite of the great whacks his Grace dealt himself'); and the pumping-up of the poor Duc's bitten flesh to be stung even worse than in Daudet ('continued to apply an unrelenting sting to surfaces already completely distended'). James knows he is addressing himself here to what is a sore point for much of his readership in the thin-skinned Anglo-Saxon world.

If Daudet's original text of *Port-Tarascon* was 'very freely handled' by James in 1890, so in the next year was his own original novel, *The American* of 1876, in his dramatization of it: more a new work than a revised text. He first wrote a version for Edward Compton's company in which the tragic conviction he had expressed to W. D. Howells in 1877, that Christopher Newman and Claire de Cintré 'would have been an impossible couple, with an impossible problem before them' (*HJL* ii. 104), seems to be contradicted by a happy ending in which they are united: Claire declares 'that I shall marry Mr. Newman', and Newman kisses her hand, with an 'Ah, my beloved!'[41] Apparently, though, this version wasn't quite happy enough, for in 1892 James wrote it a new fourth act 'in a comedy-sense—heaven forgive me!', as he confided to his brother William; 'the fourth is now *another* fourth

---

[40] Alphonse Daudet, *Port Tarascon: The Last Adventures of the Illustrious Tartarin*, trans. Henry James, New York, 1891, pp. 49–50.
[41] *The Complete Plays of Henry James*, ed. Leon Edel, London, 1949, p. 237.

which will basely gratify their artless instincts and British thick-wit-
tedness' (*HLJ* iii. 397). In this new act Claire's brother Valentin does
not die of the wound sustained in his duel with Lord Deepmere
('DOCTOR: Great news—great news! He's *better*!').[42] In this case the
commercial motive for revision is nakedly confessed, and we might
see some degree of mischievous self-reference in the early scene introduced by the play between Noémie the pretty copyist and her innocent
patron Newman, where she shows him the further work she has put
in on the painting he liked:

NOÉMIE. I think I've improved it.
NEWMAN. Well, yes, I suppose you've improved it; but I don't know but I
    liked it better before it was quite so *good*![43]

This picks up a suggestion in the original novel, where, when the
picture arrives, 'It had been endued with a layer of varnish an inch
thick, and its frame, of an elaborate pattern, was at least a foot wide'
(*1883*, i. 49). Though the play of *The American* seriously rethinks, like
The Reverberator of 1888, the aesthetically unsatisfactory relation
between the American suitor and the grand Parisian family, and contains ingenuities like the economical doubling-up of Lord Deepmere
as Newman's rival for Claire *and* Valentin's for Noémie, the reviser's
varnish is a bit thick in it. Unlike Noémie and Tennyson, moreover,
James does not seem to fancy that he has really 'improved' it.

Before each work could be 'finished and dismissed' in publication,
it had to *be* 'finished', and James's fidelity to the 'expansive, the
explosive principle in [his] material' (*LC* ii. 1278) often made finishing
a long-drawn-out business. On 12 June 1900, for instance, he was
writing to his agent Pinker that he was on the point of sending off the
last bit of copy for *The Sacred Fount* 'for reproduction with embodied
new inspired last touches'.[44] 'Inspired' is an inserted late thought in
the text of the letter, itself a last touch of self-advertisement. Seven
days later he was writing again to say that 'I have found it a more
protracted matter to *end* it—I mean finish & super-finish it—than I
expected at the moment I originally wrote you about it'.[45] The par-
enthetic phrase—with its self-mockingly inflationary overdoing—is
another insertion, another 'inspired last touch'.

The New York Edition is James's main piece of finishing and super-

---

[42] *The Complete Plays*, p. 250.
[43] *The Complete Plays*, p. 196.
[44] HJ to Pinker, 12 June 1900 (Yale MS).
[45] HJ to Pinker, 19 June 1900 (Yale MS).

finishing. As an act of revision it differs significantly from those of Wordsworth and Tennyson. It is not an habitual activity, renewed periodically for each work over a number of years (as with Wordsworth's 1850 *Prelude*), but a single massive project, self-consciously undertaken at a particular point in time as the review of a whole career. Equally, it is not in any serious sense a response to external criticism: James frequently expresses his disgust with the level of contemporary literary debate. It is rather a self-motivated, perfectionist attempt to bring an *œuvre* created over a period of thirty-seven years up to a standard satisfactory to the author produced by that long development.

For a novelist to take his phrasings so seriously, devoting such painstaking attention to the adjustment of cadence and nuance, required a considerable break with the philistine tradition about English fiction James had characterized in 1884 in 'The Art of Fiction': 'a comfortable, good-humoured feeling ... that a novel is a novel, as a pudding is a pudding' (*LC* i. 44). Puddings are for immediate consumption, and to reheat old puddings is to make a poor show; so to write a novel and revise it seems to the philistine way of thinking a defiance of proverbial common sense. In one of the *Stories Revived* of 1885, Mark Ambient, an artist besieged by Philistines, and the eponymous *Author of 'Beltraffio'* (1884), utters a lament to his young admirer about the imperfections of his work:

There are horrible little flabby spots where I have taken the second-best word, because I couldn't for the life of me think of the best. If you knew how stupid I am sometimes! They look to me now like pimples and ulcers on the brow of beauty![46]

The author of *The Author of 'Beltraffio'*, reviving and revising this story in 1908 for the *NYE*, finds here what he feels is a better word than 'best' and, indeed, a better word than 'word'.

There are horrible sandy stretches where I've taken the wrong turn because I couldn't for the life of me find the right. If you knew what a dunce I am sometimes! Such things figure to me now base pimples and ulcers on the brow of beauty! (*NYE* xvi. 43–4.)

The multiple and various 'right' turns made by James in the course of his work on the *NYE* are attempts to cleanse the brow of beauty; they

---

[46] *Stories Revived*, i. 40.

show us an author who is not so much of a 'dunce', one doing his new best to be 'cleverer than ever' in the pursuit of beauty of expression.

In a story which first appeared the year before *The Author of 'Beltraffio'*, *The Siege of London* of 1883, James's American hero Waterville is asked to denounce his compatriot Mrs Headway, an adventuress disreputable back home, by the English *grande dame* Lady Demesne, whose son is on the point of marrying this truly named social climber. Waterville resists the pressure, and demands how Lady Demesne can be hurt by the woman he knew in Texas as Nancy Beck: 'It hurts me to hear her voice', Lady Demesne replies. Waterville answers that

'Her voice is very sweet.'
'Possibly. But she's horrible!'[47]

In the *NYE* Waterville here thinks of the best word, where 'sweet' had been 'the second-best'—or so his new feeling implies:

'Her voice is very liquid.' He liked his word (*NYE* xiv. 240).

Waterville's new sense of the pleasantness of his choice of expression presumably reproduces James's new sense of it; James obviously likes what is *his* word as well as Waterville's; but primarily it has a dramatic force in the context, for the descriptive precision of 'liquid' avoids explicitly praising like 'sweet' but steers equally clear of the crudely requested denigration. The combination of accuracy and evasiveness is good reason for Waterville's satisfaction under the circumstances; and 'He liked his word' works dramatically, for Waterville in his tight corner and therefore for James in his portrayal of it.

James does *The Siege of London* another good turn at its end. Mrs Headway succeeds in marrying Lord Demesne through an ingenious and daring bluff, and the ambivalent Waterville ends in 1883 by hearing from New York that 'people were beginning to ask who in the world was Mrs. Headway'.[48] But this strikes the wrong note, for the marriage (the latest of many for her) has already taken place. The *NYE* reports instead that 'people were beginning to ask who in the world Lady Demesne "had been"' (*NYE* xiv. 271). Thus the besieging American multiple-divorcée finally takes over (for the first time in the text) the title of her enemy and mother-in-law; and the pluperfect tells us that

---

[47] *The Siege of London; Madame de Mauves*, London, 1883, p. 80.
[48] *The Siege of London*, p. 104.

her 'past' is indeed past—she is now safely a new person. At the end of *Pandora* (1884), the stiffly logical German hero similarly hears that the similarly pushy American heroine, with whom he has primly been in love, has married. She has charmed the President into making her fiancé an ambassador; and Vogelstein tells the fact to his mercilessly witty Washington friend, who has been observing his puzzled observations of Pandora Day.

He communicated this news to Mrs. Bonnycastle, who had not heard it, with the remark that there was now ground for a new induction as to the self-made girl.[49]

We do not get her reaction to his 'remark', and the 'remark' itself is incongruous. If 'ground for a new induction as to the self-made girl' is intended to render a rueful self-mockery on his part it means an unprepared access of new ironic flexibility in his character. If, on the other hand, it is to be taken straight, it brutally scorns his Teutonic rationalizations. The *NYE* notes this difficulty and makes him at *its* end a mute victim, with the deftest and most incisive of changes:

He communicated this news to Mrs. Bonnycastle, who had not heard it but who, shrieking at the queer face he showed her, met it with the remark that there was now ground for a new induction as to the self-made girl (*NYE* xviii. 168).

We can know here, more certainly than in the closing scene of *King Lear*, that the reallocation of a final speech to another speaker is decisively authorial; and the introduced shriek of Mrs Bonnycastle at his 'queer face' gives us a darker tone, harsh and parodic, with which to read the conclusion of a story that has drawn with strong lines a peculiarly modern and international tangle of competing values. Because Vogelstein has been in love with the mystifying Pandora, however ineffectually, his loss of the last word, and his passivity before what becomes a gratuitous joke at his expense by his supposed friend, combine to confirm the defeat of his romantic and philosophical efforts to get on to terms with her.

James's revisions in the *NYE* often spin significant jokes that revolve on the central axis of a whole fiction. *An International Episode* of 1879 follows two English aristocrats to America, where they are baffled by the social and sexual code of manners, with ultimately disastrous results. The younger, who is too encouraged by the openness of

[49] *Stories Revived*, i. 143.

American girls, falls in love and is at the last wounded to find he is (because a picturesque lord) not taken seriously. At the end of the first chapter their New York host Westgate sends them to join the women of his family at Newport.

> I hope you'll have a good time. Just let them do what they want with you. I'll come down by-and-by and look after you.[50]

The *NYE* steps up the 'American humour' in Westgate's alarming advice, adding a jovially threatening anticipation of the women as manipulative and predatory.

> I hope you'll have a good time. Just let them do what they want with you. Take it as it's meant. Renounce your own personality. I'll come down by and by and enjoy what's left of you (*NYE* xiv. 291).

It is young Lord Lambeth's failure to 'Take it as it's meant' that is his undoing; he has not a sufficiently cosmopolitan imagination to understand that he is only a romantic unreality for the novel-reading Bessie Alden. 'Enjoy what's left of you' extends the pleasant but unsettling aggression of American humour by making Westgate himself also a predator, rather than a protector as before. It is such sharpness that wins from F. R. Leavis, no admirer of late James, grudging praise of the *NYE* revisions in spite of Keatsian qualms: 'in revising he does, for the most part, improve, much as one might have expected the contrary of any systematic meddling by the late James with the work of his early prime'.[51]

James made great claims, however, for the *NYE* revision as establishing correctness, claims which are indisputably excessive. He wrote to Scribners on 12 May 1906 that he must see proof of the revised text of *Roderick Hudson* 'to ensure that absolutely supreme impeccability that such an Edition must have & that the Author's eye alone can finally contribute to'.[52] Since most of my subsequent chapters concentrate on the nature of James's achievement in the *NYE*, I close this introductory chapter with a few reminders that he failed, in revising and proof-reading, to 'ensure that absolutely supreme impeccability'.

In the *1882* text of *The Portrait of a Lady* from which James worked in his revision there remained some errors of reference (very possibly

---

[50] *Daisy Miller, An International Episode, etc*, 2 vols., London, 1879, i. 235.

[51] F. R. Leavis, 'The Appreciation of Henry James' (review of F. O. Matthiessen, *Henry James: The Major Phase*), *Scrutiny*, 14/3 (Spring 1947), 229.

[52] HJ to Scribner, 12 May 1906 (Princeton MS).

compositorial) to characters and places which had been brought into line in the 1883 Macmillan collected edition; and he had enough vigilance to apprehend them again in 1906. Thus where Isabel Archer has predicted that her cousin Ralph will fall in love with Henrietta Stackpole, the 1882 text puts it that

It was not apparent, at the end of three days, that his cousin had fallen in love with their visitor (*1882*, p. 74).

The NYE clears this up with a battery of firm and right possessives.

It was not apparent, at the end of three days, that her cousin had, according to her prophecy, lost his heart to their visitor (*NYE* iii. 122).

And not long after this *1882* has Lord Warburton telling Isabel he fell in love with her 'When you came to Gardencourt the other day' (p. 89), whereas she came *from* Gardencourt to his house at Lockleigh: the NYE gives the right name (*NYE* iii. 147). So far, so 'supreme': but peccability resurfaces.

Later on Isabel is considering the relations between her American journalist friend Henrietta and the extremely English Mr Bantling, 'these harmless confederates', or as the revision extravagantly makes them 'these groping celibates'.

It was as graceful on Henrietta's part to believe that Mr. Bantling took an interest in the diffusion of lively journalism, and in consolidating the position of lady-correspondents, as it was on the part of her companion to suppose that the cause of the *Interviewer*—a periodical of which he never formed a very definite conception—was, if subtly analysed (a task to which Mr. Bantling felt himself quite equal), but the cause of Miss Stackpole's coquetry (*1882*, p. 190).

This is a complex sentence, and James gets it wrong in the NYE, as he hadn't in the 1883 edition (the manuscript in the Houghton Library shows the mistake is his own). 'Her companion' becomes 'his companion' (*NYE* iii. 312), so that the sentence, even if less than subtly analysed, loses its sense and its balance. Some malign law of texts seems to demand that for a wrong masculine possessive made rightly feminine ('his' to 'her' cousin), James has to pay with a right feminine possessive made wrongly masculine ('her' to 'his' companion).[53]

---

[53] Another of these rare inadvertences (again involving a possessive) afflicts him later on, where Warburton, talking to Ralph, first 'was lighting a cigar' and then a moment later is 'puffing his cigar' (*1882*, p. 347). The NYE forgets the cigar has been lit up and brought into play, and so shifts unhappily to 'puffing a cigar' (*NYE* iv. 148).

Such errors may be part of the penalty of revision, a punishment
for the perfectionist urge which attempts 'absolutely supreme impeccability'. And the instances I have given are easily identifiable *as* 'errors'
because they are matters of fact within the work, violations of internal
consistency about what is going on. There is a much more serious,
and much less certain area of revision where the author's '*beautiful*
addition' may be to many readers an intrusive blot; and because the
author has often already given the work to the public, seemingly
'finished and dismissed' it, his right to add or omit or alter 'what [he
has] written, when almost inspired' may appear to have lapsed. The
criteria for judgement of his success, if we don't simply allow his latest
self to dictate them, are challengingly relative.

3

Confidence in Revision

i.   Hooking on Again

On 9 August 1900 *The Sense of the Past* was running into serious difficulties and James resorted to his notebook so that the close working-out of detail, as in his dramatic period, could see him on his way to a subject.

I must proceed now with a more rigorous economy, and I turn about, I finger other things over, asking, praying, feel something that will do instead. I take up, in other words, this little blessed, this sacred small, 'ciphering' pen that has stood me in such stead often already, and I call down on it the benediction of the old days, I invoke the aid of the old patience and passion and piety. They are always there—by which I mean *here*—if I give myself the chance to appeal to them (*Nks.*, p. 190).

The move from 'there' to '*here*' enacts the steadying presence of the old virtues; to regain the sense of continuity with past strengths and successes, here by the tried and testing elaboration of scenarios, is a means of restoring a shaken confidence in the currency of the imagination. For the fact that works have been produced in the past makes it *probable* that works will be produced in the future without a break of the sequence, but is no guarantee of it. What literary powers are— how far they can be possessed—is not clear in this context. So that in a crisis it will be necessary but difficult to invoke them, in order to re-establish the confidence for continuing activity. James does this nine and a half years later when drawing up another plan:

A sense with me, divine and beautiful, of hooking on again to the 'sacred years' of the old D.V. Gdns. time, the years of the whole theatric dream and the 'working out' sessions, all ineffable and uneffaceable, that went with that, and that still live again, somehow (indeed I *know* how!) in their ashes:—that sense comes to me, I say, over the *concetto* of fingering a little what I call the C.F. and Katrina B. subject (*Nks.*, pp. 202–3).

The old virtues do 'still live again'; the mysterious renewal is renewed, in a miraculously literal version of the immortal line from Gray's 'Elegy', 'Ev'n in our ashes live their wonted fires'.

What is it that James knows to be kindling the life of the past here, and what is the force of the confidence we find in his unhesitant account of the experience of revision in the Preface to *The Golden Bowl*?

No march, accordingly, I was soon enough aware, could possibly be more confident and free than this infinitely interesting and amusing *act* of re-appropriation; shaking off all shackles of theory, unattended, as was speedily to appear, with humiliating uncertainties, and almost as enlivening, or at least as momentous, as, to a philosophic mind, a sudden large apprehension of the Absolute (*LC* ii. 1330).

Revision especially involves confidence, for it brings up with peculiar sharpness questions of possession, re-possession, and self-possession, as well as the possibility of loss. Revision is a test of a life's development, and requires (but endangers) a trust in the continuing value of what has been done. As Theodora Bosanquet, James's secretary, puts it, 'it was Henry James's profound conviction that he could improve his early writing in nearly every sentence. Not to revise would have been to confess to a loss of faith in himself.'[1] The rehandling of past works challenges, then, but may unpredictably confirm, the temporal integrity of a literary career. To reappropriate something is to resume a relation with it, involving a sense of it as objectively there, a sense of yourself as self-possessed enough to possess it, and a sense of what it is to possess this thing. You could under the stress of revising quite imaginably lose any of these senses: the literary work might turn to ashes, you as an author might go to pieces, or you and it might no longer have anything to say to each other. It speaks, moreover, as an earlier manifestation of you; and in its dialogue with you this strange kinship may be painful, embarrassing, or charming. This structure of relations is important for James's confidence, both in revision as such, and in some other imaginative activities.

ii. Revisiting, Testing

The James family often summered in Newport, Rhode Island, and James wrote a travel piece about it, called simply 'Newport', in 1870 for *The Nation*. June 1905 thus found James conscious of an advantage in returning to get and write 'The Sense of Newport', which became

---

[1] *Henry James at Work*, p. 14.

Chapter 6 of *The American Scene*, the work immediately preceding, and overlapping with, the New York Edition. He had known the place before it became very fashionable, and now he knew it after it had gone out of fashion, something he realized in passing and repassing along the whole front on a June day without seeing another person. In this, 'I recognized matter for the intellectual thrill that attests a social revolution foreseen and completed' (*AS*, p. 213). To be 'on the spot' here, with memory's 'control' to check against the present experiment, induces a proper confidence:[2]

I saw, beyond all doubt, on the spot—and *there* came in, exactly, the thrill; I could remember far back enough to have seen it ['the whirligig of time'] begin to blow all the artless buyers and builders and blunderers into their places, leaving them there for half a century or so of fond security, and then to see it, of a sudden, blow them quite out again, as with the happy consciousness of some new amusing use for them, some other game still to play with them. This acquaintance, as it practically had been, with the whole rounding of the circle (even though much of it from a distance), was tantamount to the sense of having sat out the drama, the social, the local, that of a real American period, from the rise to the fall of the curtain—always assuming that truth of the reached catastrophe or *dénouement* (*AS*, p. 213).

The stretch of personal memory encompasses all the necessary differences of angle and contains 'the whole rounding of the circle'. Knowing the rounding of the circle is then 'tantamount' to feeling you have experienced the independently determined dramatic form of 'a real American period', gives a sense of being in a position to take in a substantial historical phenomenon, a full revolutionary action. The syntax expansively and then firmly enacts the rise and fall of so well-defined an American period—with the conscientious proviso that there not be another twist in the plot (as in fact there has been). The mastery of historical phases brought by such a knowledge makes James free of history, as well as subject to it; his sentences, his inclusive periods, subordinate the passage of the ages to the continuity of the observer.

The American Scene is also, however, a work in which his present sensibility and powers, and his personal history, are put to the test by his confrontation with a vast and miscellaneous subject—with regard

---

[2] Cf. James's instructions to Alvin Langdon Coburn in Dec. 1906 about taking a photograph in Venice for the New York Edition. 'You must judge for yourself, face to face with the object, how much, on the spot, it seems to lend itself to a picture' (quoted in Alvin Langdon Coburn, *Alvin Langdon Coburn, Photographer*, ed. Helmut and Alison Gernsheim, New York, 1978, p. 56).

to which, moreover, his long expatriation might be thought to put him in an uneasy position. In Newport and New York and Boston James is faced with his own past and what has become of it: which also raises the question of what has become of him. The late stories *The Jolly Corner* (1906), *Crapy Cornelia* (1908–9), and *A Round of Visits* (1909), written over the same period as *The American Scene* and the New York Edition, face their protagonists with varied forms of just such a question.

Seeing how the impressive Castle Garden theatre of his youth had been reduced to insignificance by the towering modernity of a revisited New York could produce in him 'a horrible, hateful sense of personal antiquity' (*AS*, p. 80), but the interest of observing and expressing the process practically justifies 'this superfluous consciousness' (*AS*, p. 190) of origins.

I had had my shudder, in that same Fourteenth Street, for the complete disappearance of a large church, as massive as brown stone could make it, at the engaging construction of which one's tender years had 'assisted' (it exactly faced the parental home, and nefarious, perilous play was found possible in the works), but which, after passing from youth to middle age and from middle age to antiquity, has vanished as utterly as the Assyrian Empire. (*AS*, p. 190).

The disappearance is 'complete', and a tacit comparison runs the life of the Fourteenth Street church against James's own: in the play from personal 'tender years' to figurative 'youth'; between an individual and the historical middle age; and from jocular to absolute antiquity. The sentence which contains this cycle of growth and extinction is a gauge of James's continuing empire, but empires come to an end. The same church was to provoke, six years later in *A Small Boy and Others*, another three-aged sentence, as a building 'which it now marks for me somewhat grimly a span of life to have seen laboriously rear itself, continuously flourish and utterly disappear' (*Autobiog.*, p. 132). James's sense of the still-flourishing powers of his own mind to frame sentences is poignantly put in perspective: the long view points 'somewhat grimly' towards the prospect of utter disappearance for minds and sentences alike.

iii.   A Sense for Impressions

The American Scene is self-confessedly and self-confidently a book of travel impressions, and the value James sets on impressions is high:

I would take my stand on my gathered impressions, since it was all for them, for them only, that I returned; I would in fact go to the stake for them—which is a sign of the value that I both in particular and in general attach to them and that I have endeavoured to preserve for them in this transcription (*AS*, Preface).

James finds a complex structure in the word 'impression'. He here primarily takes it as referring to the mental reception of external stimuli, a sense, however, metaphorically reinforced by drawing on the technical use of the word in printing (a 'Third Impression' and so forth). It is also backed for him by cognate ideas: 'pressure', 'impressiveness', 'impressionability'. The fact that 'impression' can be a technical term seems to be consciously recalled in James's uses of the word, which are less rigorous, to make it feel particularly pointed and to defend it against the casual reductiveness of phrases like 'just an impression'. James is stirred, in *The American Scene*, by the way his writing can convey perceptual impressions of American reality, through the impression of type on paper, into the various 'impressions' of a book. The continuity in the word 'impression' corresponds to the endeavour to preserve a value across 'transcription.'[3]

But there may be a dismissive response to this, which may also be the writer's own tormenting doubt: that there's 'nothing in' a mere 'impression'. After all, how can one 'substantiate' an impression? How 'real' is the imaginative realm? A literary artist's impression, so liable to the accusation of weightlessness, has to answer these charges on their own terms. And since it is exactly a question about 'terms' and their weight, it is to terms of weight that the artist often resorts. He has his 'material', as we say, and can appeal to the linguistic community for a practical sanction of such a figure of speech. It may be of a higher or lower degree of generality or abstraction, yet the fact that we call it 'material' has diverse metaphorical weightings, not only makes it the relevant raw material for mental industry, but may also insist on its substantiating materiality (and the sense of the word as 'cloth' can offer—as in the word 'stuff'—a particularity of texture to go with

---

[3] I am indebted, here and elsewhere, to William Empson's *The Structure of Complex Words*, London, 1951.

this). Hence the delicate play of these senses to evoke James's gratitude when he speaks of London as a source of themes in a Preface: 'It was material ever to one's hand' (*LC* ii. 1152). Primarily, of course, this means that things in London are available for fiction and that living in London puts them always within reach; but a more physical sense of it is also there, one made possible by the expansion of the offhand phrase 'to hand' into the thoughtful 'to one's hand'. In this sense 'material' is not a noun meaning 'accessible themes', but an adjective meaning 'real and substantial', and 'to one's hand' means not just 'there whenever one wants it', 'handy', but actually 'to the touch'. Eliot's 'Donne in Our Time' elucidates his relevant and difficult aphorism about James that 'He had a mind so fine that no idea could violate it':[4] 'Donne was, I insist, no sceptic: it is only that he is interested in and amused by ideas in themselves, and interested in the way in which he *feels* an idea; almost as if it were something that he could touch and stroke.'[5] James gravitates towards expressions which play with the elusive solidity of ideas (thus in the *Notebooks* 'I pick up for a minute the idea of the portrait *à la* Gualdo' (*Nks.*, p. 179)); that is, he often contrives to have the senses of touch and grasp within the metaphorical reach of his words about the processes and products of the imagination. Expressing to Scribners his confidence in *The Golden Bowl*, for instance, he declares that 'I hold the thing the *solidest*, as yet, of all my fictions.'[6]

Holding things, or rather expressing yourself so it seems you *could* hold them if you wanted, is related to the etymological or conceptual grounding of many apparently abstract words or concepts on physical and spatial relationships. If it were not for these basic relationships we could not 'grasp' the meanings of the words and concepts derived from them, and many of the ways in which we speak abstractly are implicitly drawn from a realm of objective substance. James's developed style habitually suggests the concrete even as it refines on

---

[4] 'On Henry James', collected in *The Question of Henry James*, ed. F. W. Dupee, New York, 1945, pp. 108–19, at p. 110.

[5] In *A Garland for John Donne 1631–1931*, ed. Theodore Spencer, Cambridge, Mass., 1931, pp. 11–12. Eliot uses similar terms to introduce his contrast between James and the unsensuous Henry Adams: 'It is probable that men ripen best through experiences which are at once sensuous and intellectual; certainly many men will admit that their keenest ideas have come to them with the quality of a sense-perception; and that their keenest sensuous experience has been "as if the body thought"' (*Athenaeum*, No. 4647, 23 May 1919).

[6] H J to Scribners, 17 Sept. 1904 (Harvard MS).

it, and his stylistic density gives rise to a sense of 'great matter'—
according to the account of his brother William, the most perceptive,
though not most balanced, critic of his later manner. In a letter William
says about *The American Scene* that

the complication of innuendo and associative reference on the enormous scale
to which you give way to it does so *build out* the matter for the reader that
the result is to solidify, by the mere bulk of the process, the like perception
from which *he* has to start. As air, by dint of its volume, will weigh like a
corporeal body; so his own poor little initial perception, swathed in this
gigantic envelopment of suggestive atmosphere, grows like a germ into something vastly bigger and more substantial.[7]

William is at once admiringly attracted to and pragmatically dubious
about his brother's manner of writing; the parody tactfully expresses
this combination of surrender and anxiety. He accurately expresses
the effect of the process as the arousal in the reader of 'the illusion of
a solid object, made ... wholly out of impalpable materials'. The airy
things or nothings of the imagination are not in fact things you can
pick up or sit on like the solid things of the physical world. A fertile
imaginative treatment of them as if you could really do so, however,
gives them body, promotes them from mere germhood up to the higher
standing of grown plants or fruit.

A solidifying of air into something more substantial occurs in the
very first section of *The American Scene*. James, back in his native
New York after a long absence, finds on page four that 'The whole
impression had fairly a rococo tone', and writes of 'this perceptibly
golden air, the air of old empty New York afternoons of the waning
summer-time' (*AS*, p. 4). Page 5 is about James's growing pleasure at
the evident wealth of impressions available to him. The first sentence
on page 6 is

It was perhaps this simple sense of treasure to be gathered in, it was doubtless
this very confidence in the objective reality of impressions, so that they could
deliciously be left to ripen, like golden apples, on the tree—it was all this that
gave a charm to one's sitting in the orchard.

The 'golden air' comes to weigh as much as a corporeal 'golden apple',
is thought of as literally able to bear fruit (without necessarily doing
so—on page 8 we find again 'an harmonious golden haze', 'gold-dust

---

[7] *The Letters of William James*, edited by his son Henry James, 2 vols., London, 1920,
ii. 277–8 (letter of 4 May 1907).

in the air'). James does not yet pluck these possible apples; evoking them as tokens of his confidence in the objective reality of impressions (they are exemplary *objects*), he ensures that they are there within his reach but does not lay a hand on them. He establishes, that is, that the orchard is 'all one's own to pluck' (page 6) and this makes him capable of abstention from irritable reachings; 'he can afford to wait, since the apples were surely going to drop into one's hand, for vivid illustration, as soon as one could begin to hold it out' (page 6).[8] The substantial imaginative existence of such things as impressions is valid enough; its chance to persist, however, is conditional upon an abstention from rough handling. To insist on anything like real tangibility in impressions would be (on the model of ripening) to interfere with their natural growth, to pick them prematurely; you would find their solidity just imaginary. Nothing can guarantee the duration of imaginative substantiality in artistic material, which is always subject to attrition and decay. Indeed, the very composition of *The American Scene* offers a case where the literary accessibility of memories is thrown into question.

iv.   Melting and Fading

When James was settled back in Lamb House after his American trip, writing *The American Scene*, the need became acute to preserve in spite of continual absence an intense mental possession of the impressions he had gathered. He had to keep in mind something irrevocably out of sight. He sailed from the United States on 5 July 1905—and on 3 November he wrote to his niece Peggy that he was 'squeezing out' *The American Scene*

in a kind of panting dread of the matter of it all melting and fading from me before I have worked it off. It does melt and fade, over here, in the strangest way—and yet I did, I think, while with you, so successfully cultivate the impression and the saturation that even my bare residuum won't be quite a vain thing (*LHJ* ii. 36).

The 'matter of it', which can melt and fade, is one solid metaphor for his store of impressions; another, liquid, metaphor applies punningly to the 'expression' of 'impressions', expanding into the image of James

---

[8] This concern with being patient about knowledge runs through much of James's fiction: it especially shapes his novel *Confidence* (Boston, 1880) and the later reworking of the themes of that book in the 1899 story 'The Great Condition'.

as a sponge 'saturated' with them and then 'squeezed out'. To Edith Wharton on 8 November he wrote, recalling the cave in Book Seven of Plato's *Republic*, that his impressions of his native republic 'tend exceedingly to melt and fade and pass away, flicker off like the shadows from firelight on the wall' (*HJL* iv. 375). And the anxiety about losing his grip in this sense was still with him on 23 November in a letter to William:

the effort of *holding rather factitiously on* to its (after all virtual) insub-stantiality just only to convert it into some sort of paying literature is a very great tension and effort. It would all so melt away, of itself, were it not for this artificial clutch! (*HJL* iv. 381.)

So unconfident is his state here that he explicitly acknowledges the 'factitiousness' of speaking as if you could 'hold on to' something which is in fact an 'insubstantiality'; what could be confidently seen as an imaginative grasp here becomes 'this artificial clutch', the metaphor losing its reassuring value. Again the material melts away.

On 23 December, in his long Christmas letter to W. E. Norris, James gives a grim bravura turn to his holding on.

All my consciousness centres, necessarily, just now, on a single small problem, that of managing to do an 'American book' (or rather a couple of them), that I had supposed myself, in advance, capable of doing on the spot, but that I had there, in fact, utterly to forswear—time, energy, opportunity to write, every possibility quite failing me—with the consequence of my material, my 'documents' over here, quite failing me too and there being nothing left for me but to run a race with an illusion, the illusion of still *seeing* it, which is, as it recedes, so to speak, a thousand lengths ahead of me. I shall keep it up as a tour de force, and produce my copy somehow (*LHJ* ii. 45–46).[9]

He can't, he goes on, allow his concentration to wander—'My subject—unless I grip it tight—melts away.' The achievement of *The American Scene*, described by William as the evocation in the reader of 'the illusion of a solid object, made ... wholly out of impalpable materials', seems equally on this evidence to have required the active preservation of the same illusion, the maintenance of an internally projected image, by the author himself. The 'fading', the desolating failure, of the material was apparently insuperable. Looking back, in

[9] In a still unpublished letter to W. D. Howells (in the Houghton Library) of May 1906 James complains that 'The trouble is it all fades from me so before I slowly *do* it'; by this time he had finished *The American Scene* as we know it and was preparing the abortive second volume.

a letter to William on 17 October 1907, he explained why he could not write the planned companion volume about the Mid-West and California.

My Western journey was ... too brief and breathless for an extended impression or an abiding saturation, a sufficient *accumulation* of notes; and though even this wouldn't have prevented my doing something could I have got at that part of my scheme *quickly*, the earlier mass of the same delayed me till so much time had elapsed that here, and at a distance, and utterly out of actual touch, the whole thing had faded, melted for me too much to trust it as I should have needed to. I should have to go back for six months; and embark on impossible *renewals*, to do that second volume (*HJL* iv. 466–7).[10]

For phenomena to abide with you, you must abide with them a certain time—the brevity of James's visits outside the East Coast area handicapped him for what he calls his race with the illusion. 'Actual touch' is something that *in absentia* you cannot keep up; when you have lost the necessary trust in your material and failed to preserve imaginative contact, you are left, as James is here, mourning the impossibility of the renewals 'actual touch' would effect.

The recurrent proximity of 'melted' and 'faded' here, in connection with the failing power of imagination and memory, recalls a passage from *The Tempest* which lyrically imagines the dissolution of other scenes than just the American, those of a play and by extension of the world:

> These our actors,
> As I foretold you, were all spirits, and
> Are melted into air, into thin air;
> And like the baseless fabric of this vision,
> The cloud-capped towers, the gorgeous palaces,
> The solemn temples, the great globe itself,
> Yea, all which it inherit, shall dissolve;
> And, like this insubstantial pageant faded,
> Leave not a rack behind.   (IV.i.148–56)

The 'material' is here, then, a 'baseless fabric'; it goes beyond possible recovery. Such a loss gives a force of contrast to James's praise of Stevenson in an essay of 1900: that Edinburgh remains intensely there

---

[10] For an account of what might have been in the second volume, see James's letter of 5 Mar. 1907 to Elizabeth Jordan in 'Henry James and the *Bazar* Letters', ed. Leon Edel and Lyall H. Powers, in *Howells and James: a Double Billing* (repr. from the *Bulletin of the New York Public Library*), New York, 1958, pp. 27–55, at p. 47.

in his writings despite his long exile from it. This possession is the equal of Scott's.

Edinburgh, in the first place, the 'romantic town', was as much his 'own' as it ever was the great precursor's whom, in 'Weir of Hermiston' as well as elsewhere, he presses so hard; and this even in spite of continual absence—in virtue of a constant imaginative reference and an intense intellectual possession (*LC* i. 1258).

To feel a body of things you have experienced as available to memory in this way, remaining there because of 'constant imaginative reference', is necessary for confidence in your identity.

'Reference' etymologically means a carrying or bringing back; James often speaks of things as coming back to him, and some reliance on the solidity of memory—a reliance threatened in the writing of *The American Scene*—must be possible for the writer, whose powers presumably derive from his relation to his experience. The power of the imagination lies in its overcoming of distances in space and time, its grasp of the absent and the past. James had reason to be anxious, 'nervous' and 'brooding' (*LC* ii. 1332), as he looked apprehensively forward from *The American Scene* to the next task, the New York Edition; where he would rehandle one by one a whole pageant of works, check the validity of reference in fictions written up to thirty-five years earlier.

v. Imaginative Grasp and Unconscious Cerebration

James answers the constant threat of blankness put by the possible melting of material with an emphasis on the negative capability proper to a writer's dealings in such spectral materialities—on the cultivation of a confidence that things are within your reach in order to abstain from irritable, impatient, or anxious reachings after them. What the emphasis really refers to is the necessity of understanding the limits of imaginative grasp, and of learning to refrain from being over-possessive, since it brings you no closer to a state of real possession. To clutch at things whose only-metaphorical materiality is in doubt can do no good. James is particularly insisting in such cases on the necessity of not insisting, and it is not inconsistent sometimes to do this and at other times to express your imaginative grasp by more straightforward metaphors of grasp, always provided that you understand the terms on which you do it.

One manifestation of this consciousness of the exact status of metaphor in James is the way he pushes metaphors to their limits by
extravagant flirtations with the literal, testing and defining and expanding the sense (meaning) of a word or image by his sense-impressions
of it. Thus 'The Sense of Newport' is evoked in an image of mild
sensuality, a beautifully mediated incarnation; James treats Newport,
in Eliot's phrase, 'almost as if it were something that he could touch
and stroke'. It

had simply lain there like a little bare, white, open hand, with slightly-parted
fingers, for the observer with a presumed sense for hands to take or to leave.
The observer with a real sense never failed to pay this image the tribute of
quite tenderly grasping the hand, and even of raising it, delicately, to his lips;
having no less, at the same time, the instinct of not shaking it too hard, and
that above all of never putting it to any rough work (*AS*, p. 210).

At first a simile ('like a ... hand'), the idea (describing Newport's
fingers of land) becomes an 'image', to which the observer with 'a real
sense' for (metaphorical) hands pays the tribute of 'quite tenderly
grasping the hand'—as if the imaginary hand itself were real as well
as the observer's sense of the image's value. The negative capability
here is the tenderness, the delicacy, the instinct of not shaking it too
hard or putting it to any rough work; it is artificial, but it is not a
'clutch'. If you read James with 'a real sense' of what he means, it is
implied, you will pay his image the tribute of understanding ('grasping') the special refinement of his relation to Newport; the image of
the hand here is beautiful, its function in the writing, like Newport's
in American society, to display its practical functionlessness by not
being put to any rough work. To attempt to apply the image other
than tenderly, without James's delicate wit, would be to misunderstand
as other 'developers' have misunderstood the true charm of Newport
in piling money into it—the true lover 'winces at the sight of certain
other obtruded ways of dealing with it' (*AS*, p. 211). The image of
intimate dexterity offered in this hand-kissing conveys easy reach and
the assurance of familiarity, but also a due respect.

There is another image, used by James three times in connection
with *The American Scene*, which, while it conveys easy reach, suggests
also the assurance not so much of familiarity as of faith in a mysterious
provenance—which is appropriate, as it is specifically an image for
the writer's grasp on the items stored in the recesses of his imagination.
In Charleston, James describes the local knowledge of his companion

Owen Wister (author of *The Virginian*); Wister

knew his South in general and his Carolina of that ilk in particular, with an intimacy that was like a grab-bag into which, for illustration, he might always dip his hand (a movement that, had the grab-bag been 'European', I should describe rather as a plunge of his arm: so that it comes back again to the shallowness of the American grab-bag, as yet, for illustrations other than the statistical) (*AS*, p. 410).

A 'grab-bag' is the American equivalent of a 'Lucky Dip', a receptacle in which prizes can be groped for and grasped with the assurance that prizes are there. Writing to William on 24 May 1903, James had used the same term in asserting the value to himself of the planned visit to America, calling it

my one little ewe-lamb of possible exotic experience, such experience as may convert itself, through the senses, through observation, imagination and reflection now at their maturity, into vivid and solid *material*, into a general renovation of one's too monotonised grab-bag (*LHJ* i. 417).

The process of conversion suggested here with lucid concision is richly expanded on in a notebook entry made by James at Coronado Beach, California, on Wednesday 29 March 1905 (a month and a half after his Charleston visit). He begins by worrying that he has not written down many of his impressions in the notebook—but then reassures himself that 'the history is written in my ... heart' (*Nks.*, p. 237):

Everything sinks in: nothing is lost; everything abides and fertilizes and renews its golden promise, making me think with closed eyes of deep and grateful longing when, in the full summer days of L[amb] H[ouse], my long dusty adventure over, I shall be able to [plunge] my hand, my arm, *in*, deep and far, and up to the shoulder—into the heavy bag of remembrance—of suggestion—of imagination—of art—and fish out every little figure and felicity, every little fact and fancy that can be to my purpose. These things are all packed away, now, thicker than I can penetrate, deeper than I can fathom, and there let them rest for the present, in their sacred cool darkness, till I shall let in upon them the mild still light of dear old L[amb] H[ouse]—in which they will begin to gleam and glitter and take form like the gold and jewels of a mine. x x x x x (*Nks.*, p. 237).[11]

---

[11] Cf. the kind of storage which allows James to be confident without notes in *The Princess Casamassima*: 'My notes then, on the much-mixed world of my hero's both overt and covert consciousness, were exactly my gathered impressions and stirred perceptions, the deposit in my working imagination of all my visual and all my constructive sense of London' (*LC* ii. 1101).

The alliteration of fishing out figures and felicities, facts and fancies, pleasantly imagines James making 'grabs' from the bag and drawing out plentiful material for writing down; and then, having envisaged possession, he can 'let them rest for the present', as when his very first impressions 'could deliciously be left to ripen, like golden apples, on the tree'.[12] By the time James applies the figure again in *The American Scene*, though, he denies Owen Wister the pleasurable plunge of hand, arm, *in*, deep and far, up to the shoulder—revising it with demonstrative exactitude (this is America, after all) to a dip of the hand. As we have seen, the anticipated vividness and solidity of material had partly faded and melted away back in England; the hopefulness in the progression from 'deep and grateful longing' to '*in*, deep and far' to 'deeper than I can fathom', the movement from wish to gesture to objective state, necessary as a prospect in California, had not been entirely fulfilled in the act of retrospection. For James at Coronado Beach, however, the darkness and depth in which the things are packed away are to effect—or at least prepare—some transmutation in them; not here like organic growth, but like the formation of jewels by a process of crystallization, a process perhaps also by which they take shape from the indefiniteness of 'remembrance' and 'suggestion', through 'imagination', to the form of 'art'. And to 'mine' them will be to take possession of them, to recover as personal property something presently lodged 'deeper than I can fathom'.

In the Preface to *The American*, James writes of the deliberate surrender of his initial idea for the novel to the unconscious processes of the imagination, a surrender to a presumed enrichment in similarly impenetrable depths (watery rather than mineral).

I was charmed with my idea, which would take, however, much working out; and precisely because it had so much to give, I think, must I have dropped it for the time into the deep well of unconscious cerebration: not without the hope, doubtless, that it might eventually emerge from that reservoir, as one had already known the buried treasure to come to light, with a firm iridescent surface and a notable increase of weight (*LC* ii. 1055).

The 'unconscious cerebration' (a phrase caught up from William's *The*

---

[12] An image close to that of the grab-bag comes up on p. 292 of *The American Scene*, where James has such a sense of the large intensity of meaning in Independence Hall 'that I grope, reminiscentially, in the full basin of the general experience of the spot without bringing up a detail'.

Varieties of Religious Experience[13]) which here returns an idea or impression with such additional substance and definition needs to be distinguished from the Freudian version of the unconscious, at any rate if the Freudian version is to be represented by the 1908 essay 'The Relation of the Poet to Day-Dreaming'. Freud claims there that the imaginative activity of day-dreaming (the construction of 'phantasies') is essentially indistinguishable from the imaginative activity of a writer, so that it's true of literature as of day-dreams that 'Unsatisfied wishes are the driving power behind phantasies; every separate phantasy contains the fulfilment of a wish, and improves on unsatisfactory reality.'[14] A concentration on fairly direct wish-fulfilment—Freud's indulgently expressed assumption in most of the essay that ego-centricity determines all unconscious thought—distracts from the possibility of an unconscious cerebration which would shape and substantiate germinal artistic ideas by subjecting them to the workings of instincts built up over a lifetime of literary experience. There is no a priori reason, after all, for supposing either that the imaginative work that goes into the creation of a literary sentence is all conscious or all takes place in the few minutes immediately before the sentence is written down. There *need* be no profound opposition between an unconscious imagination and the conscious act of writing; choices and judgements from the past—comparatively conscious acts—stored in the memory, can contribute to the sense of artistic rightness and the apparently spontaneous emergence of formal or verbal solutions to problems in the present act of writing.

Instinct, for James, produces an imaginative inevitability (here making the difference between romance and reality):

The determining solution would at any rate seem so latent that one may well doubt if the full artistic consciousness ever reaches it; leaving the matter thus a case, ever, not of an author's plotting and planning and calculating, but just of his feeling and seeing, of his conceiving, in a word, and of his thereby inevitably expressing himself, under the influence of one value or the other (*LC* ii. 1062).

The artistic process may not be all conscious, but it can be all artistic,

---

[13] William James, *The Varieties of Religious Experience* (first pub. 1902), London, 1960, p. 210 (in Lecture IX, 'Conversion').

[14] Sigmund Freud, 'The Relation of the Poet to Day-Dreaming', in *On Creativity and the Unconscious*, New York, 1958, selected, with introduction and notes, by Benjamin Nelson (first collected in *Papers on Applied Psycho-Analysis*, 1925, ed. Ernest Jones), p. 47.

covered by intentions. Freud at the end of his essay refers to the
artistically turned fiction of Zola and others as at least *more* complex
than day-dreams in its treatment of erotic or ambitious wishes, but
without acknowledgement of the qualitative difference such a complexity might make. James's un-Freudian view suggests that some
degree of 'unconscious intention' of a not irresponsible kind is necessary if a writer is to work at the height of his powers (indeed, if he's
to work at all). Presuming a limit to the number of factors which can
be consciously weighed at any moment, we must also presume that
choices and experiences from the past can weigh as well in the form
of habits or predilections, arriving in the consciousness as decisions
already made, convenient limitations or extensions of possibility which
serve as working definitions of the value of experience. (A less cheerful
corollary of this is that there may be *in*convenient limitations set by
the contours of the past.) James himself describes the process in respect
of *The Pupil*:

The whole cluster of items forming the image is on these occasions born at
once; the parts are not pieced together, they conspire and interdepend; but
what it really comes to, no doubt, is that at a simple touch an old latent
and dormant impression, a buried germ, implanted by experience and then
forgotten, flashes to the surface as a fish, with a single 'squirm', rises to the
baited hook, and there meets instantly the vivifying ray. I remember at all
events having no doubt of anything or anyone here; the vision kept to the end
its ease and its charm; it worked itself out with confidence (*LC* ii. 1166).

(Compare, for pleasure in the catch, 'fish out every little figure and
felicity', quoted above.) It is an objectively described process; the
reflexive, as so often, functions to justify the confidence. James pushes
his metaphors together ('germ' up against 'fish') for a startling equivalent to the miraculous animation he sees; and the first 'no doubt', not
literal, and provisional, comes back in full force when he has 'no doubt
of anything or anyone'. We can take 'on these occasions' to allow for
others on which the germ stays buried and the surface unbroken.

Any idea of literary creation which doesn't account for what is
unconscious in all thought will leave the present consciousness of the
writer terribly isolated, as for instance most Freudian versions do,
diminishing its role by suggesting that it is exceeded in the flood of
unconscious wishes. Language itself, we might point out, presumes in
each use of a word a knowledge of past uses of it, a knowledge which
would be intolerable and destructive if it all had to be brought to

consciousness in order to construct a sentence. The conscious imagination and the unconscious co-operate, then, and a writer wishing to
draw fully on his past experience will have to find some balance,
putting confidence in these mysterious processes. It is thus with interest
but not alarm that James notes of *Julia Bride* that his original 'careful
formula or recipe' was in the event supplemented from somewhere:
'The fumes exhaled by the mixture were the gage, somehow, of twenty
more ingredients than I had consciously put in' (*LC* ii. p. 1267). 'Somehow', as elsewhere, is his tribute to the abiding resourcefulness of his
whole sensibility; and the image here is like the repeated figure in *The
American Scene* according to which the 'total' a given scene amounts
to is in excess of the sum to be added up on the slate (for example,
AS, p. 308). Things go on in James's imagination deeper than he can
fathom, with the unpredictability of the actions of others; and these
other things, these strange processes, have to be trusted. An efficient
organizer has to delegate: James's way of writing on these matters
suggests repeatedly that it is not all his own work. He 'cherishes ...
any proved case of the independent life of the imagination' (*LC* ii.
1166), makes space for other-than-conscious agencies of thought which
he sometimes calls, aptly, his 'Muse'[15]—and confidence in these agencies could only dubiously be called self-confidence.

vi.   Other Agencies

James writes of revision, in the Preface to *The Golden Bowl*, that the
new 'array of terms ... simply looked over the heads of the standing
terms' (*LC* ii. 1332–3). This is striking, but his indirect way of putting
it may seem irresponsible or evasive. After all, James must have had
something to do with it. It is a potentially puzzling characteristic of the
later Jamesian style that active human verbs are applied to impersonal
subjects, especially in speaking of the processes of the imagination.
Thus in a letter to Howells on 8 January 1904 James suspects that
hates and loves, those emotional categories and rebounds, won't be
active in his appreciation of America when he returns: 'somehow,
such fine primitive passions *lose* themselves for me in the act of
contemplation, or at any rate in the act of reproduction' (*LHJ* ii. 9).

---

[15] In the *Notebooks*, for instance: 'the thing, only, now is to let the matter Simmer.
Muse it out till light breaks' (p. 187, *his* emphasis). The *OED* suggests that this sense—
'to meditate'—may actually derive from Clio, Euterpe, and the others.

Active verbs, and particularly reflexives, when used of non-human subjects, remove things from the sphere of human choice and action; used of abstract or intangible nouns—that is, of things which we can't literally conceive as *doing* anything—they assume but conceal an agency, are strictly only a manner of speaking. Here James has hates and loves lose themselves 'for me', but in most cases 'for me' is understood, one minute equivalent of the way in which the indirect free style in his novels often keeps the point of reference for its statements delicately implicit (so that what might be a sentence by the narrator is understood to be a character's thought—'for him' or 'for her'). The reader must understand what the rules of omission are in such phrasings in order to follow the contours of meaning in the prose.

The metaphorical force of reflexives used with apparently 'imposs-ible' subjects helps James to a sense of the independent capabilities of the imagination; and their form itself holds a possible emphasis to consolidate his assurance.[16] Reflexive verb forms require at least two words, either of which can be stressed, the verb or the reflexive pronoun. If the latter is stressed the form points up the agency of a particular verb. Describing the genesis of *The Ambassadors*, for instance, James speaks as if he had been guided by an action indepen-dent of himself: 'All of which, again, is but to say that the *steps*, for my fable, placed themselves with a prompt and, as it were, functional assurance' (*LC* ii. 1311). These '*steps*' are perhaps both those of James's feet, which leave the prints on the page later to be traced in rereading,[17] and the various stages of his progress and ascent. They are described as acting with a life of their own, so that James is left with little to do—their 'assurance' is qualified as 'an air quite of readiness to have dispensed with logic had I in fact been too stupid for my clue'. Shortly after this they are said to 'fall together, as by the neat action of their own weight and form'. They are allotted, then, their own substance, shape, and agency, at least metaphorically; but 'as by' keeps this status metaphorical, means 'literally *not* by', since the 'steps' here are described as acting to bring about their own existence. What's going on in the statement 'I strike myself on the nose' is, motive apart, clear enough—but what it means to say (as this in effect does) that 'the

---

[16] It is a particular version of the way in which 'The metaphoric verbs animate and sometimes even personify abstract nouns which are their subjects' (Seymour Chatman, *The Later Style of Henry James* (Language and Style Ser.), Oxford, 1972, p. 111).

[17] See section on 'Recovering Tracks', p. 93.

book's structure determines itself', for example, is another, and mysterious matter. When the determining remains to be done, the book's structure only exists at all in the mind of its author (and perhaps on paper); so long as what something is to be remains undetermined we have trouble in saying that *it* 'is' at all, and if it doesn't have existence as such it's hard to see how it can do anything, let alone to its dubious self. The reflexive here then is a convenient grammatical fiction, meaning something like 'this deed has taken place and appears to conform to a pattern, but the agency of it is mysterious.'

The guarding and cherishing of the 'how' in such creative mysteries can be seen in James's fondness for the word 'somehow', often used in connection with imagination and memory (as in the letter to Howells above). Thus in one Preface James holds on to an idea for years, 'continuing to believe that fond memory would still somehow be justified of this scrap too, along with so many others' (*LC* ii, 1243). For *The Princess Casamassima*, to revisit the place of composition 'was somehow to taste afresh, and with a certain surprise, the odd quality of that original confidence that the parts of my plan *would* somehow hang together' (*LC* ii. 1100). Both the original imaginative process and the present recovery of it arise from undefined developments, perhaps the same one. In the case of *The Wings of the Dove* 'It isn't, no doubt, however ... that the pattern didn't, for each compartment, get itself somehow wrought' (*LC* ii. 1297); where 'get itself' can hint that the pattern used James as a hired wright—not that he minds (it's a proof of the book's aesthetic independence from him and it's *his* metaphor). James has an implicit part in all these processes, but the rhetorical presentation of the agencies as independent suggests that there is a respect in which the whole story is not what he wants to call his. This independence serves as a partial justification of the result—for instance in his strong letter of reply to Shaw's socialistic attack on the sad ending of *The Saloon*, where James declares that 'the imagination ... absolutely enjoys and insists on and incurably leads a life of its own, for which just this vivacity itself is its warrant' (*HJL* iv. 512).

For a critic like Mark Seltzer, in his Foucault-inspired *Henry James and the Art of Power*, James is simply not to be credited here: the novel is, like the social structure, a form of prison based on surveillance, and the novelist's moral investigations are a sophisticated social policing. 'Finally,' for Seltzer, 'the very autonomy of the novelist's characters is merely a function of the virtually automatic mechanism of

control and exposure in which they are inscribed.'[18] This interpretation
derives from a politically orientated account of the genre of the novel:
'Even as it speaks out against systems of coercion, the novel reinvents
them and makes them acceptable in another form, in the form of the
novel itself.'[19] Seltzer's sharp insight into the tyrannies of freedom fails
to give due weight to the tyrannies of tyranny, and, with its political
grid, does not enter sympathetically into the novel's project of rendering life as something *beyond* authorial control. James's ideal, as
expressed in 'The Lesson of Balzac', of a novelist's 'respect for the
liberty of the subject' (*LC* ii. 133), is therefore taken, by analogy with
the hypocrisy of the State, as a blind for covert manipulations and
disciplines. As in all versions of the free will debate, one's belief in
such a case is unlikely to be settled by the production of decisive proof
on either side; and whether we sympathize or not James is attempting
the miraculous, a parallel to God's allowance of free will to mankind.
But if control is inevitable, we will at any rate be wise to choose the
best kind; so that James's account of how the characters in the drama
of Dumas the younger fail to attain what Seltzer calls 'autonomy', for
example, operates a criterion we would do well to take seriously:

His characters are all pointed by observation, they are clear notes in the
concert, but not one of them has known the little invisible push that, even
when shyly and awkwardly administered, makes the puppet, in spite of the
string, walk off by himself and quite 'cut', if the mood take him, that distant
relation his creator.[20]

The wit of 'cut' is relevant here, for James admits that the 'string'
can't be severed while asserting that the artist's created character, even
if only through the dictates of consistency with himself or herself, can
put up an authentic resistance to the artist's will. It will always be
open to the reader to take the author's creation of the illusion that the
characters walk off by themselves as sinister, but for James and his
sympathetic readers it is morally valuable.

Attributions of agency can focus such questions of control and
freedom; turns of agency, acts done by unexpected or unexpectedly
defined agents, become highly significant in James's writing on the

---

[18] Mark Seltzer, *Henry James and the Art of Power*, Ithaca and London, 1984, p. 89.
[19] *Henry James and the Art of Power*, p. 149.
[20] 'Dumas the Younger' (1895), in *The Scenic Art: Notes on Acting and the Drama
1872–1901*, ed. Allan Wade, London, 1949, p. 275.

imagination. About the origin of hero and plot in *The American* he recalls a confident materialization:

I have, I confess, no memory of a disturbing doubt; once the man himself was imaged to me (and *that* germination is a process almost always untraceable) he must have walked into the situation as by taking a pass-key from his pocket (*LC* ii. 1056).

James is the subject of the first, negative and weakened, syntactic unit; in the succeeding adverbial phrase he is only the recipient of the 'imaging', while the character is the subject of a passive verb (so that the process happens *to* both of them); and in the main clause Newman becomes an active subject, endowed with independent movement. The image of easy entrance used for Newman's relation to the situation is an incongruous one, not just because the situation has immediately before been described as 'the whole trap', but because the novel is largely about Newman trying and failing to get a proper social entrée. The photograph which James specially commissioned Alvin Langdon Coburn to take in 1906 as the frontispiece to *The American*[21] is of the closed *porte-cochère* of an aristocratic mansion in the Faubourg St Germain—an image of exclusion and exclusiveness. There is a disconcerting antithesis between the happy way Newman fits artistically into the situation for James, then, and the form this takes, Newman's own unhappy incapacity to fit into the social situation. Turns of agency in the Prefaces and *The American Scene* often metaphorically enact such distinctions between aesthetic success (Newman as the key to the novel) and human failure (Newman's loss within the action); they create an irony, a dual consciousness, in the precisions they force.

Turns of agency between one party to a relation and another, the active and the passive, the transitive and the intransitive, often convey moral refinements and minute plots for James. Page 383 of *The American Scene* has the authorial page-heading 'The Refusal of Legend' over a discussion of the absence of romance, and of interest, in the South: we take it at first that the gist of this heading gives the Southern leaders as refusing, by the failure of their imagination and the extreme dullness of their lives, the conditions by which Legend could survive them. The title 'The Refusal of Legend' would thus be like the refusal of an offered option. But then the relations we may have presumed in this page-heading are violently reversed and revised:

[21] His keenness is recorded in *Alvin Langdon Coburn, Photographer*, ch. 5, p. 52.

It was positively as if legend would have nothing to say to them; as if, on the spot there, I had seen it turn its back on them and walk out of the place (*AS*, p. 383).

What this means is that *they* don't even get the chance to turn their backs on *it*—the personification and activation, the metaphorical enlivening, take it out of their hands, denude them even of grammatical pride of place, switching round who it is that Refuses in the page-title and putting them quite out of it. The 'as if' which presents this indicates that James is reading a history into visible effects; 'for me' or 'in my thoughts' must again be understood. When James writes of his own imagination, such turns to personal passivity deliver him to benevolently active processes, of whose benefits he becomes the grateful recipient.

   Revision has him as the beneficiary of such processes. The Preface to *The Golden Bowl*, looking back over the project of the New York Edition, discusses the act of revision, the 'finer appeal of accumulated "good stuff"' and ... the interest of taking it in hand at all' (*LC* ii. 1334). Taking something in hand suggests a conscious act of grasp and manipulation. Then James qualifies the phrase, relinquishes this description:

For myself, I am prompted to note, the 'taking' has been to my consciousness, through the whole procession of this re-issue, the least part of the affair: under the first touch of the spring my hands were to feel themselves full; so much more did it become a question, on the part of the accumulated good stuff, of seeming insistently to give and give (*LC* ii. 1334).

James has a grasp, but not by an act of grasping; the important hinge is 'to my consciousness', and what is presented here is the phenomenal 'seeming' (as in the indirect free style). The impersonal and objective realm in the imagination is that of unconsciously functioning processes, and revision registers the results of these as they emerge into consciousness under the pressure of James's intelligent attention to his past works.

vii.   A Wild Logic of its Own

Leon Edel quotes from a letter which James's fourteen-year-old niece Peggy sent home to her elder brother from Lamb House on 26 April 1901.

Uncle Henry, Mama and I used always to go for a long walk in the afternoon, that is to say when Nick allowed us to go, by not chasing sheep or chickens, and having to be brought home again. It is too funny for words sometimes when this happens and it nearly drives Uncle Henry to distraction and he yells in a terribly loud voice 'Oh! oh! oh! oh! oh! you little brute! you little brute! you beast! oh! oh! oh!' Then he hurries home with the unfortunate wretch and leaves Mama and me to follow on at our own sweet pace.[22]

This sort of incident finds its way into James's writing: discussing the deceptive appearance of docility for which he favoured the subject of *What Maisie Knew*, and the way such subjects actually escape their supposed proper bounds, he evokes just such a situation.

Once 'out', like a house-dog of a temper above confinement, it defies the mere whistle, it roams, it hunts, it seeks out and 'sees' life; it can be brought back but by hand and then only to take its futile thrashing (*LC* ii. 1159–60).

There is a partial conflict of interests between the artist and his imagination; it resists the formal constraints he attempts to set, following its own nose and its own instincts.[23] Dryden had used the same figure in arguing for the discipline of rhyme against the freedom of blank verse:

that benefit which I consider most in it, because I have not seldom found it, is, that it bounds and circumscribes the fancy. For imagination in a poet is a faculty so wild and lawless, that like an high-ranging spaniel, it must have clogs tied to it, lest it outrun the judgment.[24]

Dryden's attitude to spaniels is not *merely* restrictive here; but in the 'Account' of *Annus Mirabilis* (1667) the freedom of spaniels is expressly seen as having a necessary function:

The composition of all poems is, or ought to be, of wit; and wit in the poet, or *Wit writing*, (if you will give me leave to use a school-distinction), is no other than the faculty of imagination in the writer, which, like a nimble spaniel, beats over and ranges through the field of memory, till it springs the quarry it hunted after.[25]

---

[22] Quoted in Leon Edel, *Henry James: A Life*, London, 1987, p. 542.

[23] An extreme figure for this is used of the composition of the story 'The Middle Years', which James compares to 'the anxious effort of some warden of the insane engaged at a critical moment in making fast a victim's straitjacket' (*LC* ii. 1238). The imagination is here so independent and other that it's thought of as *aliéné*.

[24] John Dryden, 'Epistle Dedicatory of *The Rival Ladies: A Tragi-Comedy*' (1664), in *Essays of John Dryden*, selected and edited by W. P. Ker, 2 vols., Oxford, 1926, i. 8.

[25] John Dryden, Preface to *Annus Mirabilis*, in *Essays of John Dryden*, i. 14.

'Wit writing' is a distinction that James, with his preference for impersonal terms in describing creative processes, would have concurred in;
and making allowance for the fact that Dryden uses the simile for
the imagination pursuing a phrase (something which the simile itself
demonstrates), and James uses it for a theme in the imagination
pursuing its own ends, we cannot think James would really be
angry that his house-dog has energetically ' "seen" life' (as he said in
'The Art of Fiction', 'the good health of an art which undertakes so
immediately to reproduce life must demand that it be perfectly free.
It lives upon exercise, and the very meaning of exercise is freedom'
(*LC* i. 49)).

This is independent life, at any rate, and proved cases of it legitimate
a writer's continuing confidence 'in himself': James congratulates
Howells in September 1902, after *The Kentons*, on 'so acclaimed and
attested a demonstration of the freshness, within you still, of the spirit
of evocation' (*LHJ* i. 398), as if—and because—such freshness is not
only inward but mysteriously other. In a letter to Howells four years
later, a short time after completing *The American Scene*, he implies,
again without specifying, a mysterious, even mystical source for this
freshness: 'Wooing *back* freshness is hard—but we live (or we write
at least, I think) from one vouchsafed miracle to another.'[26] When the
idea for *The American* comes back from 'the deep well of unconscious
cerebration' it is 'This resurrection' (*LC* ii. 1055), and remembering
the detailed circumstances of the writing of *The Reverberator* impresses James with the power of memory in retrieving 'the all but lost,
... the miraculously recovered, chapter of experience' (*LC* ii. 1194).
The independent power allowed for in these ways of speaking is what
makes James exceed his conscious self in the Baltimore section of *The
American Scene*; the charm of the town bypasses the adding up of its
various causes in a sum on a slate, which is what he has at first
conscientiously tried to do.

What happened then, remarkably, was that while I mechanically so argued
my impression was fixing itself by a wild logic of its own, and that I was
presently to see how it would, when once settled to a certain intensity, snap
its fingers at warrants and documents. If it was a question of a slate the slate
was used, at school, I remembered, for more than one purpose; so that mine,
by my walk's end, instead of a show of neat ciphering, exhibited simply a
bold drawn image (*AS*, pp. 308–9).

[26] H J to Howells, 13 Sept. 1906 (Harvard MS).

The imagination's separate existence is the condition for the reflexive here ('my impression was fixing itself'); its independent life and purposes are paid a passing tribute in 'wild' logic. This friendly supplanting of arithmetic by imagination occasions a forceful statement of confidence in the power of 'sensibility' running to the end of the section; James calls this 'the real way to work things out', unfavourably comparing the journalistic approach which is lost without its 'items'.

Writing to A. C. Benson in 1898, James revealed that *The Turn of the Screw* had its 'germ' in an anecdote told by Benson's father, the Archbishop of Canterbury—and offered a sociable cliché to register the transformation it had gone through into art—'quite gruesomely as my unbridled imagination caused me to see the inevitable development of the subject' (*LHJ* i. 280). When in the Preface to *The Birthplace* James thinks he's repeating the house-dog simile from the *What Maisie Knew* Preface, what he gives is a metaphorical extension of the horsey commonplace 'unbridled imagination'. In the process of art, he says, the original character of an impression taken from real life or history (in this case, of Shakespeare) is quite altered by its 'new employment':

It has been liberated (to repeat, I believe, my figure) after the fashion of some sound young draught-horse who may, in the great meadow, have to be re-captured and re-broken for the saddle (*LC*. ii. 1252–3).

Both the change of employment and the unbridling are made literal here; the horse is liberated from the toils of haulage, has a freedom in the great meadow, and then has to be redisciplined for the more elegant motions of riding. What produces this liberation in the context has just been called (using the chemical or alchemical analogy) a 'felt fermentation'—what goes on during the period of storage of the original quantity in the deep well, or the passing of it through 'the crucible of [the novelist's] imagination' (*LC* ii. 1236).[27]

A phrase James uses here suggests how 'that mystic, that "chemical" change' he describes as being wrought by the imagination in an original impression of life may be like the imaginative process of which the

[27] 'Crucible' is used again in the Preface to *The Altar of the Dead* (*LC* ii. 1257); and James is very explicit about it in a letter to Wells on 3 Mar. 1911: 'There is, to my vision, no authentic, and no really interesting and no *beautiful*, report of things on the novelist's, the painter's part unless a particular detachment has operated, unless the great stewpot or crucible of the imagination, of the observant and recording and interpreting mind in short, has intervened and played its part—and this detachment, this chemical transmutation for the aesthetic, the representational, end is terribly wanting in autobiography brought, as the horrible phrase is, up to date' (*LHJ* ii. 181–2).

revision of an original text is the register. The process, James says,

enables the sense originally communicated to make fresh and possibly quite
different terms for the new employment there awaiting it (*LC* ii. 1252).

'Fresh and possibly quite different terms'—these have their justification, if one were needed, in their necessity—in following from
the combination of the original 'small cluster of actualities' and the
imaginative process they have been put through. James feels an un-
chilled 'confidence' in *The Birthplace* on this account. And the 'terms'
which arrive from the original 'sense' will include the general method
and approach resulting from James's awareness of a given fact, *and*
the particular words which express the meaning initially conveyed
to him. The independent animation of a work can thus extend its
determinations to the detail of its expression: its pressure of meaning
gives initial expression to the material, and later revises it by the same
agency, by 'some strange and fine, some latent and gathered force' (*LC*
ii. 1333).

viii.   The Test of Expression

The impersonal processes James is delivered over to in writing are not
separable from the details of literary expression.[28] It is in a writer's
sense of his 'array of terms', which includes his sense of their proper
limitations, that the value of his experience (both generally human and
specifically artistic) will reside and emerge. Correspondingly, it would
be impossible and undesirable that more than a certain amount of this
potentially vast experience should be consciously present to the writer
at any time—its effect would be merely inhibiting. The mental economy
which calls forward into consciousness a measure of experience at the
appropriate time in the form of, say, an instinctual sense of the
rightness of a word in a particular context, without formulating
reasons or pausing for reflection, presumably makes up part of what
Wordsworth calls 'a healthful state of association'. Writers depend
on such an economy, which works through invisible and intangible
agencies; a dependence which requires repeated acts of faith and tries
the nerves.

   It is primarily in the act of literary expression that such instinctual
reserves of value can be fully drawn on, that a writer can discover in

---

[28] As argued in Ch. 5 below, on the revisions of *The American*.

himself something which has not previously existed. This is the force of James's repeated appeal in the Notebooks to 'the application of the particular firm and gentle pressure that has seen me, in the past, through so many dark quandaries, difficult moments, hours of more or less anguish ("artistic" at least)' (*Nks.*, p. 207). The act of writing floats him 'back into relation with the idea, with the possibility, into relation again with my task and my life' (*Nks.*, p. 243). The firm and gentle pressure of pen on paper is a means to expression, corresponds to a mental pressure which it helps to sustain, has a solidity of result which cannot easily fade or melt away. We find here again the grouping impression-pressure-expression, associated with some mechanical imagery (in contrast to the other images of squeezed sponges and oranges which the grouping also produces).

In the Notebooks James reminds himself of the empirical value of the test of expression: 'one doesn't know—ideally—till one has got into real close quarters with one's proposition by absolutely ciphering it out, by absolutely putting to the proof and to the test what it will give' (*Nks.*, p. 259). He goes on to ask what his present subject will give 'under the pressure and the screw'. *The Turn of the Screw* is a triumph of expression and a *tour de force*; and the more formally tight it is in its expressive logic and economy, the more fear and tension it squeezes out of its reader (like the thumbscrew to which its title alludes). Another turning of a screw occurs in *The American Scene*, to squeeze out a full expression, when James is in a Richmond hotel:

the strong vertical light of a fine domed and glazed cortile, the spacious and agreeable dining-hall of the inn, had rested on the human scene as with an effect of mechanical pressure. If the scene constituted evidence, the evidence might have been in course of being pressed out, in this shining form, by the application of a weight and the turn of a screw. There it was, accordingly; there was the social, the readable page, with its more or less complete report of the conditions (*AS*, p. 408).

Though this passage is an expression of the revealing intensity of the light thrown, what it actually describes is the making of an impression in James's sensibility by the hotel's expression of its own character; the possible gulf between impression and expression is denied in 'the readable page', including this one in *The American Scene*; the printed impression of James's expression can also be the printed expression of James's impression,[29] in a pleasant continuity.

---

[29] James plays between the terms in the 'Florida' chapter, parenthetically revising one

The phrase 'Dramatise, dramatise!', which crops up everywhere in the Prefaces, refers to the high value James places on the application of ideas: an empirical test of their value, 'that test of further development which so exposes the wrong and so consecrates the right' (*LC* ii. 1181). When in the Notebooks he is bothered by 'hovering little ghosts of motives', he resorts to the primary experiment of development and amplification and expression, which is the condition for confident continuation or confident dismissal of them:

Attempt to *state* them—and then one sees. This *test* of the statement is moreover in any case such an exquisite thing that it's always worth making, if only for the way it brings back the spell of the old sacred days (*Nks.*, p. 207).

'Statement' can be both a preliminary scenario for a work of fiction (such as that for *The Ambassadors*) and the act of stating; the latter being the scrupulously detailed thinking-through in language which goes to make up the former. The units of expression at a novelist's disposal are various, to do with relations of characters, relations of plots, the handling of dialogue, the staged revelation of information, the construction of arguments or patterns of allusion, and so on right down to the minutiae of phrasing; and his experience of dealing with these will emerge to give him a sense of what's right and what's not once an idea is put into play. 'These are intimate truths indeed', James says in *The Tragic Muse* Preface, 'of which the charm mainly comes out but on experiment and in practice' (*LC* ii. 1111), and in the Notes for *The Ivory Tower* the 'intimacy of composition' allows truths to emerge with the independence of reflexives, so that 'pre-noted arrangements, proportions and relations, do most uncommonly insist on making themselves different by shifts and variations, always improving, which impose themselves as one goes and keep the door open always to something *more* right and *more* related'.[30]

The idea for a novel or story requires the door to be kept open in this way. Of the theme of *Julia Bride*, James declares in the Preface,

What it might have to say (of most interest to poet and moralist) was certainly meanwhile no matter for *a priori* judgment—it might have to say but the most charming, the most thrilling things in the world; this, however, was exactly

---

of them to the other: 'it was wondrous that if I had there supposed the apogee of the impression (or, better still, of the e*x*pression) reached, I was here to see the whole effect written lucidly larger' (*AS*, pp. 438–9).

[30] *The Ivory Tower*, London, 1917, p. 341.

the field for dramatic analysis, no such fine quantities being ever determinable till they have with due intelligence been 'gone into'. 'Dramatise, dramatise!' one had, in fine, before the so signal appearance, said to one's self: then, and not sooner, would one see (*LC* ii. 1266–7).

Such an attention and submission to the internal logic of a subject, to the unfolding of its development 'from its own "innards"' (*LHJ* i. 408) accounts for the expansion of so many works beyond their initially forecast limits—*The Awkward Age* being the most notable case of this (hence 'the singular interest attaching to the very intimacies of the effort' (*LC* ii. 1129)). The act of expression, of amplification, of development, of statement should thus be a progressive and ordered bringing to consciousness of stored artistic experience; it should be 'the sacrament of execution' (*LC* ii. 1135), the marriage of idea with treatment. The realm of expression is a realm of responsible conduct; as James strongly puts it in the climax to the *Golden Bowl* Preface, at the end of his discussion of the values at stake in revision,

we recognise betimes that to 'put' things is very exactly and responsibly and interminably to do them. Our expression of them, and the terms on which we understand that, belong as nearly to our conduct and our life as every other feature of our freedom; these things yield in fact some of its most exquisite material to the religion of doing (*LC* ii. 1340).

This statement of faith in the ethical seriousness of our behaviour in the realm of language follows James's assertion that the value of a literary work is best tested by a '*viva-voce*' reading, a subjection to the rhythms and accents of the voice: a passage on the page will 'give out its finest and most numerous secrets', he says 'under the closest pressure—which is of course the pressure of the attention articulately *sounded*' (*LC* ii. 1339). The pressure of attention in a vocal ex-pression—a reading-out and intonation—allows a test of tones and cadences, the registering of true notes and falsities in the minute inflections and inspections of which articulate speech can consist. Depths and shallows are skilfully '*sounded*'. The practice of dictation is likely to have a relation to this announced value in its constant accommodation of the spoken and the written; Theodora Bosanquet reports James as saying that 'It all seems to be so much more effectively and unceasingly *pulled* out of me in speech than in writing.'[31] Expression in speech involves given quantities in a finely adjusted

[31] *Henry James at Work*, p. 7.

medium of judgement, and yields James, according to Theodora Bosanquet, 'a final confidence'.[32] In his lecture on *The Question of Our
Speech* (1905) James has an account of the evolution of a 'state of
sensibility to tone' by 'Contact and communication, a beneficent
contagion'[33]—by the social experience of the possibility of nuance—
and then refines on what he means by 'speaking well':

I mean, then, by speaking well, in the first place, speaking under the influence
of *observation*—your own. I mean speaking with consideration for the forms
and shades of our language, a consideration so inbred that it has become
instinctive and well-nigh unconscious and automatic, as all the habitual, all
the inveterate amenities of life become.[34]

Many of the ways in which he writes about the independent life of the
imagination in revision are metaphorical versions of 'well-nigh ...
automatic' here—as if revisions automatically wrote themselves, which
is not quite the case. 'Instinctive and well-nigh unconscious' carefully
doesn't equate the two, just approximates them in the economical
mastery which makes speech like an instrument for regular improvis-
ation, something you can develop an ear for. And the developed ear
is part of the novelistic capacity instinctively evolved in James during
the time between the original composition and the revision of works;
it is with this developed ear that those works are reheard, retried,
judged again.

ix. Not Rereading

He had cultivated the habit of forgetting past achievements almost to the
pitch of a sincere conviction that nothing he had written before about 1890
could come with any shred of credit through the ordeal of a critical inspection
(Theodora Bosanquet, about the New York Edition).[35]

Until the New York Edition James regularly claimed that once he had
written a book it was dead to him. Thus, about *The Bostonians*, he
wrote to William on 13 June 1886 that

after one of my productions is finished and cast upon the waters it has, for
me, quite sunk beneath the surface—I cease to care for it and transfer my

---

[32] *Henry James at Work*, p. 10.
[33] *The Question of Our Speech, The Lesson of Balzac: Two Lectures*, Boston, 1905,
p. 17.
[34] *The Question of Our Speech*, pp. 19–20.
[35] *Henry James at Work*, p. 12.

interest to the one I am next trying to float (*HJL* iii. 121–2).[36]

After the disastrous first night of *Guy Domville* on 5 January 1895 this capacity for immediate separation was particularly necessary: on 2 February 1895 James wrote to William that

If, as I say, this episode has, by this time, become ancient history to me, it is, thank heaven, because when a thing, for me (a piece of work), is done, it's done: I get quickly detached and away from it, and am wholly given up to the better and fresher life of the next thing to come (*LHJ* i. 233).

The awkwardness of the phrasing and the refusal of the commas to have done suggest the effort of escape from responsible suffering. As with Lady Macbeth's 'What's done is done' (*III*. ii. 12), the insistence struggles against a rooted sorrow. We have Leon Edel's word (though not reference) for it that in the middle of February 1895 James said the affair was 'rapidly growing to seem to have belonged to the history of someone else'.[37] But no one ever gets *quite* detached from his own history.

A serious writer's attitude to his existing *œuvre* directly bears on his sense of his life's worth; and James's violent emotion on 2 July 1905 at the prospect of having his early unsigned reviews 'unearthed' by the bibliographer Frederick Allen King shows the weight of emotion that could attach for him to the exhumation of works from the past, even (or especially) as he was beginning to revise *Roderick Hudson* for the first volume of the New York Edition. The idea 'fills me only with the bitterness of woe. I would much rather myself, with my own hand, heap mountains of earth upon them and so bury them deeper still and beyond *any* sympathetic finding-out' (*HJL* iv. 359–60).[38] James remembers Hamlet and Laertes in Ophelia's grave, piling up the grief, to express the extremity of his own distress. The products of an author's youth are here referred to as 'his early aberrations, his so far as possible outlived and repudiated preliminary' (*HJL* iv. 359). The

---

[36] See also a letter to Stevenson, *HJL* iii. 206 (5 Dec. 1887), where James makes his works infants who 'dwindle when weaned', and 'only flourish, a little, while imbibing the milk of my plastic care'. The word 'sunk' figures frequently in the Prefaces to register James's anxiety about the real state of his earlier works, but in the phrase ' "sunk" picture', where the surface itself sinks.

[37] Quoted in *Henry James: A Life*, p. 433.

[38] On 8 Sept. 1904 James's response to a request for bibliographical leads from Le Roy Phillips (cousin of his friend Morton Fullerton) had been more politely measured but had made the same point, that authors have many writings 'that they desire to forget and keep buried' (*HJL* iv. 320).

works of early maturity suffer a similar neglect, as is clear from James's reply to an inquiry from Mrs Frances Carruth Prindle on 1 August 1901:

I haven't either The Bostonians or The N. E. Winter under my hand, haven't seen them for years, nor re-read them since they were published—which must have been some fifteen years since; and I so detest, as it were, my books after they are done, and I've got rid of them, that I cherish no remembrances and can pass no examinations.[39]

He has not examined them and thus can't be examined on them; they give him examination nerves.

A powerful attraction, however, is closely connected to the hyperbolic revulsion; as, strikingly, in James's reactions on 11 March 1898 to A. C. Benson's praise of *The Turn of the Screw*. He supposes that Benson's note

is intended somehow to make up to me for the terror with which my earlier— in fact *all* my past—productions inspire me, and for the insurmountable aversion I feel to looking at them again or to considering them in any way (*LHJ* i. 278).

This seems a strange (even if ironically overstated) feeling to have; James goes on to give it a turn in the other direction: 'This morbid state of mind is really a blessing in disguise—for it has for happy consequences that such an incident as your letter becomes thereby extravagantly pleasant and gives me a genial glow' (*LHJ* i. 278-9). A version of the morbid state of mind is offered by James in the Preface to *The Golden Bowl*, when he is looking back on the difference between the anxious anticipation of rereading his novels and the act of revision itself—though in the context morbidity similarly turns to confidence:

Since to get and to keep finished and dismissed work well behind one, and to have as little to say to it and about it as possible, had been for years one's only law, so, during that flat interregnum, involving, as who should say, the very cultivation of unacquaintedness, creeping superstitions as to what it might really have been had time to grow up and flourish (*LC* ii. 1330).

The anxious reluctance 'To expose the case frankly to a test—in other words to begin to re-read' (*LC* ii. 1332) presumably stems from a sense of the magnitude of the discovery about his own career an ambitious

---

[39] Letter to Mrs Frances Carruth Prindle, 1 Aug. 1901, cited in *Yale Review*, 13/1 (Oct. 1923), 208.

author's sincere test will bring one way or the other. The *œuvre* could manifest itself as an insubstantial pageant faded. We may think of the emotion imagined in Dencombe's rereading in 'The Middle Years', before which he is 'conscious of a strange alienation' so that he 'couldn't have turned with curiosity or confidence to any particular page'—'something precious had passed away'[40]—but during which 'He read his own prose, he turned his own leaves, and had, as he sat there with the spring sunshine on the page, an emotion peculiar and intense. His career was over, no doubt, but it was over, after all, with *that*'.[41] (The commas after 'had' and 'page' are removed in the New York Edition for an onrush of emotion.)

The fear of inadequacy to his own criteria can produce a correspondingly intense relief at such reassurances as A. C. Benson's: the Preface to *The Awkward Age* offers the fear and its relief as, respectively, a sense of death and a surprising sense of life. 'The thing done and dismissed has ever, at the best, for the ambitious workman, a trick of looking dead, if not buried, so that he almost throbs with ecstasy when, on an anxious review, the flush of life reappears' (*LC* ii. 1120). He 'almost throbs with ecstasy' when life becomes visible in the thing; this account has James not coolly detached from his past work after all, but momentously attached to it. 'Terror' gives way to 'ecstasy'; 'superstitions' give way to a sufficient faith in 'the thing done'.

x. Rewriting

In the Preface to *The Golden Bowl* James says of 'the term Revision' that

I had attached to it, in a brooding spirit, the idea of re-writing—with which it was to have in the event, for my *conscious* play of mind, almost nothing in common. I had thought of re-writing as so difficult, and even so absurd, as to be impossible—having also indeed, for that matter, thought of re-reading in the same light. But the felicity under the test was that where I had thus ruefully prefigured two efforts there proved to be but one—and this an effort but at the first blush (*LC* ii. 1332).

The congruence of rewriting and rereading here, the way that revisions seem to take place in the act of reading so that effort is halved and then annihilated, can make us curious about how James read, both

---

[40] *Terminations*, p. 170.
[41] *Terminations*, p. 171.

others and himself. In the same Preface he speaks of himself, revising his own works, 'as a reader' following by a strange alienation the work of someone else, an imaginative 'historian' (*LC* ii. 1329).

His letters to other writers about their work, as one might expect, are suggestive about the kind of activity reading the work of another was for him, and establish a precedent for the experience he describes in the preparation of the New York Edition. Mrs Humphry Ward often received his comments on the books she sent him. 'As he often said to me, he could never read a novel that interested him without taking it mentally to pieces, and re-writing it in his own way. Some of his letters to me are brilliant examples of this habit of his.'[42] Such a speculative rewriting is likely to have something in common with the registering of the 'vision ... that experience had at last made the only possible one' (*LC* ii. 1332) in revision. When he had prematurely advised Mrs Ward (after a misunderstanding) on her barely-begun novel *Eleanor* in 1899, she complained of his rough handling and he excused himself on the grounds of

my irresistible need of wondering how, *given* the subject, one could best work one's self into the presence of it. And, lo and behold, the subject isn't (of course, in so scant a show and brief a piece) 'given' at all—I have doubtless simply, with violence and mutilation, *stolen* it. It is of the nature of that violence that I'm a wretched person to *read* a novel—I begin so quickly and concomitantly, *for myself*, to write it rather—even before I know clearly what it's about! The novel I can *only* read, I can't read at all! (*LHJ* i. 325).

To H. G. Wells he said that 'I rewrite you, much, as I read—which is the highest tribute my damned impertinence can pay an author' (*HJL* iv. 133). If, as he wrote in 1878 'The teller is but a more developed reader' (*HJL* ii. 193), the analogy between the processes of reading and writing seems to allow James—as a highly developed reader—to retell or rewrite the works of other authors as he goes over them. He repeatedly declares that this is the only way he can read. Writing to Mrs Cadwalader Jones on 20 August 1902, about two works by her sister-in-law Edith Wharton, he says that 'If a work of imagination, of fiction, interests me at all (and very few, alas, do!) I always want to write it over in my own way, handle the subject from my own sense of it' (*LHJ* i. 396). 'Writing it over' is of course very literally what James does in the New York Edition to the sheets of the early editions

---

[42] Mrs Humphry Ward, *A Writer's Recollections (1856–1900)*, London, 1919, p. 333.

of *Roderick Hudson* and *The American* and *The Portrait of a Lady*, covering the original text with ink (paradoxically called 'ablutional fluid' (*LC* ii. 1331)). Readings of the works of others are like imaginative rewritings of them for James. When he describes the process in a letter to Wells of 21 September 1913, he makes the analogy with revision closer than ever:

To read a novel at all I perform afresh, to my sense, the act of writing it, that is of re-handling the subject according to my own lights and over-scoring the author's form and pressure with my own vision and understanding of *the* way—this, of course I mean, when I see a subject in what he has done and feel its appeal to me as one: which I fear I very often don't. This produces reflections and reserves—it's the very measure of my attention and my interest (*LHJ* ii. 334).

Again the 'over-scoring' could apply to James's technique of revision in the New York Edition; and again his deviations from the text on the page represent a developed difference of measure, are the measure of his present mode of attention. The pre-condition for such rewriting is that he should be able to recognize a 'subject' in a work at all (his essay on 'The New Novel' frequently alleges that modern novels lack subjects), so that the differences will be more differences of treatment than of matter. In such active readings James demonstrates a truth too often theoretical: that the reader imaginatively co-operates in the creation of a work of fiction.

James is one of those writers whose divergent vision of a work often carries him from his creatively critical readings of others into critically creative works of his own. Thus for example we may suspect part of the impulse for *Notes of a Son and Brother* to be derived from his reading in 1907 of Edmund Gosse's autobiographical *Father and Son*. Writing to the author, he had his doubts about the degree of filiality and kindness in Gosse's tone—but

On the *whole*, however, let me add, I think the tenderness of the book is, given the detachment, remarkable—as an intellectual, reflective thing: I can conceive the subject treated with so much more uneffaced a bitterness. I can conceive it treated too, on a side, I may further add, with a different shade of curiosity, a different kind of analysis—approached, as it were, at another angle—but at one that is a bit difficult to express—so that I must wait till I see you.[43]

---

[43] *Selected Letters of Henry James to Edmund Gosse*, p. 231.

The kind of reading James does in the work of other authors seems
to result in new conceptions of related subjects, ideas for treatment
from different angles or for versions which will bear his own contrastive emphasis. F.R. Leavis has drawn general attention in *The
Great Tradition* to the way in which *Daniel Deronda* hands on to and
is rethought in *The Portrait of a Lady*, and to the refinements of
Eugénie Grandet that are achieved in *Washington Square*. Hawthorne's *Blithedale Romance* is visible behind *The Bostonians*, Turgenev's *Virgin Soil* behind *The Princess Casamassima*.[44] The Prefaces
themselves explicitly give a reaction to other literary works as the germ
of two stories, *The Siege of London* and *Paste*. The former James
traces back to his anger at the moralistic behaviour of the hero of the
younger Dumas's *Le Demi-Monde*, and to his consequent vision of a
different order of things and another turn of events, his 'wondering
whether the general situation of the three persons concerned, or something like it, mightn't be shown as taking quite another turn' (*LC* ii.
1219). The content of *Paste* is 'the ingenious thought of transposing
the terms' (*LC* ii. 1242) of Maupassant's 'La Parure', so that the false
diamonds thought to be real become real jewels thought to be fakes.
Again James gives his personal version: 'It seemed harmless sport
simply to turn that situation round—to shift, in other words, the
ground of the horrid mistake' (*LC* ii. 1243).

These large versions of the subjects of other works usually go some
way from the work which is their original stimulus; the text James has
read and reacted against is always only a starting-point; while the way
in which he imaginatively rewrites the novels of H. G. Wells and others
as he reads permits no closer register to be kept of it than in his half-
imperious, half-apologetic letters. The impulse to transcribe differences
of emphasis from another writer, to which both these forms of rewriting testify, is one accommodated with peculiar aptness and demonstrated with special clarity in the technique he evolves to revise the
work of his earlier self in the New York Edition.

[44] Marius Bewley, *The Complex Fate: Hawthorne, Henry James and Some Other
American Writers*, New York, 1954, pp. 11–30; W.H. Tilley, *The Background of
'The Princess Casamassima'*, (University of Florida Monographs, No. 5), Gainesville,
1961.

xi. The Test of Rereading

Two kinds of literary behaviour, then, repeat themselves in James before the New York Edition—the refusal to read over his own previous works and the incapacity to read the works of others without 'writing them over'. The decision to do the Edition at all, whatever its motive, made these habits problematic. As the task of revision approached, James was anxious, according to the Prefaces, in case on rereading his past works he would either be unable to read them at all or would be impelled to rewrite them entirely. Such anxiety anticipated a possible loss of 'life' in them, a deterioration of value over time or a revelation that they were worthless from the start.

The *Roderick Hudson* Preface, for instance, gives an account both of the possible satisfaction of rereading and of its possible disastrous outcome. The test of reperusal is a 'pressure' under which a past work may 'break down'—and the fact that this sometimes happens and sometimes does not is at least a partial proof of the test's engagement with real differences in the works.

The author knows well enough how easily that may happen—which he in fact frequently enough sees it do. The old reasons then are too dead to revive; they were not, it is plain, good enough reasons to live. The only possible relation of the present mind to the thing is to dismiss it altogether (*LC* ii. 1046).

The failure of such works and their reasons to 'revive' on this day of judgement leads to their redismissal, their remaining dead: as where, in a letter to Robert Herrick about the New York Edition, 'I have tried to read over Washington Square and I *can't*, & I fear it must go!'[45]

The traditional alternative to a perpetuity of death is resurrection, and in other cases the process of rereading miraculously inspires works with life, revives for the author the values of the past:

It helps him to live back into a forgotten state, into convictions, credulities too early spent perhaps, it breathes upon the dead reasons of things, buried as they are in the texture of the work, and makes them revive, so that the actual appearances and the old motives fall together once more, and a lesson and a moral and a consecrating final light are somehow disengaged (*LC* ii. 1045–6).

---

[45] Printed in Robert Herrick, 'A Visit to Henry James', *Yale Review*, 12 (July 1923), 724–41, p. 736.

Such a mysterious retrieval of past life from the dead and buried ('somehow') is equally the subject of the section of *The American Scene* which deals with the old State House in Philadelphia, where James is concerned with a test of the imaginative life remaining— again through the permanence of 'consecration'—in an exposition of value in real history, the Declaration of Independence. He refuses to apologize for his excitement about so commonly acknowledged an historic place; his ground could just as well apply to reading a novel written in the past; it is 'that, in general, one is allowed a margin ... for the direct sense of consecrated air, for that communication of its spirit which, in proportion as the spirit has been great, withholds itself, shyly and nobly, from any mere forecast' (*AS*, p. 288).[46] This empirical patience and generosity is what keeps up 'the freshness of individual sensibility and the general continuity of things'. In the Preface to *The Golden Bowl*, the assessment of the surviving value of the works to be revised similarly requires a clear margin, the direct sense you get from reading, which can't be 'forecast'; so that James attributes his anxiety to

> my but too naturally not being able to forecast the perfect grace with which an answer to all my questions was meanwhile awaiting me. To expose the case frankly to a test—in other words to begin to re-read—was at once to get nearer all its elements and so, as by the next felicity, feel it purged of every doubt (*LC* ii. 1332).

James submits himself to the trial of reperusal, in which differences and/or congruences between vision and expression emerge spon- taneously: the test resolves his doubts, not predictably. 'I couldn't at all, in general, forecast these chances and changes and proportions; they could but show for what they were as I went' (*LC* ii. 1335). The spontaneity of the results 'means, obviously, that the whole thing was a *living* affair' (*LC* ii. 1335).

The presence of the spirit (something which leaves the body after death) manifests life, and the final imaginative revivification of the Declaration of Independence in the old State House is described in much the same terms as the revival of the imaginative life of a reread novel:

---

[46] James told Edith Wharton in her marital crisis to 'remember that nothing happens as we forecast it—but always with interesting and, as it were, refreshing differences' (*HJL* iv. 519; letter of 19 Apr. 1909).

The lapse of time here, extraordinarily, has sprung no leak in the effect; it remains so robust that everything lives again, the interval drops out and we mingle in the business: the old ghosts, to our inward sensibility, still make the benches creak as they free their full coat-skirts for sitting down; still make the temperature rise, the pens scratch, the papers flutter, the dust float in the large sun-shafts; we place them as they sit, watch them as they move, hear them as they speak, pity them as they ponder, know them, in fine, from the arch of their eyebrows to the shuffle of their shoes (*AS*, p. 293).

The dropping out of the interval perfects a continuity of present and past. Life returns to what was dead, as in James's moving account in the Notebooks of his visit to his sister's Cambridge grave in 1904, where 'Everything was there, everything *came*; the recognition, stillness, the strangeness, the pity and the sanctity and the terror, the breath-catching passion and the divine relief of tears' (*Nks.* p. 240); or in Dencombe's rereading of 'The Middle Years' at Bournemouth, where 'Everything came back to him, but came back with a wonder, came back, above all, with a high and magnificent beauty.'[47]

When James returns to a work or place, the sense of the work or place comes back to him in a renewal of ties which is the 'revival of an all but extinct relation' (*LC* ii. 1039). What is 'there' for James's knowledge, like the physical demeanour of Franklin, Hancock, *et al.*, is often described as if palpable, in the terms of imaginative substance discussed above (so that 're-handling' is a way of feeling the past).

The 'old' matter is there, re-accepted, re-tasted, exquisitely re-assimilated and re-enjoyed—believed in, to be brief, with the same 'old' grateful faith (since wherever the faith, in a particular case, has become aware of a twinge of doubt I have simply concluded against the matter itself and left it out) (*LC* ii. 1333).[48]

While a work remains un-reread, then, James's confidence can only be conditional; once the test has been passed the faith becomes absolute,

---

[47] *Terminations*, p. 171. In *Scribner's* in 1893 'wonder' had been 'strangeness' (on its p. 611).

[48] The coming to life of the past in Independence Hall has a connection with James's unfinished *The Sense of the Past*, which he started in 1900 and worked on again at the very end of his life. Ralph Pendrel in the novel fetishizes the particularity of history, the exact sense of the past, and returns by a supernatural exchange of identity from 1910 to the 1820s—his imaginations are uncannily vivid. About an unknown relative 'he heard for an instant, hallucinated, the scrape of her stiff petticoat on the floor, and the tap of her shoes, if it weren't rather the click of her small crutch, on the stone stair' (*The Sense of the Past*, London, 1917, p. 70)—which is as immediate as but less ironic (on Ralph's part) than James's vision of Franklin *et al.*

the continuity re-established. The 'matter' of past values is in these cases found to stand up to the 'pressure' of attention in a rereading. The pleasure of this is partly relief, at the discovery that the anxiety James feels before turning back, before revisiting or revising, has been unfounded.

xii. 'Sunk' Pictures

The analogy of fiction and painting, the novelist and the painter, appears on nearly every page of James's NYE Prefaces in phrases like 'a picture of life'. A particular version of the analogy carries a burden of anxiety in respect of rereading and revision—the idea of a past novel as an old canvas, a 'sunk' picture which has lost its lively surface, to which the restorer's wet sponge and varnish bottle need to be applied. Some more or less submarine connections to other images and words give this analogy a place among those which most commonly figure James's attitudes to the act of revision.

'Sunk' pictures have lost their life with time; they are discoloured, lack their original finish and definition, no longer express what was intended in them, and so are available to James in the Prefaces as expressions of the apparent mortality of art. One of the things a 'sunk' picture does is fade, and the special desirability of the image for him comes in part from the way that there are technical processes for treating some 'sunk' pictures, countering the damages of time. (While in the cases of 'fading' and 'melting' examined above the process is irreversible, it is the surface, not the substance, that fades here.) James uses the image in the very first Preface, that to *Roderick Hudson*, to convey the artist's solicitous anxiety about his long-neglected work: it is

put back on the easel for measure of what time and the weather may, in the interval, have done to it. Has it too fatally faded, has it blackened or 'sunk', or otherwise abdicated, or has it only, blest thought, strengthened, for its allotted duration, and taken up, in its degree, poor dear brave thing, some shade of the all appreciable, yet all indescribable grace that we know as pictorial 'tone'? (*LC* ii. 1045).

Putting it back on the easel re-establishes the artist's relation to it—'the creative intimacy is reaffirmed' (*LC* ii. 1046)—and when he passes a wet sponge 'over his old sunk canvas' the 'momentary glaze' of a first rereading 'shows him what may still come out again'.

If the work '*has* kept a few buried secrets, he proceeds to repeat the process with due care and with a bottle of varnish and a brush'. This presumably corresponds to the written registering of the deviations in expression which are dictated by the renewed imaginative life of the work as he closely rereads. It may, however, remain dead: 'The sunk surface has here and there, beyond doubt, refused to respond: the buried secrets, the intentions, are buried too deep to rise again, and were indeed, it would appear, not much worth the burying' (*LC* ii. 1046). 'Sunk' and 'buried' are close here, as they are in the last Preface (that to *The Golden Bowl*), where James speaks of writers who unhappily reread 'to the effect ... of seeing the buried, the latent life of a past composition vibrate, at renewal of touch, into no activity and break through its settled and "sunk" surface at no point whatever' (*LC* ii. 1335). The delay of the emphatic negatives enacts the anxiety and then disappointment of such cases—a disappointment intense here because part of the 'intention' of a literary intention is to *continue* to have an effect, to create something with independent life. Like the buried, the sunk has an unpredictable worth: the two most commonplace things to bury are corpses and treasure, so that at one pole you have dead and buried, at the other, secret and valuable;[49] while we think of both corpses and treasure as characteristic of the bottom of the sea.[50] In *The Tempest*, a play which ends with the master Prospero announcing that 'I'll drown my book' (v. i. 57), Ariel sings to Ferdinand of a transmuting of corpses to treasure (bones to corals, eyes to pearls).

---

[49] The dual potential of what is dug up is dramatized in James's early story 'The Last of the Valerii' (1874). Reworking *La Vénus d'Ille* by Mérimée, which James had translated in his youth, it has a buried statue of Juno being excavated—and equivocates about its coming to life.

[50] The classic statement of this association comes in Clarence's dream of drowning, which anticipates the Song in *The Tempest*:

> Methought I saw a thousand fearful wrecks;
> A thousand men that fishes gnawed upon;
> Wedges of gold, great anchors, heaps of pearl,
> Inestimable stones, unvalu'd jewels,
> All scattered in the bottom of the sea:
> Some lay in dead men's skulls; and in those holes
> Where eyes did once inhabit there were crept,—
> As 'twere in scorn of eyes,—reflecting gems,
> That woo'd the slimy bottom of the deep,
> And mock'd the dead bones that lay scatter'd by.

> (*Richard III*, I. iv. 24–33.)

ARIEL'S SONG

Full fathom five thy father lies.
   Of his bones are coral made;
Those are pearls that were his eyes;
   Nothing of him that doth fade
But doth suffer a sea-change
Into something rich and strange.
Sea-nymphs hourly ring his knell:
SPIRITS [within]. Ding dong.
ARIEL. Hark, now I hear them.
SPIRITS.   Ding-dong bell.   (I.ii. 400–8).

The lines are important to James (as to Hawthorne before him and to Eliot after him) because of his interest in deep transformations.

The Wings of the Dove, for instance, is partly about the change in Milly Theale's consciousness made by her immersion in a particular social group—so that 'the elements were different enough from any of her old elements, and positively rich and strange' (W.o.D., p. 123)—and partly about the changes she makes in those round her—like Susan Stringham, for whom, wittily, 'She was alone, she was stricken, she was rich, and, in particular, she was strange' (W.o.D., p. 89). It ends with tracing Milly's after-effects on Merton Densher, her survival in his imagination and his refusal to read the letter which would have revealed the exact turn she had given her sacrifice.

That turn had possibilities that, somehow, by wondering about them, his imagination had extraordinarily filled out and refined. It had made of them a revelation the loss of which was like the sight of a priceless pearl cast before his eyes—his pledge given not to save it—into the fathomless sea, or rather even it was like the sacrifice of something sentient and throbbing, something that, for the spiritual ear, might have been audible as a faint, far wail (W.o.D., pp. 569–70).

The proximity of 'pearl' and 'eyes' and 'fathom' remembers 'Those are pearls that were his eyes' (and 'somehow' cherishes the mystery of the process of accretion), at the same time as 'pearl cast before' calls up the word 'swine' for Densher's guilty contemplation; while the parenthesis arrests the pearl in mid-flight, specially delaying the completion of the verb phrase 'cast into the sea'. (The second simile, revising the first, goes back before the inanimate pearl to 'something

sentient and throbbing', a *life* which is being sacrificed.) Talking
generally elsewhere about the 'curious conversion' caused by Europe
in all his young American heroines, James alludes to the same context;
'their share of the characteristic blankness underwent what one might
call a sea-change' (*LC* ii. 1199). These immersions and alterations
suggest a special imaginative value for what comes on the resurgence
from a sinking; in his 1907 Preface to *The Tempest* (mainly about the
mysteriousness of Shakespeare's genius) James says that in his last
play 'he sinks as deep as we like, but what he sinks into, beyond all
else, is the lucid stillness of his style' (*LC* i. 1209). This cluster of
meanings helps to suggest possible ways for a 'sunk' picture to rise
again in revision.

In the letter to William about his abandonment of *The Bostonians*
after finishing it, past works have 'quite sunk beneath the surface'
(that of his conscious mind); the parallel of painting and book suggests
that the revised expression of intention and nuance is like the restoration of original colour or outline. The connection seems to provide
a visible and technical equivalent to the imagination's intangible processes in revision. The analogy raises an important difficulty, though.
James is highly tendentious in equating the pictorial restoration of
paint on a canvas (which only uses varnish to bring up dead colours)
with the literary process of revision, which involves the actual alteration of verbal expression; and thus the analogy has again a prop-
ositional force, suggests an automatic ease. An artist's materials are
more defined when he is a painter than when he is a writer—but to
claim as James does that altering the words of a text (really the only
equivalent to paint) is equivalent to varnishing and bringing out the
original colours and lines of a picture—*without* changing the actual
paint-work—seems to suggest that the equivalent of actual paint-work
in a text is something more essential or less superficial than its verbal
expression. The slippage in the analogy is of kind rather than degree,
and to wonder if James may not have thought of the larger elements
of structure and composition as constituting the real paint-work will
not solve the problem. What seems to be at stake is the issue of
the separability of style and content, surface and substance—strange
though this might seem in a writer so emphatically in favour of 'the
sacrament of execution'.

Robert Herrick, in his account of 'A Visit to Henry James', comments triumphantly on the apparent contradiction in James's phrase
'a mere revision of surface and expression' (*LHJ* ii. 55), which comes

in a letter reassuring Mrs Dew-Smith about what he had done to
Roderick Hudson.

'Brother William's' philosophy should have convinced the novelist of the
impossibility—above all in his peculiar case—of making a 'mere revision of
surface and expression' without inevitably affecting 'the substance', when the
two are so inextricably fused as Henry James under other circumstances
would be only too delighted to admit that they are fused in his own work.[51]

The anomaly seems a glaring *naïveté* in one as critically intelligent as
James, and a straight contravention of his emphasis elsewhere.[52] But
we should understand this localized acceptance of the division of
surface and matter by reference to the predilection for a palpably
material metaphorical language I have already suggested. That is, the
force of James's sense of 'the "old" matter' as matter comes exactly
in the fact that he has a *sense* of it; the recovery in revision of a grasp
on the imaginative substances of the past requires, as much as the
other processes I have looked at, a metaphorical language of the
material. The seeming inaccuracy of the way James talks of revision—
as a recovery of old matter or a 'twitching, to a better effect, of
superannuated garments' on original bodies (*LC* ii. 1331)—performs
a metaphorical function, then. What returns to him is not actually the
old matter, since even when it was old it was only metaphorically
matter (it's all fiction); but rather the shape of the imaginative processes
through which this imaginative matter was passed. The 'real' matter
of a 'sunk' picture in this version is therefore the body of original
intentions and nuances recoverable from underneath its surface
expression, that is, the original imaginative life of it; and the assertion
that *this* is regrasped (as the matter) gives the condition for understanding how James can claim to be only varnishing when we might
think he was in effect repainting.

xiii. *The Return of Life*

In *The American Scene* James is at the very first not sure about
Baltimore: but 'What occurred betimes, and ever so happily, was

---

[51] 'A Visit to Henry James', pp. 736–7.

[52] In his 1907 essay on *The Tempest*, for example: 'the phrase, the cluster and order
of terms, *is* the object and the sense, in as close a compression as that of body and soul,
so that any consideration of them as distinct, from the moment style is an active, applied
force, becomes a gross stupidity' (*LC* i. 1212).

simply that the delicate blank of those first hours flushed into animation, and that with this indeed the embroidery of the fine canvas turned thick and rich' (*AS*, p. 317). From resembling the 'canvas that was a mere dead blank' of *The Madonna of the Future* (see the chapter below on *Roderick Hudson*), the blank scene flushes into life (and by implication it is the *tabula rasa* of James's imagination of it that is animated). In the Preface to *Daisy Miller* James gives an account of the principle of life in art: he attributes to even the simplest truth about something in life an independent tendency to struggle against constraints of form for complete representation and expression (in the artist's imagination, presumably); and then goes on, luridly mixing his metaphors:

Any real art of representation is, I make out, a controlled and guarded acceptance, in fact a perfect economic mastery, of that conflict: the general sense of the expansive, the explosive principle in one's material thoroughly noted, adroitly allowed to flush and colour and animate the disputed value, but with its other appetites and treacheries ... kept down (*LC* ii. 1278).

The surface of the work of art, that is, is controlled and composed, its limiting margins justified by the felt tension of the mass of relations it economically holds at bay, our sense of the artist's effort to select and focus; the illusion of depth is evoked in this compactness by what James calls 'foreshortening'. In painting this is one means of producing in the viewer a sense of a resistantly material and three-dimensional reality 'behind' the surface of the work of art; in literature, more metaphorically, the surface is the writing and the substantiality we are called on to reproduce or allow for in our own minds is that in the author's imagination. The aim of literary art, James goes on, is to make 'the surface iridescent, even in the short piece, by what is beneath it and what throbs and gleams through' (*LC* ii. 1278). Writing of *Julia Bride*, James refers to 'the achieved iridescence from within', again something arising from a materiality. And here is what happens in rereading:

Such value as may dwell in 'Julia Bride', for example, seems to me, on re-perusal, to consist to a high degree in the strength of the flushing through on the part of the subject-matter, and in the mantle of iridescence naturally and logically so produced (*LC* ii, 1264–5).

It is this that presumably happens under the 'momentary glaze' of the wet sponge (in a first rereading) 'when the moistened canvas does obscurely flush and when resort to the varnish-bottle is thereby immediately indicated' (*LC* ii. 1046). The independent life of the subject again makes itself felt: rereading *Roderick Hudson*, James says, he finds that 'A whole side of the old consciousness, under this mild pressure, flushes up and prevails again' (*LC* ii. 1042). The word 'flush' hints at a pathetic fallacy about the life of the subject (James sometimes uses 'blush' in the same way); anything can have a colour, that is, but usually only people can 'colour'. In revision the original colours are brought up; some of his works have 'all joyously and blushingly renewed themselves' (*LC* ii. 1338). What can come through in a 'sunk' picture, then, first under the 'wet sponge' of rereading and then under the varnish of revision which fixes the recaptured colours, is an intention, a 'buried secret', a quantity of extant imaginative life. The act of revision is presented by the picture analogy as simply the restoration of original colour.

James has things humanly blush and flush less than he has them botanically bloom and flower; and the organic process by which a plant goes from seed to full-blown maturity offers a perceptible continuity to render that of the reviser's imagination over the years in a way which neither the 'sunk' picture analogy nor that of a secularly miraculous resurrection can approach. James frequently uses the analogy to describe the primary growth of works of fiction in his imagination—the way in which hints germinate, or in which a stir of the air causes 'a "subject", to my sense, immediately to bloom there' (*LC* ii, 1286)—but the final flower of the process is not necessarily a first edition, coming out and then soon withering. Rereading *The Ambassadors*, James finds 'The old intentions bloom again and flower' (*LC* ii. 1314)—the products of the imagination can be hardy perennials, even ever-lasting flowers, and the process has no necessary end with its arrival in print. Thus, in *The Golden Bowl* Preface,

the act of revision, the act of seeing it again, caused whatever I looked at on any page to flower before me as into the only terms that honourably expressed it; and the 'revised' element in the present Edition is accordingly these terms, these rigid conditions of re-perusal, registered; so many close notes, as who should say, on the particular vision of the matter itself that experience had at last made the only possible one (*LC* ii. 1332).

If the act of revision brings about a flowering, the first edition can't have been a final bloom, can't have completed the process of imaginative growth. The inevitability asserted in 'caused', 'only terms', 'rigid conditions' and 'only possible one' apparently derives from the undeviating logic of nature's changes. The element of conscious choice in revision is denied, for a rhetorical purpose. James makes this explicit a few pages later, where he discusses the virtual immediacy of each single manifestation in mature rereading of 'the growth of the immense array of terms':

> The term that superlatively, that finally 'renders', is a flower that blooms by a beautiful law of its own (the fiftieth part of a second often so sufficing it) in the very heart of the gathered sheaf; it is *there* already, at any moment, almost before one can either miss or suspect it—so that in short we shall never guess, I think, the working secret of the revisionist for whom its colour and scent stir the air but as immediately to be assimilated (*LC* ii. 1335).

'*There* already' evokes and cherishes independence and existence simultaneously; 'a beautiful law of its own' (recalling the 'wild logic of its own' by which James's impression of Baltimore fixes itself) makes the act of revision the right culmination of a natural sequence of cause and effect. The analogy, then, has a special force which James needs to express his sense of what he does and what his elements do for him in revising. Where the resurrection analogy suggests its effect and the faith you might have in it, and where the 'sunk' picture analogy offers a tendentious version of what the technique of revision might amount to, the organic analogy gives an account of the presumed process which produces beauty, in which 'the working secret of the revisionist' is like the secret of life itself.

xiv. Recovering Tracks

A final analogy drawn on and drawn out by James for talking about particular aspects of the process of rereading is that of an original walk and a present following-over of its traces. Many of James's metaphors rely for extending their significance on constant reversions to the literal or etymological implications of usual ways of speaking. Thus the analogy of gait is a literalized version of a literary 'manner of proceeding'; in rereading you go over an original passage; you re-cover the ground; you retrace the steps of your argument; and at one point James talks of rereading as following tracks left in the snow (the white page). The Prefaces use the idea very largely, mainly in words like 'retracing', for what is in effect a double movement—both a temporal tracing back *to* the original 'germ' of a work, and also, presuming that germ found, tracing its growth forward through the imaginative process and through the actual plot which attempted to render it.

The analogy is specially apt for revision because of the intimate relation between a gait and the footprints a gait leaves (foot*prints*); a man's gait changes as he ages (his paces become heavier or his strides first longer and then shorter) but hardly ever—except perhaps in adolescence—by conscious choice; it is the very manner of his characteristic movement, but is also instinctive, well-nigh unconscious and automatic, and so has much in common with the developing mode of a writer's imagination. The register kept on the page of a writer's imaginative processes can be conveniently likened to the register kept by earth or snow of the nature of a man's stride; rereading early works, James is fascinated by 'that so shifting and uneven character of the tracks of my original passage' (*LC* ii. 1334). His mature imagination has a different way of covering the ground, a 'developed difference of measure' (*LC* ii. 1335), and it is the interest of noting the early works as in or out of step with it that occupies him in rereading.   .

In the Preface to *The Portrait of a Lady*, James says that some of the advantages of the fabulist's art come with the opportunity of re-perusal; they lie in 'these fine possibilities of recovering, from some good standpoint on the ground gained, the intimate history of the business—of retracing and reconstructing its steps and stages' (*LC* ii. 1072). And while the ordinary reader goes over the story and has the illusion of that, James in rereading gets back to the illusion which he had in mind as its author, including his intentions: 'As always—since the charm never fails—the retracing of the process from point to point brings back the old illusion' (*LC* ii. 1314). The larger retracing of a route here approximates to the general scheme and movement of a novel, its method as much as its detailed expression. For a novel like *The Awkward Age*, with its particularly strenuous formal demands of writer and reader, the image calls up an alert and trained attention, a capacity for close pursuit.

The revived interest I speak of has been therefore that of following critically, from page to page, even as the red Indian tracks in the forest the pale-face, the footsteps of the systematic loyalty I was able to achieve (*LC* ii. 1135).

The manner of proceeding which a rereading retraces may not be presented as so consciously 'systematic' as this, though; in another Preface, pointing out his instinctive predilection for the most responsible reflector of a given situation—here Maggie in *The Golden Bowl*—

James uses the tracking image to indicate a more generally characteristic sense for directions:

I track my uncontrollable footsteps, right and left, after the fact, while they take their quick turn, even on stealthiest tiptoe, toward the point of view that, within the compass, will give me most instead of least to answer for (*LC* ii. 1323).

'Uncontrollable' and 'stealthiest' here suggest respectively the independent artistic instinct and the technical subtlety which characterize a profoundly personal, over-determined gait (a 'quick turn' James may be thinking of is the transition from The Prince in Book One to The Princess in Book Two, where Maggie takes all on herself). Rereading such latest works James the reader makes the same imaginative steps—thinks along the same lines—as James the historian; the traces fit with perfect congruence.

Into his very footprints the responsive, the imaginative steps of the docile reader that I consentingly become for him all comfortably sink; his vision, superimposed on my own as an image in cut paper is applied to a sharp shadow on a wall, matches, at every point, without excess or deficiency (*LC* ii. 1329).

In the short term the author easily re-finds an identity over time; third and first persons satisfyingly match up in an ideal continuity of vision. First 'my' steps sink into 'his very footprints'; then, reciprocally, 'his vision' is 'superimposed on my own'—so that present and recent past fit exactly. But James goes on that such a case is simply 'the accepted repetition', and that in cases where revision has been needed 'the interest of the watched renewal has been livelier' (*LC* ii. 1338). Something quite different happens with these earlier works:

thanks to the so frequent lapse of harmony between my present mode of motion and that to which the existing footprints were due. It was, all sensibly, as if the clear matter being still there, even as a shining expanse of snow spread over a plain, my exploring tread, for application to it, had quite unlearned the old pace and found itself naturally falling into another, which might sometimes indeed more or less agree with the original tracks, but might most often, or very nearly, break the surface in other places. What was thus predominantly interesting to note, at all events, was the high spontaneity of these deviations and differences, which became thus things not of choice, but of immediate and perfect necessity: necessity to the end of dealing with the quantities in question at all (*LC* ii. 1330).

He finds himself walking in a different way (manner and direction): the original gait may have come from a set of instincts, but the mature gait, to cover the same ground, instinctively ('naturally') diverges from the tracks previously left. James presents the process as it manifests itself to him—phenomenologically, or 'dramatically'—so that revisions arrive ready-formed in the consciousness without being chosen, choose themselves, are the inevitable results of a developed imaginative and stylistic manner of proceeding. The analogy of gait further enforces his presentation of revision as 'the particular vision of the matter itself that experience had at last made the only possible one'.

xv.   Continuity and Immortality

The logic of a plant's growth from seed to flower can be a model of organic identity and continuity, a controlling version of the possibility of change without the sacrifice of unity of intention. The faded colours of a 'sunk' picture which flush with varnish in revision are intentions, and the flower that blooms in the act of revision with the arrival of the right term is satisfying because adequate to a past intention. It is therefore important for the revising James that changes in him over time should be accommodated within a continuum of intention and fulfilment. He feels it necessary, that is, to confirm the essential identity of the self of 1874, say, who intended an effect in *Roderick Hudson*, with the self of 1906 who sees himself as truly fulfilling that effect. The particular question of the continuity of authorship here is an aspect of the general question about the continuity of human identity, which may involve the power of human lives to sustain a meaning across their span.

In his 1910 essay 'Is There a Life After Death?', James's doubts about immortality centre on the survival of the personality (the 'subject'), and on the kind of conditions under which one's living self could have any continuity with a dead-but-persisting self:

I practically know what I am talking about when I say, 'I', hypothetically, for my full experience of another term of being, just as I know it when I say 'I' for my experience of this one; but I shouldn't in the least do so were I not *able* to say 'I'—had I to reckon, that is, with a failure of the signs by which I know myself.[53]

---

[53] 'Is There A Life After Death?' (1910), in *The James Family*, ed. F. O. Matthiessen, New York, 1947, p. 607.

Rereading involves a similar suspense as to whether, and if so how, 'life' survives: the Prefaces are partly a tracing of the signs by which James knows himself as an integrity defined by his development. They follow through large continuities of concern and treatment over James's career, encompassing for instance the 'whole passage of intellectual history' (*LC* ii. 1276) between *Daisy Miller* (1878) and *Julia Bride* (1908). Sometimes they fail to recover an evolution—as when James is faced by 'Intervals of thought and a desolation of missing links' (*LC* ii. 1284) between him and *The Story In It*—but the idea of a continuity, a personal tradition, is persistently sought.

I should even like to give myself the pleasure of retracing from one of my own productions to another the play of a like instinctive disposition, of catching in the fact, at one point after another, from 'Roderick Hudson' to 'The Golden Bowl', that provision for interest which consists in placing advantageously, placing right in the middle of the light, the most polished of possible mirrors of the subject (*LC* ii. 1095).

The repeating pattern has an instinctive basis; the variety of the manifestations is made coherent, part of a process of development, by the continuity of instinct—perceived with hindsight and played up in the *NYE* selection. The sensibility is moulded and modified, but never becomes something else, and the work is an object on which—or rather a complex of relations *within* which—this essential identity is tested. The original imaginative relation of author to work, that of intention (and correspondingly of responsibility), *need* not be broken off in his lifetime, James's revision asserts, despite time's attrition. Some of the force of this is conveyed by the image of parenthood in the Preface to *The Golden Bowl*, whereby James's refusal of any unrevised, any 'vulgarly irresponsible re-issue' (*LC* ii. 1331) completes a persistence of care presented as a solicitude for his issue. To revise his brood, his 'progeny', is to clothe and clean them for the drawing-room.

Throughout his career James is concerned with extending the author's relation to his work, with the endlessness of his art. He wrote to Mrs F. H. Hill on 21 March 1879, defending himself against having his meanings fixed and finalized and simplified:

Nothing is my *last word* about anything— I am interminably supersubtle and analytic—and with the blessing of heaven, I shall live to make all sorts of representations of all sorts of things (*HJL* ii. 221).

Revision makes it literal that a first edition is not his last word,

that his 'analysis' is interminable. He asserts both the flexibility and
conditionality of the things in his existing texts, and the importance
of continuing to write more, with a perfectionism—a pressure to
increasingly precise readjustment on behalf of an ideal vision—which
at once refuses to leave its products prematurely alone and places a
high value on a 'finished' product. This is not a contradiction—you
have to keep on working to put a 'finish' on something. There are risks
of imbalance and excess here, as the connotations of 'perfectionism'
suggest; but even if these are avoided, there are costs: of strenuous
attention, of restless analysis, of self-contradiction.

Dencombe, the dying author in 'The Middle Years', urgently desires
a 'better chance'[54] at writing other books, and is correspondingly
concerned with revision, struggling against the finality of print and its
threat to the author's power of amendment.

Dencombe was a passionate corrector, a fingerer of style; the last thing he
ever arrived at was a form final for himself. His ideal would have been to
publish secretly, and then, on the published text, treat himself to the terrified
revise, sacrificing always a first edition and beginning for posterity and even
for the collectors, poor dears, with a second.[55]

Dencombe's desires here give rise to paradoxes; the wish to 'begin'
with a second edition, to 'publish secretly'. It is an ironic idiom that
redeems 'the last thing . . . was a form final for himself' from tautology;
the understatement in the expression moves us to believe he never
would reach an end ('the last thing he ever' as a version of 'the one
thing he never').

To stick close in this way, making changes even after the point at
which the public is usually thought to have a work fixed in its view,
and yet to continue to be prolific, is to maximize responsibility and
the related state, to conceive and attempt an *œuvre* for the whole of
which one can answer. We can compare the achievement of Balzac,
given in the Preface to *The Golden Bowl* as the great example—its
double movement of repossession and fresh conquest dialectically
bringing it to an equivalent of rest:

He (and these things, as we know, grew behind him at an extraordinary rate)
re-assaulted by supersessive terms, re-penetrated by finer channels, never had
on the one hand seen or said all or had on the other ceased to press forward

---

[54] *Terminations*, p. 173.
[55] *Terminations*, p. 181.

... We owe to the never-extinct operation of his sensibility, we have but meanwhile to recall, our greatest exhibition of felt finalities, our richest and hugest inheritance of imaginative prose (*LC* ii. 1336).

We note the paradoxical linking of 'never-extinct ... sensibility' and 'felt finalities'; one of the conditions for the sense of a work of art as finished ('definitive', like James's Edition) is a sense of its imaginative life as capable of being extended. You can only feel it properly to cease if it hasn't ceased to feel.

On the final page of his final Preface, that to *The Golden Bowl*, James laments the irrevocable loss in time of pieces of social behaviour, but contrasts the different and more responsible permanence of pieces of art. Social performances leave little trace.

Not so on the other hand our really 'done' things of this superior and more appreciable order—which leave us indeed all licence of disconnexion and disavowal, but positively impose on us no such necessity. Our relation to them is essentially traceable, and in that fact abides, we feel, the incomparable luxury of the artist. It rests altogether with himself not to break with his values, not to 'give away' his importances. Not to *be* disconnected, for the tradition of behaviour, he has but to feel that he is not; by his lightest touch the whole chain of relation and responsibility is reconstituted. Thus if he is always doing he can scarce, by his own measure, ever have done (*LC* ii. 1340–1).

Revision for James is a practical version in the literary realm of such an impulse to make connections, of the sense of the continuity of relations; in a way which reaches down to the smallest details it exemplifies a working belief in the immortality of the things of the imagination, and in the endlessness—till death, at least—of the author's relation to such things. The 'lightest touch' here is the tiniest of amendments to a text, one which serves to renew the creative intimacy; it is a touch, moreover, felt with serious relief to be within his imaginative grasp and to save James from the limbo of disconnection, from the 'strange alienation' which afflicts Dencombe as he begins to reread his own work. James had imagined an artist suffering just such a disastrous alienation more than thirty years before in the novel that heads the New York Edition, *Roderick Hudson*.

4

Roderick Hudson and the Beginnings of Genius

i. The Veiled Face of the Muse

In the Preface of 1907 to this novel of 1875 James remarks that revision, his 'revival of an all but extinct relation with an early work', illuminates for the artist 'that veiled face of his Muse which he is condemned for ever and all anxiously to study' (*LC* ii. 1039). Such an anxious scrutiny is the project of the maturely resourceful James in rereading, revising, and prefacing; but it is also—and in their case the scrutiny is unrewarded—what Roderick Hudson and Rowland Mallet are doomed to in the novel itself. The fictional young sculptor's misfortune in the book is the extinction of his relation with his work, his loss of that 'continuity of an artist's endeavour' (*LC* ii. 1039–40) which the real resuming James notes as extant in himself.

When the young James had written on 28 June 1869 during his European initiation that his tale *Gabrielle de Bergerac*, composed in America about Europe and at last published in the *Atlantic*, 'strikes me as the product of a former state of being' (*HJL* i. 126), his hyperbole benignly differentiated present adequacy from previous wishfulness within a development which is progressive. The unfortunate Roderick Hudson, in this novel of six years later, suffers rather the difference which is the measure of decline. In Chapter 21 Rowland looks from the helpless and alarmed Mrs Hudson to the alarmingly changed Roderick,

but Roderick had his back turned, and, with his head on one side, like a tourist in a church, was gazing at his splendid 'Adam' (*1883*, ii. 121).

Two pages later in the 1883 edition (from which James probably revised for the New York Edition)

Roderick, who had hardly removed his eyes from his statue, got up again and went back to look at it (*1883*, ii. 123).

The time that has set this distance between Roderick and his earlier, creative self detaches him from his own work as the passage of centuries detaches the modern tourist from the works of past masters. The James of 1906, faced with *his* own earlier work in this novel, gets further to grips with Roderick's loss of touch by retouching both these moments.

[Rowland's] eyes, for a moment, took in Roderick—Roderick who had his back turned and, with his head on one side like a tourist in a church, was lost in the consideration of his own proved power. The proof, meeting him there in its several forms, had made him catch his breath (*NYE* i. 434).

Having now at this first moment invoked 'several forms' of proof rather than just one, James saves the contemplation of the individual 'Adam' for the second.

Roderick, who had hardly removed his eyes from the exhibition of his work, got up again and went back to the great figure in which, during his divine first freshness, he had embodied his idea of the primal Adam (*NYE* i. 437).

The revision brings in 'the primal Adam' only *after* Mrs Hudson has given her account of Roderick's disastrous egotistical passivity—seen in his suggestion that she should sell her house to pay his debts—and after Roderick has 'serenely' pronounced himself 'fallen'. The second of the revised moments makes us hesitate between recalling in Roderick something like the 'divine first freshness' of God in creating man, and seeing in him the much more precarious, and only vicariously 'divine', first freshness of the created Adam[1]. In this evocation of the gap between the former achievement of the artist and the revealed fallibility of the man, James finds for the *NYE* a pathos in Roderick's situation that takes strength from its tacitly contrastive relation to something that escapes being pitiful in his own; for James's career has not been a fall. 'Divine first freshness' is a phrase of his maturity, one giving first freshness its due acknowledgement but, as a revision there only in a late bloom, itself constituting an act which implicitly qualifies the value of that first freshness as not exclusive of other values.[2] James feels his revision, moreover, as a more appropriate embodiment of an

[1] A revision correspondingly aligns Christina Light with Eve when at the end of the eighth chapter, sitting for Roderick, 'She looked divinely beautiful' (*1883*, i. 128) becomes 'She looked divinely fair' (*NYE* i. 170), recalling *Paradise Lost*, ix. 489 ('She fair, divinely fair, fit love for gods').

[2] This recalls the tone of James's 'Note' on the papers collected the year before the *NYE* in *English Hours* (1905)—'the earliest in date more than thirty years ago' (*EH*, p. v). They represent thoughts and feelings 'the fine freshness of which the author has—

original idea, a successful continuation of relations where Roderick's sense of past success leaves him numb with his consciousness of discontinuity. James is not, as Roderick is, 'lost in the consideration of his own proved power', but is rather concerned with finding extensions and reinforcements of the sense and the fictional situation which are incidentally a proof of power. '*His own* proved power', for instance, takes up from elsewhere in the book the suggestion that Roderick has been irresponsibly confident of possessing his faculties. It points both to what it is that Roderick has lost and to why it may be that he has lost it—a presumptuous failure of tact causing him to handle as irrevocably his own a mysteriously conditional gift.

In the Preface to the novel James confesses to an error (not of conception but of composition and expression) in the timing of Roderick's collapse: 'at the rate at which he falls to pieces, he seems to place himself beyond our understanding and our sympathy'. He then develops the relation of timing and sympathy by voicing 'our' objections on this score. 'These are not our rates, we say; we ourselves certainly, under like pressure,—for what is it after all?—would make more of a fight' (*LC* ii. 1047). The intimation that sympathy functions by a process of comparison with oneself and an engagement with a community suggests at least in part a rationale for James's imaginative act in revising: he invests his sense of the thirty-two years lived between the spring of 1874, when he began writing, and February or March 1906, when he finished revising, *Roderick Hudson*, in his alteration of the text. 'Our rates,' then, and our feelings about our rates, are brought into relation with what befalls Roderick: the great divide from his past self which afflicts him within two years benefits in expression—and with ironic turns—by the partially bridged divide in James's own thirty-two further years of experience.

ii.   Genius in Practice

Though *Roderick Hudson* is not exactly an autobiographical novel, much of its life—in *1883* and in the *NYE*—springs from its intimate relation to James's own career. At the beginnings of his career James

---

to his misfortune, no doubt—sufficiently outlived' (p. vi). 'No doubt' hears and politely concedes the nostalgist's comment, but 'sufficiently' is not going to cry over the water which has flowed under the bridge. James quotes this 'Note' in the Preface to *Roderick Hudson* (*LC* ii. 1046).

was repeatedly preoccupied with beginnings, and with premature ends, of careers; with the idea of, and the delusions of, genius; and with artists' relations to their imagination. The sense of mental operations as bafflingly other had been with James already in the years preceding *Roderick Hudson*, years during which he had cultivated a consciousness of vocation and at the same time contained his ambitions within the bounds of a deliberate apprenticeship. As he put it in 1873 in a letter to William, 'Mysterious and incontrollable (even to one's self) is the growth of one's mind. Little by little, I trust, my abilities will catch up with my ambitions' (*HJL* i. 385). When James wrote this he had just stayed on into the 'mortally flat and dead and relaxing' Roman spring (*HJL* i. 365) to get impressions—those incorporated in *Roderick Hudson*, where Roderick's relaxation plays so large a part in his decline. And a significant part of James's impression of such relaxation was the experience of its effect on his own powers. 'My winter in Rome was a poor working winter and I have done less than I hoped: but it was very educative and will tell before long' (*HJL* i. 395). The rebound here from inactivity to production means not just that James collected material for future work while failing to work at the time; it comes to mean, even, that not working was an education for him—an experience which 'told' for him in his first acknowledged novel, where an artist's Roman spring sees the end of his career. In Rome James's confidence had strangely asserted itself at the heart of his relaxation: 'the languor that one continually feels has something harmonious and (intellectually) profitable in it' (*HJL* i. 362). Being able to tell sympathetically of Roderick's collapse was a harmonious consolation and an intellectual profit of this stay: James's exposure to what thirty years later in *William Wetmore Story and His Friends* he was to call the 'Borgia Cup' held out by the Roman atmosphere, the overtaking of the artist by a delusive complacency about his achievement, yielded him with a shift of gear a feeling of his powers actually *not* delusive, a confidence grounded in his possession of a sense of that Roman predicament. An ironic doubling of perspective allows him to make a true joke of saying in retrospect that 'I feel as if I had left my "genius" behind in Rome' (*HJL* i. p. 396):[3] not

---

[3] A reluctance to speak directly of his own genius was still strong in James at the end of his life—as in a letter of 11 Nov. 1912 declining the chairmanship of the English Association: where he has referred the question to 'the very essence of any poor thing that I might, or even still may, trump up for the occasion as my "genius"' (*LHJ* ii. 270).

'that I have' but 'as if I had', and not 'my genius' but 'my "genius"'.
The feeling is real, but part of something more complex. To feel a
pressing vocation like that of 'genius' (in the Romantic sense) is one
thing and to take off the inverted commas another, so that perhaps it
is thinking about this latter plain display of one's gifts, the shameless
act to which the 'Borgia Cup' seduces, that makes James write thus of
leaving Rome. He knew by experience, that is, something *like* Roderick's attitude to his genius and the collapse of it; but knew it, with a
difference, as not final and even as artistically profitable.

The young American painter whose incipient career is run against
Roderick's in the novel, Sam Singleton, offers a version of the artist's
start that corresponds to a complementary aspect of James's thinking
and practice. In the characterization of this figure as so pedestrian we
can see an alternative, painstakingly patient way of handling the lag
between ambitions and abilities. Roderick belittles this 'humble genius'
(*1883*, i. 203), who is often (if less in the *NYE*) 'little' Singleton till a
trick of the light makes him half-truly appear a 'colossal figure' (*1883*,
ii. 158) near the end in Switzerland. His apprenticeship takes him
steadily on beyond the fallen Roderick, and Rowland Mallet recognizes
in him a startling capacity for advance. Apprenticeship means practice—'practice' which means preparing to do the thing by the discipline
of doing it—and Singleton's steady work aligns him in this respect
with the James who wrote in 1873 that

With practice I shall learn to write more briskly and naturally. Practice tells
slowly with me and it seems, as yet, the successive difficulties that chiefly
dawn upon me. But eventually I shall write none the worse for having learned
slowly (*HJL* i. 344).

In the first description of Singleton we learn that he had begun by
painting 'worthless daubs', but that 'Improvement had come . . . hand
in hand with patient industry' (*1883*, i. 82); after a summer of further
hard work—'happy frugality' revised to 'successful economy' (*NYE* i.
144)—gathering 'a wonderful store of subjects' in Italy, Rowland
forces him to admit that 'I feel much more sure of myself' (*1883*, i.
108); and near the end Roderick is awed, irritated, and depressed
by Singleton's quiet ability to develop and continue producing. The
eventual contrast of the two careers comes as a reversal of the earlier
situation, where the humble Singleton ingenuously admired the confidence of Roderick's genius.

'Ah, there's a man,' cried Singleton, 'who has taken his start once for all and doesn't need to stop and ask himself in fear and trembling every month or two whether he is going on. When he stops it's to rest!' (*1883*, i. 109).

James himself had not quite this self-effacing relation to other artists. His appreciations of artistic precocity (especially in poets) combine warmth and tenderness with the reservation exacted by his sense of the fragility of youthful promise. Ironic distance keeps a space open for another, more apparently prosaic relation of the artist to his sensibility.

The account of Singleton's progress, however, does offer striking similarities to James's way of writing about his own imaginative profits from his time in Italy. When Singleton is called home to America by his family 'he submitted to destiny the more patiently that he had laid up treasure, which in Buffalo would seem infinite' (*1883* ii. 107). The treasure laid up here is nine hundred sketches; James in September 1872 noted of his progress in a letter home from Rome that 'I have had too little time to write, to lay up any great treasure to commence with' (*HJL* i. 297), profanely changing the religious value of the Beatitude into the worldly currency of pages covered and of payment by magazines. Yet the 'successful economy' of Singleton is not merely literal, but a way of attaining the 'felicity' of 'facility' (words occurring frequently in the book); while James's applications of the idea of saving up treasure sown by Christ's words in Matthew's Gospel are capable of 'wild' metaphorical ramification. In 1870, at the end of his first European visit, he wrote of his Italian experience that

I had far rather let Italy slumber in my mind untouched as a perpetual capital, whereof for my literary needs I shall draw simply the income—let it lie warm and nutritive at the base of my mind, manuring and enriching its roots (*HJL* i. 208).[4]

This is an unruly stir of associations about 'lying'—'slumbering' into 'untouched capital' into 'manuring'—but its juxtaposition of the unconscious with the economic with the organic around 'the growth of one's mind' suggests a way in which the preludial frugality and necessary self-discipline of the apprentice (the elements most noted in Singleton) need to be complemented by a relaxation before 'mysterious

---

[4] This application of the Beatitude about laying up treasure to a writer's imaginative resources connects with James's use of *The Tempest*'s language about sunken treasure.

and incontrollable' processes, a sense of the imagination as other. In Singleton, a minor character, we are left to imagine artistic growth from the outside, and know it by its putative fruits; the relaxation, and the live possibility of bafflement, are explicitly dealt with only in the handling of Roderick.

What is dramatized is Roderick's miserable exclusion from the pleasures of production. In Switzerland the two artists are brought together, and Roderick's original amusement at Singleton's intentness is severely punished by the turn of events:

he watched the little painter's serene activity with a gravity that was almost portentous (*1883*, ii. 160).

he might have been listening, as under a sombre spell, to the hum of some prosperous workshop from which he had been discharged for incompetence (*NYE* i. 484).

The revision's 'hum' sounds as both the noise of work and the musical by-product of the worker's joy; 'prosperous' cuts back against Roderick's earlier description of himself as 'bankrupt'; and the yoking of 'work' with 'shop' reflects on Roderick's fatal scorn of the respects in which his career might have been, among other things, a trade. Remaining an amateur in what has to be, for him at least, a profession, Roderick is left out of the employment he loves. In this final scene confronting the two artists a revision generous to Singleton turns his 'unflagging industry' (*1883*, ii. 160)—of which the effort might be greater than the achievement, so that we would still be left to judge of its all-important success—to 'successful method' (*NYE* i. 484), in which hard work is wedded with intelligence.

In being fairer to Singleton, of course, the revising James shifts our sense of what happens to Roderick: exclusion from happiness is a predicament that can yield the sufferer some consolation through a sense of being grandly doomed to it, but 'discharged for incompetence' renders it as a case of undignified just deserts, even if only in Roderick's desponding view. The book is true to the nature of Roderick's failure, moreover, in so far as it seriously contrasts it with a case in which not only does the artist work (hard) but his imagination works for him and his works work; the latter workings being mysteriously oblique rewards of the former effort. Singleton's power to keep going awes Roderick and repels him; he says to Rowland 'that their friend reminded him of some curious insect with a remarkable mechanical instinct in its antennae' (*NYE* i. 484),[5] and this mechanical appearance of the maturing artist's activity, in which so much of the functioning of intelligence is invisibly instinctive, seemingly outside the scope of consciousness, is further noted in the second thing Roderick finds the industrious Singleton reminding him of.

This is Singleton's account of the first and last time the two artists speak at any length in the book.

'Are you *always* just like this?' Roderick had asked in almost sepulchral accents.

'Like this?' Singleton, startled, had repeated with a guilty blink.

'You remind me of a watch that never runs down. If one listens hard one hears you always at it. Tic-tic-tic, tic-tic-tic.'

'Oh, I see,' Singleton had returned while he beamed ingenuously. 'I'm very regular.'

'You're very regular, yes. And I suppose you find it very pleasant to be very regular?'

Singleton had hereupon turned and smiled more brightly, sucking the water from his camel's-hair brush. Then with a quickened sense of his indebtedness to a Providence that had endowed him with intrinsic facilities: 'Oh, most delightful!' he had exclaimed.

Roderick had stood looking at him a moment. 'Damnation!' was the single word that then had fallen from him; with which he had turned his back (*NYE* i. 484–5).

Singleton is provokingly unaware of Roderick's different position, and the *NYE* takes care to catch Roderick's fretted and desolate ironies: *1883* lacks in its 'one hears you always—tic-tic, tic-tic' (*1883*, ii. 160) the resentment of enforced idleness in 'at it' and the disturbed irritability of the triplets in 'tic-tic-tic, tic-tic-tic'; while a revision takes *1883*'s 'And do you find it pleasant to be equable?', with its po-faced flatness of probable mockery, and twists it with a presuming 'I suppose' and a double 'very' into a pained sneer. Singleton's 'equable' in the first version is an ingenious pun—or perhaps rather an agile stretch across the range of the word's meanings, from 'of unvarying motions' to something like 'placid'; while its replacement, 'regular', makes rather the shorter and more relevantly witty span between 'you can tell the time by me' and 'I follow the rules'. The religious analogy of successful and unsuccessful artists with the elect and the damned— whereby the condition of creative felicity is paralleled with a state of

---

[5] He is a 'curious little insect' in *1883*, ii. 160.

grace—is at its most concentrated here in both *1883* and the *NYE*, and the mysterious Christian triangle of grace, faith, and works finds equivalences of configuration in the artist's predicament with regard to his—secular—aspirations. Thus we have seen Singleton work for, and merit, his present felicity of facility; yet his grateful sense of indebtedness need not represent an absurdly exaggerated failure of self-reliance, since the terms on which one *can* 'merit' such a happiness will remain obscure of provenance. Roderick's swear-word 'Damnation!' takes on in this context some of the traditional weightiness of spiritual despair—and we could see his readiness of surrender to disaster as a straight repossession of him by the New England he has struggled to escape; were it not for James's subtle chemistry in overdetermining the book's action, in so truly and bafflingly compounding plausible causes in a complex interreaction.

'You remind me of a watch that never runs down' may remind *us* of Roderick's eloquent development of the same image a couple of hundred pages earlier, in conversation with Rowland at the Villa Mondragone. The vertiginous draw of the just-possible fall preoccupies him at that stage; he 'delivered himself of a tissue of lugubrious speculations as to the possible mischances of one's genius' (*1883*, i. 172), 'gave himself up to a free and beautiful consideration of the possible mischances of genius' (*NYE* i. 230). (The explicitly 'lugubrious' is banished, but 'delivered himself of' is creatively turned to account in the dangerous liberty of 'gave himself up to a free ... consideration'.)

'What if the watch should run down', he asked, 'and you should lose the key? What if you should wake up some morning and find it stopped—inexorably, appallingly stopped? Such things have been, and the poor devils to whom they happened have had to grin and bear it. The whole matter of genius is a mystery. It bloweth where it listeth, and we know nothing of its mechanism. If it gets out of order we can't mend it; if it breaks down altogether we can't set it going again. We must let it choose its own pace and hold our breath lest it should lose its balance ...' (*1883*, i. 172; *NYE* i. 230).

Roderick's first hypothesis here functions as the premiss of the rest of his long speech; losing the key is what makes the stopping of a watch into an irremediable conclusion, the key being the vital medium of relation between two divergent scales, between clumsy human grossness and the vulnerable mechanism of inaccessibly minute adjustments which Roderick imagines as the operative part of genius. Such a metaphor, though, of perplexity before resistant physical objects, renders only the helplessly passive aspect of one's relation to the imagination, and loses sight of the sense in which, as James argues in his 1907 essay about *The Tempest* and Shakespeare's career, the artist's genius is an organic part of himself as a psychological subject. Roderick's notion here partakes of what James calls there 'that strangest of all fallacies, the idea of the separateness of a great man's parts. His genius places itself, under this fallacy, on one side of the line and the rest of his identity on the other' (*LC* i. 1216–7). James goes on: 'The genius is a part of the mind, and the mind a part of the behaviour; so that, for the attitude of inquiry, without which appreciation means nothing, where does one of these provinces end and the other begin?' (*LC* i. 1217). Roderick's metaphor has a truth but is not the truth; much of the impetus of *Roderick Hudson* goes into James's close and intelligent qualification of the way in which the fatalism of Roderick's inspirational aesthetics, superstitiously based on the language of boundary-lines and unmitigated imaginative separations, fatally handicaps his artistic practice. Rowland himself, moreover, for the most part healthily sceptical about the special rights and exemptions of original genius, is nevertheless not intact from some of the delusions associated with the idea; so that Roderick's version of a rude awakening looks back to Rowland's early words, repeated from a book, suggesting that a genius is a somnambulist and 'performs great feats in a lucky dream. We mustn't wake him up lest he should lose his balance' ('lucky' arrives in the *NYE* i. 26; *1883*, i. 21). In this account the imagination goes like a dream but then goes, like a dream; and not believing that his genius is seriously continuous with his mind and his behaviour, Roderick falls victim to the glamorously easy images which insinuate that the highest artistic achievement takes place when the artist is most passive.

James himself had early been capable of a stern resistance to relaxation in general: in a letter to the just-widowed Charles Eliot Norton on 6 May 1872 he had proclaimed his faith in 'the grim residuum of conscious manhood with which we stand face to face to the hard reality of things' (*HJL* i. 275–6), feeling his earnestness of tone justified because

I have in my own fashion learned the lesson that life is effort, unremittingly repeated, and because I feel somehow as if real pity were for those who had been beguiled into the perilous delusion that it isn't. Their hard day when it comes, is hard indeed (*HJL* i. 276).

Norton's difficult circumstances and the moral tone of Cambridge, Massachusetts, may stiffen James's attitude into a courage more stoical and muscular than his usual one; but this enliveningly tragic intuition about effort runs deep in him, and his essay on 'Ivan Turgénieff', written just before *Roderick Hudson*, attains a similar urgency of phrase as it elicits the Russian's own developed sense of the hard reality of things—an aesthetic in which waking up and conscious, active balance are valued more than delusions and lucky dreams.

But the world as it stands is no illusion, no phantasm, no evil dream of a night; we wake up to it again for ever and ever; we can neither forget it nor deny it nor dispense with it. We can welcome experience as it comes, and give it what it demands, in exchange for something which it is idle to pause to call much or little so long as it contributes to swell the volume of consciousness (*LC* ii. 998).

James is suggesting here a manner of taking life as the case which renders superfluous the tags of 'optimism' and 'pessimism' regularly attached by his contemporaries—general attitudes which fall into abeyance with the effort of attention to the variety and complexity of particular facts. Roderick's perilous delusion that effort need not be unremittingly repeated engenders in James, who is sure that it cannot, a 'real pity'.

Yet Roderick's idea of genius as all subject to external determination has the interest and the residual validity of a half-truth, or a truth seen from the wrong perspective; it is, since even the most disciplined of geniuses is liable to accidents, an illuminatingly heretical version of the relations involved. When he says in enumerating its possible mis-chances that genius 'bloweth where it listeth', Roderick startlingly enlists Christ's beautiful words to Nicodemus in John 3:8 and uses them for the inspiration of a much more secular elect:

The wind bloweth where it listeth, and thou hearest the sound thereof, but canst not tell whence it cometh, and whither it goeth: so is every one that is born of the Spirit.

The second half of Roderick's sentence—'and we know nothing of its mechanism'—steps awkwardly across again to the watch metaphor, an ungainly lurch from the airborne to the solid which might leave us wondering about a wind machine. Roderick is reluctant, as this misfit of metaphors shows, to imagine a role for personal effort in narrowing the distance between high ideals and practical possibilities. A stopped watch offers a technical difficulty, rather than an impossibility; whereas the wind blowing where it listeth genuinely leaves us nothing to do but hope and pray. Roderick's spectatorial attitude to his genius—he takes up Rowland's earlier 'lest he should lose his balance' about the somnambulist and turns it into 'lest it should lose its balance'—has him counterproductively 'holding his breath' in suspense about the inspiration which might be the medium he breathes. Evidently his speech is indeed in tone a 'free and beautiful consideration' (*NYE*) of the possibilities enumerated in what *1883* was yet accurate in calling 'a tissue of lugubrious speculations': he pursues the morbid implications of his idea with a charmingly disinterested passion and wit.

Set beside Singleton, Roderick has the unholy 'grace' of the noble spendthrift with self-straitening bourgeois virtue as his foil: the novel's patience sees us through to a chastened sense of the demands of an artistic career, and to a stricter, a less romantically inflated account of 'genius'. In so far as the word survives with a value, it is left much closer to *OED* 1's neutral 'tutelary god or attendant spirit', or *OED* 4's prosaic 'special endowments which fit a man for his particular work', than to the 'native intellectual power of an exalted type' given in *OED* 5 as 'often contrasted with *talent*'. This last grandiose notion—where the highest creative powers are disastrously 'contrasted with the aptitudes that can be acquired by study'—apparently has its origin in eighteenth-century German aesthetics, where it became attached to 'that particular kind of intellectual power which has the appearance of proceeding from a supernatural inspiration or possession, and which seems to arrive at its results in an inexplicable and miraculous manner'. In the previous chapter we saw how the mature James's developed style of reference to intangible imaginative processes characteristically described operations performed by his mind *on* objects as actions perceived taking place *in* those objects in an inexplicable and miraculous manner. *Roderick Hudson*, then, the work standing in 1906 at the head of the New York Edition, offers in its sustained test, through an individual career, of a *really* passive attitude to the creative process a warning against taking such language too straight. This novel shows James as intelligently conscious of the dangers that reside in—and responsibilities incurred by—the superstitiously effortless versions of artistic endeavour implicit in the perilously appealing metaphors associated with 'genius'.

iii.   The High Level of Perfection

In terms of practical belief James sympathizes in *Roderick Hudson* more with Singleton's long apprenticeship than with Roderick's inspirational impatience. It is a book which consciously brings together the preoccupations and achievements of many of his earlier stories, as the works of the trained artist's attained maturity resume and consummate the themes and techniques of the apprentice works which have preceded them. It draws also on James's travel-sketches, sometimes with considerable directness;[6] and on sections of his experience (like his relaxation in the Roman spring) which had been the subject only of letters. Just as several of James's previous tales, furthermore, had taken a lively start from admiring but disagreeing with other literary works—*Madame de Mauves* running against *Madame Bovary*, *The Last of the Valerii* against Mérimée's *La Vénus d'Ille*, *The Madonna of the Future* against Balzac's *Le Chef-d'œuvre inconnu*—so the writing in *Roderick Hudson* often gets a vital heat from its friction with that of authors who had differently treated similar matters. The relations between Roderick and the Lights at a number of points remarkably resemble those in the Dumas novel, *Affaire Clémenceau: mémoire de l'accusé*, to which he had devoted a friendly review in the *Nation* on 11 October 1866;[7] the figure of the young sculptor Schubin in Turgenev's *On The Eve*, called by James 'a deeply ingenious image of the artistic temperament' (*LC* ii. 980), offers a less brittle prototype of Roderick Hudson's rangy eloquence; the characterization of Christina Light can be seen as James's show of his hand on the high bid implicit in his remark, apropos of *Smoke*, that 'there is always a certain languor in our intellectual acceptance of the grand coquettes of fiction' (*LC* ii. 984); and the conception of the Cavaliere seems to have its origin in another misleadingly servile character, one from Turgenev's play *Alien Bread*, 'a poor old gentleman who has long been hanging about the place as a pensioner' and who in a scene praised by James 'breaks out into a passionate assurance that, baited and buffeted as he is, he is

---

[6] Thus for instance in sect. V of 'Florentine Notes', first printed in the *Independent* on 18 June 1874, 'I have been told of fine old mouldering chambers of which I might enjoy possession for a sum not worth mentioning' (*TS*, p. 301); and in ch. 21 of *Roderick Hudson* Rowland's friend in Florence 'enjoyed for a sum not worth mentioning the possession of an extraordinary number of noble, stone-floored rooms' (*1883*, ii. 124).

[7] The review is reprinted in *LC* ii. 275–80. Viola R. Dunbar points out the indebtedness in 'A Source for "Roderick Hudson"', *Modern Language Notes*, 63 (May 1948), 303–10.

nothing less than the father of the mistress of the house' (*LC* ii. 993–4).[8] The letters of Henri Regnault, Turgenev's *Rudin*, and novels by George Sand and George Eliot are long-recognized sources; Robert Emmet Long has added Hawthorne's *The Marble Faun*[9] of 1860, as well as specifying *Smoke* and *On The Eve*. This catholic collation of literary models, and the deliberate pulling-together of his own literary practice hitherto, indicate the sense in which the composition of *Roderick Hudson* was for James in 1874 a self-conscious literary act, a fulfilment of the years of preparation which only then, in the words of the later Preface, 'permitted me at last to put quite out to sea.'

The metaphor of the long voyage in this retrospective description, which is then elaborated in some detail to distinguish this first novel from the author's earlier short trips, might seem to align James puzzlingly with the reckless Roderick—whose career is described in terms of voyaging, quite significantly in *1883* and much extendedly in the *NYE*; but the elaboration of the metaphor tells us how James had until 1874—up to the age of thirty—been 'bumping about, to acquire skill, in the shallow waters and sandy coves of the "short story" ', had 'but hugged the shore on sundry previous small occasions' (*LC* ii. 1040). That this chimes with Rowland's reassuring words to Singleton in Chapter Nine, comparing his situation with Roderick's—'You sail

---

[8] In *Roderick Hudson* some such revelation is imagined as taking place *behind* the scenes; the borrowing gives an imaginative depth. James had already used a dramatic revelation of paternity in *Master Eustace* (1871).

[9] Cornelia Kelley, *The Early Development of Henry James* (Urbana, Ill., 1965), pp. 187–9. Long's *The Great Succession: Henry James and the Legacy of Hawthorne* (Pittsburgh, 1979) shows *The Marble Faun* as a major antecedent for *Roderick Hudson* (*The Great Succession*, pp. 38–53). The set-up of James's novel, with its four young people in Rome but with only one of them an artist (instead of three), and with a sexual angle of some kind rendered between each of the men and each of the women, has been shown by Long as a Turgenev-inspired romantic complication (one might polemically say 'fulfilment') of Hawthorne's scheme where the four are relatively clear-cut as two couples. Roderick is in part a blend of Kenyon the mood-ridden sculptor and the fascinated Donatello. Hawthorne's fascinating Miriam springs 'from English parentage, on the mother's side', yet is 'connected, through her father, with one of those ... princely families of Southern Italy' (*The Marble Faun*, Centenary Edition, Ohio, iv, 1968, pp. 429, 430); James's Christina is Anglo-Saxon on her mother's side and Italian on her father's (though she has to *marry* into a 'princely family of Southern Italy'). She also suffers from a (less hideous) family secret. Mary Garland's connection with Hilda, called by James 'This pure and somewhat rigid New England girl' (*LC* i. 446), is striking—compare Mary's possession of 'the purity and rigidity of a mind that had not lived with its door ajar upon the high-road of thought' (*1883*, ii. 53)—though James goes further than Hawthorne in his reservations about the rigidity (and recognizes a force of passion quite compatible with it). Rowland's hovering between moralism and speculative relaxation seems to derive from Kenyon's (and, not impossibly, Hawthorne's own).

nearer the shore, but you sail in smoother waters' (*1883*, i. 143)—
offers a distinction which clarifies any apparent inconsistency: 'to
acquire skill' before so demanding a journey is only prudent. Roderick
doesn't wait to acquire it before setting out, and ends up quite at sea;
Singleton is still acquiring it; James himself *has* painstakingly acquired
it, enough of it, as he recollects in the Preface, and is conscious of the
demands of the ocean voyage he is undertaking in the form of a
novel—something the very subject of the book makes clear.

One of the concerns around which James had been 'bumping about',
moreover, in the conscious apprenticeship which was constituted by
his short stories and produced the skills exercised in *Roderick Hudson*,
was in fact already the danger of delusion and failure for those too
readily confident of their own powers, the possible pathos of 'inspired'
states. Searle in *A Passionate Pilgrim* (1871) is fatally driven by a febrile
imaginative responsiveness which he takes as a vocation. Colonel
Gifford in *Professor Fargo* (1874), the mathematical thinker who is
robbed of his daughter, has an 'unbargained abundance of inspiration'
which half convinces the narrator 'that his claim to original genius
was just' (*THJ* ii. 405–6), but disaster tips the precarious balance of
his sanity and he ends in an asylum. Briseux in *The Sweetheart of M.
Briseux* (1873) turns out to be a good painter, but the story recollects
the time of his still-putative 'awakening genius' (*THJ* ii. 233), and
much of its drama lies in the momentous concatenation of events that
makes possible 'the very work which had made the painter famous'
(*THJ* ii. 234). Briseux speaks of himself in the language kept to describe
genius; 'Once the brush in my hand, I felt the divine afflatus' (*THJ* ii.
255). Another story published in the same year starts with an introductory narrator and a group of friends reminiscing:

We had been talking about the masters who had achieved but a single
masterpiece,—the artists and poets who but once in their lives had known the
divine afflatus, and touched the high level of the best (*THJ* ii. 202).[10]

This is *The Madonna of the Future*. In 1879 'the high level of the best'
became, more elevatedly, 'the high level of perfection' (*THJ* ii. 505).
'But once', in relation to the story of the unfortunate painter Theobald,
is already misleading, since he has his inspiration—of which he speaks

---

[10] We may compare, in Roderick's speech on 'the possible mischances of one's genius',
'You can number them by the thousand—the people of two or three successes; the poor
fellows whose candle burnt out in a night' (*1883*, i. 172.)

unstintingly[11]—quite apart from any question of what he calls 'superficial, feverish, mercenary work' (*THJ* ii. 206). The main narrator asks Theobald if his long years in Florence have been 'productive', and Theobald's reply—'Not in the vulgar sense!'—manifests the perilous ease with which an artistic integrity proud of its high conceptions can flip into neurotic disdain for the trials of actual labour.

James's insight into the relation of this psychological dead end to the noble rhetoric of genius deals with a less special case in *Roderick Hudson*, where Rowland's response to Roderick's extravagant forecast of the possible mischances of genius is a tacit wish that 'his companion had a trifle more of little Sam Singleton's vulgar steadiness' (*1883*, i. 173–4)—which becomes in revision 'little Sam Singleton's pedestrian patience' (*NYE* i. 232). 'Vulgar steadiness' combines Rowland's ironic scepticism about, and his simultaneous grudging allowance of, Roderick's claims to the special conditions of genius; both his sense that Roderick is capable of more than Singleton and his sense that he does less. The revision to 'pedestrian patience' looks back to Roderick's complaint that 'Nothing is more common than for an artist who has set out on his journey on a high-stepping horse to find himself all of a sudden dismounted and invited to go his way on foot' (*1883*, i. 172). It keeps on in 'pedestrian' Roderick's look down on the earthbound strenuousness of walking; but 'patience' more acutely than 'steadiness' anticipates an end to the journey, something it is worth Singleton's while to wait for—and it also implies, or lets Rowland imply, that Roderick's speech stems from *im*patience. Impatience is a matter of responsible conduct, where 'unsteadiness' would be more a matter of temperament—and the distinction is germane, for Roderick's crucial fatalism about the inefficacy of the will is newly noted by Rowland in the *NYE* as 'the unalloyed respect that he entertained for his temperament' (*NYE* i. 173).

The word 'vulgar' is replaced here in revision, but in the rest of *Roderick Hudson* it occurs as a mark of the wish to be superior—valuably aspiring as well as destructively fastidious—entertained by the ambitious failures Roderick and Christina[12]. *1883* pairs them at

---

[11] Theobald's announcement that 'This is one of my nervous nights' (*THJ* ii. 205) is given in the *NYE* the anxious excitement of the flattering rhetoric: 'This is one of my—shall I say inspired?—nights' (*NYE* xiii. 443).

[12] It is in respect of Christina that the *NYE* mostly brings in the word. Madame Grandoni's statement that she says 'her mother is an idiot' (*1883*, i. 124) wittily turns on itself—'she wouldn't mind her mother's idiocy if it wasn't for her vulgarity' (*NYE* i. 165). Christina, being modelled, beautifully (and literally) lets her hair down: Rowland

the Coliseum as 'airy adventurers' (*1883*, i. 193), revised to 'high climbers' (*NYE* i. 258), and the novel makes us conscious of the slides by which those who want to rise above themselves may only be giving themselves airs, and in which their too-uplifted wishes may end up in the air. Theobald's conception of the 'vulgar' in *The Madonna of the Future* is a desperate manœuvre at this altitude, walking a tightrope so high-strung that the consequence of coming down to earth is no longer a bruising of self-respect but a shattering of sanity. The story's narrator sympathizes to a degree with Theobald's high instincts about art: the little mock-human cats and monkeys made by the Italian sculptor who is a crude prototype of the knowing Gloriani in *Roderick Hudson* 'seemed to me peculiarly cynical and vulgar. Their imitative felicity was revolting' (*THJ* ii. 227): yet it is by this high standard— Theobald's own—that he judges the much-vaunted model for the great picture, after twenty withering years of procrastination, to suffer from 'a rather vulgar stagnation of mind' (*THJ* ii. 218). In other words, Theobald's aesthetic is admirable so long as it enables him to make valid distinctions in reality; but what the story shows is a rhetoric demanding more than the world can provide and by an insidious process detaching itself and its user from reality, from what Theobald is fatally ready to call 'vulgar fact' (*THJ* ii. 209). The narrator's own sensible appreciation of noble artistic achievement, then, gives him a point of view from which he can see as 'cynical and vulgar' the artisan's mass-produced 'cats and monkeys'; yet from which he can deploy the ventriloquial irony of wondering if his wounding mistake of 'you've *dawdled!*' has startled Theobald into 'the vulgar effort and hazard of production' (*THJ* ii. 222)[13]. As by Rowland's phrase 'vulgar steadiness', we are presented here with an outsider's rightly sceptical attitude to the claims to multiple exemption made by self-conscious genius.

stares, but she 'manifested no consciousness of it' (*1883*, i. 134), 'showed no vulgar perception of anything she was so little concerned with' (*NYE* i. 178). The response muffles Christina from the degrading scheme into which her mother has worked her ('I have had a horrible education' (*1883*, ii. 11); 'a horrid vulgar life' (*NYE* i. 287)); but it also, by visibly distancing her from her mother's marriage-plans, co-operates with those plans by making her an attractive free spirit.

[13] In one revision Roderick's pleasure in 'the downright act of production' (*1883*, i. 78) gets taken rather in 'the sublime act of creation' (*NYE* i. 102).

iv.   The Suggestion of Unattainable Repose

The narrator of the tale shows an attitude to genius which is, like Rowland's, ambivalent. The story's title sets Theobald's projected work against Raphael's famous round 'Madonna della Sedia' in the Pitti Palace at Florence, and Raphael is for Theobald an exemplary genius. The narrator gives an enthusiastic account of the 'Madonna of the Chair' early in the tale which sets his later scepticism in relief by expressing an attitude whose qualifications only later fall into place. Raphael's work has had the art to conceal its art. No fine painting, he says,

betrays less effort, less of the mechanism of effect and of the irrepressible discord between conception and result, which shows dimly in so many consummate works. Graceful, human, near to our sympathies as it is, it has nothing of manner, of method, nothing, almost, of style; it blooms there in rounded softness, as instinct with harmony as if it were an immediate exhalation of genius (*THJ* ii. 208).

This idea about the painting's creation is taken up in 'Florentine Notes' the following year: James is going through the Pitti.

Raphael is there, strong in portraiture—easy, various, bountiful genius that he was—and (strong here is not the word, but) happy beyond the common dream in his beautiful Madonna of the Chair. The general instinct of posterity seems to have been to treat this lovely picture as a kind of semi-sacred, an almost miraculous, manifestation. People stand in a worshipful silence before it, as they would before a taper-studded shrine (*TS*, p. 293).

The narrator of *The Madonna of the Future* understands how the vertigo of the 'irrepressible discord between conception and result', something which the process of art has to redeem, can give rise to a belief in the possibility of an 'immediate exhalation of genius',[14] where the mediating 'as if it were' gets impatiently forgotten. James's descriptions in both story and travel-sketch flirt with, but keep their distance from, such a belief in the 'immediate': the painting only '*betrays*' little or no effort; it has 'nothing, *almost*, of style'; and it is only 'the general

---

[14] We can compare Hazlitt's very germane essay, 'Whether Genius Is Conscious of Its Powers?' (1823), where Correggio's creations are described in the same terms: 'The whole is an emanation of pure thought. The work grew under his hand as if of itself, and came out without a flaw, like the diamond from the rock. He knew not what he did; and looked at each modest grace as it stole from the canvas with anxious delight and wonder' (*The Complete Works of William Hazlitt*, ed. P. P. Howe after the edition of A. R. Waller and Arnold Glover, 21 vols., London, 1931, xii. 119).

instinct of posterity', not necessarily James's own, which inclines only to the '*semi*-sacred', the '*almost* miraculous', interpretation of the work's arrival in the world.

Roderick Hudson's attitude to the arrival of his own works in the world has a disturbing congruence with this pseudo-divine language of outsider's praise: a complement to the account in which inspiration pays unpredictable visits is that whereby 'I have an idea' (*1883*, i. 192) becomes, impersonally, 'An idea has come to me, by a miracle' (*NYE* i. 256) and where in the 'eclipse of his genius' (*1883*, ii. 129; *NYE* i. 444) 'it was as if he believed that an inward miracle—but only a miracle—might yet take place for him and was perhaps worth waiting for' (*NYE* i. 445). 'But only a miracle' is a sulky stipulation introduced in the *NYE* revision.

Back on 27 December 1869, James had written to William from Rome, comparing the genius of Raphael with that of a figure he regards as much greater, Michaelangelo. Raphael

was incapable of energy of statement. This may seem to be but another name for the fault and not an explication of it. But *enfin* this energy—positiveness—courage,—call it what you will—is a simple, fundamental, primordial quality in the supremely superior genius ... So far from perfection, so finite, so full of errors, so broadly a target for criticism as it sits there, the *Moses* nevertheless by the vigour with which it utters its idea, the eloquence with which it tells the tale of the author's passionate abjuration of the inaction of fancy and contemplation—his willingness to let it stand, in the interest of life and health and movement as his *best* and his only possible,—by this high transcendent spirit, it redeems itself from subjection to its details, and appeals most forcibly to the generosity and sympathy of the mind. Raphael is undecided, slack and unconvinced (*HJL* i. 180–1).[15]

It is unlikely that James's versions of the theories about Raphael's genius in *The Madonna of the Future* and 'Florentine Notes' have no significant relation to this intensely felt early intuition (which he may well have somewhat refined) about the supremacy of creative effort: the 'inaction of fancy and contemplation' (taken up later in 'strong here is not the word'), of which Theobald and Roderick Hudson are both victims, presumably attaches to Raphael in the contrast with Michaelangelo, and attaches specially to the process by which Raphael's works are supposed to have been created. The fictions carry

[15] For a consideration of this contrast in relation to James's sense of his career, see R. W. B. Lewis, 'The Names of Action: Henry James in the Early 1870s', *Nineteenth Century Fiction*, 38/4,(Mar. 1984), 476–7.

the same conviction as the letter about energy of statement; they dramatize, though, the account of Raphael into an ironically reserved admiration, in the interest of rendering more vividly the question— about the activity of the imagination—James contemplated in his letter of 1869.

'Ainsi a procédé Raphaël', says the mad genius Frenhofer in Balzac's story *Le Chef-d'œuvre inconnu* (1831), 'en ôtant son bonnet de velours noir pour exprimer le respect que lui inspirait le roi de l'art' (*CHEP* ii. 10). This is 'that terrible little tale of Balzac's' to which the clever Mrs Coventry alludes in *The Madonna of the Future*, hypothesizing that Theobald's so pre-publicized picture will be, like Frenhofer's, 'a mere mass of incoherent scratches and daubs, a jumble of dead paint!' (*NYE* xiii. 461.)[16] In fact Theobald's disaster is different; his canvas is significantly 'mere' (complete as an instance, negligible as an achieve- ment) at another end of the process from Frenhofer's overworked, too-thickly repainted one: it is rather 'a mere dead blank, cracked and discoloured by time' (*THJ* ii. 228; a picture 'sunk' before even launched).[17] The narrator's '*dawdled!*' has driven him back to the 'little room it seemed such cruel irony to call a studio' (*THJ* ii. 229) to face the blank screen on the easel. Found there in 'absolute lassitude and dejection', he laments the grim truth of his failure in a speech which takes up James's concerns from the letter of 1869, without the liberating force of James's preference.

I waited and waited to be worthier to begin—I wasted my life in preparation. While I fancied my creation was growing it was only dying. I've taken the whole business too hard. Michael Angelo didn't when he went at the Lorenzo. He did his best at a venture, and his venture's immortal.

Then Theobald tries half-heartedly to salvage his high thoughts.

To convince you, to enchant and astound the world, I need only the hand of Raphael. His brain I already have ... I'm the half of a genius! Where in the wide world is my other half? Lodged perhaps in the vulgar soul, the cunning ready fingers of some dull copyist or some trivial artisan who turns out by the dozen his easy prodigies of touch! (*NYE* xiii. 486–7.)[18]

---

[16] In *THJ* ii. 215 it's simply 'that tale of Balzac's'.

[17] We may note the recurrence of this figure, not for a past wasted but for an emptied future, in Roderick's despairing words to Rowland and his mother: 'the future is a dead blank' (*1883*, ii. 126).

[18] *THJ* ii. 229; several small changes sharpen the points of his self-rebuke, so I quote the later version.

In 1873 James, at thirty, was still 'bumping about, to acquire skill', preparing for a first novel; we should be conscious of the anxious closeness this trial of his patience allows him in respect of Theobald's waiting and wasting.[19] But—not least in writing this story with its energy of statement about 'energy of statement'—he keeps his distance; the truth of Theobald's citing of Michaelangelo's *not* vulgar 'effort and hazard of production', which has some of the force of a tragic recognition, is dramatically qualified by his reversion to the super-stitious admiration of Raphael as an easy achiever. '*Only* the hand' is a giveaway of his predicament, the sign of a still-clinging disdain for the practicalities of the art, and 'His brain I already have' (the *NYE*'s cracked magniloquent inversion of the earlier 'I have his brain') implausibly lays claim to a thing we should not readily value if it were distinct from technique.

Theobald is stuck with the seductive consolations of his attitude and its terms, even when the next moment he seeks to regret the seduction: 'Well for me if I had been vulgar and clever and reck-less ...'. The attitude takes a punishing toll, however: the only thing Theobald manages to do before collapse and death is a visit to the Pitti Palace, where the situation makes Raphael's work take on the characteristics of another's: 'the celestial candour, even, of the Madonna in the Chair, as we paused in perfect silence before her, was tinged with the sinister irony of the women of Leonardo' (*THJ* ii. 230).[20] Raphael's masterpiece produces a similar taunting effect for Rowland Mallet in the later work. He retreats tormentedly to Florence to confront his strong temptation: to speed Roderick's ruin, and thus make Mary Garland available for himself.

There were times when the beautiful things about him only exasperated his discontent. He went to the Pitti Palace, and Raphael's Madonna of the Chair

---

[19] In Dec. 1875, the month after *Roderick Hudson*'s publication in book form, James's essay in the *Galaxy* on 'Honoré de Balzac' reflected on long waits justified by eventual masterpieces, and on the mistake it would have been—for a novelist—to start too soon. 'Good observers, we believe, will confess to a general mistrust of novels written before thirty ... Walter Scott, Thackeray, George Eliot, Madame Sand, waited till they were at least turned thirty, and then without prelude, or with brief prelude, produced a novel that was a masterpiece. If it was well for them to wait, it would have been infinitely better for Balzac' (*LC* ii. 33).

[20] It is corrected to 'of the Chair' from 1879 onwards; and the *NYE* phrases Theobald's exclusion more tamely and more tactfully with 'broke into the strange smile of the women of Leonardo' (*NYE* xiii. 487).

seemed in its soft serenity to mock him with the suggestion of unattainable repose (*1883* ii. 29–30).

The painting's mocking function in *Roderick Hudson* recalls the last bafflement of Theobald's 'idealism', then: and we can give a general sense to Rowland's exasperation by 'its soft serenity' if we juxtapose with it the *NYE*'s rueful expression, later on, of his perplexity at finding that *his* noble intentions have bitten off more than they can chew. 'The ideal life had been his general purpose, but the ideal life could only go on very real legs and feet, and the body and the extremities somehow failed always to move in concert' (*NYE* i. 364). To continue supporting the perverse and ungrateful Roderick, directly against the sexual ambition he has resolved wholly to suppress, is an insufferable strain for Rowland, and the chapter in Florence shows him nearly ceasing to allow it to make him suffer.

Yet Rowland's area of endeavour is the shiftingly provisional one of personal relations, not that of art. Rowland here manages to resist temptation and sustain, albeit awkwardly, his very difficult position. His conduct, so far from perfection, so finite, so full of errors, so broadly a target for criticism,[21] yet by its conscious effort at integrity manages at least partially to redeem itself from subjection to its details, and appeals most forcibly to the generosity and sympathy of the mind. His advice to Roderick after the speech about the possible mischances of genius does not treat art as a separate domain where effort is useless and inappropriate, but urges the young sculptor to abjure the inaction of fancy and contemplation: 'If you have work to do, don't wait to feel like it; set to work and you *will* feel like it' (*1883*, i. 174). Rowland's character and capacities determine—enable *and* limit—his ethical achievement; the virtue which the novel demonstrates in him, flawed as it is, and overstretched by his interference with the course of Roderick's life, comes from his good faith in regard to this fact of necessary limitation—his willingness to let his conduct stand, in the interest of life and health and movement, as his *best* and only possible. This ethic of effort and good faith, this belief in attempting to reconcile the ideal with the possible, has a bearing on the issue of revision—an issue whose important puzzles make the heart of Balzac's 'terrible little

---

[21] See, for instance, Sacvan Bercovitch's 'The Revision of Rowland Mallet', *Nineteenth Century Fiction* 24 (Sept. 1969), 210—21, which takes a relatively unforgiving line on Rowland that stems from an attempt to fix his character rather than follow his story.

tale'. The practice of revision involves a degree of perfectionism, but not all perfectionism need involve a belief in practical perfectibility. The idea of 'perfection' is associated on one hand with a belief in the ideal and yet on the other, in so far as it has a meaning within the ordinary bounds of the possible, means something more accessibly human like 'the state where all that can usefully be done has been done'. The ideally perfect is a state of completeness; the practically perfected comes when a process is completed.

The two parts of *Le Chef-d'œuvre inconnu* have each a vivid scene about repainting. The first shows a successful art of repainting, where Frenhofer's theories about the techniques for attaining the ideally illusive, his 'secret de donner de la vie aux figures' (*CHEP* ii. 13), allow him to go at the 'Marie Egyptienne' of the court painter Porbus and bring it to life (a scene very closely recalled by James in *The Sweetheart of M. Briseux*, published three months after *The Madonna of the Future*, where the young genius passionately paints over Harold Staines's dull portrait of his fiancée).[22] Frenhofer confidently offers to show the young Poussin 'combien peu de chose il faudrait pour compléter cette œuvre' (*CHEP* ii 12); as he works, he remarks how, 'au moyen de trois ou quatre touches et d'un petit glacis bleuâtre, on pouvait faire circuler l'air autour de la tête de cette pauvre sainte'. 'Compléter' here takes an excitement from Frenhofer's perception of the short distance to be covered in the process of painting before that process can transcend itself, resolve itself into a state, *a* painting; minimizing, by some refinement of ingenuity, by an adjustment of means to ends, the 'irrepressible discord between conception and result'. The language describing Frenhofer's excited act anticipates James's imagery of revision in the *NYE* Prefaces: the repeated emphasis on touch, the importance of glaze, the emergence of figures into the relief of apparent three-dimensionality, the suggestion of some external

---

[22] Balzac's sentences are directly matched by James's in the story. 'Le petit vieillard retroussa ses manches avec un mouvement de brusquerie convulsive, passa son pouce dans la palette diaprée et chargée de tons que Porbus lui tendait; il lui arracha des mains plutôt qu'il ne les prit une poignée de brosses' (*CHEP* ii. 12); 'And, as if possessed by an uncontrollable impulse, he seized poor Harold's palette' (*THJ* ii. 253). 'Puis il trempait avec une vivacité fébrile la pointe de la brosse dans les différents tas de couleurs dont il parcourait quelquefois la gamme entière plus rapidement qu'un organiste de cathédrale ne parcourt l'étendue de son clavier à l'*O Filii* de Pâques' (*CHEP* ii. 12); 'As I watched his motions grow every moment broader and more sweeping, I could fancy myself listening to some ardent pianist, plunging deeper into a passionate symphony [*sic*] and devouring the key-board with outstretched arms' (*THJ* ii. 254).

(or internal) agency working through and even in spite of the artist,[23] and especially the miraculous idea of restoring life ('en réchauffant les parties où il avait signalé un défaut de vie' (*CHEP* ii. 13)). Frenhofer is here strangely successful.

Shortly after this, though, the story follows Frenhofer to his own house and contemplates a relation to revision much more vertiginously doubtful about just how to perfect works—or when to stop. Porbus asks him if he will show them the masterpiece of which he has so lovingly spoken, and Frenhofer is alarmed.

Montrer mon œuvre, s'écria le vieillard tout ému. Non, non, je dois la perfectionner encore. Hier, vers le soir, dit-il, j'ai cru avoir fini. Ses yeux me semblaient humides, sa chair était agitée. Les tresses de ses cheveux remuaient. Elle respirait! Quoique j'aie trouvé le moyen de réaliser sur une toile plate le relief et la rondeur de la nature, ce matin, au jour, j'ai reconnu mon erreur (*CHEP* ii. 17).

The ambivalence of the French 'encore', and the instability of the notion of perfection, yield more than one sense to Frenhofer's phrase: 'I still have to perfect it' is his intended one, but the story encourages us to hear also the mocking echo of that, 'I have to "perfect" it again,' with 'perfect' and 'again' unhappily yoked together. Balzac's imagination of Frenhofer's artistic predicament seizes us when we recognize the pathos of the Sisyphean labour imposed on the painter by his radical self-discontinuity of judgement and thus of intention; he loses control of his work in an increasingly tyrannous mechanical shuttle between 'j'ai cru avoir fini' and 'j'ai reconnu mon erreur'.

The tale relates this psychological arrest to the tempting theory of aesthetic perfectibility, of capturing life itself, which catches Frenhofer. There will only be an irrepressible discord between conception and result if the original conception fails to take account of the limits of artistic representation (here, fails to see how the metaphor of 'Elle respirait' works); but only by pressing against those limits, by empirically establishing the bounds of the possible in any given case, will a work of art satisfy us as having reached an inevitable *state*, something with an internal equilibrium that rescues it in some sense from being 'in progress'.

For an artist to know when this stage has been reached is a difficult ethical achievement, involving him in a disinterested judgement of his

[23] 'Il semblait qu'il y eût dans le corps de ce bizarre personnage un démon qui agissait par ses mains en les prenant fantastiquement contre le gré de l'homme' (*CHEP* ii. 13).

work as if it were detached from himself. T. S. Eliot, who worked strenuously on drafting and redrafting the encounter with the 'familiar compound ghost' in the second section of *Little Gidding*, was evidently much taxed by these questions, recognizing that art may impose in places diverse formal requirements which are incompatible with each other (there may *be* no rhyme-word that makes exact sense): the artist must be humble and conscientious in meeting such situations, must not give up easily yet must at some point renounce the attempt at perfection. On 9 September 1942 Eliot wrote to John Hayward, who had made a number of suggestions about phrasing in the passage.

This time I accept nearly everything: perhaps it means that my resistance is weakening, at this stage; but chiefly I think because I perceive that these belong to that almost inevitable residue of items, in a poem of any length, for which the ideal is unattainable. I am still however wrestling with the demon of that precise degree of light at that precise time of day.[24]

'Un ouvrage n'est jamais *achevé* ... mais *abandonné*',[25] Valéry's famous ironic and metaphorical overstatement of the perfectionist view in 'Au Sujet du "Cimetière Marin"', is placed (rather than refuted) by the light of Eliot's weary but intact scrupulousness in practice, his conscientious weighing of 'perhaps' against the clarity of 'I perceive', his residual effort in '*almost* inevitable', his quasi-heroic, mildly self-mocking move from 'the ideal is unattainable' to 'I am still however wrestling'. Eliot's judgement about Valéry that 'He had ceased to believe in *ends*, and was only interested in *processes*',[26] which derives from Valéry's self-diagnosis in that essay detailing 'this sickness, this perverse taste for endless revision',[27] correctively draws

---

[24] Quoted in Helen Gardner, *The Composition of 'Four Quartets'*, London, 1978, pp. 177–8.

[25] Paul Valéry, 'Au Sujet du "Cimetière Marin"' (1933), *Variété*, iii, Paris, 1936, p. 60. Eliot's 'Introduction' to the selection of Valéry's essays in English, *The Art of Poetry*, translated from the French by Denise Folliot, New York, 1961, refers to these words in a way which usefully amplifies the letter to Hayward, and outlines any artist's human predicament: 'To me they mean that a poem is "finished", or that I will never touch it again, when I am sure that I have exhausted my own resources, that the poem is as good as *I* can make *that* poem. It may be a bad poem: but nothing that I can do will make it better. Yet I cannot help thinking that, even if it is a good poem, I could have made a better poem of it—the same poem, but better—if I were a better poet' (*The Art of Poetry*, p. xiii).

[26] T. S. Eliot, 'From Poe to Valéry' (1948), *To Criticize the Critic and Other Writings*, London, 1965 (repr. 1978), p. 40.

[27] *The Art of Poetry*, p. 141. The French is 'ce mal, ce goût pervers de la reprise indéfinie' (*Variété*, iii. 60).

attention to the seriousness with which the artist must sustain a faith in the possibly unattainable repose of a finished work—even at the same time as he must tirelessly seek out all that can be improved in the one to hand.

In Frenhofer these two attitudes alternate, without any longer having a real reference to their object; his mental illness takes him back and forth between assertive self-confidence and defensive self-dissatis-faction, each reversion leaving the picture further buried under another repainting. Valéry has not Frenhofer's misleading ideal of an exact correspondence of representation with reality; but he has also, in Eliot's words, no deep concern 'with the question of how [the poem] is related to the rest of life in such a way as to give the reader the shock of feeling that the poem has been to him, not merely an experience, but a serious experience'.[28] Hence the manner of his apparently un-repentant acknowledgement of his 'sickness', his avowal of the con-suming self-attention by which the process—the means of art—has become to him an end in itself, and the production of actual works—traditionally the point of it all—only a means to that end. Valéry describes each of his poems in progress as only being stopped when 'some outside intervention or some circumstance ... [broke] the enchantment of never finishing with it':[29] thus the decision to end is not his and a considerable responsibility is abrogated. The effect of this critical attitude on Valéry's poetic practice does not concern us here: more to the point is Eliot's strong insistence on its dangers.

As any advice, literally and unintelligently applied, can lead to disastrous consequences, it is as well to point out that while the poet should regard no toil as too arduous and no application of time as too long, for bringing a poem as near perfection as his abilities will take it, he should also have enough power of self-criticism to know where to stop. As with the painting in Balzac's *Le Chef-d'œuvre inconnu*, there may be a point beyond which every alteration the author makes will be for the worse.[30]

It is not just that perfection is not attainable by endless revision; you may end up multiplying imperfections, and the climax of Balzac's story

---

[28] *The Art of Poetry*, p. xxiii.

[29] *The Art of Poetry*, p. 144.

[30] *The Art of Poetry*, p. xii. Eliot's last letter to Hayward about the 'familiar compound ghost' passage sees this point as imminent; he remarks that 'to spend much more time over this poem might be dangerous. After a time one loses the original feeling of the impulse, and then it is no longer safe to alter. It is time to close the chapter' (*The Composition of 'Four Quartets'*, p. 196).

comes appropriately to Eliot's mind as a pattern for the loss of valuable intentions through overwork.

In the insane pride of his insistence on perfection, Frenhofer does not see that he has gone beyond the point where improvement is possible and has ruined his work: when Poussin and Porbus, in his studio, grotesquely cannot even see where the 'chef-d'œuvre' is, he finds his own reason for their confusion; 'Vous ne vous attendiez pas à tant de perfection!' (*CHEP* ii. 30.) He points them to the right one, and Poussin suspects a joke—the canvas does not amount to a picture, let alone give the advertised sense of air circulating 'inside' it; rather, 'Je ne vois là que des couleurs confusément amassées et contenues par une multitude de lignes bizarres qui forment une muraille de peinture' (*CHEP* ii. 31). 'Une muraille de peinture' is a metaphor by which the world of illusory things behind or inside the representational surface is closed off, and by which you see the paint but do not see through it. This presents the failure of excessive revision in terms that recall both the imagery of pictorial depth in James's prefaces and Rowland's vision of bafflement in *Roderick Hudson*.

They say that old people do find themselves at last face to face with a solid blank wall and stand thumping against it in vain. It resounds, it seems to have something beyond it, but it won't move! (*1883*, i. 67).[31]

By an anxious scrutiny Poussin and Porbus make out a beautiful foot still unburied in a corner of the picture; it is as if Catherine Lescault, its courtesan subject, has been walled up, deprived of life by being revised. They cry out in astonishment or mockery. 'Il y a une femme là-dessous! s'écria Porbus en faisant remarquer à Poussin les couches de couleurs que le vieux peintre avait successivement superposées en croyant perfectionner sa peinture' (*CHEP* ii. 31–2). The grotesque force of the Balzac story which so held James, dramatizing the disastrous consequences of endless revision, makes only more remarkable the bold turn which he gives to the premiss of *Le Chef-d'œuvre inconnu* in answering it with *The Madonna of the Future*.

---

[31] This takes up James's favourite 'face to face' from Theobald's account of his harrowing confrontation with the blank canvas: 'I've been sitting here for a week face to face with the truth, with the past, with my weakness and poverty and nullity' (*THJ* ii. 228). Gloriani gives a version of the idea, not long after Rowland's, as part of his worldly, pessimistic view of the artist's situation: 'Some day every artist finds himself sitting face to face with his lump of clay, with his empty canvas, with his sheet of blank paper, waiting in vain for the revelation to be made, for the Muse to descend. He must learn to do without the Muse!' (*1883*, i. 94).

Where Frenhofer had a masterpiece but didn't know where to stop, Theobald might have a chance at one but doesn't know where to start. The arduous toil and long application, in James's tale, are what the artist has to do first; he can worry later about being over-fussy. In certain contexts—as where the will to finish a work is in question—to revise 'en croyant perfectionner sa peinture' may really endanger one's creative power to achieve; but when James came to revise *The Madonna of the Future* for the *NYE*, probably in March–April 1908,[32] thirty-five years after its original composition, he did not act as if he thought himself to have reached the point where every alteration is for the worse.

A sense of the difference between a revision that lays down a stifling impasto of rouge and one that lets the life of the subject flush through the expressive surface was evidently active in him in the scene where the narrator at last meets the model, Serafina, who has herself altered for the worse in the twenty years over which she has been parasitic on Theobald. The deluded artist solemnly conducts the narrator—'with an air of religious mystery' (*THJ* ii. 216)—into the presence of her beauty. In the text of 1873:

As he bent his head, she looked at me askance, and I thought she blushed (*THJ* ii. 217).

In the *NYE*:

As he bent his head she looked at me askance and had, I thought, a perfectly human change of colour (*NYE* xiii. 465).

The 'blush' of 1873—only a suspected one—has the touching and grotesque incongruity of virginal modesty persisting into the stoutness of matronly middle age, as well as the embarrassment of the confidence trickster caught taking advantage of a child or imbecile; it allows us to see how Theobald's real first impression has persisted into his present deluded state. 'A perfectly human change of colour' is James's light retouch here on the representational surface (set in relief the next moment with a change for contrast from 1873's 'Behold the Serafina!' into 'This is the sublime Serafina!'); and it is alive with the story's relations. The canvas originally set aside for the masterpiece, we should

<hr />

[32] He dispatched some revised copy to Scribner on 23 Apr. 1908, saying that 'The second half of ["A Passionate Pilgrim"], with "The Madonna of the Future" & "Louisa Pallant" immediately follow' (Princeton MS). He had previously revised the story for book publication in 1875 and 1879.

recall, is later found to be 'cracked and discoloured by time'; James's revision links the two changes of colour in Serafina—the loss of her complexion and her 'colouring' at, among other things, having lost her complexion—with the decomposition of Theobald's 'mere dead blank'. The contrast of 'perfectly human' with 'sublime' doubly notes the mistakenness of Theobald's vision of things: 'perfectly human' from one angle means 'fallibly undivine', both in stout body and in immoral conduct, and is disapproving about Serafina's long acqui-escence in her patron's delusion; from another angle, though, 'perfectly human' acknowledges that you could hardly expect anything else, for what girl *wouldn't* age in twenty years, or accept an un-'compromising' pension, and yet blush to admit either the ageing or the dependence? These two angles—one sympathetic to the idealist's vision, the other forgivingly conscious of the nature of real human beings—meet satisfy-ingly, moreover, because 'perfectly human'—in another regard a mir-aculous oxymoron—is also what the first Madonna was and what Theobald thinks Serafina is. The complex life of the fictional situation gives colour to the new phrasing; even at this moment, where the passage of twenty fictional years is being seen to have mortifyingly affected Theobald's conception, the passage of thirty-five real ones somehow yields a version of James's original conception which is more alive than ever. The woman is not underneath, 'là-dessous', but there on the surface, 'perfectly human'.

v. The Life of Relations

The 'dead blank'[33] which preoccupied the young James and which is so vividly imagined in both *The Madonna of the Future* and *Roderick Hudson* primarily refers to the death of an artist's powers, but it is more generally associated also with the sense of a wasted or terminated life, an apparent end to value and significance, a completeness of mortality. Isabel Archer's predicament, discovered in Chapter 42 of *The Portrait of a Lady*, has exemplarily the pathos of this confrontation with the void, returning metaphorically to the 'blank wall', the 'high-shouldered blank wall' which in *The American* had literally enclosed Claire de Cintré (*1883*, ii. 161, 203). Isabel 'had taken all the first steps in the purest confidence, and then she had suddenly found the infinite

---

[33] The words occur when Roderick has retreated to Frascati: 'It is worse out here than in Rome, . . . for here I am face to face with the dead blank of my mind!' (*1883*, i. 170).

vista of a multiplied life to be a dark, narrow alley, with a dead wall at the end' (*1882*, p. 371). The 'relaxation' of Roman experience mentioned above is in part the specially vivid consciousness of the transience of human works called up by the 'eternal city' (where Isabel faces her dead end). The generalizing narrator—or paraphraser of Rowland—in *Roderick Hudson* expatiates (in the manner of *The Marble Faun*) on the psychological process by which, in Rome, one can arrive at an anaesthetized despair about the matter.

Whether it be that one tacitly concedes to the Roman Church the monopoly of a guarantee of immortality, so that if one is indisposed to bargain with her for the precious gift one must do without it altogether; or whether in an atmosphere so heavily weighted with echoes and memories one grows to believe that there is nothing in one's consciousness that is not foredoomed to moulder and crumble and become dust for the feet and possible malaria for the lungs of future generations—the fact at least remains that one parts half willingly with one's hopes in Rome and misses them only under some very exceptional stress of circumstance (*1883*, i. 129).

This sense of Roman ruin as a particularly persuasive and seductive emblem of the inevitable passing away of one's life's value (persuasive as a massive obsolete materiality) allows Roman walls vividly to render James's interest in the failure of artistic careers and human lives. 'A Roman Holiday' (1873) describes the staircase of the Ara Coeli. 'The sunshine glares on this great unfinished wall only to light up its featureless despair, its expression of conscious, irremediable incompleteness' (*TS*, pp. 116–17). An 'incompleteness' consciously irremediable is repeatedly attributed to Roderick Hudson; and this collocation may be set beside the scene in the Coliseum in which Roderick tries recklessly to pluck an inaccessible flower for Christina— 'a delicate plant of radiant hue, which sprouted from the top of an immense fragment of wall', a fragment further described as 'a rugged surface of vertical wall, which dropped straight into the dusky vaults behind the arena' (*1883*, i. 197, 198).[34] Roderick's thwarted attempt to

---

[34] 'A Roman Holiday' mentions that the Coliseum's 'high-growing wild-flowers have been plucked away by the new government, whose functionaries, surely, at certain points of their task, must have felt as if they shared the dreadful trade of those who gather samphire' (*TS*, p. 121). This use of *King Lear*, iv. v. 15, renders the vertigo of the flower-picker with a vividness anticipating that of the scene in the novel. A *NYE* revision turns the Roman gossips' question about Roderick and Christina—'whether he really supposed that beauties of that quality were meant to give themselves to juvenile artists' (*1883*, i. 148)—to catch the light of this later scene: 'if he really supposed flowers of that rarity to be pluckable by mere geniuses who happened also to be mere Americans' (*NYE* i. 199).

scale the wall's face is matched later by Rowland's successful one in dangerously reaching a flower for Mary Garland in the Alps, a parallel prepared by the remark at the start of the Coliseum chapter that some 'accidents of ruggedness' in the ruin 'offer a very fair imitation of the mighty excrescences in the face of an Alpine cliff' (*1883*, i. 193). These lines of thought reach a conclusion in the moment at the end when Rowland and Singleton, discovering Roderick's body in the Alps,

> looked up through their horror at the cliff from which he had apparently fallen, and which lifted its blank and stony face above him, with no care now but to drink the sunshine on which his eyes were closed (*1883*, ii. 191).

This animation of what was on the previous page 'a great rugged wall', suggesting by 'now' a previous malevolence, makes the resistance of the world to Roderick something with which he can appropriately come 'face to face'. The blankness of stone here fits his checked profession of sculptor: the imagery of the dead wall gives an inhuman face to the death of the imagination.

Frenhofer dies when he recognizes the 'muraille de peinture' behind which his ruinous repaintings have immured his originally vivid subject, shutting him off from the living reality he sought to render: many accounts of James's *NYE* revisions, drawing on the imagery of repainting in the prefaces, accuse him of similarly eclipsing the early light touch of an artistic start seen as 'spontaneous' and 'natural', burdening us with 'a feeling of effort, of deliberate striving for effect which spoils the youthful production and robs it of what was fresh and easy and sincerely unaffected'.[35] These words are the conclusion of Hélène Harvitt's study of the revisions of *Roderick Hudson*.

Clearly James can never again be the young original author of *Roderick Hudson*, and that loss is a matter of necessary regret, the source of an elegiac sense of how things are forever going. But pressing on with a stoical determination, and taking the risk that it may spoil

---

[35] Hélène Harvitt, 'How Henry James Revised "Roderick Hudson": A Study in Style', *PMLA* 39 (1924), 227. Her categories are highly suspect; she quotes the two versions of Rowland's response to Christina's sudden rebellion against the arranged marriage (*1883*, ii. 86–7; *NYE* i. 388–9), then: 'The above is a typical example of how James applied his varnishbrush. He took a straightforward, natural paragraph and introduced into it his characteristic psychological analysis, rendering it extremely obscure. The result, as the reader can see for himself, is that all life and spontaneity vanished' (p. 211). The early version, though, is full of 'psychological analysis'; and words like 'youthful', 'fresh and easy', and 'spontaneity' gives a misleading impression of what *1883* (the version she refers to) is like. The prose sense, at least, of the revised version is perfectly clear.

what has been done in the past, revision acts out the faith in spiritual progress to which Wordsworth gives voice in his great ode, a faith braced against the death which is its alternative:

> We will grieve not, rather find
> Strength in what remains behind.[36]

Not that we should be made to feel a literary work just as 'deliberate striving for effect': 'striving' implies failure and 'effect' implies the showy. Yet literature is a process which demands deliberate striving for effects; and the intricacy of studying revisions should not tempt us into too impatient an assumption that the complexity of the final product is excessive.

We are confronted, in paying critical attention to James's revisions, with serious questions about the possible functions of verbal texture in our reading of a novel: questions to which Hélène Harvitt gives a plain answer. 'In collating the two texts one wonders why he should have preferred one word to another ... It is merely a question of personal taste and something which an outsider cannot judge.'[37] She lists as if in self-evidence—but in isolation from their contexts—some of the individual words superseded and superseding: one's response to which may well be to wonder why she bothers to wonder on this slim basis, since the 'life' which is supposed to have gone out of James's novel in revision must inhere in the structure of mutual relations, connotative, syntactic, psychological, and so on, of the words of that novel; and because the most valid test in such cases is therefore a test of context. James's remark of 14 November 1878 that 'the teller is but a more developed reader' (*HJL* ii. 193), regarding the novelist as his own 'outsider', suggests that we should not take his choice of words as 'merely a question of personal taste'. What can make us feel that James, revising *Roderick Hudson* in 1906, is not, in Rowland's words, one of the 'old people' who come 'face to face with a solid blank wall', is the imaginative alertness to the original intentions, conscious and instinctual, of the work, to its complex of internal relations, manifested in the details of the *NYE*'s intensive reconsideration of phrase and proportion.

The reconsideration involves a number of changes not only of phrasing but of event also, though it is difficult in speaking of a

---

[36] 'Ode', *'Poems in Two Volumes'*, p. 276.
[37] 'How Henry James Revised "Roderick Hudson"', p. 225.

narrative to distinguish very persuasively *between* phrasing and event. Thus in the Villa Borghese Mary Garland, jealously curious about Christina Light, yet hesitates to appeal to Rowland for information.

For some minutes, as she sat scratching the brilliant pavement with the point of her umbrella, it was to be supposed that her pride and her anxiety held an earnest debate (*1883*, ii. 84).

In the *NYE* 'scratching' becomes 'pressing' (*NYE* i. 385); what Mary does alters; and we get a gesture—or rather, in place of a gesture, an intensity expressed in a posture—which is eloquent both as characterization (suggesting a strength of earnestness) and as an indirect record of Rowland's close attention to her. The later gesture with which it aligns Mary in *1883* (as, presumably, an anxiously unloved lover) is that of Prince Casamassima, impatient and embarrassed as Rowland speaks with the recklessly sarcastic Christina on her last appearance in the book, at Engelberg: the Prince 'dropped his eyes, and fretted the earth with the point of his umbrella' (*1883*, ii. 167). The revision of Mary's gesture (while 'fretted' here remains in the *NYE*) yields us a truth contrasting their temperaments, repays with amplitude any wonder we might entertain as to why James preferred one word to another. This instance is minute enough; on a larger scale James's sense of the novel's proportions and dynamics shifts Christina's dramatic *1883* conversion to Catholicism, for instance, into a significant resumption—'embraced the Catholic faith' (*1883*, ii. 49) becoming 'begun again to *pratiquer* religiously' (*NYE* i. 338). Two paragraphs of *1883*, ii. 72, giving Madame Grandoni's account of the conversion and Rowland's speculation on Christina's motives, correspondingly drop out of the *NYE*.[38]

---

[38] We might connect this with James's never reprinting the unimpressive schematic tale *Adina* (1874), whose American heroine in Italy becomes a convert—as Hawthorne's Hilda might but wouldn't—in the course of going native. Just before the confession-scene which James so praised in *Hawthorne* (*LC* i. 446), Hilda is put off. 'Seeing a woman, a priest, and a soldier, kneel to kiss the toe of the brazen Saint Peter (who protrudes it beyond his pedestal, for the purpose, polished bright with former salutations), while a child stood on tiptoe to do the same, the glory of the church was darkened before Hilda's eyes' (*The Marble Faun*, p. 351). James evidently attached much weight to this: the narrator of *Travelling Companions* (1870) lingers 'near the brazen image of St. Peter' with its 'well-worn toe'. 'Near me stood a lady in mourning, watching with a weary droop of the head the grotesque deposition of kisses.' This turns out to be his American friend Miss Evans, who is 'in sorrow and trouble' like Hilda in the same place (*THJ* ii. 38). Most of this sense of oppression is retained in *Roderick Hudson*, even in the conversionless *NYE*, when Christina 'kissed the brazen toe' (*1883*, ii. 49; *NYE* i. 338).

The actions of the Cavaliere also change. In *1883*, when Rowland is leaving the Lights' after speaking to Christina about her sudden refusal of Prince Casamassima, he has a long talk with the Cavaliere about the situation. The old man volunteers both an admission of his own ambivalence, and some melodramatic allusions to the mysterious threat, the 'sword of Damocles' (*1883*, ii. 105) hanging over Christina's head. His obscure motives for this confessional urge to transmit confidential information to the novel's centre of consciousness are probably supposed to be suggested by the allusions to the Ancient Mariner's 'glittering eye' in preceding descriptions: of his 'little black eye which glittered like a diamond' (*1883*, i. 71), and later of his 'contracted eyelids, through which you saw the glitter of his intensely dark vivacious pupil' (*1883*, i. 150). The narrator of *Professor Fargo* (1874), like Rowland here, is much aided in his grasp of the story by the not quite accounted-for volubility of one of the protagonists, who breaks out to him 'with eyes that fairly glittered with the pleasure of hearing himself speak the words' (*THJ* ii. 396). The plausibility of the narrator's vantage-point in many of James's apprentice stories is compromised by the too-visibly convenient readiness of these confidings in a stranger (in *At Isella* (1871), for instance, 'I say to you what I wouldn't say to another' (*THJ* ii. 118)). In the *NYE*, however, the Cavaliere's speeches insinuating that there is a threat to Christina are reduced to an evasion of Rowland's guess at the threat (*NYE* i. 412). We still have the Cavaliere's bottled-up pride (as Christina's father) and his special rapport with Rowland—the presumable motives of his half-revelation of *1883*—in the revised text, but the *NYE*, more enigmatically, includes no action on his part for which these would have to be produced as sufficient reasons. The Cavaliere keeps his own counsel. In the *NYE* Rowland's speculation is unconfirmed, like so many of our speculations about others' secrets.

In some places James's empirical reimagining of the fictional experience and its conditions produces results in the *NYE* acutely different from those of *1883*, and precipitates a new attitude or reaction. When Rowland, having admired Christina for her generously admiring Mary at Madame Grandoni's party, is primed for a revulsion against her by Mary's (notedly unfair) expression of dislike, he is then triggered into incommensurate anger and distrust by the news that Christina has broken off her engagement to Casamassima. The excessiveness of his reaction is also in proportion to his virtuously-suppressed self-interest *vis-à-vis* Mary, which is in fact well served by the prospect of a reunion of Roderick and Christina. Rowland's attitude to Christina, whose action thus happens inconveniently to co-operate with the temptation that shortly before in Florence he has been at such pains to resist, is complex, then: when he goes to see her his indignation is sharpened by *self*-distrust, and his strong delusive idea that Christina's gesture is an irrationally jealous act designed to wound Mary has presumably crystallized out of his own false position. James's sense of Rowland's need to repudiate her redirects in the *NYE* the detail of his feelings about the grotesque Mrs Light, who is in despair at the loss of the great match: in *1883*

Rowland greatly pitied her, for there is something respectable in passionate grief, even in a very bad cause; and as pity is akin to love he felt rather more tolerant of her fantastic pretensions than he had done hitherto (*1883*, ii. 93).

In the *NYE* the pity takes a different complexion.

Rowland greatly pitied her—so respectable is sincerity of sorrow. She too was in the blighting circle of her daughter's contact, and this exposure, shared with the others who were more interesting, almost gave her, with the crudity of her candour, something of their dignity (*NYE* i. 396–7).

The feelings in 'very bad cause' and 'fantastic pretensions' are absorbed into the new view's stress in '*so* respectable'; and Rowland's current preoccupation, Christina's perfidy, presents Mrs Light at a sympathetic angle the dignity of which only the devastating reserve of 'almost ... something' (equalling 'nothing') reasonably retracts.

When Rowland utters to Christina six pages later his suspicion of her motive, the *NYE* makes his accusation blunter and Christina's response less controlled. In *1883*:

'It seemed to me that you had consciously cruelly dealt a blow at that poor girl. Do you understand?'
'Wait a moment!' And with her eyes fixed on him she inclined her head on one side meditatively. Then a cold brilliant smile covered her face, and she made a gesture of negation (*1883*, ii. 99).

In the *NYE* Rowland takes up Christina's statement that Mary Garland 'helped' her and challenges it:

'Provoked you, you mean, to hurt her—through Roderick?'
For a moment she deeply coloured, and he had really not intended to force the tears to her eyes. A cold clearness, however, quickly forced them back (*NYE* i. 404).

Our understanding of Rowland's conduct is seriously changed by this redistribution of 'forces'; his unforgiving additional specification '— through Roderick?' has none of the reticence of 'It seemed to me', and 'he had really not intended' suggests his own provoked desire to hurt. Christina's tears, conversely, seem to testify to the sincerity of her high good intentions and her regard for his respect. In this scene Rowland weighs 'his sympathy against his irritation' (*1883*, ii. 103), 'sympathy against suspicion' (*NYE* i. 409); at its end in *1883* he inclines to the former, but in the *NYE*, very strikingly, to suspicion. He has been impressed by Christina's aspirations to virtue; then she asks for his judgement of her; and he assumes she has been only acting. In *1883*

she blushed as she perceived his smile, and her blush, which was beautiful, made her fault venial.

'You are an excellent girl!' he said, very positively; and then gave her his hand in farewell (*1883*, ii. 103).

In the *NYE*

she blushed as she guessed his fine comment, and her blush, which was beautiful, carried off her betrayal. He turned his back (*NYE* i. 410).

In both versions he perceives her behaviour as acting; but where in *1883* he sympathetically understands Christina's compulsion to dramatize her own sincerest impulses, and makes a gesture of forgiveness, the *NYE* gives him an ironic admiration of her histrionic art which forgives nothing and is used as if it released him from the ties of common politeness. The revision shocks us with Rowland's unkindness (which recalls Winterbourne's cutting of Daisy Miller); but it comes as the climax of a carefully rethought and intricately readjusted dramatic movement. Rowland has set himself too demanding a task of self-abnegation—good intentions can do evil—and the feelings he has forcibly repressed surface here to Christina's harm. The *NYE* in this chapter extends its contemplation of the disastrous consequences of Rowland's too strenuously optimistic attempt at virtue, in a similar spirit to that in which the novel as a whole— both in *1883* and the *NYE*—contemplates in Roderick the disastrous consequences of too grandly optimistic an attempt at artistic greatness.

There are certain relations and tones of reference through which the *NYE* adjusts details of characterization recurrently in the novel: one especially concerns the question of Roderick's psychological constitution and the collapse of his confidence. Roderick's mother is in

1883 mostly feeble and dependent and Roderick's resentment of her unconvincing; the *NYE* reconsiders Mrs Hudson and makes her more substantially constricting than before. In the more melodramatically eventful short tale *Master Eustace* (1871), James had handled a claustrophobic mother-love with violent consequences; *Roderick Hudson*, more ample and with less obvious contrivance, is careful to give us accounts of the parentage of its three main characters, and our sense of their submerged frames of reference and habits of mind, though not exactly their predetermined courses of action, is correspondingly intense (it is perhaps partly the lack of this parental dimension in Mary Garland—whose family is generally and sociologically described—which makes her, as treated, less than a full counterweight to Christina). The now-internalized tyranny of Mrs Light over Christina is explicitly discussed in the novel, and in Rowland's dispassionate moments this visible oppression makes him sympathetically admire Christina for her strainings at freedom. In the chapter of her decision not to marry as her mother wishes, the *NYE* introduces a sequence of thoughts in which the virtuously resolved daughter explains the power of Mrs Light's indoctrination, how much she is tempted—'I thrill with the idea of high consideration. Mamma, you see, has never had *any*. There I am in all my native horror' (*NYE* i. 407). This is the internal equivalent to the external compulsion which Mrs Light soon brings to bear, and the turns of thought exert a sense of the magnetic draw, for Christina, of a great marriage: her attempt to match up to a high ideal here is a brief triumph over her own 'native' instincts, and is perceived by Rowland in terms of Icarean aspiration and inevitable fall which align her with Roderick.

Christina, meanwhile, had really for the time been soaring aloft, to his vision, and though in such flights of her moral nature—the energy of which now affected him as real—there was a certain painful effort and tension of wing, it was none the less piteous to imagine her being rudely jerked down to the base earth (*NYE* i. 410).[39]

---

[39] Reviewing Trollope in 1875, James complains of the limitations of unstretched talent: 'cleverness is certain of success; it never has the vertigo; it is only genius and folly that fail' (*LC* i. 1315). The high aspirations of genius produce a vertigo in Roderick Hudson also: this imagery of strain is there already in *1883*, where Roderick strides 'as if his thoughts had lent him wings' (*1883*, i. 52), Christina remarks that 'You have gone up like a rocket in your profession, they tell me; are you going to come down like the stick?' (*1883*, i. 196), and Gloriani calls him 'our high-flying friend' (*1883*, ii. 66). The *NYE* raises this image to further perilous heights of powers: Christina makes Roderick feel he can not just 'do all sorts of great things' (*1883*, i. 194), but 'scale the skies' (*NYE*

This comes just before Rowland's revulsion and turning of his back. 'Really for the time been soaring aloft' and the 'real' energy come in with the *NYE*, setting his reaction in the light of the debate between suspicion and sympathy which in the revised version of the scene comes to so different a conclusion from *1883*. Mrs Light's suspected unfair advantage has just been called (in a revision) 'a means of influence too base to be used save under sharp coercion' (*NYE* i. 409–10), making the 'base' forces which threaten Christina's ideal doubly maternal, from within and without.

Mrs Hudson is a less shady figure than the grotesque Mrs Light, and readers are liable to take Roderick's early complaints about her, as Rowland does, for fuss about nothing: the weight of rebuke she turns on Rowland and even on Mary when Roderick's collapse is publicly acknowledged may in *1883* come then as something of a shock. In the *NYE* a series of glancing revisions has prepared us for this (still surprising) tenacity of family self-interest, which may help us to understand how Roderick has in his own words 'an almost unlimited susceptibility to the influence of a beautiful woman' (*1883*, i. 106), and how his disappointment by Christina Light comes to have so catastrophic an effect on his artistic self-confidence (his analogy of her gratifying compliance with 'a perfect statue shaping itself in the block' (*1883*, ii. 158) suggests that he is habituated to and dependent on a low level of resistance in women and in marble). Roderick's collapse returns him to the filial relation within which his value is reliably stable only because it is protected from commerce with the real world of success and failure: where this relation is reasserted the *NYE* turns 'the clasp of his mother's hand' (*1883*, ii. 112) to 'his mother's locked clasp' (*NYE* i. 422), rendering the truth in Roderick's sense of her as oppressively attentive. He seems to escape this confining

---

i. 260)—which is related to the way her 'indifferent tread' (*1883*, i. 190) becomes her 'Olympian command of the air, as it were, not less than of the earth' (*NYE* i. 254). In *1883* Christina, in the Coliseum, 'pointed ... into the blue air' (*1883*, i. 197) at the blue flower for which Roderick tries to 'scale the skies'; this stands in the *NYE*, and newly recalls Gloriani's judgement after seeing Roderick's figure of the lounging woman—not 'he couldn't keep up the transcendental style, and he has already broken down' (*1883*, i. 110), but 'he couldn't keep up that flapping of his wings in the blue, and he has already come down to earth' (*NYE* i. 146). And this in turn looks back to Gloriani's warning to Roderick, revised to bring in the idea of Icarus: 'Your beauty, as you call it, is the effort of a man to quit the earth by flapping his arms very hard. He may jump about or stand on tiptoe, but he can't do more ... You can't fly; there's no use trying' (*NYE* i. 119). The ominous phrase 'come down to earth' (also introduced at *NYE* i. 361) anticipates Roderick's fatal fall and relates it to the common sense of the practicable.

relation early in the action by setting out on his artistic career; but then Rowland's expectant patronage comes to irk him in a way which, as the *NYE* brings out, represents a transference of the domestic conflict. 'You are watching me; I don't want to be watched!' (*1883*, i. 96) becomes 'You're watching me, my dear fellow, as my mother at home watches the tea-kettle she has set to boil, and the case is that somehow I don't want to be watched' (*NYE* i. 127).[40] The proverbial perversity of things, its being the 'case' that watched kettles never do come to the boil, is the fatalistic premiss of Roderick's complaint, used to put pressure on Rowland; 'somehow' draws our attention to the obscure movement of thought and feeling by which he associates Rowland with his mother in a pattern where dependence and rebellion are profoundly involved with each other.

The dependence expresses itself in Roderick's first experiment with vice at Baden, reworking that of *Eugene Pickering*, which reworks that (also at Baden) in *The Newcomes*. As he tells his patron and friend about it 'Rowland was reminded of Madame de Cruchecasseé in Thackeray's novel' (*1883*, i. 105)—to which the *NYE* adds 'but of a Madame de Cruchecasseé mature and quasi-maternal, attached as with a horrible sincerity to her prey' (*NYE* i. 139). 'Quasi-maternal' makes the connection sinister, sees Roderick's susceptibility as dangerous: when later he is working on the bust of his mother, his final work, the *NYE* develops our sense of what the connection means to him. 'He evidently found it a deep personal luxury to lounge away the hours in an atmosphere so charged with feminine tenderness' (*1883*, ii. 61) becomes 'he clearly liked again, almost as he had liked it as a boy, in convalescence from measles, to lounge away the hours in an air so charged with feminine service' (*NYE* i. 353). 'Deep personal luxury' seems to suggest to James here the reminiscence of childhood, of weakness, and of 'service'; the shift from 'tenderness' to 'service' and the imagination of proneness alert us particularly to the now-renewed passivity of the spoiled child. It is again to the peculiarity of the relation that a revision soon after this draws our attention, when Gloriani has

[40] Rowland himself comes later to suffer from the moral pressure of Mrs Hudson's attention, and in the Florentine villa he is relieved when she 'promised to be diverted from her maternal sorrows by the still deeper perplexities of Maddalena's theory of roasting, sweeping and bed-making' (*1883*, ii. 128). The *NYE* wittily tightens the screws: 'her maternal sorrows' becomes 'the study of his predicament', and 'perplexities' are reprobated for their difficulty as 'perversity' (*NYE* i. 444). In the 1875 book edition, one of the chapter-titles was 'Mrs. Hudson' (See *Henry James: Novels 1871–1880*, ed. William T. Stafford, New York, 1983, p. 437).

seen the successful bust and instead of asking as in *1883* 'is he very fond of his mother—is he a very good son?' (*1883*, ii. 67–8) asks rather 'has he a special worship for her, is he one of your sons in a thousand?' (*NYE* i. 362–3). The *arrière-pensée* of the *1883* question is Gloriani's suspicion of Roderick's artistic sincerity; the *NYE* question also has a sceptical bearing but 'special' and 'one … in a thousand' signal a detected intensity in Roderick's work by also registering how much Gloriani is impressed. (This exemplifies, incidentally, the way in which the *NYE*'s Gloriani, having reappeared in the interim as the established Parisian celebrity of *The Ambassadors* (1903) with 'a personal acuteness that life had seasoned to steel',[41] speaks with a more disinterested authority than in *1883*.) Roderick's maternal preoccupation, as a knot of feelings that intertwines dependence and rebelliousness, is not, though, ever given any direct causal function in his collapse. We feel it rather—especially in the revisions—as the material of his passive temperament, and by extension, since his passivity involves fatalism, as a tendency to despair about that passivity. This gives a depth of available reference by which we glimpse a solidity of psychological structure, a valid sense of a personal mystery, there behind the novel's story.[42]

vi. His Eternal Second Thought

In the Preface to *Roderick Hudson* James writes of the painter's 'relation to the old picture, the work of his hand, that has been lost to sight and that, when found again, is put back on the easel for measure of what time and the weather may, in the interval, have done to it' (*LC* ii. 1045). In the time between writing the novel and revising

---

[41] *The Ambassadors*, London, 1903, p. 146.

[42] James's lively sense in rereading of the relations of this to the course of the action manifests itself in some suggestive cross-glances, as when at the ball the Cavaliere tries to warn Roderick off Christina: ' "Let me speak to you as a friend." "Oh, speak even as an enemy and I shall not mind it", Roderick answered, frowning' (*1883*, i. 152). ' "Let me speak to you as a father." "Oh, speak even as a mother and I really shall not mind it!" ' (*NYE* i. 204). The Cavaliere speaks, in fact, as *Christina*'s father, not Roderick's— 'a Virginian gentleman' who is mentioned only once, in Cecilia's account of their family history. 'He turned out, I believe, a dreadful rake, and made great havoc in their fortune' (*1883*, i. 22); the *NYE* enlivens this with Cecilia's doubts about Mrs Hudson's reliability: 'He turned out, I believe, quite a dreadful sort of person and made great havoc with the resources, whatever they were, that she always speaks of as their fortune' (*NYE* i. 27–8). Mrs Hudson's nervous distrust of Roderick is thus set in perspective as a possible consequence of her unhappy marriage.

it James had included just such a scene, a literal version of the metaphors in the *NYE* Prefaces, at a crucial point in *The Tragic Muse*
(1890), where Nick Dormer brings out 'his young work' for Gabriel
Nash's judgement, in order to decide whether to become an artist.
Nervously, Nick 'rubbed old panels with his sleeve and dabbed wet
sponges on surfaces that had sunk',[43] while waiting to receive Nash's
(in the end encouraging) verdict. This scene itself is a replaying of the
one written sixteen years earlier for the second chapter of *Roderick
Hudson*, where Roderick exhibits his work to Rowland in order to
reach a conclusion about his momentous opportunity for a career—
'looking at them himself with a strange air of quickened curiosity'
(*1883*, i. 28). Within *Roderick Hudson*, moreover, this scene of promise
is answered later by that where the defeated Roderick inspects his past
works in Rowland's apartments as from a great temporal distance:
'Once upon a time I did those things, and they are devilish good!'
(*1883*, ii. 125).

It can be peculiarly poignant to look on the evidence of powers you
have lost, because the death of a part of yourself, to which such a loss
amounts, suggests or recalls to the mind an idea of the mind's own
mortality. Only the thought—in some circumstances one might say
the illusion—that you are still essentially the same person, that the
passage of time has essentially left you untouched, offers immunity
from the damage this kind of confrontation makes vivid. When the
lost powers are great this thought of one's persisting integrity is hard
sanely to entertain; the wide gulf between past and present conditions
seems to tell against our lived premiss that people have a continuous
identity (an essential sameness) over time. James revised Roderick's
words more than thirty years later, making a connection of self with
work in which, despite age, continuing powers were manifest; but in
this case such a connection could not be truly made without a wondering sense of what more might easily have been lost: 'Once upon a
time I did those things—if it's possible to believe it' (*NYE*, i. 439).
This retracts *1883*'s desperately assertive attempt to yoke present self
with past 'things', and rather gives Roderick a calm loss of faith in the
value of the pronoun 'I' as a means of pulling himself back together
as an artist. Some moments later Rowland hopes Roderick will work
in Florence. In *1883* ' "I hope I may!" said Roderick, with a magnificent
smile' (*1883*, ii. 125): in the *NYE* ' "I hope to heaven I may!" ' It was

---

[43] *The Tragic Muse*, 3 vols., London, 1890, ii. 126.

full of expression, but he might have been speaking of some interesting alien' (*NYE* i. 440). The revision, with the sad acknowledgement in its 'but', extends the doubt about the continuity of past and present Rodericks into a metaphorical hypothesis of somebody else altogether, as if that were the sole possible explanation of his strange tone.

On reading *Gabrielle de Bergerac* after a short interval during which he had come to the Europe in which the tale is set, James felt that it was 'the product of a former state of being'—meaning that he now felt himself capable of a maturer account of the same subject. He never reprinted that story, whereas in rereading and revising *Roderick Hudson* he was able to feel it as the product of a state of being still lively enough to revive for republication. As he puts it in the Preface to *The Golden Bowl*, 'Not to *be* disconnected, for the tradition of behaviour, [the artist] has but to feel that he is not' (*LC* ii. 1340): 'the tradition of behaviour' makes the revising writer the heir of his old, his younger self—a self-inheritance which is an inward process discernible only by the capacity to 'feel' Roderick has forfeited. The 'tradition' hands down to James, that is, a confidence of touch about 'the related state, to each other, of certain figures and things' (*LC* ii. 1040). Roderick is for him one of these figures, and a revision in his numb scene with Mrs Hudson re-economizes with a twist James's sense of what he is doing to *Roderick Hudson* as something Roderick cannot do either in his art or in his life. Mrs Hudson pleads with Roderick not to speak violently 'before Mary, before Mr. Mallet!'

'Mary—Mr. Mallet?' Roderick repeated, almost savagely (*1883*, ii. 112).

'Mary—Mr. Mallet?' He took up these names as after a long disuse and seemed to look at them as at objects of obscure application (*NYE* i. 422).

James turns Roderick's apparently fierce egotism of *1883*, his sarcastic impatience of social ties, into a hollow echo that can discover no immediate answer, no responsibility, for the application (punning on 'appeal') of the seriously related figures named: his evident bemusement is imagined as the amnesia of one who, having forgotten a skill, finds its tools strangely familiar. The situation in James's art, his lucid reapplication of the 'names' after a long disuse—inverted to meet Roderick's situation—movingly contributes here to the novel's life:[44]

[44] As it does where the phrase used of the revising artist—'taking up the old relation, so workable apparently, yet' (*LC* ii. 1046)—comes in with a revision for a touching intimation of what may still survive of the relation between Roderick and Rowland, even in the penultimate chapter. 'Roderick's face, on the other hand, took up, even

the fact of the span in James's own life between 1874 and 1906 gives him access to a newly enlarged account of the spans within the action— an enlargement of perspective we can register as sensitive common readers of the NYE without having to collate the early and late texts.

When Rowland sees Christina again at Engelberg for the last time (and the first since the scene of her rebellious high flight about her marriage), *1883* delicately takes up his feeling about her ('You are an excellent girl!') at the end of the earlier scene.

In the clear outer light Rowland's first impression of her was that she was more beautiful than ever. And yet in three months she could hardly have changed; the change was in Rowland's own vision of her, which that last interview on the eve of her marriage had made unprecedentedly tender (*1883*, ii. 163).

'Tender' hardly applies, though, to the vision of Christina implied in the NYE scene where Rowland admires her performance but turns his back; and the last clause here correspondingly inflects to equivocate between liking and wonder at power: 'in which that last interview on the eve of her marriage had sown the seeds of a new appreciation' (*NYE*, i. 488). 'Appreciation' is the business of the critic, and the notion of Christina's behaviour as performance is amplified in the NYE's version of the first sentence:

In the clear outer light Rowland's first impression of her was that her beauty had received some strange accession, affecting him after the manner of a musical composition better 'given', to his sense, than ever before (*NYE*, i. 488).

Rowland inwardly pays, as in the earlier scene, a high compliment with a devastating reservation attached; the revision draws, for its version of Christina's cogency of attitudinizing,[45] on James's awareness of it as a 'strange accession', a better rendering of 'more beautiful than ever' in the original 'composition' *Roderick Hudson*.

before he spoke, something that evidently figured to him as their old relation' (*NYE* i. 498). This derives from 'Roderick stood looking at him with an expression of countenance which had of late become rare. There was an unfamiliar spark in his eye, and a certain imperious alertness in his carriage' (*1883*, ii. 170). The revision makes it a tender rather than a provokingly 'imperious' renewal, takes up old relations both of author to text and of character to character.

[45] Later Rowland's brooding on 'all that was tragic and fatal in her latest transformation' (*1883*, ii. 169), concerns instead 'something sinister in this fresh physiognomy she had chosen to present' (*NYE* i. 497)—with 'chosen' committing Rowland to the histrionic view of her behaviour.

The danger of self-congratulation in the self-reflexiveness of this better giving is relieved, as elsewhere, by the discipline of the characters' related state, the ethical turn by which words associated with the author's own situation are subjected to and altered by the situation of his 'figures and things'. (This subjection to context means that we do not need to recognize a new wording *as* a revision in order to be aware of its potency.) Rowland's difficult equilibrium—when he sustains it—is the result of such a habit of thought, as a revision makes clear when, having felt a momentary elation at Roderick's eventual announcement of his failure to Mary and his mother, he curbs the impulse to utter it: 'But in a moment his conservative instincts corrected it' (*1883*, ii. 114) becomes 'But the next instant his eternal second thought, his vision of the case for others, had corrected it' (*NYE* i. 424). The flickering irritability of 'eternal' catches Rowland's self-division, his discomfort at yet again subordinating his own interests to responsibility of speech; but the second thought of the revision—itself a correction of the mechanical 'conservative instincts' and a sharp vision of the case for Rowland—is embodied in a second clause, the steadyingly punctuated-off appositional reminder of 'his vision of the case for others'.

None the less, Rowland's strenuous virtue, analogous in certain respects to that of a disinterested author, is a strain hard to keep up; when it gives way under stress the consequences are serious. Thus in the last scene between Rowland and Roderick, where he is provoked by the latter's refusal to allow that he might have had interests and desires of his own with regard to a woman,

Rowland felt an immense desire to give him a visible palpable pang. 'Her name is Mary Garland', he said.
Apparently he succeeded. The surprise was great; Roderick coloured as he had never done (*1883*, ii. 180).

The *NYE* refines on Rowland's punitive impulse and on its effects.

Rowland felt the temptation to give him a palpable pang. 'With whom but with the nearest—?'
'The nearest—?' Roderick maintained his cold, large stare, which seemed so to neglect and overshoot the near. But then he brought it down. 'You mean with poor Mary?'
'I mean with Miss Garland.'
At the tone, suddenly, he coloured; something had touched him somewhere. He gave, however, at first, under control, the least possible sign (*NYE* i. 510).

Rowland's first insinuating words here, in themselves a cruel indirection, become particularly eloquent about his mental processes when we recall what, in the *NYE*, Roderick said to him years before straight after declaring his engagement: 'I felt an extraordinary desire to spill over to some woman, and I suppose I took the nearest' (*NYE* i. 82). The parallel with and reversal of the earlier scene on the boat is registered in Rowland's pointing of these words back at Roderick, and can be felt as psychologically present to him. James gives us a sudden chilling perspective on Rowland's long bitterness by reaching back for this far echo, and the pause for thought in Roderick's own echo of the words—and then the halts of the four commas as he keeps 'under control'—suggest that 'something had touched him somewhere' may render a vague pained recollection on his part of an occasion when they were used before.[46]

Such stretches of thought and feeling over time are part of the generously and ambitiously inclusive conception of the novel: the 'eternal time-question' (*LC* ii. 1048) about the representation of change in human lives is one of James's basic premisses. Moments of looking backward and forward within the represented span therefore work as tests of the novel's success, but also bear testimony to the poignancy and conviction of James's idea, to the depth of life we can feel ready to stir beneath the fictional surface. In revising he is alive to the text's possibilities of internal reverberation for character as for reader: so that for example at Como an action of Roderick and Rowland comes to recall a former series of such actions.

One day, in the afternoon, the two young men took a long stroll together (*1883*, ii. 144).

One afternoon the two young men wandered away together as they had wandered of old (*NYE* i. 464).

The *NYE* ends, in fact, with a new sentence of reminiscence turning our thoughts back over the action: Rowland assures Cecilia, as in *1883*, that he is the most patient of mortals;

---

[46] A much shorter temporal gap is crossed by the echo of Mary Garland's 'You are very generous' to Rowland on the picnic (*1883*, i. 58) in Augusta Blanchard's 'You are very generous' to him at Rome (*1883*, i. 92). The *NYE* revises this latter to 'You're most awfully splendid, you know—to be so generous' (*NYE* i. 122), and turns 'He had heard the words before' into 'He had heard something like it, and yet so unlike, before.' The revision changes the words, and has Rowland note the difference in them—as well as the difference to him.

And then he talks to her of Roderick, of whose history she never wearies and whom he never elsewhere names (*NYE* i. 527).

This intimates the aptness of the novel's procedure in telling Roderick's history from Rowland's point of view; offers the formal satisfaction of recognizing a particular original pattern for the relation between author and reader in that between Rowland and Cecilia; and, allowing a range of imaginable motives for Rowland's reticence, closes *Roderick Hudson* with a potent delimitation of the context in which the name is ever treated.

James's poetic sense for experience past, missed, and to come—for the poignancy of moments on which the pressure of an accumulated mass of life comes to bear—informs equally his revision of the earlier passages of the novel, where we are prepared for feeling the lapse of the action as a period within which the potential felicity of a number of lives may be mainly realized, irrevocably diminished, or cruelly cancelled. This is again not just our grave sense, but that of the characters; as on the farewell picnic before the new friends set off for Europe.

Roderick had chosen the feasting place; he knew it well and had passed many a summer afternoon there, lying at his length on the grass and gazing at the blue undulations of the horizon (*1883*, i. 55).

Roderick had chosen his happy valley, the feasting-place; he knew it well and had passed many a summer afternoon there, lying at his length on the grass in the shade and looking away to the blue distances, the 'purple rim' of the poet, which had the wealth of the world, all the unattainable of life, beyond them (*NYE* i. 72).

'His happy valley' here, recalling *Rasselas*, suggests a restlessness which the world cannot fulfil; while the 'purple rim', coming in from Tennyson's 'The Day-Dream' (to the following section of which Roderick jokingly alludes in the earlier text of the book),[47] brings a new substance to Roderick's day-dreaming:

> Across the hills, and far away
> Beyond their utmost purple rim,

[47] 'He had once quoted Tennyson against her—"And is there any moral shut | Within the bosom of the rose?" "In all Miss Blanchard's roses you may be sure there is a moral"' (*1883*, i. 144). In the course of the book Roderick also quotes *The Princess*, and lotus-eaters are mentioned more than once. Christina is associated with a Tennyson princess here; she is associated with Tennyson's *Princess* in *The Princess Casamassima*, where her country-house, Medley, recalls Tennyson's subtitle for that poem, *A Medley*.

> And deep into the dying day
> The happy princess followed him.[48]

Christina makes Roderick and herself unhappy in the novel by becoming a princess and giving him up: the movement of thought in 'the
wealth of the world, all the unattainable of life' is a small enactment
of the sad progression from wishfulness to bafflement and resignation
in the book, an intimation of the fate of Roderick's ambitions.

Even nearer the start James, looking back at the words he had
written more than thirty years before, finds Rowland looking forward
beyond the New England horizon to a time when he will look back
yearningly at *this* time. James recognizes that there is a relation
between Rowland's imaginative anticipation of a sadder and wiser
retrospect, and his own sense in 1906 Rye that he is at the far end of
an analogous perspective within his own life and career; and the
recognition allows him to produce a touching imaginative extension
of the elegiac emotion.

He sat up beside his companion and looked away at the far-spreading view.
It seemed to him beautiful, and suddenly a strange feeling of prospective regret
took possession of him. Something seemed to tell him that later, in a foreign
land, he should remember it with longing and regret (*1883*, i. 25).

He sat up beside his companion and looked away at the far-spreading view,
which affected him as melting for them both into such vast continuities and
possibilities of possession. It touched him to the heart; suddenly a strange
feeling of prospective regret took possession of him. Something seemed to tell
him that later, in a foreign land, he should be haunted by it, should remember
it all with longing and regret (*NYE* i. 32).

'For them both' revises to catch Rowland's 'eternal second thought,
his vision of the case for others'; we feel the 'beauty' of the view to be
connected to the rich potentialities it evokes as an image of the future
of their friendship; and we retain the flat, but beautiful, turn by
which 'prospective regret', both an anticipation of a regret not yet
experienced, and the emotion of regret as itself part of the act of
anticipation, gets looked back to by the prospect of 'longing and regret'

---

[48] *The Poems of Tennyson*, ed. Christopher Ricks, ii. 55. This section is called 'The
Departure'. The sense of Roderick's American dreams of remote foreign futures (and a
remote foreign past) comes in also apropos of Roderick's design for his brother's tomb:
'The young soldier lay sleeping eternally with his hand on his sword—like an old
crusader in a Gothic cathedral' (*1883*, i. 29). This ends in 1906—'his hand on his sword,
the image of one of the crusaders Roderick had dreamed of in one of the cathedrals he
had never seen' (*NYE* i. 37).

in *1883*. This doubling is redoubled in the *NYE*, where 'possibilities of possession' for Rowland and Roderick give way to a sudden seizure of passiveness when the prospective regret takes 'possession' of him. The small changes which give us 'should be haunted by it, should remember it all'—where the passive idea of being 'haunted by it' fills out to the active response of 'remember it all'—deliberately carry through a shift of agency the reverse of that in the repeated 'possession', and pause for a swelling cadence to call up the imagined process of recollection. In these revisions we see James moved by a sense of his own history as the words of his first acknowledged novel bring it home to him; but these words sympathetically deal with the situation of a character, and the distinction of his treatment in 1906 of the retrospective emotion which stirs him lies in the consistency over more than thirty years of his vision of that situation, in the intense self-discipline with which he directs his own feelings into a vision of the case for others.

5

The American: Henry James at Work

i. Good Intentions

James later believed that he had written *The American*, the novel which followed *Roderick Hudson*, too hastily in 1875–6. He had certainly begun at speed. To F. P. Church, editor of the *Galaxy* where he hoped his novel would appear, he wrote on 1 December 1875 that 'I have got at work upon one sooner than I expected, and particularly desire it to come out without delay' (*HJL* ii. 8–9).[1] On 3 February 1876 he referred to his hurry in a letter to Howells (in whose *Atlantic Monthly*, after a disagreement with Church, the novel eventually came out), noting that 'It was the only subject mature enough in my mind to use immediately' (*HJL* ii. 22). When he reread the story for the New York Edition, however, thirty years later, the value of the subject struck him as a reason to regret his previous treatment of it. His general 'yearning reflexion' about the chance to rehandle, as he says in the Preface to *The Golden Bowl*,

> was to reach its maximum, no doubt, over many of the sorry businesses of 'The American', for instance, where, given the elements and the essence, the long-stored grievance of the subject bristling with a sense of over-prolonged exposure in a garment misfitted, a garment cheaply embroidered and unworthy of it, thereby most proportionately sounded their plaint (*LC* ii. 1337).

What he thought of in 1876 as a 'mature enough' subject had as he later judged received an inadequate treatment, giving rise to a 'long-stored grievance'. James felt his 'good intentions baffled by a treacherous vehicle'. The massive 1906 revision of *The American* is then an attempt to refit the 'garment' of expression, or to make the 'vehicle' go better; it was conceived, in other words, as a reconsidered continuation of his rendering of 'the elements and the essence', things seen

---

[1] The letters show that there was a financial motive to his urgency of composition ('it was the money question solely that had to determine me', *HJL* ii. 22). In the 1906 Preface James talks of how he 'began to write it that December day' (*LC* ii. 1057)—the 1 Dec. letter to Church seems to have been written on the day he began.

as bristlingly alive to their own unseemliness, to the maltreatment they have suffered.[2]

Such restitution has its limits: in particular, the plot which is designed to express 'the elements and the essence', determining the sequence and disposition of scenes and chapters, can undergo little alteration (since initially worked out as a unity) without demanding a different book altogether. James's career is full of completely new works which take over, and build new structures on, the premises of previous ones.[3] His revision, on the other hand, has 'in the event, for my *conscious* play of mind, almost nothing in common' with 'rewriting' (*LC* ii. 1332). It therefore lays no claim to the comprehensiveness which might secure more than a decent perfection: the Preface, enjoyed by Howells for the candour with which 'you rounded upon yourself, and as it were took yourself to pieces, in your self-censure',[4] frankly points out faults in the structure too large-boned to be entirely reset by the instruments of revision. James draws attention, for instance, to the 'inordinate leak' (*LC* ii. 1053) of the Bellegardes' motive for breaking off Newman's engagement.

James also points in the Preface to the unreality of the family's 'power' over Claire de Cintré and Newman's over them (*LC* ii. 1067), and to the weird effect given by the temporal hiatus in Newman's relation to Claire immediately after their public engagement. That this had troubled him over the intervening years is suggested by the reworking of this aspect of the plot in *The Reverberator* (1888), where

---

[2] The revisions of *The American* have been studied by Royal A. Gettman, in a thesis and in 'Henry James's Revision of "The American"', *American Literature*, 16 (Jan. 1945), 279–95; by Isadore Traschen in a thesis and in 'An American in Paris', *American Literature*, 26 (Mar. 1954), 67–77, 'Henry James and the Art of Revision', *Philological Quarterly*, 35 (Jan. 1956), 39–47, and 'James's Revisions of the Love Affair in "The American"', *New England Quarterly*, 29 (Mar. 1956), 43–62; by Max F. Schulz in 'The Bellegardes' Feud with Christopher Newman: A Study of Henry James's Revision of "The American"', *American Literature*, 27 (Mar. 1955), 42–55; by William T. Stafford in 'The Ending of James's "The American": A Defense of the Early Version', *Nineteenth Century Fiction*, 18 (June 1963), 86–9; and by Larry J. Reynolds in 'Henry James's New Christopher Newman', *Studies in the Novel*, 5/4 (Winter 1973), 457–68. R. W. Butterfield uses some revisions in his essay on the novel in *The Air of Reality: New Essays on Henry James*, ed. John Goode, London, 1972, pp. 5–35.

[3] In the Preface James imagines how the Bellegardes' *acceptance* of Newman would have been an interesting subject—'only it wouldn't have been the theme of "The American" as the book stands, the theme to which I was from so early pledged' (*LC* ii. 1067). *The Reverberator* of 1888 is in several respects a reworking of the theme of *The American*: see 'Introduction', *A London Life and The Reverberator*, ed. with an intro. and notes by the present author, Oxford, 1989, pp. xxx–xxxii.

[4] W. D. Howells to Henry James, 2 Aug. 1908 (Harvard MS).

the American heroine is accepted, because wealthy, by the French aristocratic family into which she wishes to marry; only to commit a major social gaffe which threatens the acceptance. The dramatic version of *The American* (1891) adroitly revises the situation by making Newman's rival Lord Deepmere at least as rich as he is, and thus (with his title) a preferable *parti*—only to save Valentin from death and have Claire end in Newman's arms.

In spite of the reservations about the novel's plot which these reworkings might be taken to imply, the Preface ends by offering the unity of Newman's point of view—in the *NYE* text—as the work's main value, a consistency in the perceiver which may be felt partly to redeem the falsity of what he perceives. In addition, the revisions not only work hard to 'drug' (*LC* ii. 1065) our sense of these supposed implausibilities, but actually reduce their implausibility.[5]

James had the 411 pages from two copies of the 1883 Macmillan two-volume edition pasted on to larger sheets on which he then revised. The manuscript survives as evidence of his procedure. The revisions are handwritten in black ink, mostly in the wide margins, but with most of the changes which only affect punctuation, as well as some alterations of wording, registered in the body of the text. The new wordings often appear at some distance from their place on the original page; James puts them in balloons and leads the eye back to their context with long wavy lines attached to the scratched-out words of *1883* or (for insertions) squeezing between words left intact. Sometimes these revisions entirely fill a sheet or spill over to the next; sometimes, to regain a clear presentation of sequence, typed or handwritten transcriptions of revised portions of text replace the pasted-down pages. It seems from the comparative neatness of the handwriting in most balloons that James may have roughed out some or all revisions before transcribing them into the margins; but in any case the manuscript cannot be called a fair copy, since the wording of the balloon is often later altered or cancelled. Rodney Dennis, in his Introduction to the

---

[5] The changes which affect the Bellegardes' change of mind, and some which substantiate their power over Claire, are usefully described in Max F. Schulz's 'The Bellegardes' Feud with Christopher Newman'. Newman's 'power' over the Bellegardes becomes in the *NYE* more questionable, or their demeanour at any rate less melodramatically ruffled. James turns the restrictions of intimacy between the fiancés to account in revision as a symptom of Claire's anxiety—as a result, in ch. 17, of the family attempt to replace Newman with Lord Deepmere at the ball in ch. 16 (see esp. *NYE* ii. 356).

facsimile of the Houghton Library manuscript, notes that 'Although the revision was carefully prepared for the printer by James, the text of the New York Edition as issued contains many variants from the version here presented.' He goes on, speculating, to suggest that 'The corrected proofs which would presumably represent a further process of revision are not known to exist' (*HMS*, p. 4).

The 'further process of revision' shown by collation of the various texts is, however, extremely heavy in places. The correspondence between James and the Scribners, now at Princeton, shows that after the Riverside Press compositors had difficulty in deciphering James's manuscript revisions of *Roderick Hudson*, he offered to have the sheets for that novel typed out. Though this offer was not taken up, he wrote to Scribner on 9 May 1906 that 'I shall send you the *American* completely re-typed, as I am here also obliged to riddle the margins practically as much as in the case of *R.H.*' (*HJL* iv. 402). James's agent J. B. Pinker wrote to Scribner on 15 June 1906 that 'the revision of "The American" is proceeding, and we are having it typed as it leaves Mr. James's hands'.[6] The first volume of revised copy for the novel was sent by Pinker to Scribner on 16 November 1906, and the second on 14 February 1907—in what James called 'complete type-copy'.[7]

That the surviving manuscript represents so intermediate a stage in the production of the final *NYE* text both makes it less straightforward to use and, much more importantly, gives it a unique critical interest as detailed evidence of James's working process in revision. The exhaustively intense manner in which James materially handles his original text, giving himself a margin and then freely deviating into it, offers us a critical grasp on the substance of his art. We have here a special chance to compare versions and elicit the rationale of change; to investigate the nature of the relation of the words of *1883* to the words of the *NYE*, and some of its significance for the meaning of *The American*.

ii.   *In Other Words*

The final thirteen pages of the Preface to *The Golden Bowl* turn explicitly on the importance of revision and think back over the works

[6] Pinker to Scribners, 15 June 1906 (Princeton TS).
[7] Pinker to Scribners, 16 Nov. 1906 (Princeton TS); Pinker to Scribners, 14 Feb. 1907 (Princeton TS); HJ to Scribners, 15 Feb. 1907 (Princeton MS).

as they appear in the New York Edition, considering the nature of the transformations in the text, changes wrought by James, and their relation to the changes in James himself wrought by the years. The metaphors he uses to convey his wondering sense of ease in the recovery and redisposition of past meanings derive much of their force (as I have suggested) from their purchase on the organic independence of mental processes, from their representation (here) of the earlier work as the seed from which James grows the revised work printed in the *NYE*. They also seem to coincide, again and again, with the format of James's procedure of revision, variously to render and meditate on the physical relation on the page of earlier words to those of the *NYE*.

James habitually follows, or leads, his metaphors back to their roots, and an idea which comes often to his mind and pen to describe revision is that of connection. Frequently his imagination dwells on the line that links the balloon of new words for the *NYE* with the superseded words of the earlier text in order to think about the continuity of his self-relation—as reviser to original author. They are all his own words, but in a way which reflects on the development in his self which is the condition of his active development of the early into the *NYE* words. The difficult conclusion of the *Golden Bowl* Preface concerns the special permanence of literary works as 'conduct minutely and publicly attested', using the previous discussion of writers who do and don't revise to define our possibilities of relation to our own past writings. Literary works

leave us indeed all licence of disconnexion and disavowal, but positively impose on us no such necessity. Our relation to them is essentially traceable, and in that fact abides, we feel, the incomparable luxury of the artist. It rests altogether with himself not to break with his values, not to 'give away' his importances. Not to *be* disconnected, for the tradition of behaviour, he has but to feel that he is not; by his lightest touch the whole chain of relation and responsibility is reconstituted (*LC* ii. 1340).

The author's relation to his own works, 'the tie that binds us to *them*' as he calls it just before this passage, is at his own disposal. James is accounting here for his own emotion in revising, the abundant return of his own sense of the works; and the 'chain' his 'lightest touch' (delicately, the result of his 'feeling') can reconstitute in the retouching of a phrase fastens on him as no undesirable burden. To break with the values would be not to revise, not to believe the values (or yourself) capable of fuller expression and not to take that responsibility: the condition of confidently revising is a belief that your revision makes a connection, that the matter to which you are now giving a surface is essentially the same as before. The emphasis here turns against the temporal direction of the practical process of revision (a progress from early to late) to look back and see that progress less as a superseding than as a respectful continuity, in which the early and the late have a co-operative relation as part of a large organic scheme.

James construes the connection of early words and wavy line and late words into an organic flourish earlier in the Preface: 'the act of revision, the act of seeing it again, caused whatever I looked at on any page to flower before me as into the only terms that honourably expressed it' (*LC* ii. 1332). James looks over the pages again, but what he *sees* again is the matter of which the page is only the surface. In this respect the words of the first text serve as the seed, which gives rise to a stem, on the end of which comes the revision as a flower. How exactly James's mind comes up with the new form of words in a revision is as mysterious as such an arrival:

The term that superlatively, that finally 'renders', is a flower that blooms by a beautiful law of its own (the fiftieth part of a second often so sufficing it) in the very heart of the gathered sheaf (*LC* ii. 1335).

This 'gathered sheaf' matches the piled sheets on which James worked—'in the very heart' of which a new term strangely blooms out of the soil of an old one.

In another image seemingly also drawn from the appearance of his revised sheets, the new term 'breaks the surface', 'breaks out' (*LC* ii. 1330), erupting from a small page into wide margins. James's mind runs on the significance of his crowded sheets, on the pressure in himself which forces the novel into a multitude of new expressions; he writes of his old matter

for due testimony, for re-assertion of value, perforating as by some strange and fine, some latent and gathered force, a myriad more adequate channels (*LC* ii. 1333).

Soon after this James describes Balzac's revised texts as 're-assaulted by supersessive terms, re-penetrated by finer channels' (*LC* ii. 1336); the 'channels' here, suggested by the maplike lines running from main text to revisions, convey in effect the flow of sense between text and reader, the expression of a sense of the object. 'Latent and gathered' pointedly equivocates between being something in the text, something dammed up in it and amassing pressure with the years, and being something in James, a secretly accumulated feeling of how to direct the traffic of meaning in his long-past works that only now emerges in a new delineation of the assumed matter, doing justice to its 'value'. The supersession which takes place in a revision is here put by James as benign. Even when the 'operative terms' in a reread work turn out to be misfits,

The misfits had but to be positive and concordant, in the special intenser light, to represent together (as the two sides of a coin show different legends) just so many effective felicities and substitutes (*LC* ii. 1335).

'Represent' here startlingly makes the old wrong terms—when 'positive and concordant'—not simply suggest but somehow directly *show* James (in his reseeing of the matter, which he gets from his rereading of them) those that should come in their place. The bargain James reports 'the blest good stuff ... in its myriad forms' as proposing is: 'Actively believe in us and then you'll see!' (*LC* ii. 1334). Such an emphasis on the continuity of essential intention which alone can make sure revision's substitutions are felicities suggests forcibly James's view of the nature of the relation between an early wording and a late. The original wording which he rereads makes him see again the action it expresses; and then, with the resources of his maturity, he re-expresses that action in more appropriate words.[8]

The American's Preface calls a novel 'a complex of fine measurements' (*LC* ii. 1062), and ends, with James looking back over his copious revisions of Newman's experience, referring to them modestly as 'any occasional extra inch or so I might smuggle into his measurements' (*LC* ii. 1069).[9] The measurements made in a James novel mostly coincide, through the indirect free style, with those made by the character acting as centre of consciousness: we can see this in a scene

---

[8] This idea of revision as a return to the action might seem contradicted by the changes in particular actions, facts, and emotions—which I discuss below: but on a larger scale James's reasoning would allow for a reseeing of a *general* action, a set of proportions, in such a way that the gestures and reactions of a particular moment would count as expressions of that general action. These are distinctions, that is, not of kind but of degree.

[9] I take it that James is punning on this as an extension of Newman's physical *height* (rather than his power to measure) when shortly afterwards he describes himself as 'clinging to my hero as to a tall, protective, good-natured elder brother in a rough place'; the intensity of point of view given by the extension of one kind of measurement (one which protects the novel's illusion of reality) is wittily transformed into a personal dependence for which the important dimensions are physical.

in Chapter 17, where Newman sees the heartlessly ambitious Noémie de Nioche after she has indirectly caused a dangerous quarrel involving his friend Valentin. In *1883*

'They can't come off without crossing swords. A duel—that will give me a push!' cried Mademoiselle Noémie, clapping her little hands. '*C'est ça qui pose une femme!*' (*1883*, ii. 62).

In the NYE

'They can't come off without its going further. A meeting and a big noise— that will give me a push!' said Noémie, clapping with a soft thud her little pearl-coloured hands. '*C'est ça qui pose une femme!*' (NYE ii. 350).

The act here is essentially the same, but the language of the NYE has a sudden access to all sorts of relations: 'duel' separates with a delayed report into 'a meeting and a big noise' (as if seen from a distance); the delight of 'cried' is flattened into 'said' and she becomes only 'Noémie'; and for a closely contrastive echo of 'a meeting and a big noise' we get 'clapping with a soft thud', where her loud elation deadens into a sickening anticipation of its consequences. The lurid vividness of this, where 'pearl-coloured' notes Newman noting this harm of her prettiness,[10] realizes for the central figure, in a finely adjusted verbal structure of internal relations, the meaning of a *femme fatale*. The imaginative connection James makes in rereading between 'duel' and 'clapping' in *1883*, as a way of thinking about causes and effects, ramifies into a set of implications and parallelisms (like 'going further' and 'push') which minutely affect our response and denote Newman's. This is an extension, not a denial, of the meaning of *1883*, meta- phorically 'an extra inch'—James connects with the old matter by seizing on the moment when Noémie's hands connect with their soft thud, and expresses that connected sense to render Newman's sense, a reliving which freshly sees the relation of a small act to a large action.

   HMS does not represent the complete set of revisions transforming *1883* into the NYE—but the fact of its *not* doing so makes it yield more interest than if it did. We gain thereby intermediate stages of revision between *1883* and the NYE which throw light on James's

---

[10] The idea has occurred earlier in a revision about the unpleasant Urbain de Belle- garde's gloves: 'Newman for a few moments watched him sliding his white hands into the white kid' (*1883*, i. 150). In the NYE 'Newman for a few moments watched him sliding his fair, fat hands into the pearly kid' (NYE ii. 190). The novel is full of feeling about manipulation.

procedure in revising.[11] A collation of the final *NYE* text with that arrived at from *HMS* shows certain rough categories of revision as particularly frequent between *HMS* and *NYE* (though by no means invariable); quite a few of the Americanisms of Newman and his friend Tristram, for instance, arrive after this stage,[12] and a number of dialogue directions are similarly altered after the completion of *HMS*.[13] From the occasional passages which in *HMS* James hardly retouches from *1883* and revises to any extent only in the *NYE*, it can be deduced that a primary process (to which they *were* submitted) was the introduction of many more contractions and the thinning of punctuation, especially of commas: When James speaks of revisions happening in 'the fiftieth part of a second', therefore, we are not to believe they occurred to him spontaneously at a single rereading; the revision for the *NYE* emerges from the manuscript as a progressive accretion of significances, a regathering and adjustment of proportions in which any single revision is a part.

The process of thought by which James turns up his final terms, moreover, is by no means necessarily single for any instance, and

[11] To my knowledge the only critic to have made use of this intermediate stage of revision is Stephen Heath in *The Sexual Fix* (London, 1982, pp. 99–100), where he discusses, as a sign of an evolving modern consciousness about sexuality, the successive revisions which produce an embrace between Newman and Claire de Cintré (*1883*, ii. 4; *HMS* ii. 4; *NYE* ii. 272).

[12] Thus for instance when Tristram tells him in *1883* that he wants to be his own master in Paris, he replies 'Oh, I have been my own master all my life, and I'm tired of it' (*1883*, i. 16); in *HMS* he replies 'Oh, I've enjoyed that blessing, or that curse, all my life, and I'm tired of it' (*HMS* i. 16); and in the *NYE* the answer is 'Oh, I've skipped about in my shirt all my life, and I've had about enough of it' (*NYE* ii. 20). When Tristram asks him 'Where are you staying?' (*1883*, i. 19), this is unchanged in *HMS* but becomes 'Where are you hanging out?' (*NYE* ii. 23.) These revisions make Newman less aggressive and more modestly ironic. Tristram asks him how he made his fortune—in *1883* he replies 'I have worked!' (*1883*, i. 20), in *HMS* 'I've worked, worked, worked!' (*HMS* i. 20), and in the *NYE*, 'Well, I haven't done it by sitting round this way' (*NYE* ii. 24). In *1883* Newman tells Mrs Tristram 'And then I'm lonely, and helpless and dull' (*1883*, i. 38); in *HMS* 'And then I'm lonely, and I wasn't made really for solitude' (*HMS* i. 38); and in the *NYE*, 'And then I'm lonely, and I really kind of pine for a mate' (*NYE* ii. 48). On several occasions the American 'Well, . . .' arrives at the start of a sentence between *HMS* and the *NYE* (e.g. *HMS* i. 90, *NYE* ii. 116; *HMS* i. 106, *NYE* ii. 135; *HMS* i. 109, *NYE* ii. 139).

[13] Thus for instance 'asked' (*1883*, i. 6) becomes 'said' (*HMS* i. 6) becomes 'inquired' (*NYE* ii. 6); 'rejoined' on the same *1883* and *HMS* page only becomes 'objected' in the *NYE* ii. 7. 'Said Newman' (*1883* i. 40) becomes 'Newman returned' (*HMS* i. 40) and then in the *NYE* 'Newman granted' (*NYE* ii. 50). At the ball the Duchess asks Newman his courting methods; in *1883* ' "The secret is with Madame de Cintré", said Newman' (*1883*, ii. 40); in *HMS* this becomes 'Newman said' (*HMS* ii. 40); and in the *NYE* 'Newman found a face to answer' (*NYE* ii. 321).

HMS permits us to trace stages in the evolution of a 'definitive' NYE wording. Thus in the second chapter Newman's honourable ambition is foreshadowed by his interest in a particular painting in the Louvre: I give the three versions of its description.

The great canvas on which Paul Veronese has depicted the marriage feast of Cana (*1883*, i. 13).

The great canvas on which Paul Veronese has set swarming and glowing forever the marriage feast of Cana of Galilee (*HMS* i. 13).

The great canvas on which Paul Veronese has spread, to swarm and glow there for ever, the marriage-feast of Cana of Galilee (*NYE* ii. 16).

'Depicted' first gives way to 'set swarming and glowing forever', which has Veronese give permanent active life to the painting's subject; and then the hint of setting a table develops into 'spread' to render its scale as well as its swarm and glow ('spread' being not only something you do to feasts but, with graphic equivalence, another, slangy, name *for* a feast). The commas newly pause to set the painting apart ('there') in a cadence enacting the arrest of admiration. The associations of the words there on the page act, that is, as James's stimulus at each stage in this incremental process; his feel for the terms and cadences which most significantly relate the elements of a sentence repeatedly refines and rehears the successive versions until satisfied (though 'if he is always doing he can scarce, by his own measure, ever have done' (*LC* ii. 1340–1)).

When Claire de Cintré tells Newman after the settling of their engagement that she can't marry him, in *1883* we have a description of his physical response as if seen by an observer:

Newman dropped her hand and stood staring, first at her and then at the others (*1883*, ii. 73).

In *HMS* the sentence imagines a further, metaphorically physical act to which this motion now comes as a pained response.

Newman dropped her hand—as if with the others she had planted a knife in his side; he stood staring, first at her and then at them (*HMS* ii. 73).

The NYE yet further extends the shock in this, enactively finding a stunned delay of the blow:

Newman dropped her hand—as if, suddenly and unnaturally acting with the others, she had planted a knife in his side: he stood staring, first at her and then at them (*NYE* ii. 363).

The transformations carry back the 'others' to a confrontation coming dramatically sooner in the sentence—the 'others' at whom Newman stares in *1883* only at its end. This repositioning gives, in the grammatical *rapprochement* of 'the others, she', his shocked sense of the relation revealed as existing between 'her' and 'them'. The *NYE* arrangement gives a strongly segregated clause to her 'acting with the others', isolating 'planted' as a verb in the singular for what she alone can do to him. The use of 'unnaturally' even in a case where she reverts to family ('natural') ties catches the poignancy of Newman's miscalculation of her nature; 'suddenly' prepares the violence of the image as a correlative of the abruptness of the (not physically violent) revelation. James's revision returns for its first image through *1883* to the 'matter' of the scene, the relative positions of Newman and his betrothed—thinking of a possible violent physical cause for what is a physical response—and then in the *NYE* gives equal and stunning weight to the collaboration and the deep wound, which come to the same thing.

HMS often affords such an opportunity to trace the imaginative development of a final expression, to appreciate the recurrence of attention which seeks out the closest correspondence of sentence to experience. The usefulness of its evidence when its revisions diverge from those of the *NYE* may serve only as an incidental aid, a special cue to reflection on the general process which produces the text of the *NYE*. Yet the freedom with which the *NYE* often rehandles readings in *HMS* that already represent one layer of revision marks James's persistent concentration on the object, his investment in the imaginative 'matter' of character, situation, and plot.

iii.   A Range of Revision: I

The *NYE* revisions of *The American* make changes in actions; in the words spoken by characters and the substance of what they say (which count as events in the story); in tones and relations and emotions and responses. The customary distinction between matter and substance is severely tested here, in the significant alteration of what would usually be thought the matter rather than the surface of the action—the movements, gestures, words, and attitudes of the characters.

It is indeed philosophically impossible to maintain the distinctions between matter and surface, action and wording. While the wording of fiction expresses its actions, the actions themselves express its action.

After a story has been written, its primary intentions elaborated into a finished form, every element, including the plot, is in some sense expressive. A revision of an event in the story can therefore still be thought of as a revision of expression, because every part of the book is an expression of the whole.

Even so, the philosophical categories of the critic need to be adjusted to recognize the imaginative requirements of the novelist. James's secretary, Theodora Bosanquet, describes his feeling his occasional crossings of the notional boundary between matter and surface as transgressions:

> He allowed himself few freedoms with any recorded appearances or actions, although occasionally the temptation to correct a false gesture, to make it 'right', was too strong to be resisted.[14]

This is a difficult area. We can at any rate feel that the justification of a change in gesture will require the measuring of the particular act against the general action: and since the contribution made by single acts to the whole lies in their effect, the relevant criterion for such changes will want them better to produce that effect as intended, more happily to fulfil their functions.

The example offered by Theodora Bosanquet comes from *The American* and illustrates this principle: Newman meets his possible mother-in-law for the first time.

> Valentin presented his friend, and Newman walked up to the old lady by the fire and shook hands with her ... Madame de Bellegarde looked hard at him, and returned his hand-shake with a sort of British positiveness which reminded him that she was the daughter of the Earl of St. Dunstan's (*1883*, i, 143).

> Valentin presented his friend, and Newman came sufficiently near to the old lady by the fire to take in that she would offer him no handshake—so that he knew he had the air of waiting, and a little like a customer in a shop, to see what she *would* offer ... Madame de Bellegarde looked hard at him and refused what she did refuse with a sort of British positiveness which reminded him that she was the daughter of the Earl of St. Dunstans (*NYE* ii. 181–2).[15]

---

[14] *Henry James at Work*, p. 14. The 'bargain' James describes the fictions as offering, which will make revision possible, requires him to entertain the illusion that they are not fictions: 'Actively believe in us and then you'll see!' (*LC* ii. 1334.)

[15] The idea of a refusal to shake hands could have come from *The Aspern Papers*, written in 1888 between *1883* and the *NYE*—there the narrator asks Juliana 'May I shake hands with you, on our contract?' and she 'only said coldly, "I belong to a time when that was not the custom"' (*1888*, i. 48–9). But it seems more likely that the unfriendliness draws on Newman's introduction to Urbain de Bellegarde five pages

Theodora Bosanquet comments that

> There were good reasons why the Marquise should have denied Newman a welcoming handshake. Her attitude throughout the book was to be consistently hostile and should never have been compromised by the significantly British grip. Yet it is almost shocking to see her snatching back her first card after playing it for so many years.[16]

The near-shock here connects with an honourable sense of the finality of print; yet the revision demonstrates the continuing life of the action in the author's imagination, the workings of which brought us the handshake and its manner in the first text. *1883* gives us Newman's presumption and (with a puzzling delay about 'returned his hand-shake', since when people shake hands with you, you mostly shake hands with them) Madame de Bellegarde's manner of taking it. The *NYE* prepares us for larger refusals in the action. Newman's intuitive knowledge, tracking James's sense on close rereading of the likely fate of such an overture, brings him up short and leaves him 'waiting' on the other side of a dash which has him cut off from any response to his intention, facing him with a disturbing blank. 'He knew he had the air' renders a finer consciousness on his part of the effect he produces, a sympathetic embarrassment at the situation; and with a turn of wit the Marquise's 'sort of British positiveness' applies in the *NYE* not to what she does but to what she doesn't do, what she sturdily negates. The tidiest criterion of equivalent effects might here be satisfied with the ingenious leading back of the syntax to Newman's same recollection about the old woman's ancestry; but more generally the principle of referring effects to their context in the larger scheme, the 'matter' or intention of the work as a whole, exacts no such precision.

Thus when Newman confronts his enemies in the Parc Monceau towards the end, the Marquise's more or less unchanged stony reaction

---

later. There: ' "I am delighted to know Mr. Newman", said the Marquis, with a low bow, but without offering his hand. "He is the old woman at second-hand", Newman said to himself, as he returned M. de Bellegarde's greeting' (*1883*, i. 148). The *NYE* has 'said the Marquis with an unaccompanied salutation', and 'Newman reflected with the sense of having his health drunk from an empty glass' (*NYE* ii. 187). The *1883* move from 'without offering his hand' to 'the old woman at second-hand' seems to suggest to James a further possible relation within the chapter (Newman's thought here becoming aptly an echo of his sense of the *mother*'s refusal). Newman in the *NYE* doesn't bow back.

[16] *Henry James at Work*, p. 15.

to his threat has on him quite a different effect—he has quite a contrary affect—in *1883* and the *NYE*:

Newman had an exasperating feeling that she would get the better of him still; he would not have believed it possible that he could so utterly fail to be touched by the sight of a woman (criminal or other) in so tight a place (*1883*, ii. 171–2).

He felt the pang of a conviction that she would get the better of him still, and he wouldn't have been himself if he could wholly fail to be touched by the sight of a woman (criminal or other) in so tight a place (*NYE* ii. 491–2).

In *1883* the inclusion of his 'exasperating feeling' in the same sentence as his uncharacteristic lack of emotion has the effect of an unbalancing *non sequitur*, a step out of line (though presumably the second half of the sentence gives the vindictive condition for his being exasperated in the first half). The *NYE* instead connects the two halves of the sentence (with a consequential 'and'), making it a correlative to his 'pang' that a generous and gallant accessibility to pity is rooted in his character.

James's reversal in this revision makes use in expression of its own logic: 'he wouldn't have been himself'; the author's sense that the *1883* scene's pitiless revenger is not really Newman is transformed into Newman's sense—preparing us for his final resignation and pity—that it is not in him to carry through his plan. This case, then, gives another direct reversal of an element in *1883*, but with a freedom that takes the pressure of James's sense of the action, of how the novel's ending needs to be set up, of the sensibility in Newman that we need to feel progressively discovered to be prepared for his final change of heart.

There are several themes and relations in *The American* which undergo consistent revision of a kind close to 're-writing' in the light of such larger consideration, like the friendship with Valentin, which becomes more warmly affectionate and less ironically edged. The *NYE* reworks the development of their relation with striking thoroughness in Chapters 7 and 8. The central relationship of Newman and Claire de Cintré, which the Preface frankly acknowledges was insufficiently treated in *1883*, receives some of the *NYE*'s most consistent rethinking, the fresh investigation of an intimacy that is still restricted by an ominously unbridged distance.[17] The hero's bearing as 'The American', too, alters significantly in the *NYE* for an intelligent geniality about

---

[17] The first pages of ch. 13 offer a clear example of this extensive remeasurement, as on a smaller scale does the expansion of *1883*, ii. 68 into *NYE* ii. 356–7.

things that comes over as less of an insensitive self-satisfaction than in *1883*. This density of substantial change is unique to the case of *The American*, and follows from James's sense (outlined in the Preface) of the implausibility of the Bellegardes' behaviour, of Claire's psychology, and so on; but as revision on a large scale it can still conform to the notion of a reseeing of original 'matter', even when not creatively stimulated by the local wordings of *1883*. The notion of an original 'matter' here takes James as far as the confident reappropriation of the function and movement of a long passage or chapter. However long their extension and variation, though, James's revisions always return to the original body of the text; the clue for James through this apparent labyrinth being the relation of things to Newman, through whose point of view the action is refracted—whose experience is the 'matter' of the novel.

James's developed art of fiction, the result of long and reflective experience of language, concerns itself with the close linguistic notation of the experience of characters by means of the common sense of language, the associative life of its parts. In revising, the question of expression, of the detail by which a text conveys meaning, is thrown into relief by the discrepancy between James's present 'mode of motion' and those of his past self. The previous expression James made of an element in a work is what, in his rereading, gives rise to his repossession of the 'matter'—and the sense he has reseen can then be re-expressed. This re-expression, because arising through the previous expression, stands in a close imaginative relation to it.

Often the revision teases out some implication from the earlier text, develops a latent suggestion, seeks out the possibilities beneath (or rather *in*) its expressive surface. In *The Princess Casamassima*, for example, 'Mademoiselle Vivier's son was a tiny particle',[18] expressing the short Hyacinth's sense of not counting for much, grows into a fuller metaphor of invisibility: 'Mademoiselle Vivier's son, lacking all the social dimensions, was scarce a perceptible person at all' (*NYE* vi. 6). The 'growth' of which James speaks as producing the revisions need not therefore be thought of as the maturing in his unconscious mind of every sentence in his *œuvre* in the time between its writing and the *NYE*. The development of the second nature of his 'late style' is a necessary condition of the *NYE* revision of his earlier works, but the revision is a distinct process. Two related but separate histories

[18] *The Princess Casamassima*, 3 vols., London, 1886, ii. 98.

are being invoked by the ambiguous invitation to criticism in the Preface to *The Golden Bowl*:

What it would be really interesting, and I dare say admirably difficult, to go into would be the very history of this effect of experience; the history, in other words, of the growth of the immense array of terms, perceptional and expressional, that, after the fashion I have indicated, in sentence, passage and page, simply looked over the heads of the standing terms—or perhaps rather, like alert winged creatures, perched on those diminished summits and aspired to a clearer air (*LC* ii. 1332–3).

The history of the 'growth' may be James's personal history as a writer—the development of his style over the years; but it may also be the process by which the revisions came into being. This growth of the immense array of revised terms takes place in the act of revision, in the reseeing of old stories 'in other words' (James also puns on the phrase a page before).

James's long sentence twice revises itself—first taking up 'history' for qualification, and then returning on its own simile about revision to find 'perhaps rather' an adjusted alternative, a closer version of the process. This second turn redefines the difference between a new wording and its predecessor: the figure of bodily height, by which the second term stands separate from the first and has grown to a tallness that grants it a better view, gives way to a more co-operative idea of the relation, in which the second term's advantage of height is reached by a flight (of the imagination) that takes off from the helpful perch of the former and strives from it to attain a higher clarity ('air' punning on the medium of life and 'artistic presentation'). The former of these two figures, indeed, is perched on and extended by the second.

James's witty sense of other expressions that are possible finds a 'perch' in the 'standing terms', consisting of the whole set of relations belonging to those terms: the multitude of other meanings, other contexts, different syntactic relations, puns, rhymes, alliterations, metaphors, and images—of 'other words'—that they bring within imaginative range. These 'other words' are sometimes those of another writer. In the last scene Newman throws the incriminating document, his possible weapon against the Bellegardes, into the fire.

Mrs. Tristram sat with her embroidery-needle suspended. 'What is that paper?' she asked.

Newman, leaning against the fireplace, stretched his arms and drew a longer breath than usual. Then, after a moment, 'I can tell you now', he said (*1883*, ii. 206).

Mrs. Tristram sat with her embroidery-needle suspended. 'What in the world is that?'

Leaning against the chimney-piece, he seemed to grasp its ledge with force and to draw his breath for a moment in pain. But after that, 'I can tell you now', he said (*HMS*, ii (p. 206 changed to p. 207)).

In *NYE* ii. 537, Mrs Tristram's part is exactly the same as in *HMS*: Newman though now seems, remembering, 'to draw his breath a while in pain'.[19] What we can trace here is the building-up and mapping-out of a reminiscence, a serious play on the dying words of Hamlet to Horatio:

> If thou didst ever hold me in thy heart,
> Absent thee from felicity a while,
> And in this harsh world draw thy breath in pain
> To tell my story . . .   (v. ii. 298–301)

From *1883* 'drew', 'breath', and 'tell' strike and ignite James with the sense of this other ending; *HMS* matches Shakespeare's 'world' to Mrs Tristram's question and adjusts for a proximity of 'draw' and 'breath'; and the last refinement of equivalence comes in with 'a while', remembering the felicity which Horatio is to miss for a sense of Newman's own painfully deprived survival in this world he has now learned to be so harsh. The relation between the words and the meaning here works out, by association, intricately and dialectically, to an achieved poise: a drawing-together through *Hamlet* of feelings in the novel about endings, of the bitter experience of the world and of waste, and of the difficulty for Newman of expressing his final resignation. The allusion rises from a foundation already laid in *1883*, but there only latent—though even there it perhaps marks a consciousness of the end of *Hamlet* to match the explicit consciousness of its beginning at *1883*, i. 22, where to Newman's pleasure 'A vague sense that more answers were possible than his philosophy had hitherto dreamt of had already taken possession of him.'

The structure of associations that emerges in these examples refers to an extrinsic literary fact about the words involved (that Shakespeare has famously and powerfully combined them). Mostly James's recognitions of the latent draw on an intrinsic wealth of suggestion in the

---

[19] And then 'But presently he said: "I can tell you now"' (*NYE* ii. 537).

wordings of *1883* and then, in turn, in the other wordings *1883* prompts. Thus in Chapter 7 there is a characterization of Valentin de Bellegarde, Newman's new friend:

But all that he was he was by instinct and not by theory, and the amiability of his character was so great that certain of the aristocratic virtues, which in some aspects seem rather brittle and trenchant, acquired in his application of them an extreme geniality (*1883*, i. 105).

HMS hardly touches this (or the succeeding sentences, which are all retouched in the *NYE*)—'rather' just becomes 'both' (*HMS* i. 105). In the *NYE*:

But he attained his best values by instinct rather than by theory, and the amiability of his character was so great that certain of the aristocratic virtues lost, at his touch, their rigour without losing, as it were, their temper (*NYE* ii. 134).

The transformation here involves a rethinking of the conditions of aristocratic virtues and an appreciation of Valentin's worth, taking up and retouching the relations of the implied metaphor—the suggestion of a possible rigid but vulnerable cutting edge that is made by 'brittle and trenchant' but then confusingly neglected at the end in 'extreme geniality'. Where 'his application of them' sounded methodical and heavy only to be surprised into 'extreme geniality' at the end of *1883*'s sentence, 'at his touch' suggests the gentle exactitude of instinct. *1883* gave the virtues two possible defects and then ·an 'acquisition' of something else. The *NYE*, considering that a blade (the undeclared image in *1883*) either cuts or uselessly doesn't, so that Valentin comes badly out of this version, finds a related, non-incisive idea—that of the combined flexibility and strength of steel. It takes the acquiring of *1883* and replaces it with, successively, the loss of a defect and the retention of a quality, a fine balance of relaxation and firmness. For 'brittle', the word denoting an inherent defect of some forms of the virtues, we get its converse in respect of metals, 'temper', pointedly at the conclusion of the sentence (as a tempering of the excessive 'extreme' of *1883*). In the novel as a whole the other Bellegardes are shown displaying 'rigour', but not being 'brittle' (the vulnerable side of 'rigour')—and 'rigour' can also be 'trenchant'. The final pun on 'losing ... their temper' imagines another less flexible way to lose rigour—to snap. These considerations all shed light then on the bearing of Valentin's mother and brother in the book. From the same general analogy as in *1883* James derives for the *NYE* a complex set of relations (of ease to strength, character to virtue, bending to breaking, the inherent to the manifest, the extreme to the moderate, and so on), using the reflections prompted by the standing terms as the elements for a new combination more respectful in its account of Valentin's relation to his own nobility.

The linguistic reshaping by which James's revision operates can be described, then, as a process of creating meanings as well as of expressing them, as a practised seeking-out and measurement of the relations of which meaning consists. When Newman goes to Notre Dame in the final chapter for his ambiguous moment of renunciation, his physical arrival undergoes a reseeing that elicits, in other words, a perspective on his approaching spiritual act. In all versions 'he crossed one of the bridges'; then he

stood a moment in the empty place before the great cathedral (*1883*, ii. 204);

stood a moment in the empty square that makes the great front clear (*HMS* ii. 204);

paused in the voided space that makes the great front clear (*NYE* ii. 533).

'Place' translates back from the French to 'square', and then 'square' and 'place' compact into 'space',[20] 'voided' enforcing the act of emptying (as against the fact of emptiness); this change from *HMS* to the *NYE* adjusts on its part to the flickering animation of the cathedral given by *HMS*'s 'that makes the great front clear'. This primarily means 'allows us to see clearly the cathedral's façade'; but the episode to come partly makes something clear to Newman, while the poetic (and French) sense of 'front' as brow or face,[21] here applying via a

---

[20] There is in ch. 8 another verbal evolution of which *HMS* allows us to follow the imaginative morphology. Valentin calls his sister in *1883* 'tall, thin, light, imposing, and gentle' (*1883*, i. 116); in *HMS* this becomes 'tall, slight, imposing, gentle' (*HMS* i. 116); in the *NYE* it turns to 'tall, slim, imposing, gentle' (*NYE* ii. 149). 'Thin' and 'light' turn to 'slight'; then '*sli*ght' and '*im*posing' run together into 'slim'.

[21] The associations waiting for James in the early versions often need only a slight turn. In *1883*, when Newman comes to the Bellegardes' château at Fleurières he finds Mrs Bread waiting for him. 'Her face, as usual, looked as hopelessly blank as the tide-smoothed sea-sand, and her black garments seemed of an intenser sable' (*1883*, ii. 121). *HMS* changes only 'seemed . . . sable', and its change is retained by the *NYE*: 'Her face, as usual, looked hopelessly blank, like the tide-smoothed sea-sand, and her black garments hung as heavy as if soaked in salt tears' (*NYE* ii. 425). As with 'place' and 'front' in the Notre Dame example, there is a French sense about here from *1883*, an odd tie-up of 'sea-sand' and 'sable'. The *NYE* takes up rather the notion of the relation of tide and sand as a metaphor for the effect of misery on human beings, extending the tide to seem to soak (with another imaginative reach) the garments already associated

pathetic fallacy to the cathedral and turning 'clear' into a word for the non-architectural relief of lined anxiety, intimates a correspondence between an emptying and an end to trouble that anticipates Newman's secular revelation of the peace brought by a negative capability. The linguistic process here represents a higher flight, perhaps, from a lower perch, a more diminished summit, than in my other examples; yet it equally comes about through striking up from relations there in the matter of the words of *1883* to a sense of the general relations—the place in plot and theme—of each particular sentence in *The American*.

iv.   A Range of Revision: II

The manner and extent of James's revising suggests how fully close attention to his words may be rewarded. While writing *The American* early in 1876 James was also sending regular notes on Parisian matters to the New York *Tribune*. In his remarks on Meissonier's painting of 'The Battle of Friedland' we can see (assuming his constant pre-occupation with the resemblance of picture to novel) a basis for his developing sense of works of art as organic wholes none of whose parts is insignificant. James writes of 'the great general impression which, first and foremost, it is the duty of an excellent picture to give you', and complains of Meissonier's handling of each individual figure that 'He feels under no necessity to do anything with him, to place him in any complex relation with anything else, to make any really imaginative uses of him.'[22] Praising Munkacsy's 'Intérieur d'Atelier' some months later, he specially admires the harmony of particular and general.

There is plenty of detail, and yet it is all detail in such warm, fluid juxtaposition that you are conscious of it only through your general impression of richness.[23]

The impulse to place a figure in complex imaginative relations fits James's account in the Preface of his original discovery of circumstances for Newman's crisis ('the who? the what? the where? the when? the why? the how?' (*LC* ii. 1055)); the novel, that is, was written

by 'sable' with the sand. This balances the blankness with a sense of what lies beneath it.

[22] *Parisian Sketches: Letters to the New York Tribune 1875–1876*, ed. with an intro. by Leon Edel and Ilse Dusoir Lind, London, 1958, p. 38 (22 Jan. 1876). (Repr. also in *The Painter's Eye*, ed. John L. Sweeney, London, 1956, p. 112.)

[23] *Parisian Sketches*, p. 144 (27 May 1876).

in 1875–6 with the idea of an organic unity between particular details and general impression, the notion of a 'warm, fluid juxtaposition' in which, presumably, every sentence, paragraph, and chapter would variously consort with the governing movement of the whole.

At the time of the NYE James's sense of the meaning of a novel and of what is possible to the form has developed further than this, but is not essentially dissimilar; the primacy of an individual point of view in it (as with *Roderick Hudson*) offers the revising author a continuity of general intention though not of style and execution, and the selection of detail in scene and episode holds up a structure of dramatic inter-relations and possibilities that serves the James of 1906 as a 'perch' for imaginative ascents. Such an aesthetic as that of 1876 offers a chance, that is, to the extensions of a new sense of treatment which wishes 'to multiply in any given connexion all the possible sources of entertainment' (*LC* ii. 1338). One way of multiplying these is to sharpen the sense of connections within the work, the fluidity of juxtaposition.

When Newman inadvertently forces the Marquise into the giving of the celebratory ball, it is threateningly noted in the NYE narration that

on this occasion he failed to catch a thin sharp eyebeam, as cold as a flash of steel, which passed between Madame de Bellegarde and the Marquis . . . (*NYE* ii. 285).

In *1883* he had 'failed to notice a certain delicate glance which passed' (*1883*, ii. 14; *HMS* was as the *NYE*, except that it had 'the flash', *HMS* ii. 14). The revision's steel image reworks an image that occurs 111 pages further on in the *1883* text to describe the effect of Newman's revelation, to the same pair, that their son and brother Valentin apologized for their bad conduct on his death-bed:

A quick flush leaped into the faces of Madame de Bellegarde and her son, and they exchanged a glance like a twinkle of steel (*1883*, ii. 125).

At that point in the novel the NYE brings in an alternative and triumphant image:

A quick flush leaped into the charged faces before him—it was like a jolt of full glasses, making them spill their wine (*NYE* ii. 431).

As Isadore Traschen points out,[24] *this* goes directly back to, and completes, an image used by Newman to Mrs Tristram about the Bellegardes (and retained in the *NYE*):

'They make me want to joggle their elbows and force them to spill their wine' (*1883*, ii. 12; *NYE* ii. 282).

The wine image is carried 113 pages forward for the fulfilling of Newman's expressed wish; taken with the cancellation and replacement of the steel image 111 pages back it testifies to a far-ranging comparative habit of imaginative readjustment. James feels the idea of threat in the steel image more appropriate for the immediate build-up to the Bellegardes' rupture with Newman; the perverse jostling impulse, more pointed because of Newman's intervening wound, is now satisfyingly answered in an echoing suggestion of the American's desire for revenge.

Within a chapter, more often, James's close grasp of the structure and proportions and timing of expression yields him a flexible freedom in reseeing a piece of action, so that in Chapter 12, where Newman gets the family licence for his courtship, 'receive his passport from M. de Bellegarde' (*1883*, i. 173–4) becomes 'receive, as he might say, this prodigious person's damned permission' (*NYE* ii. 223); and then ten pages later (as the basis of a joke about 'red tape') Valentin's 'Well, you have got your permit' (*1883*, i. 183) becomes 'Well, you've taken out your passport' (*NYE* ii. 236). In such cases of James's long reach we could distinguish the removal of words, phrases, and images from one context in *1883* to another in the *NYE* (something the reader of the *NYE* text will have no evidence to recognize as happening), from the giving of a new connection with all its terms in the *NYE*.

The syntax and vocabulary of causes and effects often introduce further approximations to each other of the elements of *1883* or syntheses drawn from the materials of *1883*. In Newman's eloquent declaration of his love, for instance, the closer logic of the *NYE*

[24] Isadore Traschen, 'Henry James and the Art of Revision', *Philological Quarterly*, 35 (Jan. 1956), 45. In another article, 'James's Revisions of the Love Affair in "The American"' (pp. 60–1), he draws attention to the way in which an image brought in by the *NYE* for Claire de Cintré's response to Newman is echoed by another revision over 250 pages later. It comes in first as 'the slow flushing of the east at dawn' (*NYE* ii. 271), and then returns in 'a white tower that flushed more and more as with a light of dawn' (*NYE* ii. 524).

brings in a reciprocity to take him forward into a new paragraph of persuasion:

Then she sat down in silence, and her attitude seemed a consent that he should say more. She might almost be liking it.

'Why should you say it's impossible you should marry?' he therefore continued ... (*NYE* ii. 173).

'She might almost be liking it' and 'therefore', the fact which strikes Newman and the reasoning from it which impels his resumption, are additions to *1883* (i. 136) which show him intelligently and sympathetically reacting. The *NYE* renders his pressing on more considerate: the new logic involves the possibility of his stopping. At the start of Chapter 8 a *NYE* revision (after the *HMS* stage) brings in an idea of cause and effect to match and provoke one there already in *1883*. Valentin, who has come to Newman's apartments, remarks that Newman has never asked him anything about his sister, Claire de Cintré. In *1883*:

'I know that very well.'
'If it is because you don't trust me, you are very right', said Bellegarde. 'I can't talk of her rationally. I admire her too much' (*1883*, i. 116).

In the *NYE*

'Well, I guess I know why.'
'If it's because you don't trust me, you're very right', said Valentin ... (*NYE* ii. 149).

In the *NYE* 'If it's because' seems a natural answer to 'I know why' in the now preceding sentence: this in itself enables an easier intercourse, but we can also trace on this minute scale the dexterity with which James takes 'well' from Newman's self-congratulating 'very well' of *1883* and turns it into a modest introductory note of unassertiveness—and likewise colloquially tempers the unyielding certainty of 'I know' with the genial relaxation of 'I guess' in a fluid juxtaposition. The sureness of James's retouching of these five to six words of speech constitutes a quiet triumph of characterization, the remeasured creation of a proper stimulus to Valentin's amicable response. At another end of the register from the 200-page-spanning echoes of phrase and image, such attention to nuance impresses the reader with a sense of what can properly be attended to, of an expanded possibility of tone and meaning.

v. Reading Experience

It may seem that James's ramifying intelligence in revision of the possibilities of interrelation risks top-loading the book with an authorial wit (in T. S. Eliot's sense) that cannot be sustained by, exceeds the understandings of, the characters of *1883*. What I want to suggest, on the contrary, is that the revisions, by means of the indirect free style, mostly re-economize James's intelligence of the story's relations *as* the characters', and particularly as Newman's. Such a process—an increase in ironic consciousness of relations—might even so seem to break with the genre of the book, if we take James literally at his word when in the Preface to it he extensively discusses 'romance' as a medium presenting experience without 'the inconvenience of a *related*, a measurable state' (*LC* ii. 1064); but then the Preface's emphasis on this is making an ironic point about his having been unconscious that he was participating in romance: 'I had been plotting arch-romance without knowing it' (*LC* ii. 1057)—that is, he had been intending something else.

The Jamesian International novel has necessarily an oblique relation to romance as James defines it; since romance is often associated with the foreign, and the foreign offers conditions of which an American (here) has no measure and to which he has at first no relation. Newman's experience can to this extent be romantic without *The American*'s losing touch with reality—the reality of a clash of nationalities. The romantic scenes and events of the story of 1876—the melodrama of psychological influence, past crimes, threats, and convents—are both the real matter of another culture and the stuff of the traditional genre romance, so that in responding to them as romance and unreal Newman shows his nationally bounded sense of reality. Discovering the relatively variable nature of standards, Newman becomes a sadder and wiser man, another kind of new man, in a harsh world he did not at the beginning recognize. When he visits the convent where his ex-fiancée is confined, he finds he cannot imagine the life there—he thinks of it despite himself as cheerful.

And yet he knew the case was otherwise; only at present it was not a reality to him. It was too strange and too mocking to be real; it was like a page torn out of a romance, with no context in his own experience (*1883*, ii. 161).

In the *NYE* 'romance' alters to convey Newman's impatience with it: 'a page torn out of some superannuated unreadable book' (*NYE* ii. 478).

A feeling for the comparative justice done to modern sensibilities and experience by modern forms and genres emerges by contrast from the constant references to superannuated genres in *1883*, often amplified to bring home this point in the *NYE*. When Newman discovers from the Tristrams that the Bellegardes may try to sell Madame de Cintré in marriage a second time, he responds, critically, 'It is like something in a play' (*1883*, i. 87); *HMS* provides a contraction (*HMS* i. 87); and then the *NYE* relaxes the utterance and yet sharpens its critical edge, giving 'It's like something in a regular old play' (*NYE* ii. 111), where 'regular' and 'old' both double as bland American colloquialisms and as expressions, through the metaphor of dramatic convention, of a wondering sense of the survival of rules from the past. When Valentin gives Newman his account of his sister's first forced marriage, he too has this feeling about it—that 'It was a chapter for a novel' (*1883*, i. 119), and then in the *NYE*, with a sense of his miscasting in life, that 'It was a first act for a melodrama' (*NYE* ii. 152). The *NYE* brings in a new literary touchstone for Valentin when he reminds Newman of his warning that the Bellegarde family is 'very strange' (*1883*, i. 128); *1883*'s 'I give you warning again. We are!' becomes 'Well, I give you warning again. We're fit for a museum or a Balzac novel' (*NYE* ii. 162; 'Well, . . .' arriving after *HMS*).

This painful self-consciousness of incongruity, this feeling of being part of a pointless superseded action, informs Newman's experience at Valentin's death-bed in a Swiss village after the outmoded but fatal duel. In *1883*, seated in the sickroom,

He seemed to be playing a part, mechanically, in a lugubrious comedy (*1883*, ii. 98).

In the *NYE*

He felt as if he were now playing a part, mechanically, in the most lugubrious of comedies (*NYE* ii. 396).

'Comedy' can also mean just play-acting, and the superlative 'most lugubrious of comedies' (brought in after *HMS*) suggests the ghastliness of unfunny farce. The *NYE* 'now' conveys a new contrast with two earlier points in the same revised chapter, one on the previous page where Newman restlessly takes a walk 'for two or three hours' to pass the time:

The day seemed terribly long (*1883*, ii. 97).

The day had the length of some interminable tragedy (*HMS* ii. 97).

The day had, in its regulated gloom, the length of some interminable classic tragedy (*NYE* ii. 395).

HMS gives the contrast with the feeling of sad comedy a page later; it picks up from 'terribly' an association with the terror and pity of tragedy, and starts to measure the kind of length of time involved (the genre invoked represents twenty-four-hour spans, but often so grindingly that it seems they will never end, even though they last a mere two or three hours). The *NYE*, as with 'a regular old play', brings in both the sense of rules (the unities) and of the ancient. At the start of the chapter Newman arrives at the Swiss station and meets one of Valentin's seconds in the duel, who greets him. Newman replies in *1883*, 'You are M. de Bellegarde's friend?' (*1883*, ii. 85)—a good question. An insertion mark in *HMS* allows us to see that James first made this 'You've been acting for the Count?' before from this perch taking a metaphorical leap to a further ironic phrase: 'You've been acting, in this tragedy, for the Count?' (*HMS* ii. 85; *NYE* ii. 380.) The pause given by the intervening clause grimly puns on the unreality to Newman of the real events in which the second has played his part.

These genres are unsympathetic for Newman—they don't accommodate his feelings—and the unhappiness they cause him here follows up his blither sense of their oddity (in the *NYE*) at the Bellegardes' ball. There his inadequate sense of his situation is suggested by a revision which brings in the idea of the world about him as an obscure text to be interpreted. The members of the nobility at the ball are far from beautiful.

It is a pity, nevertheless, that Newman had not been a physiognomist, for a great many of the faces were irregularly agreeable, expressive, and suggestive (*1883*, ii. 37).

The *NYE* takes the suggestion in 'expressive' (I omit the *HMS* middle stage):

It was a pity for our friend, nevertheless, that he had not been a physiognomist, for these mobile masks, much more a matter of wax than of bronze, were the picture of a world and the vivid translation, as might have seemed to him, of a text that had had otherwise its obscurities (*NYE* ii. 317).

Two pages later James revises correspondingly Newman's sense of a set of introductions to some noblemen, gentlemen who bow when named: 'they were all what are called in France *beaux noms*' (*1883*, ii.

39). In the *NYE* 'these pronouncements again affected Newman as some enumeration of the titles of books, of the performers on playbills, of the items of indexes' (*NYE* ii. 320). In the first of these revisions the remote hypothesis of 'had had' enforces a disparity for the reader between Newman's possible understanding and his actual understanding; the metaphor of translation for faces conveys the uninterpretable foreignness to him of this *monde*.[25] In the second the metaphorical description of the gentlemen themselves as '*beaux noms*' gives rise to Newman's feeling in the *NYE* (an intelligent feeling about his failure of understanding) that the people he is meeting are *just* names, some kind of irrelevant print that doesn't express anything for him, some other sort of writing 'with no context in his own experience'.

Such ideas of uncongenial texts and genres relate to the characters' searching sense of contexts and relations that *would* be appropriate. The outdated modes are played off against Newman's and Mrs Tristram's conception about his marriage and its imaginative beauty (what she calls at the end 'the highest flight ever taken by a tolerably rich imagination!' (*NYE* ii. 513))). The work of expression going on in the flexible commerce between these analogies of different representations indicates an ironically ranging awareness of situation on the part of *The American*'s characters (especially Newman) which corresponds to that of its revising author. The extensive seeking-out and inclusion of significant relations, the interpretative play of mind over points of view, which informs James's imaginative practice in revision, is a linguistic process analogous to what happens dramatically in the course of Newman's ill-fated attempt to adapt his idea of the world to an intercourse with the Parisian *monde*. James's subject-matter, New-

---

[25] The novel could be seen as the story of Newman's discovery that value is relative, that the proud and narrow Parisian aristocracy assumes the world to be the same as its *monde*. The ancient M. de la Rochefidèle tells Newman at an earlier stage that he once saw an American, and the progressive revisions refine our sense of his sense of these relations: ' "The great Dr. Franklin", said M. de la Rochefidèle. "Of course I was very young. He was received very well in our *monde*" ' (*1883*, i. 180). ' "The great Dr. Franklin", said M. de la Rochefidèle. "Of course I was very, very young. I believe I had but just come into the world. He was received very well in our *monde*" ' (*HMS* i. 180). ' "The great Dr. Franklin. Of course I was very very young. I believe I had but just come into the world. He was received very well *dans le nôtre*" ' (*NYE* ii. 232). In the last chapter Tom Tristram, an American who lives blithely and narrowly in the American expatriate circle in Paris, offers the permanently excluded Newman, with tactless insistence (only in the *NYE*) the latest news 'as to what had been going on in "*notre monde à nous*, you know" ' (*NYE* ii. 535).

man's education about self and world, and the development in him of an acute consciousness of the cultural particularity of self learned by relations with others, consorts, that is, with the stylistic business of expression, the building and refinement and readjustment of sentences as elements in a sense of things. The revision of the novel's expression takes Newman's point of view and grants him the intelligence of its own flexibility, bringing our experience of reading sympathetically close to Newman's reading of experience.[26]

vi. Rereadings of Experience

I have tried to show how James's revisions perch on the sense of the *1883* expression, returning to an original 'matter' in order to come back with a heightened sense, a new expression which extends the previous thought by a turn or a negation or a comparison. When the consciousness is a character's, then the extension is that character's also. The 'few extra inches' that James says in the Preface he has smuggled into Newman's 'measurements', in other words, often give that character a quality akin to T. S. Eliot's account of wit—a consciousness, in the expression of every experience, not only of other kinds of experience that are possible but here also of other expressions that are possible. James's impulse in revision is to make the other expression or experience that is possible (in the NYE text) that from *1883*; to carry the perch into the new flight. This is not to say that the new NYE phrasing depends for its meaning on a knowledge of *1883*, or refers explicitly to *1883* as such; rather that in comparing the texts we see the way in which the possibility represented by *1883*—of fact, of attitude, of expression, of image—is often invoked by the NYE as an element in a new process of thought which grows out of it.

In the NYE Newman's threats against the Bellegarde family seem less effectual than in *1883*. When he threatens Urbain with the knowledge given him by the dying Valentin, a revision expresses the noble-

---

[26] It may be objected that part of the point of *1883* is Newman's transcultural stupidity, and that if he weren't so innocently arrogant and provincial on his side the Bellegardes would have no reason to be viciously arrogant and provincial on theirs. James's remeasurements in the NYE, though, intensify the poignancy of Newman's betrayal by eliminating all his inessential provocations, diminishing the aggressive certainty of his tone (as in the 'Well, I guess I know why' example) and curbing his apparent self-satisfaction ('I am not intellectual', *1883*, i. 35) to a modest self-respect ('I don't come up to my own standard of culture', NYE ii. 45).

man's response in a new way, but with reference to what was said in
1883:

The Marquis almost succeeded in looking untroubled; the breaking up of the
ice in his handsome countenance was an operation that was necessarily
gradual. But Newman's mildly-syllabled argumentation seemed to press, and
press, and presently he averted his eyes. He stood some moments, reflecting.
　'My brother told you this', he said, looking up (*1883*, ii. 128).

Urbain's face looked to him now like a mirror, very smooth fine glass, breathed
upon and blurred; but what he would have liked still better to see was a
spreading, disfiguring crack. There was something of that, to be sure, in the
grimace with which the Marquis brought out: 'My brother regaled you with
this infamy?' (*NYE* ii. 434)

'Still better' refers to the appearance *1883* described as beginning but
makes it something that can—unfortunately—only be described as a
wish; the *NYE* takes up the ideas of the 'handsome countenance' and
of the surface of ice, combines them into the simile of the face and the
mirror (an image suggested—via 'reflecting'—by Urbain's self-regard),
but then does not resee in fact even the 'necessarily gradual' breaking
up of the ice that Newman wants. Urbain's facial 'grimace' realizes
momentarily the 'disfiguring crack' Newman hopes for, but then his
next remark gives away less ground than in *1883*. The *NYE* here
uses *1883* to separate Newman's wish from his actual perception—
rendering Newman's own intelligent sense of a contrast between what
he wants and what he is really getting, of a disappointing simulation
of equanimity on the Marquis's part.
　Just below, another negative turn wittily takes away another effect of
the threat: 'M. de Bellegarde gave a shrug' becomes 'M. de Bellegarde's
shoulders declined even a shrug', noting Newman's reduced sense of
what would manifest the success of his blackmail, again by contrasting
what occurs in the reseen action of the story with *1883*. (This recalls
his mother declining to shake Newman's hand in the *NYE*.) What
occurs to James in rereading as a truer note, that is, occurs to Newman
also in a remarkable parallelism of thought: a concordance we can
follow generally, in his speech as well as his flow of ideas. Still on the
same page of *1883* Newman gives an ultimatum to Urbain—'A simple
yes or *no* on paper will do'—and James, rereading, feels the need to
explain it. In the *NYE* Newman too feels the need to make clear what
he is referring to, and to add (alluding to his earlier question in the
NYE: 'What I say has no weight with you?' (*NYE* ii. 434)): 'That will

refer to your attaching or not attaching what we call weight; or better still, to your consenting or refusing to take your hands off Madame de Cintré' (*NYE* ii. 435). 'Or better still'—like 'still better' above—incorporates an equivalent to James's revision into the body of Newman's experience, into the life of the work. A moment later James adds another clause to the ultimatum and Newman further insists that 'I can give you, let me add, no *more* than the time' (*NYE* ii. 435).[27]

If the act of revision is for James a return on himself as author, for the characters it often involves returns on themselves in thinking and speaking, recognitions of another possible kind of experience or expression. One particular notation of the dramatic pause for a still better expression comes back repeatedly in the revisions. Newman is speaking to the Tristrams of his ideal of marriage as a thing 'every man has an equal right to':

'He doesn't have to be born with certain faculties on purpose; he needs only to be a man' (*1883*, i. 39).

In the *NYE*, on the brink of completing his *1883* sentence, Newman takes a meditative moment for reconsideration (this isn't after all a question of being a brute male but of sincerity and authenticity):

'he needs only to be—well, whatever he really is' (*NYE* ii. 50).[28]

Valentin is startled by Newman's unexpected announcement of intentions towards his sister:

'I will not pretend I am not surprised. I am—hugely!' (*1883*, i. 122).

In the *NYE* he swiftly recovers his self-possession and tactfully catches himself up:

'I'll not pretend I'm not—well, impressed. I am—hugely!' (*NYE* ii. 157.)

Newman proposes to Claire de Cintré, who refuses, and he then suggests a trial period of courtship, saying he will wait till she is surer of him.

'Meanwhile you can see more of me and know me better, look at me as a possible husband—as a candidate—and make up your mind' (*1883*, i. 136).

In the *NYE* Newman delicately hesitates as he thinks what the sentence

---

[27] 'Let me add', moreover, comes in as a typed revision on a typed page of *HMS* (p. 128b)—suggesting perhaps that this typed page was dictated by James.
[28] *HMS*, i. 39 has only '—well, whatever he *is*'.

of *1883*, should he go on with it, may unpleasingly mean to her, and acknowledges that by a candid pun before resuming.

'Meanwhile you can see more of me and know me better, look at me in the light—well, of my presumption, yes, but of other things too. You can make up your mind' (*NYE* ii. 172).

'Presumption' reproduces 'as a possible husband', but with a sense of social infraction—'as intrusively arrogant'—that pre-emptively disarms her aloofness before wittily suggesting the possible 'other things' that may weigh ('yes' could be an explicit nod at her possible response to *1883*'s different continuation of the sentence, a possibility of behaviour we can think of Newman as having in mind). In the final chapter Newman has returned to Paris with the intention of dwelling for ever, but his experience in Notre Dame changes his mind, makes him revise his judgement. In *1883* Mrs Bread, by now his housekeeper, is distressed by his order to pack his bags:

'I thought you said that you were going to stay for ever.'
  'I meant that I was going to stay away for ever', said Newman, kindly (*1883*, ii. 205).

In the *NYE* he confesses a mistake (the implausible reply of *1883* wouldn't convince even Mrs Bread):

'Well, I guess I omitted a word. I meant I'm going to stay *away* for ever', he was obliged a little awkwardly to explain (*NYE* ii, 535).

The 'awkwardness' of this change of wording by Newman is a counter-point to the art involved in James's change of wording and his lead-up to it (the art which shows Newman converted from revenge, compelled into inconsistency by the force of some unconscious cere-bration). The word 'well' in these examples—a word which takes the weight of some other saying before introducing a better—allows the characters, as if in dialogue with themselves, to hear the words of *1883* as another possible expression which they can choose to refine on—as part of that business of expression which constitutes a crucial part of the conduct of life. The process of revision as James puts it into effect turns regularly to a superior consciousness, a more lucid wit of situation, for the characters in speaking and for the centre of consciousness (here, Newman) in speaking and thinking: not, that is, a higher consciousness manifested only by its results (these are not polished epigrams, finished in the mind before expression), but rather one demonstrated in the act of ascent, reacting to and reflecting on the dramatic conditions.[29]

The characters' intensified interest in questions of expression does not make them dilettantes; in thought such an interest reflects particularly a concern with defining and grasping relations with others and with oneself, and in speech it particularly involves a concern with forming and sustaining these relations. Both in thought and speech linguistic self-consciousness has therefore an integral connection to plot, to drama, to the moment by moment unfolding of experience. In *The American*, where the action so concentrates on Newman's effects on people and where we mainly follow this process from his point of view (with regular authorial comments to guide us), questions of expression are already strongly charged in *1883*, and provide the *NYE* with much of the energy for its powerful variations.

When Newman first gets inside the Bellegarde house the tentative explorations in his early exchanges with Claire de Cintré feel out the possibilities of their relation and, at the same time, put them into further relation.

Newman wanted to ask her something more, something personal, he hardly knew what. 'Don't you find it rather—rather quiet here?' he said; 'so far from the street?' Rather 'gloomy' he was going to say, but he reflected that that would be impolite.

'Yes, it is very quiet', said Madame de Cintré; 'but we like that.'

'Ah, you like that', repeated Newman, slowly (*1883*, i. 91).

Here Newman's tact in expression—a matter of being polite or impolite—seems to himself sufficient (and the past tense of 'he reflected' confusingly *follows* that of 'he said', though the reflection precedes the utterance). In the *NYE* more is risked and more exchanged in this dialogue:

He wanted to ask her something more, something personal and going rather

---

[29] The dramatic possibilities of syntactic expectation redirected to accommodate impinging thoughts and facts, so developed by James, may be compared with later experiments by which Joyce, for example, allows the syntax of inner consciousness to be broken by new information: thus Bloom, after reading the love-letter from Martha, takes the pressed flower she has pinned in it. 'He tore the flower gravely from its pinhold smelt its almost no smell and placed it in his heart pocket' (*Ulysses: the corrected text*, ed. Hans Walter Gabler with Wolfhard Steppe and Claus Melchior, New York, 1986, p. 64, lines 260–1). The convention of internal utterance here has 'smelt its' registered for the start of the act before 'almost no smell' comes back on it to disconcert both real and syntactic anticipation.

far—he hardly knew what. 'Don't you find it rather lifeless here', he said; 'so far from the street?' Rather 'lonesome' he was going to say, but he deflected nervously, for discretion, and then felt his term an aggravation.

'Yes, it's very lifeless, if you mean very quiet; but that's exactly what we like.'

'Ah, that's exactly what you like', he repeated. He was touched by her taking it so (*NYE* ii. 116).

The revising James takes up from and reconstrues *1883*'s 'rather— rather quiet', 'so far' and 'reflected'. The *NYE* first conveys Newman's new impulse to go 'rather far' (compacted from 'rather—rather' and 'so far') into his question's 'so far from the street'; he makes a mistake with 'lifeless'—sensed by himself as soon as said (with no saving pause of 'rather—rather')—which registers affectingly as the awkward result of a nervous and too-rapid wish to establish some measure of frank intimacy. 'Reflected' in *1883* gives Newman time to think; the word becomes a rhyming perch for the flight to 'deflected nervously', suggesting an instinctive decision to change which, too hastily executed, exposes him to the real possibility of offending. What Newman can be newly 'touched' by in the *NYE*, therefore, is Madame de Cintré's sympathetic revision of his utterance by reference to what she kindly takes him to have originally meant (indeed, what he *said* in *1883*): he *has* now gone 'far' with the term of his *NYE* question, and the mistaken revision of 'lonesome' to 'lifeless'—which escapes him just before he feels it to be wrong—has to be redeemed by her amiable act of imagination back to 'quiet'. What happens here—in the detail of the characters' expression—is a new event in their experience, a slip and then a rescue taking place between Newman and Claire de Cintré;[30] James's tender imagination of the delicate co-operation involved comes as a creatively appropriate reinvestment of the interest yielded by his

---

[30] A similar dramatic moment where Newman thinks, speaks, and then regrets his words occurs with a revision on the next page, where he has told Claire and Valentin of his touristic visits to 'some four hundred and seventy churches'. In *1883*, ' "Perhaps you are interested in theology", said the young man. "Not particularly. Are you a Roman Catholic, madam?" And he turned to Madame de Cintré' (*1883*, i. 92). In the *NYE* Newman becomes alive with a new tension to the possibility of blunders in speech. ' "Perhaps you're interested in religion", said his amiable host.|Newman thought. "Not actively." He found himself speaking as if it were a railroad or a mine; so that the next moment, to correct this, "Are you a Roman Catholic, madam?" he inquired of Madame de Cintré' (*NYE* ii. 117–18). The reflexive of 'found himself speaking' renders Newman a reviser—though one who can only change his meaning by going on, not (as James can) by going back.

experience of revision, *his* care for the real meaning that *he* has to rescue.

In my final example James's activity in revising again finds an equivalent in a tender exchange between Newman and Claire de Cintré at a late stage in the courtship, not long before the second, successful, proposal. She is worried about Newman's aversion to her mother and brother—which Newman evasively denies. He has a suspicion, though, about their attitude to him, and hopes they 'let you alone'.

'If I thought they talked ill of me to you, I should come down upon them.'
'They have let me alone, as you say. They have not talked ill of you.'
'In that case', cried Newman, 'I declare they are only too good for this world!' (*1883*, i. 200–1.)

The *NYE* is stimulated by this to seek out a peculiar intimacy between Newman and Madame de Cintré—at a moment when the mother and brother are about to appear with their new-found alternative candidate, Lord Deepmere.

'If I thought they talked against me to you at all badly'—and he just paused—'why I'd have to come in somewhere on *that*.'
She reassured him. 'They've let me alone, as you say. They haven't talked against you to me at all badly.'
It gave him, and for the first time, the exquisite pleasure of her apparently liking to use and adopt his words. 'Well then I'm ready to declare them only too good for this world!' (*NYE* ii. 264–5.)

Newman's threat of *1883* about 'coming down upon them' (and, incidentally, of *HMS* i. 201, where it is expanded) is here felt as forthcoming in an ominous pause, but then tactfully restrained to the considerate understatement of 'have to come in somewhere'. With reciprocal tact 'She reassured him' (not in *HMS*), evoking the anxiety against which their unanimity here stands, gives in advance the tone and sense, the *intention*, of what she says—so that the exactly echoing words she chooses to utter can ring as consenting repetitions, in their very superfluity a calm refutation of his worries about her alienated idea of him. Her acceptance and reproduction of his distinctively personal word-order in the *NYE*, and her mirroring of 'me to you' in 'you to me', come then as a compliant gesture, a positive act to indicate her perfect taking of his sense. 'As you say' in *1883* is what gives James the clue to all this; the kind of pleasure he elsewhere takes in revision from a harmonious consonance of expression with meaning (one that

'matches, at every point, without excess or deficiency' (*LC* ii. 1329))
occurs to him here even, paradoxically, to provide the very point of
his deviation from his own original words (words he both adopts and
adapts). Madame de Cintré's yielding at this stage anticipates her later
acceptance of the proposal; Newman's response to the correspondence
takes its special relief from the refinement with which, after earlier
difficult exchanges like that above over 'lifeless', their dialogue has at
last 'for the first time' found an expressive common ground.[31] To a
character who feels such a pleasure, 'exquisite' but not unsexual, the
realm of verbal expression is a rich medium for the whole of experience.

The process which we have seen undergone by the 1883 text of *The
American* emerges then as neither a rewriting nor a non-committal
half-measure. We could liken its development to that undergone by a
Jamesian 'germ', first into the Notebooks and then into story form, as
an eliciting of inner logic. There is an incremental relation and re-
relation of expressive elements, progressively prompting and shifting
and metamorphosing as each makes and settles into its place in the

---

[31] The characters are often dramatically conscious of questions of expression. Where
Madame de Cintré replies to Newman's first proposal in *1883* that 'Your offer seems
strange to me, for more reasons, also, than I can say' (*1883*, i. 135), in the *NYE* she
makes this 'If I call your proposal "strange" it's also for more reasons than I can say'
(*NYE* ii. 172); in which she remembers her 'It seems very strange' from the previous
page (*1883*, i. 134), hearing her own word and consciously trying to make herself clear
to him. When Newman says privately to Valentin that 'You don't love your brother'
(*1883*, i. 120), 'You could struggle along without your brother' (*NYE* ii. 153), Valentin
politely and insincerely protests that 'well-bred people always love their brothers' (*1883*),
'A house like ours is inevitably *one*' (*NYE*); and the response of *1883*—' "Well, I don't
love him, then!" Newman answered'—becomes: 'On which Newman, after an instant,
put the matter another way. "Well, I'm glad *I'm* free not to like him!" ' (*NYE*) In
addressing Urbain in *1883* Newman declares 'I want to marry your sister, that's all'
(*1883*, i. 176); in *HMS* this becomes 'I want, very obstinately, to marry your sister, and
nobody other—that's all' (*HMS*, i. 176); and in the *NYE* he hears, with an intelligence
that does not abate his determination, what Urbain will make of his intention: 'I want,
very originally, no doubt, but very obstinately, to marry your sister and nobody
other whomsoever—that's all' (*NYE* ii. 226). 'Very originally, no doubt' works in the
American's sense of what he's up against—it's a matter of principle rather than of
incomprehension. Threatening Urbain and the Marquise in the pre-penultimate chapter
becomes signally harder in the *NYE*: ' "You had much better listen to me", Newman
went on' (*1883*, ii. 169) becomes 'he persisted with his difficult ease' (*NYE* ii. 488).
Shortly afterwards Newman turns in triumph 'to the Marquis, who was terribly white—
whiter than Newman had ever seen any one out of a picture' (*1883*, ii. 171). In the *NYE*
James perches on 'picture' and 'out of' to give Newman a distracted musing about a
matter of expression: he turns 'to the Marquis, whose face was beyond any he had ever
seen discomposed, decomposed—what did they call it?' (*NYE* ii. 490.) 'They' are the
French, whose 'visage décomposé' ('face distorted by grief or terror') is suggested, via
'composition', by the juxtaposition of 'picture', a Frenchman, and being put out.

whole, altering that whole, but as part of a single evolution, each new link connecting with something in the old matter to form a continuity of intention. We may want to ask in a few instances whether the fact of imaginative connection makes the revisions as infallible as James's confidence makes him, in the Prefaces, want to suggest, for it may be impossible to guard entirely against the trap which catches Balzac's Frenhofer, in which the necessary renewal of the illusion can become delusive and self-incited. What, moreover, are we to make of the losses which inevitably accompany the gains in any process of change? What I hope the examples here demonstrate, though, is the creative truth of James's principle as his practice mostly shows it. His conception of the novel as a coherent record of experience receives extraordinary tribute as we examine the pages documenting his vast labour—in our sense in him of the energy he ascribes to Balzac, 'the never-extinct operation of his sensibility' (*LC* ii. 1336).

These cases also show the intensity of James's imaginative dependence on and liberation by the very substance of his expressive art, the words with which he grasps the matter of fictional experience. The revisions of the *NYE*, taken together with his 1905 lecture on *The Question of Our Speech*, express his passionate belief in the value of the development of a power of nuance and exact expression as the shaping condition of a truer consciousness. In this belief the details of writing and speech are enlivened.

(It all comes back to that, to my and your 'fun'—if we but allow the term its full extension; to the production of which no humblest question involved, even to that of the shade of a cadence or the position of a comma, is not richly pertinent.) (*LC* ii. 1338.)

James allows the term its full extension.

6

Perspectives in *The Portrait of a Lady*

i. *A Considerable Infusion*

James's cousin Minny Temple died of consumption in America in 1870 while James was at Great Malvern. Ten years later *The Portrait of a Lady* was unimpededly under way; a work whose germ James recalled in his *NYE* Preface years later as residing in his 'grasp of a single character' (*LC* ii. 1075). The 'single character' in the book is Isabel Archer; but James's 'grasp', his sense of 'complete possession' as he calls it, was derived from his knowledge of the remarkable girl dead a decade before.

Minny Temple was high-minded and highly strung, interesting and unfortunate. In *Notes of a Son and Brother,* published forty-three years after her death, James quoted vivid late testimony from his recently departed brother William about the living significance of the long-gone girl: 'I find that she means as much in the way of human character for me now as she ever did' (*Autobiog.*, p. 504). This persistence of meaning, felt by those who knew her, seems to have been aided by the dramatic impact made by the early death of a person whose future life in the world had been a puzzling question for herself and her circle. Her case distinctly marked out an area of profound difficulty. As Henry James wrote to his mother from Great Malvern on 26 March 1870, hyperbolically, after hearing of Minny's death,

She certainly never seemed to have come into this world for her own happiness—or that of others—or as anything but as a sort of divine reminder and quickness—a transcendent protest against our acquiescence in its grossness (*HJL* i. 219).[1]

And on 29 March he wrote to William in terms which anticipate those to be used by William years later:

---

[1] Leon Edel in *HJL* i mistakenly transcribes (as elsewhere, and as is easily done) the 'or' in 'or that of others' as 'as'. The effect is to muffle James's frank acknowledgement that Minny Temple made others unhappy as well as herself.

I feel as if a very fair portion of my sense of the reach and quality and capacity of human nature rested upon my experience of her character: certainly a large portion of my admiration of it (*HJL* i. 223–4).

The terms of these 1870 outpourings echo through James's subsequent writing: they apply as directly to *The Portrait of a Lady* as to *The Wings of the Dove,* where Merton Densher's climactic 'aftersense', his new sense of human possibilities, is brought about by his experience of Milly Theale's magnanimous character in a manner which reworks James's own understanding of *his* bereavement long before. One sense in which the novel of 1902 differs technically from that of 1881, though, lies in its comparative restriction of the heroine's point of view, the progressive centring of the action on Densher's view *of* her and gradual comprehension of her significance. In *The Portrait,* while we are given a variety of points of view on the heroine, our primary sense of her comes from the narration's account of Isabel's own point of view, which yields us a more detailed and not only uplifting view of her character. Some half-dozen times in the novel she is said to 'flatter herself', a phrase we can take as establishing continuity with a tradition of ironic authorial distancings, from for instance Emma Woodhouse and Gwendolen Harleth, previous mistaken heroines; and this should put us on our guard against taking the 'transcendent protest' as the whole story of the novel, whatever we take to be James's personal conception of Minny Temple.

We can distinguish two complementary senses of 'character' which apply to Isabel Archer: the 'character' of individual nature (descriptive), and that of virtue (approbatory). The relation between these senses mirrors on a small scale the conflict between ethical progressivism and the resistant world. For 'the world' means not only the laws of nature but also the moral constitution of mankind; and that moral constitution embraces not only others, who may obstruct or assault from outside, but also the individual subject, whose life is a protracted confrontation with his or her own inner nature. The resources any individual like Minny or Isabel has for following through high aspirations are only ever those she already has, actually or potentially, whether innately or through external influences. The resources at a crisis may prove defective. The first 'character', the total intricate set of psychological relations and complications and fallibilities making up an individual nature, can thus circumscribe and contain the degree of the second, heroic kind of 'character' that an individual will, even with effort, be able to show. An alternative and less disheartening construction of the same idea would have it that the first 'character', the set of characteristics, is what gives body and meaning to the individual's strivings towards the second 'character', and is the condition of its value. Thus the only perfection worth aiming for is the perfecting of the given material. The relation between the two senses is significantly ambiguous, and in the case of a figure whose death and memory were as creatively stimulating for James as Arthur Hallam's were for Tennyson, it is likely to be in part the very ambiguity that is stimulating.

In the Preface James says that at the time of writing *The Portrait* he had been in complete possession of his single character for a long time, already having 'the trick of investing some conceived or encountered individual ... with the germinal property and authority' (*LC* ii. 1073). The 'so considerable' time (*LC* ii. 1076) taken for germination was almost exactly ten years, if we take the initial date as that of Minny Temple's death on 8 March 1870 and the true start of *The Portrait* as that made in Florence in the spring of 1880. James was revising Minny into Isabel, but in writing the novel he was already also revising in more literal senses. The autobiographical notes made in Boston on 25 November 1881 recall how 'At that exquisite Bellosguardo at the Hotel de l'Arno, in a room in that deep recess, in the front, I began *The Portrait of a Lady*'; but then correct themselves: 'that is, I took up, and worked over, an old beginning, made long before' (*Nks.*, p. 219). In July 1878 he had replied to a query of William's that 'The "great novel" you ask about is only begun; I am doing other things just now' (*HJL* ii. 179); and in June 1879 to the same correspondent he describes it as a work 'which, begun sometime since, has remained an aching fragment' (*HJL* ii. 244). The Preface's remark that 'all tormentingly, I saw it in motion', may well refer to the resultant sense of creative frustration. Once properly begun, moreover, the novel took time to construct, going 'steadily, but slowly, every part being written twice' (*Nks.*, p. 220). The renewals of vision in the case intricately multiply before the work's first appearance in print.

The initial impulse may date from before Minny Temple's death, but it is expressed, even if unpromisingly, in the letter of 26 March 1870 to his mother: 'what an impulse one feels to sum up her rich little life in some simple compound of tenderness and awe' (*HJL* i. 219). The tenderness possibly overpowers the awe under the stress of grief, and James makes too cosy a package of 'her rich little life' as 'some simple compound'; but in the longer term, in *The Portrait*, this impulse comes to be artistically modified by the responsible processes of fictional creation developed by him in the course of the decade. At other points in the letters of 1870 James more closely anticipates the concerns of *The Portrait*, thinking about Minny Temple's problematic future, the impossibility of any equilibrium between the mundane life of the world and her urgent vitality. He wrote to his mother: 'No one who ever knew her can have failed to look at her future as a sadly insoluble problem—and we almost all had imagination enough to say, to murmur at least, that life—poor narrow life—contained no place for her' (*HJL* i. 222; 26 March 1870). At the same time James's distance in rural England makes him conscious of a different construction of the case in which Minny's loss of Europe presents a poignant antithesis to his own initiation into it—in which her future might have seemed to contain a possibility of fulfilment.

I now become sensible how her image, softened and sweetened by suffering and sitting patient and yet expectant, so far away from the great world with which so many of her old dreams and impulses were associated, has operated in my mind as a gentle incentive to action and enterprise. There have been so many things I have thought of telling her, so many stories by which I had a fancy to make up her lack to her (*HJL* i. 221).

The things to tell here are probably James's personal anecdotes about his own experiences in Europe, but it is at least possible that the 'stories' are fictions, made-up narratives to 'make up' a lack, works of 'fancy' to supply things to Minny Temple she missed in fact.

Four Meetings of 1877 is such a story, imagining Caroline Spencer's dream of Europe momentarily fulfilled, but her life permanently stricken in consequence with exploitative relatives: the lack is made up but would have been better left void. The 1870 letters already suggest an attitude making *this* possible future, the European one, only equivocally desirable. On 8 March, the day Minny Temple died, James happened to mention her in a letter to William, for the sake of her contrast with the literalness of English girls.

I revolt from their dreary deathly want of—what shall I call it?—Clover Hooper has it—intellectual grace—Minny Temple has it—moral spontaneity. They live wholly in the realm of the cut and dried (*HJL* i. 208).

The distinction shows James's mystical valuation of 'grace' and 'spontaneity', and identification of them as characteristically American qualities. It makes the old world, also, 'the realm of the cut and dried', a place of excessive definition and prescription. This line of thought eventually makes James thankful Minny's European plans came to nothing; for there would have been a painful confrontation. 'She was a breathing protest', he wrote to William on 29 March, 'against English grossness, English compromises and conventions—a plant of pure American growth' (*HJL* i. 228). While this 'breathing protest'—when actually brought to Europe—would have had a dramatic force and inspiring implications, the breathing protest, he implies, would more likely have ended in martyrdom than victory. The way in which James writes of Minny's other possible choice of life, in the same letter, suggests an equally unsanguine view of her prospects: 'She has gone where there is neither marrying nor giving in marriage! No illusions and no disillusions—no sleepless nights and no ebbing strength' (*HJL* i. 226). The sequence of distresses avoided here actually occurs in the marriage of Isabel Archer with its vigils and despairs, save that the very end of the novel seems to bring *her* a return of strength.

James's immediate response to the death of Minny Temple is then in part an imaginative multiplication of possible alternatives to her premature ending—continuations pursued to a point that reveals their tragic or pathetic impracticability. 'Her character may be almost literally said to have been without practical application to life' (*HJL* i. 223), as he put it to William. At a time of strain such a line of thought offers obvious consolations, her death the evident best thing for it. James's reasoning works him round to the acceptance of the loss, by translating it into a translation: 'The more I think of her the more perfectly satisfied I am to have her translated from this changing realm of fact to the steady realm of thought' (*HJL* i. 226). What gets lost in translation here is life, and to be 'perfectly satisfied' about any death, no matter how ingeniously euphemized, is barely decent; but the circumstances make the announcement less intolerable, since it reads in context as a defiance of real grief thrown off at a venture and not a bland avowal of complacency ('more perfectly' is revealingly over-insistent).[2]

The creative use subsequently made by James of the girl's memory shows a fascination with enforcing the possible other fates, the prac-

[2] The terms of James's satisfaction reflect relief for suffering spared her, and the compensating constancy of image he calls on to diminish Minny's irrecoverability need not be read as charged with ghoulish pleasure—which it is by Leon Edel (*Henry James: A Life*, pp. 108–11).

tical applications, which had no chance to mark Minny's own life. The fictions she inspires both show by their following-through of projected careers what grim realities Minny has been spared, and allow their heroines, who are not Minny, an individuality which makes *their* fates matter. Figures like Madame de Mauves, Caroline Spencer, Bessie Alden, and Isabel Archer, stuck in 'this changing realm of fact', have to extricate from it what value they can, short of the simplification of dying. Minny Temple may be an original for some or all of these various figures, but an understanding of James's sense of what he was doing in invoking her is necessary to interpretation of her literary descendants. There are no direct equivalences here.

This was James's point when he wrote on 28 December 1880 to Grace Norton, who had identified Isabel with Minny in reading the instalments of the novel in the *Atlantic Monthly*. He simultaneously admitted and qualified the correctness of her guess.

It is much the best thing I have done—though not the best I shall do. You are both right and wrong about Minny Temple. I had her in mind, and there is in the heroine a considerable infusion of my impression of her remarkable nature. But the thing is not a portrait. Poor Minny was essentially *incomplete* and I have attempted to make my young woman more rounded, more finished. In truth everyone, in life, is incomplete, and it is the work of art that in reproducing them one feels the desire to fill them out, to justify them, as it were. I am delighted if I interest you; I think I shall to the end (*HJL* ii. 323–4).[3]

The warning *not* to identify Isabel with Minny has an absolute force; 'the thing is not a portrait' of her, despite its title, and whatever unconscious processes we may think drew together the cousin and the heroine, this conscious statement of a complex intention, made while he was still writing the novel, requires of the interested reader a more differentiating account of their relation and what it means for James. Accounting for the artistic process which brings into being and constitutes this relation thus becomes an endeavour central to our understanding of the writing, the constructed meaning, of the book. James makes clear that it is a *re*-writing of 'poor Minny', and his language in this letter, about completing and filling out, recalls the compensatory stories fancied ten years earlier as making up her lack to her: though

---

[3] Edel in *HJL* ii puts an '[in]' before 'the work of art', in the hope of clarification—but without success: the statement remains tantalizingly difficult. Alfred Habegger reads 'mark' rather than 'work' (*Henry James and the 'Woman Business'*, Cambridge, 1989, pp. 160, 255n.).

there the compensation was a matter of supplying her lack of the European 'great world', inventing events, and here it is a matter of amplifying her character, altering her nature, a significantly psychological extension of the imagination's precinct. Explaining 'much the best thing I have done' to Grace Norton makes James want to sum up what his art is *for* and *about*; and he is impelled towards re-presenting the idea of the perfect satisfaction of 'the steady realm of thought'; but somehow the definition he actually comes out with fails to be definitive. 'It is the work of art that in reproducing them one feels ...' etc. is syntactically disconcerting, not least because the art-*object* (work-of-art) turns out to be the artistic *process* (the *work* of art). That the labour of art is *that* one feels ... etc. doesn't tell us what the effect of feeling this desire is, what one does about it. Yet perhaps this evasion, a pragmatic veering-off from too big a statement, from something he is not prepared to say, does suggest something valuable about James's notions in the composition of this novel: that there is some limitation of the reach of wish-fulfilment that is tricky to express. '*More* rounded' and '*more* finished' stop comparatively short of the rounded and the complete.

Notes of a Son and Brother (1914) reflects on some other originals for figures in *The Portrait*, the Bootts with their Florentine hilltop— though a more striking imaginative transformation is involved. The 'germ' they represent seemed to have sunk, he recalls.

Then at last after years it raised its own head into the air and found its full use for the imagination. An Italianate bereft American with a little moulded daughter in the setting of a massive old Tuscan residence was at the end of years exactly what was required by a situation of my own—conceived in the light of the Novel; and I *had* it there, in the authenticated way, with its essential fund of truth, at once all the more because my admirable old friend had given it to me and none the less because he had no single note of character or temper, not a grain of the non-essential, in common with my Gilbert Osmond. This combination of facts has its shy interest, I think, in the general imaginative or reproductive connection— testifying as it so happens to do on that whole question of the 'putting of people into books' as to which any ineptitude of judgment appears always in order. I probably shouldn't have had the Gilbert Osmonds at all without the early 'form' of the Frank Bootts, but I still more certainly shouldn't have had them with the *sense* of my old inspirers. The form had to be disembarrassed of that sense and to take in a thoroughly other (*Autobiog.*, p. 522).

There is a conscious act of differentiation involved in the fictional creation-and-derivation of character, which takes over the 'form' but needs to disembarrass itself of the particular 'sense' of the original, retaining however the general 'essential fund of truth' James comes into from having known the Bootts. To know in detail a particular case gives the novelist's imagination a confident, an 'authenticated' grasp not only on that case but also on other possible ones with quite different bearings, cases the evolution of which is the work of the imagination, 'the work of art' as James says to Grace Norton.

That this was already James's sense of the matter at the time of *The Portrait* appears from his remarks in *Hawthorne* (1879) on the relation between the real Margaret Fuller and Zenobia in *The Blithedale Romance*:

There is no strictness in the representation by novelists of persons who have struck them in life, and there can in the nature of things be none. From the moment the imagination takes a hand in the game, the inevitable tendency is to divergence, to following what may be called new scents. The original gives hints, but the writer does what he likes with them, and imports new elements into the picture (*LC* i. 420).[4]

The 'essential fund of truth' James derives from possessing the image of the original 'in the authenticated way' gives him a confidence in his understanding of a given connection which allows his imagination to diverge, to follow 'new scents' (new 'sense'), without getting lost. It is in this way that the surface of the work flushes, showing the life beneath or behind it, in the terms suggested in James's analogy between painting and fiction. The original woman is then not buried behind a wall of paint, as in Balzac's *Le Chef-d'œuvre Inconnu*, but breathingly present in the representational surface. The detailed account in the fictitious work of the experience of a woman (by her, or by others round her) has not only a general tacit reference to the whole body of the writer's real experience (of women, books, and life), but also a particular reference to his experience of an individual woman, including the reflections and convictions and speculations she has stimulated. The imaginative deviation is the constitutively creative act, yet the firm presence of an original is the condition of value and of confidence for the deviation. Minny Temple, to use a Jamesian phrase, is 'there for' Isabel Archer.

---

[4] Cf. the image, for the imagination, of the 'house-dog of a temper above confinement', off the leash and 'seeing life' in the field, in the Preface to *What Maisie Knew,* discussed in Ch. 3 (p. 69).

ii. *Wine and Water*

James recurrently attended to the shapes taken by artists' careers, and portraits of ladies are associated for him with establishing success. In the 1873 story *The Sweetheart of M. Briseux,* the painting whose creation is narrated makes a reputation:

This was the very work which had made the painter famous. The portrait of a Lady in a Yellow Shawl in the Salon of 1836 had *fait époque* (*THJ* ii. 234).

In 1890 it is Nick Dormer's finally arranging to paint Julia Dallow—instead of marry her—that gives him his public start as an artist in the up-to-the-minute ending of *The Tragic Muse*:

every one will remember in how recent an exhibition general attention was attracted, as the newspapers said in describing the private view, to the noble portrait of a lady which was the final outcome of that arrangement.[5]

And James approached his own *Portrait of a Lady*—he already had the title by 23 August 1879 (*HJL* ii. 253)—with a self-conscious sense that it was a momentous undertaking, with the hope that it should attract general attention and make an epoch. On 29 January 1880, soon to take up the 'aching fragment' in earnest, he told Isabella Stuart Gardner, with comic exaggeration, to 'Look out for my next big novel; it will immortalize me. After that, some day, I will immortalize you' (*HJL* ii. 265–6). Writing to his mother, whose harping on his current unprofitability forced him to an embarrassing stand on his own projected merits, he had resorted on 17 February 1878 to the deliberately inflated heroic diction used by the James family for avoidance of the pompous or the solemn when self-assertion was necessary: 'It is time I should rend the veil from the ferocious ambition which has always couvé beneath a tranquil exterior'; then entered a plangent plea for sympathy, recording his silent sufferings in an unknowable tone: 'which enabled me to support unrecorded physical misery in my younger years'; and finally, with an exclamatory mark at the coolness of his own assurance, asserted the value of his future: 'and which is perfectly confident of accomplishing considerable things!' (*HJL* ii. 156).

The two or three years up to *The Portrait*, and after it those up to the disappointing reception accorded the unlucky *Bostonians,* show James buoyantly full of himself, or of his powers, 'perfectly confident'.

---

[5] *The Tragic Muse*, iii, p. 257.

'The Art of Fiction', between the two novels, has an ironic dash and pleasure in its own victorious percipience which never again surfaces so unguardedly in James's writing. The summer before the letter to his mother just quoted, on 4 May 1877, he was already announcing to her that he intended to surpass *The American,* which was still in the process of coming out and had recently been criticized by William.

I subscribe to all his objections, & shall answer them most shortly by putting forth in the course of time another glowing romance, to which the *American* shall be as water unto wine.[6]

The image returns the following spring, when James has to disappoint his mother's expectation that his next novel, *The Europeans,* was to be this other glowing romance.

The story Howells is about to publish is *by no means* the one of which I wrote you last summer that it would be to the American 'as wine unto water'. *That* is still on my hands; but I hope to do something with it this summer.[7]

Mrs James seems to have suffered some confusion in her motherly impatience for the one which, he had promised her, 'will cover you with fame'; the following year she was evidently under the same misapprehension about the serialized *Confidence,* and on 8 April 1879 he had to write that, 'No, the thing in *Scribner* is *not,* by any means, the big "wine-and-water" novel' (*HJL* ii. 229). The repeated Biblical allusion directs us to Christ's miracle at the wedding in Cana (done in some degree for *his* mother's sake), and quasi-blasphemously arrogates for James himself the Messianic power of transmutation. The use of this reference recalls too the beginning of *The American,* where the hero admires Veronese's portrayal of 'the marriage feast of Cana'—a scene which becomes with hindsight an emblem of Newman's disappointed hopes; James makes the allusion to his already written novel stand for the difference between the thinness of that work and the qualitatively incomparable vintage—matured by some obscure process—of the forthcoming masterpiece. The story of the miracle also bears a strong idea of progressive improvement, which James adapts to his career. The ruler of the feast congratulates the bridegroom:

Every man at the beginning doth set forth good wine; and when men have

[6] HJ to Mother, 4 May 1877 (Harvard MS).
[7] HJ to Mother, 15 Mar. 1878 (Harvard MS).

well drunk, then that which is worse: but thou hast kept the good wine until now (John 2:10).

Such a saving of the best till last is a model for the anxious author, keen to escape deterioration and coarsening ('then that which is worse'). The bridegroom is (miraculously) not like others; and James won't be like other writers. Such high claims as are involved in the reference here, however jocularly muffled, constitute the pledges of a confidence which is also James's challenge to himself to go ahead and *faire époque,* to attract general attention, immortalize himself.

The 'wine-and-water' phrase also looks to Tennyson's 'Locksley Hall', a favourite work throughout James's life; to the moment where the embittered and passionate narrator, deserted for another by his beloved Amy, takes refuge in misogynistic abuse:

> Woman is the lesser man, and all thy passions,
>   matched with mine,
> Are as moonlight unto sunlight, and as water
>   unto wine.[8]

In so far as James is alluding to Tennyson's words more directly than to those in the Bible, he seems to be announcing that *The American*'s successor will display greater, more glowing passions, and will be strong stuff; though the comparative judgement of the sexes in Tennyson's lines is reversed in Isabel and Newman to the disadvantage of the male. The doubtful sanity of Tennyson's narrator, and the incredibility of his melodramatic assertion, further suggest the presence of a protective covering of irony in James's prospectus for his literary future.

In the letter of April 1879 he went on, having put *Confidence* in its place, to say that 'The "wine-and-water" thing must await my larger leisure. This will come, in portion at least, I hope, from the proceeds of the just named.' His plan to 'do something with it' in the summer of 1878 had not apparently been unhindered: on 29 May 1878 he had written to his father that 'I have many irons on the fire, and am bursting with writableness' (*HJL* ii. 176); but by 23 July was telling William that 'the "great novel"' was 'only begun' and had already been set aside for 'other things' (*HJL* ii. 179). *The Portrait* is 'great' not only in quality, but in quantity too; and the 'proceeds' from the other 'irons on the fire' buy him time, a 'larger leisure' for working

---

[8] 'Locksley Hall' in *The Poems of Tennyson*, ii. 128.

the miraculous change of state and of scale. In prolifically producing, among other things, *Daisy Miller, The Europeans, Hawthorne, An International Episode, The Pension Beaurepas, Confidence,* and *Washington Square* in so short a period, James was not only writing several works of great intrinsic value but also industriously earning money, getting in practice, and establishing his marketability, in order to secure the right chance for the major work started and discontinued in 1878. This pragmatic motivation is more fully stated in a letter to Howells of 17 June 1879:

I am pledged to write a long novel as soon as possible, and am obliged to delay it only because I can't literally afford it. Working slowly and painfully as I do I need for such a purpose a longish stretch of time during which I am free to do nothing else, and such liberal periods don't present themselves—I have always to keep the pot a-boiling (*HJL* ii. 243).

'The pot a-boiling' is a professional's skirting of self-importance, and James is playing up the current concerns of the 'shop' in order to give relief to his procrastinated art; but his requirement of a 'liberal period' of freedom, a 'larger leisure' on the basis of money received, seems authentically to distinguish *The Portrait* from its predecessors. James needs financial freedom to start on Isabel Archer's adventure just as she does in the novel. There is a largesse, a liberal expenditure and investment, needed for the 'larger leisure' both of author and heroine.

Early in 1880 James could at last afford to put no new irons in the fire, and wrote to Henry James Senior on 11 January that he was declining to do a *Dickens* for the English Men of Letters series on the ground that 'I wish during several months to come to have my hands free to work upon my forthcoming long novel' (*HJL* ii. 263). He was on 15 February telling his father that he wanted 'to get vigorously forward with my long novel, which begins next August' (*HJL* ii. 273); but on 30 March in Florence wasn't yet 'settling down to the daily evolution of my "big" novel' (*HJL* ii. 277); and on 18 April, after some time in Italy, had to tell Howells that 'in respect to my novel it has been a month lost rather than gained' (*HJL* ii. 285), and to ask for a postponement of the *Atlantic* serialization. In July he resisted his mother's pressure on him to return home to America because he was unwilling to go back with the novel only half-completed (*HJL* ii. 295); and staying on, he kept at it. On 20 September 1880 he was still working on it, and still confident; he told Grace Norton that he set much less store by the 'slender' and 'narrow' *Washington Square* than

by the forthcoming *Portrait*: 'I don't, honestly, take much stock in it—
the larger story coming out presently in *Macmillan* and the *Atlantic*
will be a much more valuable affair' (*HJL* ii. 308). And on 27 November
to William he also associated the 'large' with the valuable, again
contrasting the old work unfavourably with the new. 'The other book
increases, I think, in merit and interest as it goes on, and being told in
a more spacious, expansive way than its predecessors, is inevitably
more human, more sociable. It was the constant effort at *condensation*
. . . that has deprived my former things of these qualities' (*HJL* ii. 316).
On 24 January 1881 he assured T. S. Perry that his long story, 'when
it is finished, will be the best thing I have done'; and that 'the story
contains the best writing of which I have hitherto been capable. But',
he goes on, 'I mean to surpass it, *de beaucoup* ' (*HJL* ii. 335). *The
Portrait*, while its composition is still drawing to a close, is thus already
being treated by James not only as his best so far, but also as only a
staging-post, an achievement to be exceeded—*de beaucoup*—in the
future.

As this double perspective might suggest, we can view *The Portrait*
as an especially and consciously transitional work in James's career,
facing both ways. In it James discovers a new fluency, a stylistic
expansiveness, variety, and figurative daring which produce, in his own
judgement, 'the best writing of which I have hitherto been capable'. As
in the case of *Roderick Hudson,* the big, capacious novel permits
James to bring together preoccupations and subject-matter from a
whole range of preceding work; in his confident variations realizing
on thematic investments made, treasure laid up, in earlier fiction,
travel writing, and criticism. The book also seems to herald later
developments: Isabel Archer before her marriage anticipates Milly
Theale and after it Maggie Verver, for instance, and the sustained
presentation of a social surface distorted by a secret intimacy looks
ahead to all three of the last major novels. The distance, much later,
between James's sense of *The Portrait* and his sense of *Roderick
Hudson* and *The American* is conveyed by a letter of 9 May 1906 to
Scribners, about his intentions for the dispatch of revised sheets for
the *NYE*:

I shall send you *The Portrait of a Lady* with all the worst pages (I mean the
most amended ones) re-copied—though my retouchings of this book are fewer
& *no* passages so intricately altered as in the two others. . . . And let me add
that I shall be obliged to send you the *P. of a L. before* the *American,* as it

will be the easiest revision for me to finish (not having to be so close).[9]

In fact there are in the revised *Portrait* many cases of passages just as intricately altered as in the two others; and on 12 June 1906 he confessed to Scribners that 'This has proved, in the close quarters of revision, slower (as well as really more beneficent) work than I fondly dreamed.'[10] The force of this emphasis for us is James's feeling in 1906 so much closer to *The Portrait* and easier with it, feeling presumably that its manner has more in common with his 'present mode of motion' (*LC* ii. 1330). The Preface to the book, which James mailed off to Scribner on 17 August 1906,[11] accurately puts it forward as a case of literary 'architecture', ruled by a 'technical rigour' about point of view which allows James to put up 'on such a plot of ground the neat and careful and proportioned pile of bricks that arches over it and that was thus to form, constructionally speaking, a literary monument' (*LC* ii. 1080).[12] The James of 1906, that is, chooses to treat *The Portrait* primarily (though not exclusively) as a formal experiment, comparable to such successors as *The Awkward Age* or *The Turn of the Screw*; though we could easily see it in other contexts. The transitional status of the book, and its inauguration of a new, more technically conscious phase in James's writing, are confirmed by the later author's hindsight.

iii. *Extensions and Variations*

We misread the place of *The Portrait* in James's *œuvre*, however, unless we understand its innovative liberation from the constraints of the 1870s works as coming in large part from its *consummation* of those works. A clear case of an 1870s prototype for a central relationship in *The Portrait* is the way in which the situation of *Longstaff's Marriage* (1878) anticipates that of Ralph and Isabel: the sick observer loving the girl and offering her money. The short story has a playful implausibility in the extreme reversal which is its central conceit: that lovingly to watch Diana Belfield revive the dying Longstaff, while correlatively she falls in love with him after refusing his offer of marriage and pines to death of it. Yet though the scheme is barely plausible, the will to

---

[9] HJ to Scribners, 9 May 1906 (Princeton MS).

[10] HJ to Scribners, 12 June 1906 (Princeton TS).

[11] With that of *Roderick Hudson* (see HJ to Scribners, 17 Aug. 1906, Princeton TS).

[12] There seems to have been a connection for James between Archer, arch, and 'architecture', a word the *Portrait* Preface picks up from *1882*, p. 491—where Isabel is struck by the 'architectural vastness' of 'the truth of things'.

live Longstaff finds in the interest of observing Diana—'I am dying, but for the last five weeks that has kept me alive' (*THJ* iii. 211)—looks ahead to a counterpart in the novel's quite serious statement that 'What kept Ralph alive was simply the fact that he had not yet seen enough of his cousin' (*1882*, p. 346; *NYE* iv. 146 has 'of the person in the world in whom he was most interested'). We can trace the exchange scheme in the tale back to James's sad reflection, expressed in a letter to William on 29 March 1870 about himself and the dead Minny Temple, on 'the gradual change and reversal of our relations: I slowly crawling from weakness and inaction and suffering into strength and health and hope: she sinking out of brightness and youth into decline and death' (*HJL* i. 224). No such exchange takes place *during The Portrait*, but *Longstaff's Marriage* helps an exchange to take place *before*, in its very conception: a reversal of gender between invalid and survivor (taking the James–Minny Temple relation as the original). The 1878 tale is an experiment, a playing-through of possibilities of permutation which gives James confidence for the novel by preparing the 'plot of ground' (or ground of plot) for his 'architecture'.

Diana Belfield in the story has scorned many offers of marriage: 'They had come from honourable and amiable men, and it was not her suitors in themselves that she disrelished; it was simply the idea of marrying' (*THJ* iii. 204). This elevatedly abstract or general reluctance foreshadows that of Isabel in *The Portrait*; and Diana's disastrous collapse from it into a fatal passion for Longstaff foreshadows (with a different result) Isabel's yielding of herself to Osmond. Diana, like Minny Temple, goes to an early grave, 'where there is neither marrying nor giving in marriage' (*HJL* i. 226); but many of James's 1870s heroines, like Isabel in not dying, in their various difficulties carry forward James's protracted meditation on the often impossible situation of intelligent and independently-minded young women. The refusal of Longstaff's proposal is the hinge of the symmetrical plot in *Longstaff's Marriage*; the refusal of Lord Lambeth's by Bessie Alden is the climax of *An International Episode* (1878), and that whole story is a run-through for Isabel's refusal of Lord Warburton. Initial refusals like Isabel's, or Margaret Hale's in *North and South*, or Clarissa's in *Clarissa*, have a plot function: they often show the heroine asserting her own value and her values; suggest that the proposer of marriage (Goodwood, Warburton, Henry Lennox, or Soames) fails to live up to it or them; and frame the action to follow as a sequence of figures and events to be judged in terms of the meanings such a start brings into play. Such a move can signal a departure from the most conventional concern of fictional heroines (whom to marry) in favour of a more comprehensive choice of life (including the questions: *why* and *whether* to marry). An exceptionally free play of values may be thereby indicated. It can also bring up the psychological question of the heroine's motives, her criteria for rejection and their well- or ill-foundedness; and 'a psychological reason', as James says in 'The Art of Fiction' defending *An International Episode,* 'is, to my imagination, an object adorably pictorial' (*LC* i. 61).

Bessie Alden's reason in that story is relevant to Isabel's in *The Portrait*: she refuses Lord Lambeth at last despite liking him ('I like him very much' (*THJ* iii. 263)), as Isabel does earlier in her story ('I like you very much, Lord Warburton' (*1882,* p. 90)), because she doesn't at heart regard him seriously, as an individual and an end in himself, but touristically, as an addition to what is called 'her little private museum of types' (*THJ* iii. 265). Her appreciation of him treats him as a source of impressions but is strictly unreciprocal, neglecting his human feelings in favour of his appealing Englishness: 'He would be an unconscious part of the antiquity, the impressiveness, the picturesqueness of England; and poor Bessie Alden, like many a Yankee maiden, was terribly at the mercy of picturesqueness' (*THJ* iii. 268).

Such keeping of a safe distance recalls a preoccupation of James's own travel writing at the time. The previous year, 1877, 'In Warwickshire', he had walked a pretty girl to church. The country walk, to 'the sympathetic stranger' delightfully novel, has no special meaning for her; 'But her quiet-eyed unsuspectingness only makes her the more a part of his delicate entertainment.'[13] 'Delicate' arouses our suspicions; and the following year, in 'Italy Revisited', James finds in the lively poverty of Genoa, made picturesque by the sunny smiles of the inhabitants, sufficient prompting for explicit reflection on the equivocal position of the tourist, a figure not rootedly or fully there.

To travel is, as it were, to go to the play, to attend a spectacle; and there is something heartless in stepping forth into foreign streets to feast on 'character' when character consists simply of the slightly different costume in which labour and want present themselves (*IH*, p. 116).[14]

[13] *Portraits of Places*, London, 1883, p. 253. It becomes 'her want of immediate intelligence' in 1905 (*EH*, p. 205).

[14] This revises *Portraits of Places*, p. 50: 'foreign streets' replaces 'the streets of a foreign town'; '"character"' twice replaces 'novelty'; and 'labour and want' replaces 'hunger and labour'.

He finds a partial extenuation in the case of Genoese poverty;

Our observation in any foreign land is extremely superficial, and our remarks are happily not addressed to the inhabitants themselves, who would be sure to exclaim upon the impudence of the fancy-picture.[15]

But an American's observation of English 'characters' cannot enjoy this certainty of not being addressed to the inhabitants themselves, though the material comforts of the English circumstances mitigate the offence that may be taken at an American's 'feasting'. The anxiety, in other words, that there is 'something heartless' in such observation even when refined and well-intentioned, a treatment of others as objects for a private museum of types, remains in the air; it informs Bessie Alden's story, uniting the international and personal relations by making the extent to which characters represent their nations an integrated element of the argument. 'Italy Revisited' immediately afterwards has an appreciation of a figure singing as he passes through James's vista—'exactly what was wanted to set off the landscape'. The complacency of this vision, like that of Strether's by the river in *The Ambassadors,* is at once rebuked: the figure, far from belonging in the feudal frame where it has been put, turns out 'a brooding young radical and communist'. 'This made it very absurd of me to have looked at him simply as a graceful ornament to the prospect, an harmonious little figure in the middle distance.'[16] A similar turn occurs when Bessie Alden discovers, against her self-deluding expectation, that Lord Lambeth *is* prepared to marry her, has real intentions of his own which need to be taken seriously and which make him inharmonious with her artistically ordered picture.[17]

The shift from Lord Lambeth to Lord Warburton exemplifies the speed of James's development: the young Lambeth is a touching comic conception, a bit dim and uncomplicated, who is only rendered to the point where he can be at last unhappily but inevitably discomfited; whereas Warburton is mature, intelligent, powerful, alienated from his class, and rendered with such imaginative sympathy as to remain,

---

[15] *Portraits of Places,* p. 51; *IH,* p. 116.

[16] *Portraits of Places,* pp. 52–3; *IH,* p. 117.

[17] 'Harmony' is a word which recurs throughout *The Portrait*: in the NYE Madame Merle on her musical first appearance becomes 'the source of the harmony' (iii. 244), while Osmond later puts on for Isabel, in revision, 'a particular harmony with other supposed and divined things, histories within histories' (iii. 399). The verbal recurrence can help us to see the big novel as continuing the preoccupations of the earlier, shorter fictions and travel-sketches.

after his dismissal, a haunting presence to the end of the novel. It may be that in planning *The Portrait* James had foreseen a Warburton more like Lambeth, more easily contained within his stereotype and his corner of the plot; in the event his letter to Howells on the matter, of 5 December 1880, when the book was well on in the writing and already being serialized, shows unease.

That you think well of Lord Warburton makes me regret more than I already do that he is after all but a secondary figure. I have made rather too much of his radicalism in the beginning—there is no particular use for it later (*HJL* ii. 321).

In one way we could see this as an unhappy excessiveness, a character getting too big for his function. But in another we can take it as part of the amplitude which makes the book move so affectingly through the lives of its characters; Warburton abides and returns with a truly human confusion of motive, and the portrayal of him, 'spacious' and 'expansive', takes on a dimension—that of duration—which does not apply in the case of Lambeth. Warburton is in a sense a revision of Lambeth, a representation of an analogous figure but exhibiting many more of his relations; this is a point at which the big novel visibly uses its shorter predecessor as a perch and aspires to a clearer air.

The Portrait picks up and reworks matter from the preceding novels, as well as shorter works, in ways which show James's mind running back over, repeating and reconstructing, plots and situations and scenes.[18] When Isabel is found in Albany by her aunt she is reading a book of European history, a suggestion of her own future history in Europe; as a device for beginning the action proper this looks back (with an adjustment of genre for Isabel's earnestness) to Gertrude Wentworth in *The Europeans* reading in *The Arabian Nights*, then looking up to see for the first time her exotic (European) prince, Felix Young. Like Roderick Hudson's, Isabel's eager young sensibility needs the worldly support of an external agent to realize its European ambitions; and we could see the functions of Rowland Mallet in the earlier novel being divided here between Mrs Touchett and Ralph, the former discovering her potential and the latter taking unusual

[18] As Richard Poirier says, 'There is general agreement that the novels of James from *Roderick Hudson* to *Washington Square* are the work of apprenticeship for the writing of *The Portrait of a Lady*. Most of the themes and all of the characters in this novel exist in less subtle form in the earlier works' (*The Comic Sense of Henry James,* London, 1960, p. 183).

responsibility and entering into a contract intended for her benefit but leading to disaster. The independent spirit of the dependants produces different kinds of waywardness, but the trajectories of the two works are similar: both Isabel and Roderick approach their endings in a state of moral and spiritual exhaustion that reflects their excessive idealizing aspirations, and the horizon-gazing of their beginnings. The matrilineal transfer of Mrs Light's disappointed high marital ambitions on to a fresh candidate, her daughter Christina, is reproduced in the conception of Madame Merle's relation to Pansy, albeit in submerged form. (As the Countess Gemini puts it, 'She has failed so dreadfully herself that she is determined her daughter shall make it up' (*1882*, p. 479).) The secret illegitimacy moves from father (the Cavaliere) to mother (Madame Merle); and in both novels its secrecy is preserved till the climax as a vital element of the plot, though it works more powerfully in *The Portrait* for representing a far crueller and further-reaching treachery—that of both the child's parents towards Isabel.

Pansy also offers James a means of replaying the plot of *The American* in miniature, with herself as a more *petite* Claire, her suitor Rosier as a small-scale Newman, and with Isabel finding herself like Valentin de Bellegarde in a false position *vis-à-vis* the authority of the family. James's handling of the plot in *The American* had been subject to much criticism, and his allegation of the *impossibility* of the Newman–Claire de Cintré marriage forcefully disputed. Years later the *NYE* Preface strikingly retracts the family's sudden retraction of consent ('They would positively have jumped then, the Bellegardes, at my rich and easy American' (*LC* ii. 1066)). In 1890 James was prepared (even if only for the theatrical market) to change the ending to a happy one in the dramatization; and we can see him re-covering with an altered mode of motion similar terrain—a too-assured American candidate encountering problems in marrying into a haughty European family—in *Lady Barbarina* (1884) and *The Reverberator* (1888; this also reworks *Daisy Miller*). Writing to William on 23 July 1878 about his plans for *The Portrait*, James had invoked the memory of his earlier novel: 'It is the history of an *Americana*—a female counterpart to Newman' (*HJL* ii. 179); and the adjustment of his characters' finances may sufficiently account for the differences of development between the two books—given James's revised sense of the probabilities. Isabel, that is, becomes a 'rich and easy American' and *is* jumped at; Rosier is 'not rich enough for Pansy' and is given the push—which leaves him, though weaker and less dignified than Newman, with a 'sense of injury' (*1882*, p. 329) that matches his precursor's 'sense of outrage' (*1883*, p. 118).

In *The American* the relation between the family's use of 'authority' and Claire's motives for withdrawal is unclear; it is not apparent within the novel that the situation develops as James wrote of it on 26 May 1877 to the remonstrating Lizzie Boott:

Come, now, they couldn't have married, when it came to the point, & I never meant they should, or that the reader shld. expect it. It was very well for Newman to want it, & for Mme. de C. to fancy for a few weeks it was possible: but she was *not* in love with him, &, in fact, she could never have crossed the Rubicon.[19]

This is ('in fact') an assertion of naked authorial power, or a confession of failed authorial intentions, but there is too little given of Claire, certainly in the pre-*NYE* versions, for the reader to understand her as '*not* in love with him'. We get much more of Pansy, who *is* in love with Rosier; and the way Osmond uses 'authority' is much more comprehensible. Claire goes into a convent voluntarily, against her family's wishes (recalling Turgenev's ardent Liza at the end of *A Nest of Gentlefolk*); but Pansy is sent back to hers (also felt as a prison) by Osmond's express command, her non-resistance to which is believable in the light of what we know of the rigorous demands of obedience made in the course of her education, the unyielding delineation of thresholds not only metaphorical but actual that she may not cross. Pansy and Rosier are not the central characters, and in a sense James simplifies the plot of *The American* to make it less ambiguous, a comparatively straightforward matter, a case of European patriarchal and papistically tinted manipulation of the emotional life of a daughter. If the plot in itself is simplified and relegated to secondary status, however, this is not to say that James's intentions for it are not complex, for it is on Isabel as an initially detached observer that this plot is made to bear; it brings home to her the criteria dominating the view of marriage taken by Osmond and Madame Merle. The hidden analogy between the manipulation she has unconsciously undergone and the more blatant tyranny exercised at Pansy's expense comes increasingly to the surface, until finally her action on Pansy's behalf (her keeping of her promise to return to Rome) could be seen as a vicarious means of expressing her defiant non-acquiescence in the way

[19] HJ to Elizabeth Boott, 26 May 1877 (Harvard MS).

she has been used. The *American* plot is thus subsumed into a larger structure, a more extensive 'architecture' in which it is presented at a different angle and in which its internal relations are simplified but its external ones varied and refined; it becomes a ground of plot for James's developing imagination of new 'values'.

Having made his fortune, Newman in *The American* is searching for a 'lovely being' to be 'perched on the pile like some shining statue crowning some high monument' (*NYE* ii. 49). In keeping with the reduced scale of the plot in *The Portrait*, the object of Ned Rosier's choice, Pansy, has for Isabel 'always a little of the doll about her' (*1882*, p. 363); and the narration comments that 'He thought of her in amorous meditation a good deal as he might have thought of a Dresden-china shepherdess' (*1882*, p. 313). The *NYE* the moment before (putting on the 'last touch' which it newly mentions) makes her 'a consummate piece' (iv. 90) in his eyes. The notion of 'possession', a word later to be so rich in metaphorical extensions for James, here becomes charged with moral questions about how to distinguish between legitimate attitudes to inanimate objects, *objets d'art,* and decent attitudes to other people, especially those of the other sex. To call a woman a 'piece' in other contexts is grossly disrespectful, and to 'possess' one straightforwardly sexual; here special exemptions for attitudes of artistic appreciation have to come into force in order to make the analogy of woman and 'Dresden-china shepherdess' at all acceptable—if taken seriously. The language of connoisseurship, after all, has traditionally been appropriated for the delectation (and justification) of rakes, possessors and keepers of women; though the counter-argument offers the recognition of beauty as a duty and the beauty of women as just as true as that of art objects.

James's interest in this equivocal area is particularly clear in the *blague* of *Théodolinde* (later called *Rose-Agathe*), a short story of 1878, in which the narrator observes an American friend, Sanguinetti, regularly visiting the shop of a Paris hairdresser with a pretty wife for mysterious negotiations. Sanguinetti speaks of 'her' with rapture: 'I have an intense desire to possess her' he remarks shockingly (*THJ* iii. 148), and 'he made no secret of his conviction that "pretty things" were the only things in the world worth troubling one's self about' (*THJ* iii. 144). This starts to seem too explicit, a tale very *drolatique* for James; but in fact the narrator, sure Sanguinetti has been corrupted and 'Parisianised' (*THJ* iii. 145) into proposing adultery, has the wrong end of the stick. (Years later Strether's wrong end of the stick is the *other* end.) The tale is an extended pun, a pronominal ambiguity (crude next to those of the later novels) lasting to the punch line. The 'she' is not the human wife but the hairdresser's doll in the window, and the harmlessness of Sanguinetti's passion is firmly indicated: 'She existed only from the waist upward' (*THJ* iii. 153). The narrator's mistake has a satirical point to make about French sexual attitudes, and about the diverse ethical judgements that fasten on the same expression of an attitude according to the nature of its object—human, or not.

Sanguinetti is a model for the innocence of Ned Rosier (whose loved one has 'a little of the doll about her'). Rosier, once in love with Pansy, is capable of preferring the human to the artificial ornament and selling his *bibelots* for her sake. In *The Portrait* Rosier is one of the figures run against Osmond for a characterizing contrast, a further precision of terms. Osmond and Rosier are distinct kinds of collector, pursuing for different purposes different ideas of possession. The respect and delicacy involved in a proper relation to beautiful objects, for instance, cultivated by Rosier in regard to Pansy, are neglected by Osmond in his behaviour to Isabel, which she eventually registers in an image revised to note her treatment as inferior to that he gives his fine ornaments: 'she had been a dull un-reverenced tool' (*1882*, p. 484) becomes 'she had been an applied handled hung-up tool, as senseless and convenient as mere shaped wood and iron' (*NYE* iv. 379). Isabel had actually, in the *NYE*, gone so far as to view herself as a rare object; where after her travels in *1882* she 'felt a good deal older than she had done a year before' (*1882*, p. 285), the *NYE* takes this up and points it in the direction of her relation to Osmond and its meaning for her: 'she only felt older—ever so much, and as if she were "worth more" for it, like some curious piece in an antiquary's collection' (*NYE* iv. 42). Here Isabel makes herself out a 'piece' in Osmond's eyes, with age refining her intrinsic quality and giving her an increased value for him; whereas the 'tool' metaphor more truthfully reads back her value to him only as a temporary utility, and through 'hung-up' suggests a rapid depreciation, rather than a steady appreciation, in value—that of something 'used' but not 'antique'. When Osmond is still caressing his complacency into imagining Isabel as a perfect wife, we are told that for him 'this lady's intelligence was to be a silver plate, not an earthen one—a plate that he might heap up with ripe fruits, to which it would give a decorative value, so that conversation might become a sort of perpetual dessert'(*1882*, p. 307). This statement corroborates

Isabel's initial feeling of herself as a 'curious piece' for him, silver not earthen, while overloading the image to a point of comic repletion, which expresses his desire for her as not crudely mercenary but sublimely (and ridiculously) egotistical.

The book's handling of the ethics of collecting, a topic connected with attitudes to marriage, seems as interested in differentiating the values of the various collectors as in producing a systematic critique of Victorian male sexuality. Ralph Touchett is a collector, as the embittered Madame Merle recalls early on in deploring the blank sheet presented by American men at a loose end in Europe: ' "He is very cultivated", they say; "he has got a very pretty collection of old snuff-boxes." The collection is all that is wanted to make it pitiful. I am tired of the sound of the word; I think it's grotesque' (*1882*, p. 171). This may derive some of its withering scorn from her sense of Osmond's failure (the scene precedes Isabel's inheritance and her older friend has no special reason to be cagey); at any rate we can take it as introducing a severely dubious note into the argument, offering the collector's activity as a wastefully trivial misdirection of energy. Not that Ralph is shown as neglecting human relations for object relations; the pictures at Gardencourt, 'most of them of his own choosing' (*1882*, p. 37), don't keep him from 'pausing in the middle of the gallery and bending his eyes much less upon the pictures than on her figure . . . she was better worth looking at than most works of art' (*1882*, p. 38). Confronted with Isabel, an interesting live person, Ralph, like Rosier with Pansy, devotes his attention to her rather than objects; if his secret financial arrangement is a kind of investment, it is essentially an expenditure made in order to give her freedom, and not (at all literally, anyway) to possess her. Isabel early on, still beguiled by harmonies, makes a cogent comparison between Ralph and Osmond, without yet realizing its implications: 'Ralph had something of this same quality, this appearance of thinking that life was a matter of connoisseurship; but in Ralph it was an anomaly, a kind of humorous excrescence, whereas in Mr Osmond it was the key-note, and everything was in harmony with it' (*1882*, p. 229).

In Chapter XXXVII James stresses, especially in the *NYE*, that collecting has not impaired the humanity of Rosier, either—another antitype to Osmond. Rosier's admiration for Isabel,

Like his appreciation of her dear little step-daughter, . . . was based partly on his fine sense of the plastic; but also on a relish for a more impalpable sort of merit—that merit of a bright spirit, which Rosier's devotion to brittle wares had not made him cease to regard as a quality (*1882*, p. 321).

The *NYE* imaginatively compacts the 'brightness' and the 'impalpability' here for a metaphor transcending the topic to which it refers; and turns 'quality' back on Rosier himself to give him credit for his unimpaired judgement.

Like his appreciation of her dear little step-daughter, it was based partly on his eye for decorative character, his instinct for authenticity; but also on a sense for uncatalogued values, for that secret of a 'lustre' beyond any recorded losing or rediscovering, which his devotion to brittle wares had still not disqualified him to recognise (*NYE* iv. 105).

Rosier's 'instinct for authenticity' sounds less heartless and more valuable than his 'fine sense of the plastic' in *1882*—which also risked his seeming to love Pansy only as a physical object. The revisions help to point the contrast with Osmond, whose unsociable look amid his guests, on the previous page, has been expansively revised to include his disdainful advertisement of his own superior values. 'His eyes were fixed, abstractedly' (*1882*, p. 320) has become 'his eyes had an expression, frequent with them, that seemed to represent them as engaged with objects more worth their while than the appearances actually thrust upon them' (*NYE* iv. 103). This powerful bluff is what has made Isabel, seeking to please, think of herself as 'worth more' for an increase in her antiquity. But at the mid-point of the chapter Osmond is 'seen'; Rosier goes with Pansy to Osmond's 'yellow room', and exercises his judgement to Osmond's disadvantage: 'Rosier really thought the room very ugly, and it seemed cold' (*1882*, p. 324). Pansy mentions how much taste her papa has: 'He had a good deal, Rosier thought; but some of it was bad' (*1882*, p. 325; *NYE* iv. 110 makes this 'very bad'). The more expensive purchases Osmond has been able to make since his marriage brought him money, moreover, appear not to have reached the level of the 'great prizes' he found 'during his impecunious season' (*1882*, p. 320); so that by the standards of his obsession with perfect appearances the effort made to entrap Isabel has failed to pay off. *Within* the realm of collecting, then, Osmond is seen to lapse.

The 1906 revisions refining this line of interest in the *1882 Portrait* are the fruit of a continuing concern on James's part through the intervening years: notably in *The Spoils of Poynton* (1897), where Mrs Gereth openly acknowledges 'her personal gift, the genius, the passion, the patience of the collector',[20] and where beautiful objects are the currency in which the story is transacted—a currency with disputed rates of exchange. The title of *The Golden Bowl* (1904), like those of *The Spoils* and *The Portrait*, refers to a precious art object; and this novel, the last fiction to be written by James before the *NYE*, returns to the terrain of *The Portrait* in its dialectical movement between the demands of the aesthetic sense and of the moral sense. The titular object in *The Golden Bowl* has a material flaw; and is associated with Charlotte's proto-adulterous excursion with the Prince. Standing for something deeply wrong with arrangements beneath the surface, it retrospectively connects, even in its 'central position above the fire-place', with a scene in *The Portrait*.[21] Osmond is with Madame Merle, his long-time associate, in her salon, being accused of frightening Isabel: he displays a mocking coolness.

He took up a small cup and held it in his hand; then, still holding it and leaning his arm on the mantel, he continued: 'You always see too much in everything; you overdo it; you lose sight of the real. I am much simpler than you think.'

'I think you are very simple.' And Madame Merle kept her eye upon her cup. 'I have come to that with time. I judged you, as I say, of old; but it is only since your marriage that I have understood you. I have seen better what you have been to your wife than I ever saw what you were for me. Please be very careful of that precious object.'

'It already has a small crack', said Osmond, dryly, as he put it down (*1882*, pp. 459–60).

The object so edgily comprehended in their discussion becomes loaded with significance; though Osmond's rebuke to Madame Merle for reading in, that 'You always see too much in everything', gives us some (Hawthorne-like) hesitancy about making the cracked cup too much of a Hawthornian emblem. Madame Merle appears to be right about the resistingly superficial Osmond in this scene, however; and so the accusations 'you overdo it; you lose sight of the real', accusations directed by many at James's later fiction, are not convincingly grounded. The simplicity Osmond claims for himself is an innocent one; the simplicity Madame Merle sees in him is that of monstrous

[20] *The Spoils of Poynton*, London, 1897, p. 12.
[21] S. Gorley Putt points out that 'There is a passing reference to a "cracked cup" motif which briefly prefigures the controlling image of *The Golden Bowl*' (*The Fiction of Henry James*, Harmondsworth, 1968, p. 135).

egotism; and if she is exposed to the allegation that she is indulging in over-speculative interpretation, the cause of this vulnerability is Osmond's deceptive strategy of elaborating his own account of 'the real' into a hard surface.

We could see this moment as a manifesto, a justification in advance of James's later method, where the technical complication and equivocation are means necessary for rendering the working of dramatic discrepancies, the movement between the reality of a situation and the fictitious structures evolved by the characters. Madame Merle's keeping her eye on her cup, and her insistence 'Please be very careful of that precious object', may be her ways of asking Osmond to take care in handling Pansy or Isabel, precious objects of hers entrusted to him; her ways because the truth on the topic remains unspeakable between them, yet is there between them. The dry remarking of the 'small crack' seems to signify Osmond's general refusal to take her point; it is a disagreeable devaluing of the physical object which can also convey a disparagement of the metaphorical object (Isabel or Pansy) to which the exchange may refer. In the context of such conspiratorial reticences, the discussion of realities is bound to be displaced, to appear in masked and indirect forms; those with secrets don't want to give away evidence. The later sections of *The Portrait* anticipate James's later fiction in this respect: they are full of characters unwilling to speak out what is in their thoughts.

iv. Great Scenes

When planning in his notebook the revelation that Madame Merle is Pansy's mother, James at first imagines a direct confrontation between Isabel and her older ffiend on the subject of their rights over the girl.

Isabel resents Madame Merle's interference, demands of her what she has to do with Pansy. Whereupon Madame Merle, in whose breast the suppressed feeling of maternity has long been rankling, and who is passionately jealous of Isabel's influence over Pansy, breaks out with the cry that she alone has a right—that Pansy is her daughter (*Nks.*, p. 14).

But immediately, as if this passionate cry rang melodramatically false to the cageyness established as characteristic of Madame Merle, James steps back into a questioning parenthesis:

(To be settled later whether this revelation is to be made by Mme Merle herself, or by the Countess Gemini. Better on many grounds that it should be the latter; and yet in that way I lose the 'great scene' between Madame Merle and Isabel.)

Having said this, James continues to sketch the plot up to the end of the novel; after an interval, indicated by crosses, he gives himself his well-known justification for ending *en l'air*—that 'The *whole* of anything is never told; you can only take what groups together' (*Nks.*, p. 15); and then after leaving another space he returns to the question of the maternity-revelation.

I am not sure that it would not be best that the exposure of Mme Merle should never be complete, and above all that she should not denounce herself. This would injure very much the impression I have wished to give of her profundity, her self-control, her regard for appearances. It may be enough that Isabel should believe the fact in question—in consequence of what the Countess Gemini has told her. Then, when Madame Merle tells her of what Ralph has done for her of old—tells it with the view I have mentioned to precipitating her defiance of Osmond—Isabel may charge her with the Countess G.'s secret. This Madame Merle will deny—but deny in such a way that Isabel knows she lies; and *then* Isabel may depart (*Nks.*, pp. 15–16).

The consideration that 'above all . . . she should not denounce herself' is a familiar one for readers of *The Wings of the Dove*, where the conspiring Densher stifles in conversation with Milly the exclamation that 'I know what one would do for Kate!' because 'resisting the impulse to break out was what he *was* doing for Kate' (*W.o.D.*, p. 319). The same fear of exposure pervades *The Golden Bowl*, where the confronted Prince is puzzled into a momentary lapse of dignity which makes Maggie feel, 'as in a flash, how such a consequence, a foredoomed infelicity, partaking of the ridiculous even in one of the cleverest, might be of the very essence of the penalty of wrong-doing' (*GB*, p. 424). In these late works people don't *deliberately* give themselves away, because of the 'regard for appearances' which they share with Madame Merle and Osmond.

The notebook debate of 1880 or 1881 fascinatingly shows us James revising his intentions in the process of thinking out the action—revising impulses towards melodrama and explicit confrontation which are lively in the works of the 1870s and channelling them into potent indirections which anticipate those he was master of two and three decades later. Thus 'Isabel may charge her with the Countess G.'s secret' is a resurfacing of the urge for moral statements and the making of 'scenes', recalling Newman's charge of the Bellegardes with

Mrs Bread's secret in *The American*; but it is an urge which does not get into, or rather does not get acted upon in, the *1882* scene with Madame Merle. Like Newman but at an earlier stage, Isabel experiences the bitterness of a desire for revenge only for it to pass over: 'There was a moment during which, if she had turned and spoken, she would have said something that would hiss like a lash. But she closed her eyes, and then the hideous vision died away' (*1882*, p. 484). 'Hiss like a lash' *has* the lurid pigment of a melodramatic 'great scene'— only fended off to the conditional—and the 'hideous vision' is only that, a vision. A moment later 'Isabel's only revenge was to be silent still', moreover; and we can recall how Maggie Verver, the exemplary manipulator of loaded silences, might fairly, as James comments, 'have yearned for it, for the straight vindictive view, the rights of resentment, the rages of jealousy, the protests of passion, as for something she had been cheated of not least'; a conventionally alliterating repertoire of strong affects figured, to distance the bombastic, as 'nothing nearer to experience than a wild eastern caravan, looming into view with crude colours in the sun, fierce pipes in the air, high spears against the sky, all a thrill, a natural joy to mingle with, but turning off short before it reached her and plunging into other defiles' (*GB*, p. 455). The abnegation of the vindictive as remotely romantic has a different basis from that in *The American*, where Newman seriously contemplates exacting revenge and then mysteriously and impressively refrains; for it is as 'her husband's wife' and 'her father's daughter' that Maggie finds the self-righteous mode inconceivable. She has unlike Newman a set of family responsibilities, imposed by her great 'love' for the others, which prevents any such horrified flight from the domestic complexities of her situation. It may be that the loved and fragile Pansy performs the same function for Isabel, humanly representing the necessity of limiting any damage to be done.

The undeclarative passage between Isabel and Madame Merle at Pansy's convent belies James's notebook worry that 'in that way I lose the "great scene" between Madame Merle and Isabel'. The scene works by keeping Isabel in pained silence while her betrayer puts up a monologue which is supposed to cover herself; and then having the monologue falter: 'She had not proceeded far before Isabel noted a sudden rupture in her voice, which was in itself a complete drama' (*1882*, p. 483). The *NYE* makes this 'a sudden break in her voice, a lapse in her continuity, which was in itself a complete drama' (*NYE* iv. 378). Both early and revised texts draw attention to the inferential excitement to be derived from the small crack in her consistency, 'a complete drama' making a strong claim for the dramatic potency of unspoken transactions when much is at stake. James is venturing an experiment here, and immediately glosses the moment with a polemical insistence to make clear that Madame Merle has guessed that Isabel knows, explaining just how 'This subtle modulation marked a momentous discovery.' The equivalent moment in *The Golden Bowl* again has the young heroine listening to a monologue by her treacherous friend and picking out the troubled consciousness denoted by the quality of her voice. Charlotte Stant, here, loudly acting as a guide for visitors to Fawns, does not have an actual vocal 'lapse': rather, 'The high voice went on; its quaver was doubtless for conscious ears only, but there were verily thirty seconds during which it sounded, for our young woman, like the shriek of a soul in pain' (*GB*, p. 495). 'Doubtless ... only, but ... verily' produces less explicitly *The Portrait*'s combination of the 'subtle' and the 'momentous'. Maggie is brought to tears by a quavering rather than an interruption in her rival's speech; which is a reflection of the fact that whereas in *The Portrait* a certainty is attained through intuition ('Madame Merle had guessed in the space of an instant that everything was at an end between them'), in *The Golden Bowl* Charlotte's suffering is a torment of uncertainty: she is deprived of any sense of what others know, and is thus socially and emotionally disabled. The claim entered in *The Portrait* for 'a complete drama' in a broken voice, and the registered possibility of a remark that would hiss like a lash, recognizably anticipate the acuteness with which 'it sounded, for our young woman, like the shriek of a soul in pain'. In both cases the psychological punishment is conveyed by a violent, hellish metaphor; though the crucial insight of *The Golden Bowl*, that the punishment is all the crueller for not being applied from the outside, distinguishes it from the earlier work. At all events we can see the innovative changes of mind about the structure and treatment of this climactic scene in *The Portrait*, which James's notebooks permit us to trace, as steps in an evolution towards the formal and thematic preoccupations of his 'major phase'; an evolution more *evident*, at least, in this scene than in the preceding one, that of the revelations by the Countess Gemini, which repeats patterns familiar from *Roderick Hudson* and *The American*—though doing so with an ulterior motive.

The chapter above on *Roderick Hudson* drew attention to James's problems in the 1870s with the plausible conveyance of plot information between his characters and especially with the final revelation of secrets. Coleridge's Ancient Mariner, his 'glittering eye' indicating a compulsion to speak out about a crime (and spoil the fun of a marriage, incidentally), serves James again in *The Portrait*, in the scene between Isabel and the Countess Gemini which prepares us for the confrontation with Madame Merle at the convent. In *1882* the Countess, confronting Isabel with something to say, 'had a strange smile on her thin lips, and a still stranger glitter in her small dark eye' (p. 475). But the NYE seems to want to put this quite otherwise: 'she had a strange smile on her thin lips and her whole face had grown in an hour a shining intimation. She lived assuredly, it might be said, at the window of her spirit, but now she was leaning far out' (iv. 361). In the Houghton Library manuscript of the revision, though, we can see that 'a shining' begins as 'a living'; while 'assuredly' is an insertion, a further thought. The reference to light in 'glitter', that is, at first gets suppressed but then returns in 'shining' as the idea of 'living' is transferred and expanded into the sentence about leaning out, which alerts us to a departure in the Countess from her habitual angle of inclination. But if the Ancient Mariner is here submerged, he comes back a dozen lines later in a revision, more explicitly than in his *1882* form. The earlier version reads:

She appeared to have something to say, and it occurred to Isabel for the first time that her sister-in-law might say something important. She fixed her brilliant eyes upon Isabel, who found at last a disagreeable fascination in her gaze (*1882*, p. 475).

The NYE gives this an enlivening turn or two:

She appeared to have a deal to say, and it occurred to Isabel for the first time that her sister-in-law might say something really human. She made play with her glittering eyes, in which there was an unpleasant fascination (*NYE* iv. 362).

'Really human' makes Isabel's scepticism till now about the Countess seem a matter of course rather than of pride (since she has been 'not really human' rather than 'unimportant'), and gives an emphasis which dramatically enlarges our sense of what she may say. 'Made play' suggests an expressive motion the reverse of 'fixed', and prepares us for the theatricality of her recital; while the allusion in 'her glittering eyes' intimates not only her need to speak but also the auditor's reluctance.

If the basic format of the scene is melodramatic or romantic, though, both in *1882* and in the much-amplified *NYE* version, the melodramatic or romantic element is there just in order to be discarded—in favour of the movement, in the following scene with Madame Merle, towards a complex play of silences and understandings. The combination of the Madame Merle and Countess Gemini scenes as a pair is a crucial step on from the first notebook idea of them as alternatives ('in that way I lose the "great scene" between Madame Merle and Isabel'). F. O. Matthiessen, in his pioneering piece on the revisions of *The Portrait,* comments on the Countess's 'dramatic possibilities' which James 'in his revision . . . exploited to the full'; and he quotes Lawrence Leighton observing that 'James wanted a good harangue, the sort of speech an actress could get her teeth into'.[22] He then remarks, subsequently and separately, on the way in which 'James has also built up the contrast between her and Isabel',[23] by making the young American's reactions more unexpected by her.

But there is a relation between the Countess's values—which don't have currency with Isabel—and her melodramatic presentation, one which we can see as complicating Matthiessen's claim that here James 'did everything he could to make her revelations to Isabel into the "great scene" he had missed'.[24] The Countess's revelation is not a *self-*denunciation, nor an unmotivated spilling of the beans, but a polemical denunciation of her resented brother and Madame Merle from the point of view of a partisan hostility to marriage and with a particular intention for the effect to be made on her hearer. We can be prompted by the revisions to see the Countess, already in *1882*, as an artistic figure choosing her means for producing intended effects by her revelation; like James, shown by the notebooks consciously deciding how to bring about what is also *his* revelation. Once the words have been spoken, in *1882*, Isabel, who has at first found 'the announcement . . . an anti-climax' (p. 476), says she doesn't understand.

> She spoke in a low, thoughtful tone, and the poor Countess was equally surprised and disappointed at the effect of her revelation. She had expected to kindle a conflagration, and as yet she had barely extracted a spark. Isabel seemed more awe-stricken than anything else (*1882*, pp. 476–7).

In the *NYE*, the account is pointed to give first a sharper sense of the

---

[22] F. O. Matthiessen, *Henry James: The Major Phase,* Oxford, 1944, pp. 175–6.
[23] *The Major Phase,* p. 176.
[24] *The Major Phase,* p. 175.

Countess's failure as artistic, and then of Isabel's peculiar reaction which registers the failure.

> She spoke as one troubled and puzzled, yet the poor Countess seemed to have seen her revelation fall below its possibilities of effect. She had expected to kindle some responsive blaze, but had barely extracted a spark. Isabel showed as scarce more impressed than she might have been, as a young woman of approved imagination, with some fine sinister passage of public history (*NYE* iv. 365–6).

The raising of the question of '*possibilities* of effect' can point us back to the critical calculations in the notebooks: 'effect' in *1882* might simply have meant 'result of a cause', where in the *NYE*, differently placed, it suggests a rhetorical idea of audience manipulation. 'Conflagration' in *1882* has the Countess an emotional arsonist, with 'in flagrante delicto' behind it, but as if any kind of fire would do. 'Some responsive blaze' in the *NYE* spells out the desired sympathy in indignation which is too faintly suggested by the 'con-' in 'conflagration'; the Countess wants Isabel to feel as fierce as she does.

The *NYE*'s last sentence establishes a clearer syntactic balance of values: '*scarce* more impressed than' takes us in a clearer direction than 'more awe-stricken than'; while the strong adjectival pointing of the quantities introduced—'approved imagination' and 'fine sinister passage of public history'—establishes something detached and 'scarce more than' blandly impersonal in Isabel's appreciation of the news. '*Public* history', particularly, conveys her instinctive unwillingness to associate such calculating duplicities with her own life; and the *NYE*'s near-simile here ('scarce more than') recalls that from *The Golden Bowl* quoted above where Maggie feels the vindictive view as 'nothing nearer to experience than a wild eastern caravan . . . turning off short before it reached her'. Maggie, no more inflammable than Isabel, has in the same passage been unable to 'give herself . . . to the vulgar heat of her wrong'.

In *The Golden Bowl* the revelation to Maggie of the deception and adultery comes through the unlikely agency of the little man in the Bloomsbury shop, without benefit even of the preparatory characterization we have in *The Portrait* for the Countess; and a comparable revelation is made by the vindictive Lord Mark in *The Wings of the Dove*; but these scenes, confrontations consisting of plain statements of facts previously suppressed, are not—that is are only indirectly—

presented. The stress on the 'anti-climax' of the Countess Gemini's fully staged revelation can be seen as offering a rationale for these later elisions: in the Countess's view it is a genre scene, grandly operatic, with a conventional lively delivery and a conventional passionate response (the repertoire of attitudes listed by Maggie)—but as we have noted, this is not the kind of scene in which James's American heroines, coming from another world, feel they can participate. Isabel's pitiful tears signal her refusal to accept the terms in which the Countess presents the material, and her insertion of the events narrated into a quite different sort of story. James's remark that Isabel was to be 'an *Americana*—a female counterpart to Newman' is germane to this: like Newman, only without delay, she rejects the proffered European ethic of revenge in favour of conduct more enlightened and less brutally selfish, and does so in a way related to her distance from the European conventions (attitudes struck and scenes made) in which the unacceptable values are enshrined.

James's handling of point of view in the Countess's revelation scene corresponds to the play of values thus dramatized. The scene begins from Isabel's point of view, and keeps to it from her initial sense of the revelation as 'an anti-climax' up to her stunned absorption of its main implications, at which point she nearly speaks the name of Madame Merle. Then ' "Why have you told me this?" she asked, in a voice which the Countess hardly recognised' (*1882*, p. 476). It is the *Countess*'s cognitive process that is offered here, for the first time in the scene, at a moment of traumatic strangeness for Isabel; we seem to have a withdrawal from the central character's consciousness into that of the person attempting to produce a special effect in her. Straight after this Isabel says she doesn't understand and we get the paragraph discussed above, where 'the poor Countess *was* equally surprised and disappointed at the effect of her revelation' while 'Isabel *seemed* more awe-stricken than anything else' (my emphases). After which James begins to present the dialogue as a sensitive spectator would write of a piece of theatrical action, without assuming special insight into the characters' thoughts. We are left in some doubt about Isabel's internal processes. When she bursts into tears we are authorially informed that 'It was a long time since she had shed any' (*1882*, p. 477); 'suddenly controlling herself' is an uncontroversial inference to draw from appearances, but even so is revised to the more superficial 'with a sudden check' in the *NYE* (iv. 367). In the *NYE* when Isabel asks if Osmond has been faithful 'To me—', she does so *as if* her question

... were all for herself' (iv. 367; my emphasis). On the next page 'Isabel sat staring at her companion's story as at a bale of fantastic wares that some strolling gypsy might have unpacked on the carpet at her feet' (*1882*, p. 478); which is a novelized stage direction, not an entry into her consciousness. We don't get the Countess's view either, but a comment on her which need not be directly Isabel's: 'if she lied she lied well' (*1882*, p. 478). It is not till page 479 that Isabel's feelings return to the text with the reference to Pansy as 'her daughter'— Madame Merle's; and even here it is in an account of their numb state which, in the *NYE*, has been *prepared* by the revision two pages before about 'public history': ' "It seems very wonderful", she murmured; and in this bewildering impression she had almost lost her sense of being personally touched by the story.' Then Isabel flushes 'at the thought' (the reader's minor insight) of Madame Merle's pain at seeing her own successful step-motherhood; but even so for another three-quarters of a page she and the Countess are rendered from the outside: when the Countess cries 'Why did you ever inherit money?', 'She stopped a moment, *as if* she saw something singular in Isabel's face.' Finally 'Isabel rose from her sofa again; *she felt* bruised and short of breath; her head was humming with new knowledge'; and '*she felt* weak' (*1882*, p. 480; my emphases).

We come back to Isabel, then, though not very conclusively, after what we could think of as an experimental abstention from explicit authorial insight, one which allows a suspense to build up about the nature of the heroine's response to such shattering news, and about how far her code of values will be tenable and sustaining in face of it. Such a suspense gives a go with the whip to the European vindictive view; there are occasions when we are with the Countess looking at Isabel. The scene is a test of Isabel's moral imagination, which has to come up with an alternative relation to circumstances it has not been prepared to contemplate. The complete withdrawal from the point of view of Milly Theale at the comparable juncture (Lord Mark's brutal divulging of the plot) in *The Wings of the Dove* seems to be James's furthest extension of this practice or principle: with Densher's sub-sequent burning of Milly's letter it asks the reader to supply imagi-natively the heroine's possibilities of response at a moment of ethical and emotional crisis. Even in *The Portrait*, however, where Isabel's point of view is re-entered, the authorial privilege of 'going behind', of detailing and accounting for her thoughts and feelings, is considerably limited from this point on, in the technique of 'gradual authorial withdrawal':[25] a ready proof being the controversy surrounding the novel's ending, which so many have differed about, or found frustratingly ambiguous.

v.   In the Sequel

The Portrait ends equivocally; James in his notebook anticipates the criticism that Isabel is left *en l'air,* and confidently equivocates: 'This is both true and false.' He goes on, explaining,

The *whole* of anything is never told; you can only take what groups together. What I have done has that unity—it groups together. It is complete in itself—and the rest may be taken up or not, later (*Nks.,* p. 15).

Which kind of wholeness of telling is being referred to here, temporal or philosophical—or both? What will happen when Isabel returns to Rome and Osmond is something we care about and are deprived of; the nature of Isabel's decision to return, which does fall within the temporal compass of the book, is another thing about which we care and yet are left without details. She leaves as she has entered, 'in motion and, so to speak, in transit' (*LC* ii. 1076), as James says in the Preface. She does so 'all tormentingly', for Casper Goodwood at least. Yet in the sense that the final section of the work has shown Isabel adrift and emotionally exhausted, unable to reach a decision, we can feel some finality in her having now decided, and a double propriety, to which we may have ambivalent reactions, in her thus fulfilling her promise to Pansy to return at the same time as going back to Osmond (in some sense) and thus not 'repudiating the most serious act—the single sacred act—of her life' (*1882,* p. 405). The strength of the marriage bond as a consideration for Isabel has been intensified in the *NYE*—though before the Countess Gemini's revelations: 'marriage meant that a woman should abide with her husband' (*1882,* p. 475), 'should cleave to the man with whom, uttering tremendous vows, she had stood at the altar' (*NYE* iv. 361). And the promise to Pansy has been acknowledged by Henrietta—reluctantly but without qualification—as in itself a sufficient reason to go back (*1882,* p. 496). We are not put in a position definitively to arbitrate between the force of these two promises in Isabel's decision, though the stress placed by

---

[25] Ora Segal, *The Lucid Reflector: The Observer in Henry James's Fiction,* New Haven, 1969, p. 55.

James throughout on the importance of the relation to Pansy ought to correct any interpretation of Isabel's return as merely a capitulation to Osmond's marital power and his cult of respectable appearances.

Under the influence of Freud and perhaps of some of James's own *NYE* revisions to the penultimate scene, many critics have read Isabel's return as really motivated by something different from either of these ties, as a flight from sexual passion and the 'hard manhood' of Caspar Goodwood (*NYE* iv. 436). Richard Poirier, apparently with a Lawrentian idea of fullness in mind, puts the point persuasively as an inadequacy in James's intentions: 'even his most cherished value, the idea of individual freedom from social restriction, begins to look suspiciously like an abstract rationalization by which Isabel makes her fear of sex into an ideal of conduct'[26]—a point which presumably applies as much to the quitting of Caspar Goodwood at the end as to the refusal of her suitors in the beginning. Poirier argues that James strongly endorses Isabel's principled decision: 'in talking about her return we should be talking about a novel, not about a person, about the relation of her act to James's whole intention, more than about its revelation of her individual psychology'.[27] But he sees the novel as less good for thus relegating the matter of individual psychology. In *The Portrait*, according to Poirier, James 'had reached a point of crisis in his capacity to imagine a character in all its fullness and yet to present her as an object of more ideological than psychological interest'.[28] That is, Poirier reads Isabel as a figure mistakenly presented for ideological admiration (sticking to her word *vis-à-vis* Pansy and Osmond) but in fact striking the reader as psychologically—sexually—flawed. James in this view is on the point of discovering—or artistically accepting—that psychology underlies and redefines ideology (what's shown in the action of *The Bostonians,* his next novel). Poirier sees James as insufficiently true to his insights:

James does give us, however, a very tentative suggestion about Isabel which, if developed in conjunction with all that is fully achieved, would have, for me at least, made the novel a greater work than it is. I refer to the implication that there can be no such thing as the 'freedom' which Isabel wants and which Ralph and James want for her, simply for the reason that regardless of opportunity in the world outside, there are in everyone the flaws, the fears, the neuroses that fix and confine and stifle.[29]

[26] *The Comic Sense,* p. 150.   [27] Ibid., p. 244.
[28] Ibid., p. 252.   [29] Ibid., p. 207.

The 'tentative suggestion' runs counter to what Poirier sees as the damagingly 'glamorous' movement of the book,[30] its poetic sympathy with the future-fancying of its heroine, which is said to embody James's romantically excessive 'reverence for impractical aspiration'.[31]

Anthony J. Mazzella in his essay on 'The New Isabel' takes a more sympathetic view than Poirier of essentially the same interpretation: he brings together the Osmond–Pansy promises and the rejection of Goodwood as twin aspects of a highly abstract value: the rejection is construed as coming 'from fear of control by the erotic of the mind's power to operate', while the return to Rome is 'almost' a 'positive' challenge, 'for in that constricting environment only the mind has intense and wide freedom of movement'.[32] Mazzella, that is, accepts the reading that Isabel is afraid of sex, but makes it mindless sex she fears so that her final decision can be approved by reference to the high principle of 'mind' and its freedom.

It is not necessary, however, to see James's intentions as so unambivalently ideological: we can understand the ending perfectly well as deliberately engaging our uncertainty about what frame of reference to apply to Isabel's final movement, the ideological (in which it can be noble and ethically uplifting) or the psychological (in which it can be a repressively aim-inhibited transference of sexual urges on to other ground). Such a deliberate solicitation of ambiguity need not signify reprehensible uncertainty on James's part: it puts a valuable question to the reader about the relation between the realm of ethics and the 'deeper psychology', about the roots of noble actions and the capacity of human beings for sincere selflessness. In real life there is no certainty or consensus about the status and origins of high-minded actions, so those who perform them often have to go through with them psychologically 'blind', and we have to watch the process with some mixture of scepticism and generosity. Events *may* show whether the motives were pure (or sufficiently so)—but they also may happen *not* to show this, and to leave us in doubt.

We can find something chillingly lofty about Isabel's return, as about the conduct of the comparably placed Euphemia de Mauves in the 1874 story *Madame de Mauves*, where the betrayed wife behaves so

---

[30] *The Comic Sense*, p. 223.
[31] Ibid., p. 249.
[32] Anthony J. Mazzella, 'The New Isabel', in Norton Critical Edition of *The Portrait of a Lady*, ed. Robert D. Bamberg, New York, 1975, pp. 597–619, at p. 611.

impeccably ('She was stone, she was ice' (*THJ* ii. 347)) that she drives her European husband to blow out his brains. The suitor in that case, Longmore, ends like Goodwood, waiting; but the delay is of his own making: 'in the midst of all the ardent tenderness of his memory of Mme. de Mauves, he has become conscious of a singular feeling, for which awe would be hardly too strong a name'. Yet such a chill, while accompanied with a due scepticism about the springs of virtuous behaviour, does not prevent the spectator's appreciation of the awe-inspiring acts of self-abnegation which provoke it. If Isabel can save Pansy from Osmond's manipulation she will have done real good, even if she is partly driven to keep her promise by her pride, and even if her pride is intimately associated with her capacity for error.

James's attitude at the end, veiled as it then is, presumably corresponds to his proleptic authorial statement early on, unaltered in the *NYE*, 'that, later, she became consistently wise only at the cost of an amount of folly which will constitute almost a direct appeal to charity' (*1882*, p. 88). When this statement is made (after the surprising rejection of Warburton's proposal), the emphasis falls on the folly and the charity needed; but 'consistently wise', when we recall it at the conclusion, seems to approve the final decision without qualification—though sardonic ingenuity could extend the lessons of folly and defer 'later' till *after* the novel's end, to make her return to Rome itself the 'amount of folly' so costly as a course of education; a view to suit Caspar Goodwood, whose hopes are put off into some belated future.

What is to happen 'later' is variously important for the poised and weighted ending of *The Portrait*: as James said to himself in the notebook, 'the rest may be taken up or not, later'. Consideration of the novel is haunted by calculations as to what may happen in the sequel, whether metaphorically or in a literal volume taking up and pushing on the old story. The idea of a continuation was enough in the air to receive a denial as late as 1898, when James was pleased by A. C. Benson's praise, but stated that 'I shall never write a sequel to the *P. of an L.* ... It's all too faint and far away—too ghostly and ghastly—and I have bloodier things *en tête*. I can do better than that!' (*LHJ* i. 279).[33] In the event, though, it was not to Isabel Osmond that

---

[33] These words are echoed in an unpublished letter from HJ to his niece Peggy on 19 June 1913, responding to the Minny Temple letters she had sent him for the

James turned later in the 1880s when he came to write the novel which was his nearest approach to a sequel, but to the Princess Casamassima, a figure who had ended *Roderick Hudson* in a state so far from 'consistently wise'. In a general sense *The Princess Casamassima* repeats the action of *Roderick Hudson* (Christina again fascinates and reduces to suicidal despair a sensitive young hero); and the Balzacian reappearance of a triangle of characters (Christina, Madame Grandoni, and the Prince), though the setting and the *central* concern are so different, creates resonances between texts that matter more to the meaning of the new work than those produced in *The Ambassadors* by the recurrence of Gloriani from *Roderick Hudson* twenty-six years before, or those in *The Golden Bowl* by the location of the crucial adulterous exploit at Matcham, mentioned as Lord Mark's destination in Chapter 37 of *The Wings of the Dove*. The contrast between the two women's final characters and situations vitally influences James's choice of Christina rather than Isabel for an extension of career. Christina is trapped in a loveless marriage and is romantically desperate for fulfilment and escape, and is thus a figure established as passionately uncomfortable within social rules and divisions, a ready source of plots; whereas Isabel has made her mistake and faced it, resisting Goodwood's summons to romantic flight and finding an honourable duty in her step-maternal relation to Pansy. From the vista of 'pathless lands' she dismally looked over from the train to London (1882, p. 491), she comes, on leaving Goodwood, to a clear view: 'She had not known where to turn; but she knew now. There was a very straight path' (1882, p. 519). Christina, that is, still represents aimless potentiality at the end of *Roderick Hudson*; Isabel has found direction and resolve.

At the beginning of this chapter I dealt briefly with the sense in which Isabel Archer is a creative extension and continuation of Minny Temple; and the end of *The Portrait* presents a conclusive aspect of the process. 'Minny was essentially incomplete', James wrote to Grace Norton; whereas Isabel's *Portrait* 'is complete in itself'. Whereas Isabel moves through 'pathless lands' to a vision of the 'very straight path' before her, James's last impression of Minny, recorded later in *Notes of a Son and Brother,* was 'as of a child struggling with her ignorance in a sort of pathless desert of the genial and the casual' (*Autobiog.,*

autobiography: 'what an infinitely pathetic faraway little ghostly voice it seems' (Berkeley TS transcript).

p. 514). Matthiessen, discussing *The Portrait*, quotes William James in a letter commenting relevantly on *The Tragic Muse*: 'the final winding up is, as usual with you, rather a losing of the story in the sand, yet that is the way in which things lose themselves in real life'.[34] Minny's real life story gets lost in the sand, the pathless desert, incomplete in a way that causes lamentation, and needs imaginative restoration. In *Notes of a Son and Brother*, alive to the pain of her life, James comes to the end of Minny's letters 'with a sigh of supreme relief for an end intimately felt as at hand' (*Autobiog.*, p. 534); back on 29 March 1870, writing to William, he had thought of 'the very heroine of our common scene', as he called her three days before to his mother, as 'the helpless victim and toy of her own intelligence—so that there is positive relief in thinking of her being removed from her own heroic treatment and placed in kinder hands' (*HJL* i. 223). The relief of ending as such is denied Isabel, whose 'amount of folly' has from the start taken the form of quixotically hoping for a crisis: 'Sometimes she went so far as to wish that she should find herself some day in a difficult position, so that she might have the pleasure of being as heroic as the occasion demanded' (*1882*, p. 43). The marriage to Osmond which ultimately offers this chance more immediately gives her a challenge to meet from Ralph, and he sees her 'having caught a glimpse, as she thought, of the heroic line, and desiring to advance in that direction' (*1882*, p. 300).

These earlier moments cannot necessarily be applied with any directness of irony to the actual ending, since the 'pleasure' as such of her return to Rome may well be minimal, while 'the heroic line' here involves defending Osmond from Ralph—a line she entirely abandons in the death-bed scene, where 'nothing mattered now but the only knowledge that was not pure anguish—the knowledge that they were looking at the truth together' (*1882*, p. 506). The ironic or awestruck remark that 'Women find their religion sometimes in strange exercises' (*1882*, p. 380) applies to Isabel's attempts to deceive Ralph about her suffering, which she equally drops at the close. The heroism of the ending is, at least in great part, presented as purged of its folly; 'the heroic line' is not the same as the 'very straight path' and the seeing of Ralph's spectre connotes a serious change of state, a passage through suffering to consistent wisdom. Isabel's promise to Pansy that 'I will come back' (*1882*, p. 489) is an engagement she would have to betray to go off with Caspar Goodwood, and no reader has a right to *demand*

---

[34] *The Major Phase*, p. 182.

that she break it, whatever the dismay with which her last action is regarded. Isabel can be seen as more 'complete' than Minny partly in finding a path, a worthwhile aim; and having married in the summer of 1873 at twenty-four, the age at which Minny was removed by death in 1870 from her own heroic treatment, she is very possibly by the spring of 1877, when the novel ends, 'filled out' and 'justified', in the words of the letter to Grace Norton.

We could certainly see Isabel's return to Gardencourt near the end of the novel as drawing attention to a new elegiac wisdom acquired since her first visit there. In the passage whose manuscript revisions are reproduced as the frontispiece of this book, the pictures in the gallery make her movingly conscious of the cruel contrast between human beings, who decay, and works of art, which seem so permanent—in a way which anticipates Milly Theale's tears before the Bronzino portrait in *The Wings of the Dove*.

Nothing was changed; she recognised everything that she had seen years before; it might have been only yesterday that she stood there. She reflected that things change but little, while people change so much (*1882*, p. 499).

In the *NYE* James, recognizing everything that he had seen years before, makes a change in *his* work of art, one which shows Isabel realizing a sad dissimilarity between things and people that she has wishfully ignored earlier in the action. After her travels, we recall, 'she only felt older—ever so much, and as if she were "worth more" for it, like some curious piece in an antiquary's collection'; a feeling which corresponds to her susceptibility to Osmond. Now, at Gardencourt, James expands the second sentence to give it a more disturbing pathos:

She envied the security of valuable 'pieces' which change by no hair's breadth, only grow in value, while their owners lose inch by inch youth, happiness, beauty ... (*NYE* iv. 403).

James, changing his valued 'piece' by more than a 'hair's breadth', may take some consolation from his continuing grasp of the action; but poor Isabel, who now knows herself a 'piece' *not* 'valuable' to Osmond, is unrelievedly stuck with her human mutability, and the dying Ralph's. This tragic consciousness of failure and loss seems to be the pre-condition of her closing movement towards an uncertain but more truly perceived future.

Eleven days after Minny Temple's death, when James, in Great Malvern, had still not heard the news, he wrote to his father that 'something tells me that there is somehow too much Minny to disappear for some time yet—more life than she has yet lived out' (*HJL* i. 214). The end of *The Portrait*, itself a reflection of Minny's continuing life in James's imagination, is full of very similar references to the life in Isabel's future. On the visionary journey to England she deeply senses how 'life would be her business for a long time to come' (*1882*, p. 492). And her intuition that 'she should last' (*1882*, p. 493) becomes twenty-six years later 'she should last to the end' (*NYE* iv. 393), grimly foreseeing a bound on her seeing of life and invoking an 'end' not that of the novel. When the dying Ralph asks if all is over between her and Osmond, Isabel replies, 'Oh no; I don't think anything is over' (*1882*, p. 507). *The Portrait* makes itself felt as an act of selection, of framing, which doesn't pretend to exhaust its subject when *it* is over but rather indicates how much lies outside its scope, in a way which relies on the connection it is alleging between its imaginative world and the conditions of real life. Its ' "artistic" idea', to take James's polemical terms from 'The Art of Fiction' three years later, does in a special sense 'render any ending at all impossible' (*LC* i. 48), by not including for representation what subsequently happens to Osmond and Pansy and Isabel herself. There is a mysterious life after the close of the book, and it is explicitly invoked in the conclusion, an act of reference to a larger and underlying reality behind and beyond the work of art. The conjured set of pseudo-historical data available for consultation and allusion—the imaginative world which the novelist draws up and then draws material from—shows forcefully here at the very edge of the book in James's purposeful abbreviation of the text.

The last pages of *The Portrait* formally parallel and significantly inflect two scenes from immediately previous works by James. The scene in the dark English garden with Caspar Goodwood echoes in its excitement at potential liberation the scene in the dark Genevan garden of *The Pension Beaurepas* (April 1878), whence the trapped heroine Aurora Church nearly flees with the hesitant narrator from the Europeanizing tyranny of her awful mother: 'It seemed to me, for a moment, that to pass out of that gate with this yearning, straining young creature would be to pass into some mysterious felicity. If I were only a hero of romance, I would offer, myself, to take her to America' (*THJ* iii. 330). Caspar Goodwood unhesitantly offers, himself, to take Isabel to America, and we could say tempts Isabel with the possibility of passionate surrender to him as 'a hero of romance'. We could see the point of these scenes as the resistance of a temptation to leave behind the oppressive constraints, already vividly demonstrated in both stories, of convention and duty corruptly defined (by Mrs Church and Osmond).

The closing scene between Caspar Goodwood and Henrietta Stackpole, which immediately follows, looks back to the last moments of *Washington Square* (1881), which in England first appeared in a volume together with *The Pension Beaurepas*. The heroine Catherine Sloper has taken her resolve and turned down her suitor Morris Townsend, who, implausibly encouraged by his supporter Mrs Penniman but unyieldingly dejected, sees only a bleak future for himself. Mrs Penniman asks,

'But you will not despair—you will come back?'
'Come back? Damnation!' And Morris Townsend strode out of the house, leaving Mrs. Penniman staring.
Catherine, meanwhile, in the parlor, picking up her morsel of fancy-work, had seated herself with it again—for life, as it were.[35]

The depressingly bland encouragement and the disconsolate reaction recur with a more humane and less satirical point in *The Portrait*— where, though, the heroine's future, having already been evoked on the previous page ('There was a very straight path'), is not mentioned. Henrietta grasps Goodwood's arm.

'Look here, Mr. Goodwood', she said; 'just you wait!'
On which he looked up at her (*1882*, p. 520).

1882 thus leaves the reader to provide expressions for Goodwood's (to us blank) face and mind in this gnomic final notation. The *NYE* amplifies, with an appended paragraph, the unhappiness of this ending for him:

On which he looked up at her—but only to guess, from her face, with a revulsion, that she simply meant he was young. She stood shining at him with that cheap comfort, and it added, on the spot, thirty years to his life. She walked him away with her, however, as if she had given him now the key to patience (*NYE* iv. 437–8).

This revision occurs almost 'thirty years' after *1882*, and seems to call on its own temporal distance from the first composition to imagine a life sentence of disappointment (an 'addition to' which is really a

[35] *Washington Square, The Pension Beaurepas, A Bundle of Letters,* 2 vols., London, 1881, i. 266.

subtraction from his life). Caspar knows, we are aware, that 'there are disappointments which last as long as life' (*1882*, p. 445). The view into Goodwood's future here includes Isabel's by imagining no end to his unsuccessful persistence with her. In both *The Portrait* and *Washington Square* the prospect is 'for life', and the statement of that is a way of propelling the action presented in the book forward to echo into the silence and emptiness after its final words. The *NYE*'s 'but' in 'but only to guess' quasi-pugnaciously jumps to correct any reading of this as a purely cheerful termination, and clarifies the ambiguity of *1882*'s half-line (he may look up thinking things are promising, *or* in immediate disgust) into a small narrative of hope followed by disappointment. The revision carries us a few moments and a few steps further into the hitherto blank future that begins with the words 'The End', as if to demonstrate James's continuing grasp of its substance; and these appended moments make the exchange between Isabel's friends more amply evoke things to come. The emblematic exchange of speechless views between the two, she 'shining' and he presumably glowering, is fixed as a tableau 'on the spot' and metaphorically borne into the future by the hyperbolic figure which packs into it thirty years of aroused impatience. With the long-term future thus newly spun out of a brief confrontation, James beautifully takes advantage of the fact a few lines above in *1882* that Henrietta is dressed ready to go out, and balances Caspar's passive immobility with her cheerful pushiness by having her 'walk him away with her', in a construction which leaves intact our sense of him as still really frozen, emotionally out of action. They physically leave the scene, justifying James's final scene-break with a more convincingly natural rhythm than in the abrupter and more disconcertingly authorial 'cut' of *1881*. The *NYE* makes it truer, we can feel, that 'it groups together', gives us as readers more of a 'key to patience'. From the static long perspective of the previous sentence we move out of the book with a brisk return to the short term; the crystallizing 'now', which pulls together the sentence around Henrietta's sense of a provisionally satisfactory ending, is a manuscript insertion on a last page typed for the *NYE*—maybe James's final, pointedly immediate revision in a work consciously mediating between the beginnings of his career and its later consummations.

7

Revised Judgements of Daisy Miller

i A Study

Henry James tells us that he got the hint for *Daisy Miller* while staying
in Rome in the autumn of 1877. He wrote the story early in 1878, and
had it read and rejected by the Philadelphian *Lippincott's* magazine;
it was then accepted 'with effusion' by Leslie Stephen, editor of the
Cornhill, at some time just prior to 19 April 1878. It was first published
in England, in the *Cornhill* of June–July 1878, and in book form, with
some revisions, by Macmillan the next year. Thirty years passed before
James revised the story for the New York Edition of his works,
dispatching the revised copy to Scribner on 25 September 1908;[1] it
came out in 1909 as Volume xviii.

The 1909 Preface to *Daisy Miller* remarks how the story

qualified itself in [the *Cornhill*] and afterwards as 'a Study'; for reasons which
I confess I fail to recapture unless they may have taken account simply of a
certain flatness in my poor little heroine's literal denomination. Flatness
indeed, one must have felt, was the very sum of her story; so that perhaps
after all the attached epithet was meant but as a deprecation, addressed to
the reader, of any great critical hope of stirring scenes. It provided for mere
concentration, and on an object scant and superficially vulgar—from which,
however, a sufficiently brooding tenderness might eventually extract a shy
incongruous charm. I suppress at all events here the appended qualification—
in view of the simple truth, which ought from the first to have been apparent
to me, that my little exhibition is made to no degree whatever in critical but,
quite inordinately and extravagantly, in poetical terms (*LC* ii. 1270).

Viola Dunbar, in her article on 'The Revision of "Daisy Miller"',
uncomplicatedly takes James up on this apparent invitation to share
a hindsight (even though it is because of a lapse in memory): 'In his
new interpretation of the work, he saw that it should never have been
called "a Study" and he conscientiously deleted that qualification.'[2]

---

[1] HJ to Scribners, 25 Sept. 1908 (Princeton TS).
[2] Viola R. Dunbar, 'The Revision of "Daisy Miller"', *Modern Language Notes*, 65/5
(May 1950), 312.

'Conscientiously' here does justice to the demonstrative character of James's retraction, and certainly there is nothing exhaustive in the story's mode of attention to Daisy—it is partial, offering accounts of her only via reports and Winterbourne's eight encounters with her, and conforms to William James's early account (in a letter of 1868) of his brother's method:

You expressly restrict yourself, accordingly, to showing a few external acts and speeches, and by the magic of your art making the reader *feel* back of these the existence of a body of being of which these are casual features.[3]

The evocation of such a 'feeling' in Daisy's case is naturally more a poetic than a critical process, calling not for 'mere concentration' but for 'a sufficiently brooding tenderness' to draw out its charm. There is another sense of 'study', one to which 'flatness' can offer a clue, and which links the original title with that of *The Portrait of a Lady*. In this sense the 'flatness' recalls the two-dimensional quality of the representational surface of a picture, and can refer to the temporal 'foreshortening' the story uses in portraying Daisy. William's 'making the reader *feel* back of these the existence of a body of being', with its play between surface and depth, similarly offers a pictorially organized incompleteness. Writing to William on 23 July 1878 about *The Europeans*, James mentions that

It is only a sketch—very brief and with no space for much action; in fact it is a 'study', like Daisy Miller (*HJL* ii. 180).[4]

(One notes the way 'no space for much action' recurs years later in the negation of 'any great critical hope of stirring scenes', characteristically turned to humorous self-diminishment.) It seems then that the story's treatment of Daisy is quite adequately described in the term 'study' taken in this sense.

But another sense, connoting deliberation and science and considered judgement, occurs several times in the story, even being introduced by a revision at a crucial point.

---

[3] About *An Extraordinary Case* (*The Letters of William James*, i. 271).
[4] Kenneth Graham, in *Henry James: The Drama of Fulfilment*, Oxford, 1975, is factually mistaken but generally correct when he says: 'The story is sub-titled "A Sketch", and it seems to work as fine sketches do, and with the advantage a sketch has over a finished picture, that the tentativeness and quickness of its lines can best convey the living mystery of a personality like Daisy's' (p. 16).

'I am afraid your habits are those of a flirt', said Winterbourne, gravely (*1883*, p. 55).

'I'm afraid your habits are those of a ruthless flirt', said Winterbourne with studied severity (*NYE* xviii. 70).

The two senses of 'study' have a crucial function in the construction of *Daisy Miller*: the story's sketch-like treatment of Daisy with 'a sufficiently brooding tenderness' is constantly and subtly run against the way in which Daisy is 'studied' by Winterbourne (the story's centre of consciousness, whom the Preface omits to mention).

The New York *Times* reviewer was blunt but suggestive about Winterbourne's role: 'He is supposed to be in love with the heroine, but is really nothing but a detective following her about.'[5] Something subtler than this *is* true; that for Winterbourne being in love, with Daisy at any rate, involves what one might call a detective attitude to the loved one. Both at the beginning and at the end of the story there is a collocation of love and study—at the start, there are friendly accounts which 'usually said that he was at Geneva, "studying" ', and others which

affirmed that the reason of his spending so much time at Geneva was that he was extremely devoted to a lady who lived there—a foreign lady—a person older than himself (*1883*, p. 4).

The final sentence repeats this pair of versions; Winterbourne goes back to live at Geneva,

whence there continue to come the most contradictory accounts of his motives of sojourn: a report that he is 'studying' hard—an intimation that he is much interested in a very clever foreign lady (*1883*, p. 72).

These double reports correspond to a division in Winterbourne himself, an incapacity represented in the story as related to his stiflingly respectable social milieu. His attraction to Daisy combines with her unconventionality to cause in him a crisis of judgement, a discovery of the limitations in his own education and of the failure of his usual criteria for moral evaluation. He is caught between this enforced uncertainty and the mental habits of stabilizing conclusiveness which Genevan life has instilled in him, is left with a constant 'desire for

---

[5] (Anon.), The New York *Times*, 10 Nov. 1878, 10; repr. in William T. Stafford, *James's 'Daisy Miller': The Story, The Play, The Critics* (Scribner Research Anthologies), New York, 1963, p. 104.

trustworthy information' (*1883*, p. 20) which is the index of his inability fully to trust Daisy (whom he desires). The particularity of Geneva as the source of Winterbourne's ethical focus is frequently glanced at, so that when James leaves us with the equivocation above about the reason for Winterbourne's living there, it is with the statement that he 'had an old attachment for the little metropolis of Calvinism; he had been put to school there as a boy, and he had afterwards gone to college there' (*1883*, p. 5).[6]

His confusion on first meeting Daisy makes him feel 'he had lived at Geneva so long that he had lost a good deal; he had become dishabituated to the American tone' (*1883*, p. 13). (In the *NYE* it is 'so long as to have got morally muddled; he had lost the right sense for the young American tone' (*NYE* xviii. 16); 'muddled' is picked up later again in regard to Daisy (*NYE* xviii. 73).) After Mrs Walker's officious intervention in the Pincian Garden, referring back to this, Winterbourne tells her 'I suspect, Mrs. Walker, that you and I have lived too long at Geneva!' (*1883*, p. 50.)

The reference of Winterbourne's problem of judgement to 'the little metropolis of Calvinism' recalls another historian of fine consciences, Hawthorne, whose close accounts of the allegorizing and abstracting imagination in the Puritan tradition are often present to the early James (who wrote his study *Hawthorne* in 1879, the year after *Daisy Miller*). As James saw, Hawthorne 'had ample cognizance of the Puritan conscience', and yet 'played with it and used it as a pigment; he treated it, as the metaphysicians say, objectively' (*LC* i. 363). *Rapaccini's Daughter* (1844), a story to which James explicitly alludes in *Travelling Companions* of 1870, offers an example of this process with special reference to *Daisy Miller*. The story is introduced as a translation from a French writer, Aubépine (hawthorn), with ironic disclaimers about the method of it; particularly about Aubépine's 'inveterate love of allegory, which is apt to invest his plots and characters with the aspect of scenery and people in the clouds, and to steal away the human warmth out of his conceptions'.[7] This preface both anticipates the complaints of obtuse critics and draws attention to the

---

[6] William James had gone to this college, specified in the *NYE* as the Academy, in 1859–60, and Henry had also attended courses there.

[7] *Mosses from an Old Manse* (1854), Centenary Edition, Ohio, 14 vols., x, 1974, pp. 91–2. In James's 1870 story *Travelling Companions*, also about American girls being 'compromised' in Italy, Miss Brooke has been reading *Rapaccini's Daughter* (*THJ* ii. 33).

cruelly symbolizing imagination of the hero, Giovanni, in regard to the heroine. Giovanni, a student, takes lodgings in Padua overlooking a garden where the scientist Rapaccini grows poisonous plants. Beatrice, the daughter, has become immune to their poisons, and Giovanni, though attracted to her after seeing her in the garden, is infected with distrust both by her seeming (literally) poisonous and by the innuendo of Rapaccini's rival Baglioni (about a collusion of father and daughter).

Beatrice returns Giovanni's love, but the appearances of contamination are so strong (he himself becomes poisonous) that he gives her Baglioni's 'antidote'[8]—which kills her. Her dying words turn back on him his own accusations, demonstrate the real good faith which underlay bad appearances: 'Oh, was there not, from the first, more poison in thy nature than in mine?'[9]

The allegorical element in the story is mainly placed by Hawthorne's narrative, then, and does not simply constitute it: the process of judgement by analogy in which Giovanni involves himself is both the vehicle and the subject of the work. Describing Giovanni's point of view (his distorting perceptions) at the same time as the real action he perceives, carefully drawing the judgements of the reader close to Giovanni's without misrepresenting the evidence, the movement of *Rapaccini's Daughter* has much in common with that of the more urbane *Daisy Miller*. There is equivocation in both about flowers ('It was impossible to regard her as a perfectly well-conducted young lady' (*1883*, p. 46) becomes 'as a wholly unspotted flower' (*NYE* xviii. 59)); and where Baglioni's words corrode Giovanni's capacity for trust, causing Beatrice's death, the judgement of the American community is internalized and transmitted by Winterbourne, leading (much less directly) to Daisy's death. These similarities may be coincidental, but they point to the way in which the socially and emotionally complex treatment of questions of knowledge in James's story has a precedent in Hawthorne.

To want to know the truth about someone you love may seem natural; but your attitude to such knowledge is not ethically neutral ground. Winterbourne's mistake in the story comes not so much from his not being sure about Daisy as from his lacking at a crisis the patience to rest in such uncertainties. In an 1872 review of Taine's

---

[8] *Mosses from an Old Manse*, p. 119.
[9] *Mosses from an Old Manse*, p. 127.

History of English Literature, James contrasts the approaches of Taine and Sainte-Beuve to the ethics of investigation; and the admiration for Sainte-Beuve's loving empiricism as against the rigidity of Taine bears on Winterbourne's study.

Now Sainte-Beuve is, to our sense, the better apostle of the two. In purpose the least doctrinal of critics, it was by his very horror of dogmas, moulds, and formulas, that he so effectively contributed to the science of literary interpretation. The truly devout patience with which he kept his final conclusion in abeyance until after an exhaustive survey of the facts, after perpetual returns and ever-deferred farewells to them, is his living testimony to the importance of the facts. Just as he could never reconcile himself to saying his last word on book or author, so he never pretended to have devised a method which should be a key to truth. The truth for M. Taine lies stored up, as one may say, in great lumps and blocks, to be released and detached by a few lively hammer-blows; while for Sainte-Beuve it was a diffused and imponderable essence, as vague as the carbon in the air which nourishes vegetation, and, like it, to be disengaged by patient chemistry (*LC* ii. 844).

When Mrs F. H. Hill wrote her review of the first book edition of *Daisy Miller* in the *Daily News* of 21 March 1879 she approved of *Daisy Miller* and *Four Meetings*, but, quickly and generally concluding, resented the satirical representation of Lord Lambeth's mother and sister in *An International Episode* as a slur on all English ladies. James's reply bears the trace of his early aspiration to Sainte-Beuve's 'intelligence and his patience and vigour' (*HJL* i. 77):

Nothing is my *last word* about anything—I am interminably supersubtle and analytic—and with the blessing of heaven, I shall live to make all sorts of representations of all sorts of things (*HJL* ii. 221).

Mrs Hill's too-ready interpretative habit draws her to assimilate the particular up into lumps and blocks (all English ladies); James's indignation in the letter gives his resentment of this violent detachment of figures he has represented from their particular conditions, of this pressure to last words. The image James uses in the review for Sainte-Beuve's sense of the truth recalls Eliot's praise of James's fictional achievement, his mastery 'in the chemistry of these subtle substances, these curious precipitates and explosive gases which are suddenly formed by the contact of mind with mind'.[10] And the critical opposition

---

[10] T. S. Eliot, 'In Memory' (1918), in F. W. Dupee (ed.), *The Question of Henry James*, New York, 1945, pp. 108–12, at p. 110.

between Taine and Sainte-Beuve in their conceptions of the truth has an artistic parallel in *Daisy Miller*, where Winterbourne's desire for conclusions and simplifications contrasts with the more 'patient chemistry', also concerned with flowers and fragrances, of the story's treatment of Daisy (a contrast heightened by the removal of the subtitle and the Preface's comment that Daisy is 'of course pure poetry' (*LC* ii. 1271)). For Sainte-Beuve 'the facts' need loving attention—he is 'truly devout', and 'perpetual returns and ever-deferred farewells' imagines the relation with the evidence as an intimate affair which reaches a conclusion only with the most humane and reluctant of disengagements.

It would be mistaken to suggest that Winterbourne's fallibility and urge to quick judgement are only present, or even only emphasized, in the *NYE*. But whereas the first edition offers strong intermittent hints that we should doubt Winterbourne's conclusions, the *NYE* works the doubts far more closely into the texture of the narration. I shall consider the effects of the *NYE* revisions on our view of Winterbourne in some detail; but first, to suggest that the *NYE* is imaginatively extending something already there in *1883*, I shall pick out in the earlier text what is 'the truth, for Winterbourne, as the few indications I have been able to give have made him known to the reader' (*1883*, p. 49).

The first thing Winterbourne says when he sees Daisy is a generalization—'American girls are the best girls' (*1883*, p. 7)—and remarking on Daisy's beauty he again refers it to the plural, the lump: ' "How pretty they are!" thought Winterbourne.' Winterbourne's relations to women are the object of a pseudo-scientific curiosity: 'He had a great relish for feminine beauty; he was addicted to observing and analysing it' (*1883*, p. 9); and we note the proximity of relish and analysis, pleasure and observation. When Daisy does not appreciate his hastening to Rome to see her (when the progress of his advances is checked), Winterbourne immediately refers this to a static body of aphoristic knowledge—'He remembered that a cynical compatriot had once told him that American women—the pretty ones, and this gave a largeness to the axiom—were at once the most exacting in the world and the least endowed with a sense of indebtedness' (*1883*, pp. 39–40). The treatment of people as texts to be studied, facts from which conclusions and large axioms can be drawn, is a tendency to which Winterbourne's social milieu predisposes him. It is broadly satirized in the attitude of Winterbourne's Genevan friend Mrs Walker, 'one of those American ladies who, while residing abroad, make a point, in their own phrase, of studying European society; ... she had on this occasion collected several specimens of her diversely-born fellow-mortals to serve, as it were, as text-books' (*1883*, p. 52). Such an analytic perspective is definitively called into play in the Coliseum scene at the end, where Winterbourne finally judges and 'the riddle had become easy to read' (*1883*, p. 66); Daisy has been a particularly hard problem, a difficult specimen to classify, and has not yielded the usual pleasures of facile expertise.

The things she says, in the first scene, cannot be taken by Winterbourne for what in Geneva they would be, 'a kind of demonstrative evidence of a certain laxity of deportment' (*1883*, p. 13); the evidence in this case means something different, and Winterbourne does not know what—he 'had lost his instinct in this matter, and his reason could not help him' (*1883*, p. 14). He finds a usable category for Daisy, though, even in this first scene, and brings her to book as 'only a pretty American flirt. Winterbourne was almost grateful for having found the formula that applied to Miss Daisy Miller. He leaned back in his seat...'. There is even a bodily ease, then, in the satisfaction of the desire for certainty (dwelt on in the full social title 'Miss Daisy Miller'). Classifications and formulas, social *points de repère*, are the condition of Winterbourne's urbanity, but Daisy frustrates the expectations which are the comfort in the labels attached to her. ' "Common" she was, as Mrs Costello had pronounced her; yet it was a wonder to Winterbourne that, with her commonness, she had a singularly delicate grace' (*1883*, pp. 24–5). But then less than twenty pages later the word itself comes into question: 'He had assented to the idea that she was "common"; but was she so, after all, or was he simply getting used to her commonness?' (*1883*, p. 31.) The failure of Winterbourne's sense of social value, the discontinuity between his standards and any recognized by Daisy, casts doubt on his judgement and thus—for him—attacks his self-approval: 'he was vexed with himself that, by instinct, he should not appreciate her justly' (*1883*, p. 21).

James draws attention to the contradictions caused by Winterbourne's particularity of focus in the scene with Daisy and Giovanelli in the Pincio, where the desire to be certain about Daisy makes him wish against his own interests: 'Singular though it may seem, Winterbourne was vexed that the young girl, in joining her *amoroso*, should not appear more impatient of his own company, and he was vexed because of his inclination' (*1883*, p. 46). A secure state of know-

ledge about her even becomes at certain points, perversely, more
desirable to him than Daisy's virtue: 'It would therefore simplify
matters greatly to be able to treat her as the object of one of those
sentiments which are called by romancers "lawless passions". That
she should seem to wish to get rid of him would help him to think
more lightly of her, and to be able to think more lightly of her would
make her much less perplexing.' The simplicity and ease of relations
with a member of a denominated and predictable class (one identified
by an external authority, 'romancers') constantly escape him; his single
rule comes to be the safe paradox that 'the unexpected in her behaviour
was the only thing to expect' (*1883*, p. 57), and his inability to come
to terms with Daisy's otherness, to find common ground[11] with one
held apart as 'common', threatens his reliance on his conditioned
instincts: 'he was angry at finding himself reduced to chopping logic
about this young lady; he was vexed at his want of instinctive certitude
as to how far her eccentricities were generic, national, and how far
they were personal' (*1883*, p. 62). It is a question for him of finding
the *responsible* in Daisy's behaviour, the criteria by which he can judge
her. When he finds Daisy in the Coliseum with Giovanelli (hears
Giovanelli answer her in the darkness), he takes this as the evidence
he needs to conclude, and the doubleness of his emotions is an index
of the difficulty into which he has been drawn.

Winterbourne stopped, with a sort of horror; and, it must be added, with a
sort of relief. It was as if a sudden illumination had been flashed upon the
ambiguity of Daisy's behaviour (*1883*, p. 66).

The careful 'it must be added', like 'singular though it may seem',
enters a scrupulous qualification to the singleness of his response.
Winterbourne starts to advance towards the cross in the middle of the
Coliseum, where Daisy and Giovanelli are sitting—but 'he checked
himself; not from the fear that he was doing her injustice, but from a
sense of the danger of appearing unbecomingly exhilarated by this
sudden revulsion from cautious criticism' (*1883*, p. 67). The double
affect, revulsion and exhilaration, corresponds to the division in Winterbourne's self; what revolts and disappoints him as a lover exhilarates
him as a detective. We could take 'cautious criticism' here as corresponding to Sainte-Beuve's 'patient chemistry', while the violence of

[11] Where in *1883* Daisy remarks that Mrs Costello 'never dined at the *table d'hôte*'
(*1883*, p. 22), in the NYE she calls it 'the common table' (*NYE* xviii. 28), with some of
the weight of 'common humanity'.

Winterbourne's manner to Daisy once he has made up his mind (he speaks 'almost brutally') recalls Taine's 'few lively hammer-blows'— has the excitement of a simplification which banishes perplexity.

The continuities and modifications of this mode of handling Winterbourne's judgements in the 1909 version begin to emerge in the changes made to the cases quoted above from *1883* (and in some other related revisions). The kind of connoisseurship Winterbourne indulges in his relations with women becomes more frankly, though still abstractly, sensual: where in *1883* 'he had a great relish for feminine beauty; he was addicted to observing and analysing it', the *NYE* picks up directly from the previous sentence where he notes 'her complexion, her nose, her ears, her teeth. He took a great interest generally in that range of effects and was addicted to noting and, as it were, recording them' (*NYE* xviii. 11). The physical particularity plays against 'generally' (Daisy's teeth—but also all other women's). 'Effects' renders the characteristic preoccupation of Winterbourne with his own response by treating the other person's features so spectatorially, by eliding the sense in which they are firstly causes of the effect in him and also that in which they do not exist *for* him but are part of Daisy. 'As it were, recording' yields an innuendo, and further suggests the contrast between the story's disinterested view and Winterbourne's 'interest' here by implying that he thinks of his mind as a book. The appropriating habit in him is given us by a revision shortly after this, when he considers Daisy's face: 'it was eminently delicate' (*1883*, p. 9) becomes 'it offered such a collection of small finenesses and neatnesses' (*NYE* xviii. 11). The response is translated into the special version his character gives, the narration inflecting closely to follow the particular movement of his thought ('offered' and 'collection' making Daisy seem consciously to intend his pleasure immediately before his wonder whether she's a coquette). Winterbourne becomes Giovanelli's 'critic' (*NYE* xviii. 87) when he rushes to judgement in the Coliseum scene, while the 'people' (*1883*, p. 69) who then gossip about Daisy are in the *NYE* 'these sources of current criticism' (*NYE* xviii. 89).

The image of other people as textbooks for study is answered by the image of the memory as a book of conclusions about them; in *1883*, after failing to persuade Mrs Miller of the need for vigilance, Winterbourne

said to himself that [Daisy] ... was too light and childish, too uncultivated and unreasoning, too provincial, to have reflected upon her ostracism, or even to have perceived it (*1883*, p. 62).

The cadence of the *NYE* version has the balanced finality of a Johnsonian judgement:

He set her down as hopelessly childish and shallow, as such mere giddiness and ignorance incarnate as was powerless either to heed or to suffer (*NYE* xviii. 80).

'Set her down' (the translation into his terms of 'said to himself') contains both writing and ostracizing; 'mere giddiness and ignorance incarnate' allegorizes Daisy's physical being into a receptacle for abstract absolutes. The strong beat of the binding alternatives at the end of the sentence picks up from a revision shortly before about Mrs Miller's hopeless incapacity: in *1883* Winterbourne 'gave up as utterly irrelevant the attempt to place her upon her guard' (*1883*, p. 62); in the *NYE* he 'recoiled before the attempt to educate at a single interview either her conscience or her wit' (*NYE* xviii. 80; the retention of the 'either . . . or' phrase till the end suggests the reasoned-out and inclusive view).[12]

The relation of the revisions to the original phrasings of *1883* about Winterbourne's point of view frequently involves a readjustment of the degree of finality in a judgement or of the stage a statement represents in a syllogism. Thus in Geneva 'to say such things seemed a kind of demonstrative evidence of a certain laxity of deportment' (punning on 'certain') in *1883*; what we are given in the *NYE* is the reason why this *is* evidence in Geneva but is not in New York State: in Geneva 'to say such things was to have at the same time some rather complicated consciousness about them' (*NYE* xviii. 16).[13] The change relates to the way in which Daisy cannot or will not hear her words in their European context, with the social significance of their utterance: the question for Winterbourne is accentuated in the *NYE* as being that of the consciousness Daisy has about her actions rather than the actions themselves. This revision pairs with one in the next sentence, where in *1883* he wonders 'was he to accuse Miss Daisy Miller of actual or potential *inconduite*, as they said at Geneva?' (*1883*, p. 13.) In the *NYE* 'actual or potential *inconduite*' becomes an 'actual

---

[12] Cf. too, in the Coliseum scene, James's replacement of 'a young lady whom a gentleman need no longer be at pains to respect' (*1883*, p. 66) with the emphatic cadence of 'a young lady about the *shades* of whose perversity a foolish puzzled gentleman need no longer trouble his head or his heart' (*NYE* xviii. 86).

[13] Cf. the revision of 'she blushed' (*1883*, p. 31) to 'she . . . coloured from an awkward consciousness' (*NYE* xviii. 40).

or a potential *arrière-pensée*' (*NYE* xviii. 16), wittily wondering if Daisy is capable of an ulterior motive, a sense of the meaning of what she says for the foreign situation in which she says it. For Winterbourne the laws of evidence in Daisy's case are so slippery as to make the operations of his reason useless in *1883* and in the *NYE* actively delusive: where in *1883* 'Winterbourne had lost his instinct in this matter, and his reason could not help him', the *NYE* at this point leaps on from the question he has just asked (is Daisy a coquette?) to answer another one—'Yes, his instinct for such a question had ceased to serve him, and his reason could but mislead' (*NYE* xviii. 17).

'Such a question' shows Winterbourne trying, but failing, to insert Daisy's case into a sequence of others, a familiar series. Since Daisy's case cannot be 'solved' by reason, his reasonings in the story become an index of something else (so that 'said Winterbourne' (*1883*, p. 46) becomes 'he reasoned in his own troubled interest' (*NYE* xviii. 60)). Daisy's frustration of the predictive in the labels attached to her (like 'common') is in the *NYE* much more closely related to the inadequacy of those labels: 'yet it was a wonder to Winterbourne that, with her commonness, she had a singularly delicate grace' in *1883*; in the *NYE* he acknowledges that she 'might be' common, 'yet what provision was made by that epithet for her queer little native grace?' (*NYE* xviii. 31.) In the same way, Winterbourne's mental exclamation 'that little American flirts were the queerest creatures in the world' (*1883*, p. 56) becomes 'the name of little American flirts was incoherence' (*NYE* xviii. 72), with a hyperbolic metonymy of woman and abstract noun to echo Hamlet's in 'Frailty, thy name is woman' (1. ii. 146). Quite often the *NYE* intimately engages the nature of doubts where *1883* gave certainty baffled by contradictions: 'He had assented to the idea that she was "common"; but was she so, after all, or was he simply getting used to her commonness?' is revised into the mood which most provides for contingencies, the conditional; 'If he had assented to the idea that she was "common", at any rate, *was* she proving so, after all . . .?' (*NYE* xviii. 40.) 'Proving so' is poised between the honest surrender to the facts of a proper empiricism and the urge to press the evidence to the assistance of an a priori hypothesis.

Winterbourne's feelings about his doubts are more equivocal in the *NYE*, more shifting, just as the doubts are more tightly bound in with the dramatic development of his relation to Daisy. Thus the neutral statement that 'the unexpected in her behaviour was the only thing to expect' of *1883* becomes 'he really liked, after all, not making out what she was "up to"' (*NYE* xviii. 74), a poignant small triumph of his 'liking' for Daisy before returning to suspicion (the next paragraph starts 'But she was evidently very much interested in Giovanelli' (*1883*, p. 58; *NYE* xviii. 75)). Much earlier 'he was vexed with himself that, by instinct, he should not appreciate her justly' is put with more personal edge as 'it vexed, it even a little humiliated him, that he shouldn't by instinct appreciate her justly' (*NYE* xviii. 26), so that the relation of certain judgement to self-esteem is registered. The movement here, the externalization in '*it* vexed' of the emotional agency and the removal from Winterbourne of his self-determining will, recurs with a similar force of suggestion at the climactic moment, his hearing of Giovanelli's voice answering Daisy's in the Coliseum.

Winterbourne stopped, with a sort of horror; and, it must be added, with a sort of relief (*1883*).

Winterbourne felt himself pulled up with final horror now—and, it must be added, with final relief (*NYE* xviii. 86).

The passive role he is given here in the revision suggests the way in which his arrest is the product of unconscious processes, the reflexive rendering his perception of an effect in himself whose cause is unknown. The close sequence 'final horror now' (with 'final' then repeated and paired with 'relief') intimates by association what this cause might be—the defensive wish to have an immediate end of uncertainties, mysteries, and doubts (of the conflict of attraction with judgement). The division in Winterbourne is similarly focused in an earlier (revised) moment, equally reflexive, when Daisy announces she is engaged and asks if he believes it: 'He asked himself, and it was for a moment like testing a heart-beat; after which, "Yes, I believe it!" he said' (*NYE* xviii. 84). Another construction with an impersonal subject, whereby thoughts impinge on him instead of being formulated by him, comes in the revision of his conclusion after seeing Daisy and Giovanelli drive away from St Peter's: 'he could not deny to himself that she was going very far indeed' (*1883*, p. 60) becomes 'the measure of her course struck him as simply there to take' (*NYE* xviii. 78). There is no attempt at denial in the *NYE*, where the mysterious impersonal subject refers to a complex of choices and determinations; it implies a motive in the word 'simply' (the wish easily to conclude). 'There to take' gives the perplexingly intangible (certainty about Daisy) a desired, though only momentary, accessibility to the grasp.

If Winterbourne is a detective following Daisy about, James himself evidently cannot be accused here of what T. S. Eliot claimed was his error with regard to Rowland Mallet in *Roderick Hudson*, 'the cardinal sin of failing to "detect" one of his own characters'.[14] There is an exemplary moment in the climactic scene in the Coliseum which finely renders these relations of author to character to character (I quote the revised version).

He stood there looking at her, looking at her companion too, and not reflecting that though he saw them vaguely he himself must have been more brightly presented (*NYE* xviii. 86).

'Presented' replaces 'visible' (*1883*, p. 66); the story's presentation of point of view 'organically re-economises' (*LC* ii. 1302) the process of viewing: Winterbourne's attention to Daisy is the substance of the story, is how we know her but also how we know him.

In a sense the whole action, wishfully taken by Winterbourne to be in essence his trial of Daisy, is also intimately testing his character, his ethical and perceptual means. A revision in the first few pages gives a turn in the other direction, one which is answered in the rest of the story. Winterbourne, first a schoolboy in Geneva, had 'afterwards even gone, on trial—trial of the grey old "Academy" on the steep and stony hillside—to college there' (*NYE* xviii. 5). We may start by thinking that like any other child Winterbourne is subject to examinations— but if so we discover with the comic swerve of the syntax that he is comfortably immune from scrutiny, that (because of a parental *carte blanche*?) it is the school that is on trial. The benign but unrelaxing mode of the narration which looks over Winterbourne's study of Daisy is thus a measured qualification of the self-exemption from criticism constitutive of his social attitude. The revised version introduces in the penultimate paragraph another reflexive figure, where Winterbourne is turned to inquisitively; which again epitomizes this movement in the story. Mrs Costello, Winterbourne's aunt, asks if he means that Daisy would have reciprocated his (one's) affection: in *1883*

Winterbourne offered no answer to this question; but he presently said, 'You were right in that remark that you made last summer. I was booked to make a mistake. I have lived too long in foreign parts' (*1883*, p. 71).

---

[14] T. S. Eliot, 'The Hawthorne Aspect', in *The Question of Henry James*, pp. 112–19, at p. 117. This is belied by James's account of Rowland in the Preface (*LC* ii. 1050).

In the *NYE*:

As he made no answer to this she after a little looked round at him—he hadn't been directly within sight; but the effect of that wasn't to make her repeat her question. He spoke, however, after a while. 'You were right in that remark that you made last summer. I was booked to make a mistake. I've lived too long in foreign parts.' And this time she herself said nothing (*NYE* xviii. 93).

Winterbourne has not been 'directly' within sight in the tale—and his 'no answer' might have seemed enigmatic in *1883*—but his aunt's small gesture of curiosity draws attention to the return on himself which evokes such a silence in him, and produces an answering grave silence in her.

There is a relation of this new look to the touchingly unsuccessful appeal of Daisy against Winterbourne's judgement as they leave the Coliseum. He has pronounced that, given her scandalous behaviour, 'it makes very little difference whether you are engaged or not!' (*1883*, p. 68), whereas to Daisy his indifference makes all the difference, so that her final words—'I don't care ... whether I have Roman fever or not!' (*1883*, p. 69)—will come to sound, with the echo of not caring and the finishing 'or not!', as the indirect consequence of his sentence. Daisy's appealing look in this scene, like Mrs Costello's inquiring one, comes with the pregnant silence left in the air by an unanswered utterance:

He felt the young girl's pretty eyes fixed upon him through the thick gloom of the archway; she was apparently going to answer (*1883*, p. 68).

He felt her lighted eyes fairly penetrate the thick gloom of the vaulted passage—as if to seek some access to him she hadn't yet compassed (*NYE* xviii. 89).

The interrogative look is given a dramatic dimension by the hidden presence in the *NYE* of a passage from Shakespeare, one which might be taken as asking about the humanity of Winterbourne's action: Lady Macbeth's

> Come, you spirits
> That tend on mortal thoughts, unsex me here,
> And fill me from the crown to the toe top-full
> Of direst cruelty. Make thick my blood,
> Stop up th'access and passage to remorse,
> That no compunctious visitings of nature
> Shake my fell purpose, nor keep peace between
> Th'effect and it.

> (*Macbeth*, I. v. 39–46.)

The proximity of 'thick', 'passage', and 'access' can call up 'remorse', the repentance for his hardness of heart in the Coliseum which comes over Winterbourne on Mrs Costello's last look (and 'unsex me here' corresponds to the pull in him between lover and detective). 'Fairly' in the revision contains 'pretty' from *1883* (and contrasts with the darkness of 'gloom'), but puts the accent on the emotional weight of Daisy's regard, while 'penetrate' gives her answer to the 'infinite point' (*NYE* xviii. 88) with which Winterbourne has just accused her in the revised version. Winterbourne has already been interrogated by Daisy's eyes in this scene, when he has come up to ask her— 'with conscious roughness' (*NYE* xviii. 87)—how long she and Giovanelli have been in the Coliseum.

Daisy, lovely in the flattering moonlight, looked at him a moment (*1883*, p. 67).

Daisy, lovely in the sinister silver radiance, appraised him a moment, roughness and all (*NYE* xviii. 87).

There is a subtle reciprocity of judgements here, one in which Winterbourne sees Daisy's loveliness made 'sinister' and she sees the cruelty of his vision of her; and this poignant exchange of looks, in which their possible relation gets lost, is what the story compassionately oversees.

It is not only through the ethics of perception and judgement (with these images of vision and reflection) that Winterbourne's behaviour is compromised: both structurally (in terms of matching scenes), and in terms of verbal echoes (especially in the *NYE*), the sexual improprieties his Genevan social codes impel him to condemn in Daisy are found again in his own thought and conduct. His very acquaintance with her is the result of a transgression by him of those codes (his own), and what would now be called a male double-standard informs most of his judgements of her. His aunt points out that 'Of course a man may know every one' (*1883*, p. 36), and though his repudiation of Daisy in Rome is grounded exactly on whom she chooses to associate with (it is Giovanelli's voice that brings him 'final horror'), he has picked her up at Vevey without even an introduction. The balancing of Vevey and Rome in the book, each half dramatically linking moonlight and impropriety, each half having its Byron echo ('The Prisoner of Chillon' and then *Manfred*), each half having its tolerated 'gentleman' (Winterbourne then Giovanelli), clearly points to the shakiness of his ground for judging even in the Coliseum. When he first speaks to Daisy he is 'perfectly aware' that 'a young man was not at liberty to speak to a young unmarried lady except under certain rarely-occurring conditions' (*1883*, p. 8): that is, he is *taking* a liberty. In the evening, this licence continues—he comments familiarly on Daisy's mother, 'thinking, with Miss Miller, the joke permissible' (*1883*, p. 24)—and a syntactic ambiguity allows both 'permissible with Miss Miller' and 'thinking with Miss Miller'. Also in the first scene the *NYE* strengthens this emphasis by signalling a daring personal insistence; what was in *1883*

'I should like very much to know your name', said Winterbourne (*1883*, p. 10).

becomes

'I should like very much to know *your* name', Winterbourne made free to reply (*NYE* xviii. 12).

This is another sense of 'freedom' from that in 'the Land of the Free', and the two senses—the innocent and the transgressive—are often played on in the *NYE*. Thus

there was always in her conversation the same odd mixture of audacity and puerility (*1883*, p. 57).

becomes

this easy flow had ever the same anomaly for her earlier friend that it was so free without availing itself of its freedom (*NYE* xviii. 74).

If it 'availed itself' it would be 'free' in the sense Winterbourne uses after Mrs Walker's public warning to Daisy in the Pincian Garden— 'He expected that in answer she would say something rather free' (*1883*, p. 49). The word renders an irreducible ambiguity when Daisy does not go boating with him at Vevey: 'she only stood there laughing' (*1883*, p. 29) changes to 'she only remained an elegant image of free light irony' (*NYE* xviii. 37), where 'light' similarly equivocates between 'unreliable' and 'urbane'.

In Winterbourne's first meeting with Daisy, the *NYE* gives us his consciousness that 'he had gone very far' (*NYE* xviii. 19); an expression already used on his first speaking to Daisy when 'He wondered whether he had gone too far' (*1883*, p. 8). It is also an expression applied to Daisy, first in a revision where 'it was probable that anything might be expected of her' (*1883*, p. 21) becomes with a concession to the

difference of American standards 'it was probable she did go even by
the American allowance rather far' (*NYE* xviii. 26), and then, with a
weight of condemnation (not Winterbourne's), in St Peter's, when
among the American colonists he indignantly hears 'a great deal said
about poor little Miss Miller's going really "too far"' (*1883*, p. 60). A
moment later, however, Winterbourne sees her with Giovanelli and
feels the pressure of the colonists' point of view hard to resist.

James plays twice on the word 'alone', again in a way which
ironically complicates the process of judgement; once with reference
to Winterbourne and once to Giovanelli. Both times it is specially
accentuated in the *NYE*. First Eugenio, the courier, asks about Daisy's
proposed boating trip with Winterbourne—'Does Mademoiselle
propose to go alone?'—

> 'Oh no, with this gentleman!' cried Daisy's mamma for reassurance.
> 'I *meant* alone with the gentleman' (*NYE* xviii. 37–8).

Mrs Walker asks the same question of Daisy about her proposed walk
on the Pincio: if she is going 'Alone, my dear—at this hour?' (*1883*,
p. 41); but a more telling sequel comes when Winterbourne's friend
reports on a sighting of Daisy in the Doria Palace near the Velasquez
picture of Innocent X (I give both versions):

> his friend narrated that the pretty American girl—prettier than ever—was
> seated with a companion in the secluded nook in which the great papal
> portrait is enshrined.
> 'Who was her companion?' asked Winterbourne.
> 'A little Italian with a bouquet in his button-hole' (*1883*, p. 61).

> his friend narrated that the little American—prettier now than ever—was
> seated with a companion in the secluded nook in which the papal presence is
> enshrined.
> 'All alone?' the young man heard himself disingenuously ask.
> 'Alone with a little Italian who sports in his button-hole a stack of flowers'
> (*NYE* xviii. 79).

This seems at first to the modern reader like a mistake (as if 'with a
companion' should have been deleted in the revision); but it carries
exactly the weight ('unchaperoned') of Eugenio's question, and 'heard
himself disingenuously' gives Winterbourne's consciousness of the
social meaning of his enquiry—for which he has to pretend not to
have understood 'with a companion'. The echoing transformation of
'All alone?'—already an echo of Mrs Costello's 'She went with you all

alone?' (*1883*, p. 35)—into 'Alone with' brings us what Winterbourne really wants to know, but would also rather not know. 'Heard himself', moreover, is a hint for *us* to hear him—hear him echo Eugenio's interrogatively expressed disapproval of his own earlier impropriety—hear his double standard.

The examples just given all contain some specific element of reflection—point to the doubleness and confusion of Winterbourne's standard—but many revisions in the first half of the book work to the same end by generally making Winterbourne's behaviour towards Daisy more opportunistic and manipulative. A number of them are descriptions of Daisy that suggest Winterbourne taking a rakish attitude to her: as he approaches her for the first time she is 'the charming creature' (*NYE* xviii. 8) instead of 'the young lady' (*1883*, p. 9); then she is 'this charming apparition' (*NYE* xviii. 17) instead of 'this young girl' (*1883*, p. 14); 'the charming creature' (*NYE* xviii. 42) instead of 'Miss Miller' (*1883*, p. 33); and so on. He justifies the infraction of social codes in the revised version by attributing to Daisy an intention towards himself—'a pretty American girl coming and standing in front of you in a garden' (*1883*, p. 8) becomes 'coming to stand in front of you . . .' (*NYE* xviii. 9). Daisy's actions are often rendered by the *NYE* into the language of pleasure and desire: 'she rested her eyes upon the prospect' (*1883*, p. 8) becomes 'she gave her sweet eyes to the prospect' (*NYE* xviii. 9), and 'glanced at him again' (*1883*, p. 8) becomes 'glanced at him with lovely remoteness' (*NYE* xviii. 9), the *frissons* of mock-libertine sensibility attaching themselves to her smallest gestures.

Correspondingly, Winterbourne's actions and speeches are described in the *NYE* as part of a conscious strategy of ingratiation, their insincerity much more evident.

'Are you going to Italy?' Winterbourne inquired, in a tone of great respect (*1883*, p. 8).

This is suspect but blank.

'Are you going to Italy?' Winterbourne now decided very respectfully to enquire (*NYE* xviii. 9).

We *presume* that he would have 'decided' to ask the question before speaking, naturally—but what the word-order of the revision gives us is his adept selection of a particular tone for the question (and a 'respectful' address picked out in this way is no index of real respect). When he goes to work on Daisy's brother Randolph to establish the acquaintance, ' "Tell me your name, my boy", he said' (*1883*, p. 10) becomes ' "Tell me your honest name, my boy." So he artfully proceeded' (*NYE* xviii. 12), where the indirect free style marks Winterbourne's characteristic (comic) mode of private self-congratulation.

A statement of Winterbourne's action in *1883* which could be either 'dramatic' (seen by an observer) or from his point of view (a mental fact)—'Winterbourne hesitated a moment' (*1883*, p. 15)—comes with the *NYE* revision to involve his real motive—'He pretended to consider it' (*NYE* xviii. 19). This has the effect of ironizing the tones of his speech, making us hear his utterances as calculated means to a self-interested end ('the project' (*1883*, p. 16) of going to Chillon becomes 'his chance' (*NYE* xviii. 20)). In this way the descriptions of his manner read as if they were in inverted commas, are descriptions of the appearance he wishes to produce, or versions in indirect speech of what he only says he feels. When Daisy and Mrs Miller get on to the subject of Randolph they mention Dover. ' "And what occurred at Dover?" Winterbourne asked' (*1883*, p. 26); this becomes in the *NYE* 'Winterbourne desired to know' (*NYE* xviii. 32), whereas it seems likely that he does not, at least in any spirit he would admit to. A further revelation about Randolph's late nights gets another enquiry; and 'It was of great interest to Winterbourne' (*NYE* xviii. 33), even though his great interest is not in Randolph. When Daisy hopes he will come and teach Randolph, in *1883* 'Winterbourne said that nothing could possibly please him so much' (*1883*, p. 33); in the *NYE* he 'was certain that nothing . . .' (*NYE* xviii. 42). It is *assumed* that these are things he just says, not manifested emotions. And this cumulative submission of Winterbourne's comedy of politeness to ironic scrutiny (especially in the *NYE*), with its gradual evocation of a body of ulterior motives—of *arrière-pensées*—qualifies our acceptance of the increasingly sceptical scrutiny of Daisy's behaviour conducted by Winterbourne himself.

For Winterbourne, who is in this sense the victim of his Genevan upbringing, a mode of social behaviour not dictated by hidden interests, and a habit of conversation not preoccupied with its possible effects on others, are practically inconceivable; to believe in the innocence of Daisy's conduct would require of him a radical readjustment of his sense of the world. As a result he first repeatedly seeks in her (as the examples above suggest) a guilty thrill of 'adventure' to correspond with his own (*NYE* xviii, p. 39, with its usual Victorian overtones); and has about the trip to Chillon some 'expectation of seeing her regard it in the same way' (*1883*, p. 31), of 'seeing her appear to find in it the same savour' (*NYE* xviii. 39). Then in Rome, apparently passed over for Giovanelli, he seeks (as a resolution of the giddying dialectic in him between suspicion and 'liking') some proof that she *intends* her transgressions as transgressions, that she does after all share his moral and social standards even as she infringes them. The second half of this chapter looks at the handling of Daisy on the other side of this relation, to suggest how it is that James can do justice to her even from (or rather *through*) Winterbourne's point of view, and to show how the revisions consistently aim to direct our reading to the end of this justice.

ii. The Words He Heard

It might seem reasonable to ask, given the way in which the revisions intensify the partiality of Winterbourne's point of view, intimately colouring the narration with his mental processes, how it is that we read the story and still get a true impression of Daisy. The answer lies in this very accentuation of the predatory and judicial attitudes in Winterbourne, assigned to *him* with such ironic force that we can follow the action and yet be conscious of his judgements of it as not necessarily right. Particularly in the *NYE* we are invited to consider the story as a still-open process of empirical attention, one of the first of whose discoveries about Daisy is the remoteness for her of Winterbourne's stringent standards. We recognize like Winterbourne that there may be no coquettish intention in Daisy's coming to stand near him, no impure calculation in her glances and smiles, no thought of their trip to Chillon as a 'tryst' (*NYE* xviii. 39) or an adventure. Daisy's defiance of the social conventions and restrictions Winterbourne habitually judges by (which give actions meanings and make them transgressions) may be conscious or unconscious; and, if conscious, may denote either a moral recklessness *or* a protest on behalf of ideal American freedom against a cynically narrow definition of innocence. The descriptions of the behaviour of Daisy and her family are greatly revised to point up its incompatibility with the Genevan and Roman codes, in a way which cumulatively produces a substantial sense of Daisy's social origins and the values of her native Schenectady. Many of these descriptions are freshly introduced, not just adjustments of the phrasings of *1883*; as if James wishes to prevent a repetition of the misunderstandings which had controversially attended the first appearance of the tale.

Daisy's first utterance in the book, addressed to Randolph, is revised from 'said the young lady' (*1883*, p. 7) to 'she freely began' (*NYE* xviii. 8), drawing attention to the difference that Winterbourne's presence does not make to her. She has come to stand there 'with all the confidence in life' (*NYE* xviii. 9): when Winterbourne interrogates her later his question 'tapped, at a touch, the spring of confidence' (*NYE* xviii. 13), and she talks at Mrs Walker's with 'the sweetest brightest loudest confidence' (*NYE* xviii. 69). She does not adapt her tone to the conditions or the company; after Winterbourne has spoken to her she turns to Randolph, 'whom she addressed quite as if they were alone together' (*NYE* xviii. 9). What manifests itself as sweet and trusting in Daisy can be insensitive or imposing in her family: the other Millers' tone in the *NYE* is raised in volume to a pitch of high publicity: ' "I bought it!" responded Randolph' (*1883*, p. 8) becomes ' "I bought it!" Randolph shouted' (*NYE* xviii. 9); and in the same way 'the child declared' (*1883*, p. 8) becomes 'the child rang out' (*NYE* xviii. 9). At Mrs Walker's first gathering Randolph compares her rooms unfavourably with the Millers' own: 'said Randolph' (*1883*, p. 37) becomes 'Randolph hereupon broke out' (*NYE* xviii. 48); and when Mrs Miller gloomily points out to him that he has committed a gaffe, the revision wittily turns her utterance from a hushed (Europeanized) tone—'she murmured' (*1883*, p. 37)—to a self-defeatingly public address: 'she stated as for the benefit of such of the company as might hear it' (*NYE* xviii. 48). Randolph then makes a 'proclamation' (*NYE* xviii. 48— more clamorous than an 'announcement' (*1883*, p. 38)), about the family dyspepsia, which instead of embarrassing Mrs Miller 'seemed to soothe her by reconstituting the environment to which she was most accustomed' (*NYE* xviii. 48). Daisy's volume has been set by this same environment, but she is capable within it of more musical tones, as by the Swiss lakeside, where her appeal to 'Mr. Winterbourne!' goes from being 'murmured' (*1883*, p. 27) to being 'piped from a considerable distance' (*NYE* xviii. 35). Daisy is of her family, and yet distinguishable from it.

The newly penetrating quality of the family voice extends the deep echo in *1883* between the scene in which Daisy's voice comes to Winterbourne (murmuring or piping his name) through the 'thick dusk' (*1883*, p. 23) of the Swiss lakeside, and their final meeting in the 'deep shade' and 'luminous dusk' (*1883*, p. 66) of the Coliseum (where Winterbourne has gone for 'nocturnal meditation' (*NYE* xviii. 85)): in the first scene,

his meditations were interrupted by hearing his name very distinctly pronounced by Mrs. Miller's unprotected daughter (*1883*, p. 27).

In the second,

Presently the sound of the woman's voice came to him distinctly in the warm
night air (*1883*, p. 66).

In this second instance, moreover, Daisy's distinct words (in which
she jocosely aligns herself with the Christian martyrs) are followed by
a revision associating her freedom of tone with innocence:

These were the words he heard, in the familiar accent of Miss Daisy Miller
(*1883*, p. 66).

becomes

These words were winged with their accent, so that they fluttered and settled
about him in the darkness like vague white doves. It was Miss Daisy Miller
who had released them for flight (*NYE* xviii. 85–6).

The *NYE* image recalls *The Wings of the Dove* (seven years before),
but also a probable source in Hawthorne's *The Marble Faun*, where
doves are one of the tokens of Hilda's innocence;[15] while 'winged with

---

[15] The *NYE*'s doves recall Ch. VI of *The Marble Faun*, in which the innocence of
Hilda (the antitype in the book to the corrupted and unhappy Miriam) is betokened by
doves. She lives high up in a *palazzo*, and Miriam, looking up, sees 'a flock of white
doves, skimming, fluttering, and wheeling about the topmost height of the tower, their
silver wings flashing in the pure transparency of the air' (*The Marble Faun*, p. 52). The
new echo of *The Marble Faun* gives a counterweight to another in *Daisy Miller* (there
in *1883*) which associates Daisy rather with Miriam in that novel. In his 1896 essay on
'Nathaniel Hawthorne', James said about the book that 'Hawthorne took with him to
Italy, as he had done to England, more of the old Puritan consciousness than he left
behind' (*LC* i. 465); and repeated the gist of what he had said in the 1879 book on
Hawthorne, that 'It is part of the intellectual equipment of the Anglo-Saxon visitor to
Rome, and is read by every English-speaking traveller who arrives there, who has been
there, or who expects to go (*LC* i. 444). Winterbourne takes his version of the 'old
Puritan consciousness' to Rome with him from Geneva and America; but more, he takes
with him his sense of *The Marble Faun*. When he sees Daisy emerge from St Peter's,
'get into an open cab with her accomplice and roll away through the cynical streets of
Rome' (*1883*, p. 60), he is recalling another crime committed with a young Italian. In
Hawthorne, James strongly praises 'the pages describing the murder committed by
Donatello under Miriam's eyes, and the ecstatic wandering, afterwards, of the guilty
couple, through the "blood-stained streets of Rome"' (*LC* i. 446–7). This is (mis-)quoted
from memory: Hawthorne's original reads 'They trode through the streets of Rome, as
if they, too, were among the majestic and guilty shadows, that, from ages long gone by,
have haunted the blood-stained city' (*The Marble Faun*, p. 176). The phrase 'streets of
Rome' has already occurred by the time of the St Peter's incident in the *NYE* of *Daisy
Miller*, with the revision of Winterbourne's indignant complaint about Giovanelli, 'he
would never have proposed to a young lady of this country to walk about the streets

their accent' makes it specially characteristic of Daisy's voice that it should carry so.

The loudness of the Miller family voice amounts to a failure to delimit address; an incapacity to feel the embarrassment that one might suffer when, for example, after hours of not speaking in a library, the voice mispitched at a librarian rings out round a hushed reading-room. In Daisy's case the loudness may be partly a matter of American principle, a loyalty to the voice of the homeland. The revisions describe the family's lack of the habit of thinking about the context of their utterances, of hearing what it is that they are saying (since the same words, even in the same tone, can have quite different meanings when spoken at different times, to different people, in different places). Many adverbs specifying the Millers' tone of utterance are introduced in the *NYE*, as are phrases defining their serene insensitivity to the social patternings of European speech. In his 1921 essay on 'Andrew Marvell' T. S. Eliot offers a famous account of wit: 'It involves, probably, a recognition, implicit in the expression of every experience, of other kinds of experience which are possible'.[16] We could say of the Millers' expressions, as defined by these revisions, that they dramatically involve an unconsciousness, implicit in the expression of every experience, of another kind of experience which is possible (Winterbourne's).

It is in Winterbourne's noting of these blanks and negatives that we perceive the witlessness of the Millers—what he notes being the way in which they fail—or in Daisy's case, perhaps, refuse—to recognize anything remarkable in their own behaviour (this doesn't prevent their remarking the oddity of others'). Thus, straight after he's first spoken to Daisy,

the young lady turned to the little boy again (*1833*, p. 8).

becomes

the young lady turned again to the little boy, whom she addressed quite as if they were alone together (*NYE* xviii. 9).

The kind of experience which Daisy does not recognize, because of

with him' (*1883*, p. 54), to read 'about the streets of Rome with him' (*NYE* xviii. 70). So that the spectral presence in the story of Hawthorne's 'guilty couple' puts a pressure of analogy on Daisy and Giovanelli in the Coliseum (where a dramatic scene takes place by moonlight in *The Marble Faun* just before the murder)—a pressure which the image of the white doves resists.

[16] T. S. Eliot, 'Andrew Marvell', *Selected Essays*, London, 1951, p. 303.

the environment to which she has been accustomed and which she constantly reconstitutes, is the kind in which it *does* make a difference to the tone in which you address your little brother that a stranger should be present; but then, as the obverse of this, the way Winterbourne expresses his perception of Daisy's manner—'quite as if they were alone together', which they are not—fails to recognize hers as another *kind* of experience, sees it only as an anomaly within his own. The adverbs and adverbial clauses used in the revisions to convey his sense of the Millers' behaviour are all notations of difference from the expected, ironic dwellings on the manner of their self-presentation, echoes of their actions as negatives in the terms of another culture.

When Daisy's mother does not think Daisy should go boating with Winterbourne, and then there is a digression, Daisy returns to her first wish; and ' "I want you to take me out in a boat!" Daisy repeated' (*1883*, p. 72) is said otherwise: 'Daisy went on as if nothing else had been said' (*NYE* xviii. 36). Winterbourne notes this because a Genevan young person would have been silenced by a mother's disapproval. At their reunion in Rome Daisy speaks to Winterbourne 'as if they had parted the week before' (*NYE* xviii. 47); and in the Pincian Garden she introduces Giovanelli to Mrs Walker, 'declaring with it, and as if it were of as little importance, that she had never in her life seen anything so lovely as that lady's carriage-rug' (*NYE* xviii. 61). She preserves an unaffected equanimity of tone throughout situations which might be expected to make a difference; addressing people 'quite at her leisure' (*NYE* xviii. 12) and going on 'quite as naturally' (*NYE* xviii. 13), 'with all serenity' or 'without a shadow of emotion' (*NYE* xviii. 19), with no 'awkward consciousness' (*NYE* xviii. 40) and 'with the easiest grace' (*NYE* xviii. 57), 'imperturbably' and 'blandly' (*NYE* xviii. 61). The maintenance of this equanimity, of Daisy's 'small flat monotone' (*NYE* xviii. 31), is connected with a defiant deafness to the inflections demanded by un-American social contexts: Mrs Walker may be in the *NYE* 'the voice of civilised society' (*NYE* xviii. 62), but Daisy will not hear her as that and calls her officious advice 'cool'(*1883*, p. 54) as if it had been meant as a frivolously private interference.

Daisy is not prepared to hear herself in the European way, but the Genevans hear her all right, as all wrong. The things she says (like the things she does) resonate with a difference in their world, which has another acoustic constitution, a particular rhythm of conversation, a strict diction, a set tone (the revision of 'There isn't any society' (*1883*, p. 13) to 'There ain't any society' (*NYE* xviii. 16) neatly exemplifies

Daisy's standing as an outsider in this respect). Thus the even volume at which she maintains her 'gay and audible discourse' ensures that it is imprinted, with the relevant interpretation, on the minds of Winterbourne and Mrs Walker and Mrs Costello. The story induces a sympathetic anxiety in the reader for what Daisy and her compromising family may say next by drawing attention (especially in the *NYE*, as we have seen) to this extra dimension of social meaning which she and they knowingly or innocently ignore. Her little brother asks her about Italy:

'Can you get candy there?' Randolph loudly inquired (*1883*, p. 9).

'Can you get candy there?' Randolph asked of all the echoes (*NYE* xviii. 10).

He is only conscious of asking Daisy, we presume; but this description takes a metaphoric leap to what he is actually doing in Winterbourne's terms. The revised version of the story repeatedly makes the point that the other Millers do not know what they are doing and saying in Europe, and that if Daisy knows she will not let it make any difference in her conduct.

Winterbourne and Daisy are working out who will look after Randolph while they go to Chillon:

'Then we may arrange it. If mother will stay with Randolph, I guess Eugenio will'.

'Eugenio?' the young man inquired (*1883*, p. 16).

... 'Eugenio?' the young man echoed (*NYE* xviii. 19).

The interrogative echo here questions the first-name term Daisy comes up with, cautiously suspects a male threat to the arrangement, remarks the easy familiarity to herself of her strange references. At their reunion in Mrs Walker's rooms Winterbourne makes an eloquent plea to Daisy for mercy: 'have I come all the way to Rome to encounter your reproaches?' (*1883*, p. 40); which is increased in the *NYE* to the 'generous passion' of 'have I come all the way to Rome only to be riddled by your silver shafts?' (*NYE* xviii. 51).[17] Daisy finds this pleasant.

[17] In the *NYE* the tones of the Millers and Winterbourne are pulled much further apart, the Millers' speech being even more Americanized: we find 'you bet!' (*NYE* xviii. 7), 'hanging round' and 'ain't' (*NYE* xviii. 12, 13, the latter frequently), 'he don't' (*NYE* xviii. 13), 't'Italy' (*NYE* xviii. 10, 14), 'She doesn't sleep scarcely any' (*NYE* xviii. 27), 'I guess' (*NYE* xviii. 28, 84), 'Father's got it bad' (*NYE* xviii. 48), 'Zurich's real lovely' (*NYE* xviii. 50), 'just the finest kind of Italian' and 'She's going to go it with Mr. Giovanelli' (*NYE* xviii. 52), 'We're real intimate friends' (*NYE* xviii. 72), and 'you can't see anything over here without the moon's right up' (*NYE* xviii. 90). Winterbourne's

'Just hear him say that!'—and she gave an affectionate twist to a bow on her hostess's dress. 'Did you ever hear anything so quaint?'

'So "quaint", my dear?' echoed Mrs. Walker more critically—quite in the tone of a partisan of Winterbourne (*NYE* xviii. 51).

The inverted commas round 'quaint' and the words 'echoed . . . more critically—quite' (replacing 'murmured' in *1883*) are revisions pointing up the point; that Mrs Walker refuses to 'hear' Winterbourne say *'that'* (as if it were strange) in Daisy's sense, and rather turns back on her the word, 'quaint', she has used to express the way Europeanized utterances sound to her.

Conversation, the turning of two speakers in the same direction, their coming to accord, is impossible between the Millers and the Genevans; these echoes of misapprehension repeatedly enact a turning-apart, a failure of terminological common ground. Their words are ambiguous, but often each culture is only in possession of one of the senses, and it takes James's wit to bring them together. Daisy's greeting of Winterbourne on the Palatine Hill, 'I should think you would be lonesome!' (*1883*, p. 63), is presumably an amiable attempt at a desired *rapprochement*, and maybe an attempt to see if her going round with Giovanelli has made him jealous; but this meaning does not get through.

'Lonesome?' asked Winterbourne (*1883*, p. 63).
'Lonesome?' Winterbourne resignedly echoed (*NYE* xviii. 82).

The word is picked up by him for its connection with all the previous cross-cultural misfirings of 'alone'; he resists the appeal in her sense of it, and the subsequent dialogue shows him defending his feelings by sticking aggressively to European codes, catechizing her 'compassionately' and 'patiently' (*NYE* xviii. 83: his adverbs of self-approval) into an understanding of Roman social law. The questions and answers here, the catching-up and definition of words between the interlocutors, the reluctance of Winterbourne to accept Daisy's meaning in his concentration on his own; these dramatically render the complex of relations in the story. Winterbourne's is here an authoritarian and non-reciprocal version of conversation, guarding against

syntax and diction, on the other hand, get higher and more formal: 'I don't think too much sugar good for little boys' (*NYE* xviii. 6); 'And are you—a—thinking of the Simplon?' (*NYE* xviii. 9); 'You're not disposed, madam, . . . to make the so interesting excursion yourself?' (*NYE* xviii. 35.) In the presumable indirect speech of the narration, as well, such raisings of tone are frequent.

self-engagement in an ambiguous situation; Daisy says he has 'no more "give" than a ramrod' (*NYE* xviii. 83—from 'as stiff as an umbrella' (*1883*, p. 64)), and he wants no exchange, only wants to make her take his meanings.

'You'll find at least that I've more "give" than several others', he patiently smiled.
'How shall I find it?'
'By going to see the others.'
'What will they do to me?'
'They'll show you the cold shoulder. Do you know what that means?'
Daisy was looking at him intently; she began to colour. 'Do you mean as Mrs. Walker did the other night?'
'Exactly as Mrs. Walker did the other night' (*NYE* xviii. 83).

In *1883* this was ' "Exactly!" said Winterbourne' (*1883*, p. 64); but the repetition of the whole phrase (as in James's late style, where such echoes are the medium both of conflict and accord) reflects also the sense in which Daisy is asking 'Do *you* mean . . .' Thus Winterbourne's reply is his refusal to differentiate himself from his social group.[18] His pieces of advice to Daisy in the Roman section of the book are in the *NYE* shown to be warning echoes of 'the voice of civilised society', spoken in prudent conformity to an external standard.[19] On the Palatine Hill his third-person answer to her second-person singular challenge about his attitude ('you think . . .')—'Every one thinks so'—is a conscious evasion, 'all Winterbourne found to reply' (*NYE* xviii. 83). It is with a relieved and despairing resort to this public voice that he definitively speaks to Daisy in the Coliseum.[20]

[18] An earlier version has given us ' "They don't", he declared as in full sympathy with "them", "understand that sort of thing here" ' (*NYE* xviii. 71).
[19] Thus at Mrs Walker's party he 'decided to make answer on this' and speaks 'with studied severity' (*NYE* xviii. 70); 'remained grave indeed' (*NYE* xviii. 71); 'had a touched sense for this, but it didn't alter his attitude' (*NYE* xviii. 71–2); 'judged' (*NYE* xviii. 72, 91); and 'permitted himself to growl' (*NYE* xviii. 73); cf. *NYE* xviii. 68, where Mrs Walker 'permitted herself to observe'.
[20] James's interest in the untrained voices of American girls, how they are heard and how the girls hear (or do not hear) themselves, had found further expression by the time *Daisy Miller* came to be revised (just prior to 25 Sept. 1908), when James dispatched the *NYE* copy for it to Scribners (MS letter, Princeton)—in a novel, *The Reverberator*, first published between February and July 1888. *The Reverberator* was the earlier to be revised for the *NYE* (heading vol. xiii), and copy for the *NYE* was dispatched by James to Scribners in two batches, on 13 Mar. and then on 18 Mar. 1908 (Princeton MSS): so that the revisions of *Daisy Miller* follow a *double* attention to such matters. These concerns had equally preoccupied him in his lecture to the graduating girls of Bryn Mawr on 8 June 1905, *The Question of Our Speech*. There he proposed a course of

The story is the record of the play of people's words across these dimensions of meaning, but it offers in the manner of its narration— and has to in order to narrate at all—an understanding which spans the gulf of misunderstandings between Winterbourne and Daisy. In doing this, moreover, its nuanced deployment of the resources of fiction holds open the possibility of a style of accord: the indirect free style, which can objectively and compassionately 'place' characters in their correct relation to the particular and the general, the national and the human; or, rather, correctly map their shifting relations to these disputable borders. That is, the special endeavour of the

further education: 'To discriminate, to learn to find our way among noted sounds, find it as through the acquisition of a new ear' (*The Question of Our Speech*, p. 36). This refers primarily to the act of enunciation, but Francie Dosson in *The Reverberator* undergoes 'what one might call a sea-change' (*LC* ii. 1199) exactly by acquiring a new ear. The novel's plot shows first Francie's '*state of innocence*' (*LC* ii. 1197), her initial deafness to the reverberations of what she says (made a family trait, as in *Daisy Miller*); then the way her indiscreet words about the Probert family 'go bang into the *Reverberator*' (*NYE* xiii. 127) and are transformed by the report of the journalist Flack into a social 'noise'; and finally her new consciousness of the moral implications of language-use, which emerges in her critically echoing attitude to Flack's free speeches: '"Oh—how can you say such a thing?" Francie returned with a tremor in her voice that struck her sister' (*NYE* xiii. 183). Francie speaks at first 'with a strange want of articulation' (*NYE* xiii. 16); her voice, like Daisy's 'small flat monotone' (*NYE* xviii. 31), is described as having a 'little harmonising flatness' (*NYE* xiii. 135)—and we recall James's 'Flatness indeed, ... was the very sum of her story' (*LC* ii. 1270); but towards the end she discovers real discords. As in *Daisy Miller*, but even more extensively, unselfconsciousness is amplified by the increased loudness of the Dossons' speech (and especially that of the journalist George Flack—because he speaks for 'his organ' (*NYE* xiii. 127)): the progress of the drama can almost be followed in terms of volume. Francie painfully comes to hear herself as others hear her, realizing, because of the Proberts' foreignness, that her speech is particular and not inevitable. When Mme de Brécourt talks to her alone, just before the family trial, not suspecting that Francie could have been the source for Flack's scandalous article, she wonders how he got his information. '"You told me, you told me yourself", said Francie quickly. She turned red the instant she had spoken' (*NYE* xiii. 145). The words are no sooner out than Francie hears them back (as we, reading the story, hear them); the gruelling interrogation by the Proberts is a scrutiny of her words, a use of them against her. 'He seems to have printed more', she says: '"*More*? I should think so!" And Mme. de Brécourt rebounded, standing before her' (*NYE* xiii. 146). We remember the innocence of her 'prattle' with Flack in the Bois de Boulogne, the interested interrogative echo with which, when she lets slip that Mme de Brécourt '"has told me all their histories, all their troubles and complications", "Complications?" Mr. Flack threw off' (*NYE* xiii. 136). Speech is no longer an enjoyable and irresponsible realm, but becomes serious for her by the threat this return of her words puts to her happiness with Gaston. This forcible process of education brings Francie close to the ironic, listening stance of the narration in the story, figured often as an imaginary auditor; she takes on the responsibility for what she has said, even across the gulf of the relative which divides cultures, even for consequences she could not have imagined.

revisions, which are *more* in the indirect free style, more closely adhere
to Winterbourne's thought, is to 'place' Winterbourne (by showing
more closely the struggle between his feeling for Daisy and his Genevan
origins, setting in relief his classificatory urge); and, correspondingly,
as far as Winterbourne's placing of Daisy goes, to allow her more
obviously to escape his harsher judgements, those he finally repents as
having 'done her injustice' (*NYE* xviii. 93). The final characteristic of
the revisions that I want to consider, which extends the meanings of
speech in the story, is the rehandling of the presentation of dialogue
and its relation to the indirect free style.

F. O. Matthiessen, talking about the revisions in *The Portrait of a
Lady*, called James's replacements of 'he said' and 'she said' with
various other phrasings 'evasions of the obvious'[21] and Viola Dunbar
in her short piece on the revisions in *Daisy Miller* does not mention
the revisions of the dialogue, presumably on her usual ground that
they are 'purely stylistic'[22] (a category not to be recognized). It would
be wrong to deny that much of the subtlety of James's revisions in this
area parallels and draws on that with which he handles dialogue in
his late fiction (after, that is, the dramatic experiments of 1890–5); but
it would be wrong for critics to act as if it is a corollary of this, even
in a story so closely concerned with ethical and cultural questions
about speech, that there could be no particular meanings, only a
general manifestation of 'style', in the changed treatment of dialogue.

The phrase 'evasions of the obvious' suggests that James replaced
'he said' and 'she said' with various other phrasings just because they
were the most obvious ways of introducing dialogue, and for the sake
of the exquisiteness of rarer ways of doing the same thing. 'Evasions'
insinuates that you really cannot get away from the chore of giving
this basic information. There are, though, artistically respectable
reasons for neither wanting your reader to think the question of *who*
is speaking a question merely of information (since much fiction,
including *Daisy Miller*, involves divisions in the self, so that people
can speak, for instance, in their public or private capacities); nor
wanting him or her to think the question of tone irrelevant. In *1883*,
the tags 'he said' and 'she said' are not thoughtlessly used; they conduct
the exchanges of speech between the characters with a proper reticence,
leaving to the reader the effort of working out the psychological and

---

[21] *The Major Phase*, p. 157.
[22] 'The Revision of "Daisy Miller"', p. 311.

interpersonal reactions which underlie enigmatic utterances, drawing attention to the fact of speeches and not so much to their manner. What the *NYE* revisions do to the speeches they surround is to recontextualize them by making the devices for presenting speech variously interpretative, of vocal tone and of relations to interlocutors and scenes.[23] They give many more of the circumstances of utterance; and by offering a much greater relatedness in sequences of speeches (with 'buts', 'indeeds', 'at any rates', and other logical connectives) they give a closer equivalent to an individual's sense of the movement of a conversation (with questions, answers, statement, denials, hesitations, misunderstandings, surprises, embarrassments, and so on) than the consciously discrete units of speech in *1883*, since they attend to the process of one understanding through experience.

As the intensification of Winterbourne's point of view generally might seem to work against an impartial view of Daisy, so it might seem that this much-increased specification of tone and movement in dialogue would seriously impair the story's ambiguity about behaviour. On the contrary, it defines it, exactly because the indirect free style specifies and draws attention to the troubled source (Winterbourne) from which these specifications of tone and movement come. The utterances given as direct speech in the *NYE* do not retain the 'obvious' relations to their speakers of the formulas 'he said' and 'she said', which are unable in themselves to raise or to silence the question of what it is to say a particular thing, who really says it, and so on. In the revised version the speeches stand out from the interpretative framework Winterbourne progressively tries to fit them into; their speakers are often (if deducible) left unspecified; or instead of being transitively 'said' they precede or coincide with or follow a gesture or a look. There are different modes in the *NYE* of this

---

[23] A far greater range of tones occurs in the *NYE*. Taking only the main verbs used of speech (without reference to the many adverbs of manner) we can find in fifteen pages 'returned' (*NYE* xviii. 41), 'pleaded' (*NYE* xviii. 43), 'broke out' and 'retorted' and 'whined' (*NYE* xviii. 48), 'concurred' (*NYE* xviii. 50), 'pursued' and 'commented' (*NYE* xviii. 52), 'suggested' and 'brought out' (*NYE* xviii. 53), 'piped up' (*NYE* xviii. 54) and 'protested' (*NYE* xviii. 56). Some of these ways of uttering speeches are difficult for a reader to imagine—to 'hear'—because we are not used to so variously metaphorical an application of verbs transitively to speech; when a speech is followed by 'His friend laughed' (*NYE* xviii. 49), it is not clear whether Winterbourne says it *then* laughs, laughs as he says it, or says it *as* a laugh (cf. the way he often 'smiles' his utterances (*NYE* xviii. 15, 25, 60, 83))). Such a problematic relation of main text and direct speech, a felt difficulty of voicing, of interpretation, can be understood as part of the tension between the indirect free style of narration and the speeches quoted within it.

resistance of the spoken to Winterbourne's interpretative setting down of it.

A large number of the assignations of speech used in *1883* are entirely omitted in the *NYE*; some because we know from the circumstances who is speaking, and many more because the assignation is subsumed in a revision with a different relation to the speech, one containing Winterbourne's collection of evidence or his partial judgement.[24] We find an instance of the possible power of such omission in the revision of the exchange after Mrs Walker has 'cut' Daisy:

'That was very cruel', he said to Mrs. Walker.
'She never enters my drawing-room again', replied his hostess (*1883*, p. 57).

'That was very cruel', he promptly remarked to Mrs. Walker.
But this lady's face was also as a stone. 'She never enters my drawing-room again' (*NYE* xviii. 74).

'But' gives the movement of contradiction between the two speeches; 'also' so glancingly mentions the fact that Mrs Walker has a heart of stone that her hard heart is still with us in her final word on the subject (truly the last word in the *NYE* version of the episode). 'Replied' in *1883* has a grim comic force, in that Mrs Walker's decree utterly ignores Winterbourne's remark; and 'his hostess' notes that she is no longer Daisy Miller's. Both these felicities are sacrificed in the revision (for the hard heart and the demanding rank of 'lady'); the moral question, that of sympathy, is tacit (not absent) in *1883*, and the *NYE* consistently concentrates on that question. When the things characters say are presented as grammatically complete in themselves, like Mrs Walker's entirely closed sentence here, without being readily subordinated to a larger syntactic framework, one effect will be to make them stand out with some independence from their context.

A frequent means of specifying tone in the *NYE*, the introduction of a tone-setting sentence before a speech, has a function in relating the progress of a dialogue scene to Winterbourne's point of view. 'But this lady's face was also as a stone' exemplifies this: it gives us Winterbourne's judgement of her heart, his disappointed hope of having an effect ('But' makes his words more of a remonstrance), the expression on Mrs Walker's face, the tone (stony) in which she speaks. And by coming *before* she speaks it renders his immediate perception

---

[24] e.g. 'he protested' (*1883*, p. 23) is omitted (*NYE* xviii. 30); 'said Winterbourne' (*1883*, p. 38) is omitted (*NYE* xviii. 49); and 'she said' (*1883*, p. 43) is omitted (*NYE* xviii. 56).

of her rigidity, allows her words to sound with inevitable finality. These preliminary speeches (which differ in this from stage-directions) not only specify the tone of the speaker, then, but give Winterbourne's response to that tone and direct our sense of how he listens to what is said (the *tone* of his attention, how the speech received echoes in his consciousness). Thus when he first picks Daisy up at Vevey, he asks about Randolph's education, and there immediately follows in *1883* an uninterrupted stream of 140 words on the topic. In the *NYE* this is preceded by 'It tapped, at a touch, the spring of confidence' (*NYE* xviii. 13). 'Confidence' here refers both to Daisy's trusting state and to the disclosures it leads her to make, and 'It tapped, at a touch' retrospectively gives a predictive intention ('get her talking') to what might have been in *1883* merely a polite enquiry by Winterbourne; so that the preliminary sentence sets up the space, the particular acoustic, of the relation in which the speech is to sound. In the moonlight scene by the lake Daisy's sudden change of mind about the boating trip (when Eugenio bows and gives in), which in *1883* is given straight, has a sentence prefixed in the *NYE*:

'Oh, I hoped you would make a fuss!' said Daisy. 'I don't care to go now' (*1883*, p. 30).

But Daisy broke off at this. 'Oh I hoped you'd make a fuss! I don't care to go now' (*NYE* xviii. 38).

'But' gives Winterbourne's expectation that she will press on; 'at this' suggests that the cause of her breaking-off is the collapse of opposition; and this interposed sentence interrupts the flow of the speeches for the reader, signals the change of direction in Daisy's behaviour.

Two more of these interpretative sentences come in the final pages of the *NYE* version of the story. The first case concerns Winterbourne's criminal judgement (his remorseless moment) in the Coliseum. In the crucial exchange as Daisy and Winterbourne leave the ruin, when he has decided that it makes no difference whether she is engaged or not, she reverts to the question, of what he believes about her, that arose at their previous meeting.

'It doesn't matter what I believed the other day', said Winterbourne, still laughing.
'Well, what do you believe now?' (*1883*, p. 68).

'It doesn't matter now what I believed the other day!' he replied with infinite point.

It was a a wonder how she didn't wince for it. 'Well, what do you believe now?' (*NYE* xviii. 88.)

His 'point' (his accent, presumably, on the new sanctimonious 'now') becomes potentially piercing with the revivification of the metaphor, a wound Daisy braves (in the *NYE* picking up what is *his* word, 'now'). Some degree of causal relation between his rough inaccessibility and her willed death is implied by this figuring of his words as a probing susceptible of a response; and 'it was a wonder' both catches his surprise at the time and allows for his later wondering retrospect (as well as inducing the reader to 'wonder'), the indirect free style beautifully holding together this complex of perspectives.

The second case concerns Winterbourne's bitter recognition at Daisy's funeral of what he has done. Giovanelli, approaching him with something to impart, pays a tribute to Daisy, calling her the most 'beautiful' and 'amiable' girl he has known.

And then he added in a moment, 'And she was the most innocent.'
Winterbourne looked at him, and presently repeated his words, 'And the most innocent?'
'The most innocent!'
Winterbourne felt sore and angry ... (*1883*, pp. 70–1).

In the *NYE* we have 'Winterbourne sounded him with hard dry eyes, but presently repeated his words' (*NYE* xviii. 92); so that 'sounded' carries from its initial visual sense in the interrogative look to the spoken trial in Winterbourne's questioning echo (the sceptical echo we have heard throughout)—and for the first time the echo returns on him, rings true, comes home with an unwelcome certainty. In *1883* it is not clear what the nature of the 'soreness' and the 'anger' is; in the *NYE* we get a new sentence:

It came somehow so much too late that our friend could only glare at its having come at all. 'Why the devil,' he asked, 'did you take her to that fatal place?' (*NYE* xviii. 92.)[25]

[25] The graveside scene with Giovanelli anticipates—and in the *NYE* verbally echoes— the final scene in *The Beast in the Jungle* (1903), in which John Marcher, who has failed to reciprocate a woman's love because of *his* too-rigid categories, is suddenly brought to a realization of his blindness (his wasted life) when confronted at her graveside with another mourner. The scene includes the phrases 'the raw glare of his grief' and 'the sounded void of his life' (*The Better Sort*, London, 1903, p. 177), words used in the revision of *Daisy Miller*'s equivalent scene five years later. Marcher remembers the dead May Bartram, and 'her spoken words came back to him' (*The Better Sort*, p. 178).

'Somehow' as often in James directs us to unconscious processes; and the 'glare' (continuing 'hard dry eyes') is not at 'it' (the truth) but at the fact that it's come, the irreparability of his judgement, rendered final by her death. The question he puts to Giovanelli cannot still be in the NYE (as it *could* in *1883*) the expression just of a righteous indignation at Giovanelli's compromising of an innocent girl; the sentence which precedes the speech has shown Winterbourne recognizing that he is not in a good position from which to rebuke Giovanelli, that he is himself too deeply involved.

The revisions of the handling of dialogue, so far from being 'purely stylistic', carry forward then a common artistic purpose with the other revisions examined here, a common concern with the intensification of Winterbourne's point of view in the story, at the same time as they intensify the reader's consciousness that the story is from that point of view. I have tried to suggest the way in which the speeches in the dialogue scenes are in the NYE more intimately inserted into the argumentative structure of Winterbourne's developing conception of Daisy—but there are points where the strain of this insertion shows, junctures where Winterbourne's interpretation is in doubt. Speeches given without any version of the 'he said'/'she said' formula, because of the way that formula includes what is said in a larger (narrative) sentence than that uttered by the speaker, can thus stand apart from Winterbourne's restless attempts at schematization (and these placing tags frequently disappear in the NYE revisions). Within the system of point of view, then, these speeches retain their value as 'dialogue organic and dramatic, speaking for itself' (*LC* ii. 1127).

There is another angle to this relation of the words of the characters to the interpretative attention of Winterbourne, moreover, again to do with his efforts to get his experience into sentences. It hinges on his use of relatives and conjunctions to join speeches up into his sense of them (a sense which is in turn contained by our sense of it as *narrated*— rather as the dramatic monologue in Browning puts the words of a speaker into a verse form of which he is not conscious and thus offers them for scrutiny). The NYE will sometimes replace some variant of 'he said'/'she said' in *1883* not with one of the usual tonal specifications (transitive verb plus adverb of manner, e.g. 'amiably whined' (NYE xviii. 48)), but with a split into two sentences. The first main clause is the speech of the character—and the second, given after a hesitation in the punctuation (a full stop, or semicolon, or dash) will read, for example:

With which he levelled his alpenstock at his sister (*NYE* xviii. 12).

; with which she gave him a smile and turned away (*NYE* xviii. 21).

—with which the girl radiantly took in the gentlemen on either side of her (*NYE* xviii. 61).

On which the cab-driver cracked his whip and they rolled across the desultory patches of antique pavement (*NYE* xviii. 89).

'Which' refers in these contexts to what has been said ('utterance' could be understood after each 'which'), takes it up to move on with it (there usually follows, with the momentum of onward propulsion, some turning or look or striking physical gesture). What is important in this sort of construction, what draws James to it, is the effort of grammatical resumption it involves. This feeling of (Winterbourne's) difficulty in reconciling the flow of events with the flow of his sentences about them, so that he has to take them up again after they seem to be completed, is also evoked by the way in which the *NYE* (not only in dialogue scenes) starts sentences with 'But' and 'And', syntactically abrupt and unconventional accommodations of ceaselessly encroaching dramatic information ('But this lady's face was also as a stone'; 'But Daisy broke off at this').

Such a concentration on the work Winterbourne puts into these turns between his general overview and the particular occurrence (most often in *Daisy Miller* a speech) is a gauge of the ease with which James's use of the indirect free style moves between the report of dramatic facts (what the characters actually say) and the 'subjective' response to these facts of an individual, Winterbourne. The punctuation of the *NYE* (its dashes and pivotal semicolons) constantly throws up turns, hesitations of sense and movement across which we are flexibly moved, so that as we read we can trace the various meanings of the characters, the expectations of Winterbourne and the possibly wilful unconsciousness of Daisy. We are enabled by James's imaginative reach to follow out a complex and dramatic truth quite distinct from the kind of fixed 'truth' the baffled Winterbourne is driven by his ambivalence to seek in the story. The hesitations, written by the *NYE* into Winterbourne's subordinations of Daisy's words, allow them to sound for themselves, 'in poetical terms'; keep them in the air so that 'a sufficiently brooding tenderness might eventually extract a shy incongruous charm'.

The mobility with which James puts Daisy into print, then, does her the justice—renders her the freedom—which Winterbourne's 'setting down' of her so often fails of till his final sorrowing recognition of his 'injustice'. As W. D. Howells said in 1882,

that artistic impartiality which puzzled so many in the treatment of Daisy Miller is one of the qualities most valuable in the eyes of those who care how things are done.[26]

And he goes on, 'this impartiality comes at last to the same result as sympathy'. It might seem that Winterbourne, whose uneasy double standard is so intimately exposed by James, does not benefit from the same 'impartiality' and 'sympathy'; but his difficult social and emotional position, under pressure from his own people and unsure of Daisy's motives, is given serious weight. Daisy's awful miscalculation of his likely response in attempting to make him jealous of Giovanelli is a mark of her accustomed American environment that he could hardly be expected to understand; the story is a small tragedy of error, of mutual misunderstanding determined by cultural differences.

James's revision of *Daisy Miller*, which clarifies these differences and distances thirty years after the first edition, does not just in a general sense (by a rereading of the book) refuse to abdicate his empirical attention to the facts of the tale; the revision's 'perpetual returns and ever-deferred farewells' to the facts are particular and intensive, loving rehearings of the process of judgement, James's 'living testimony to the importance of the facts'.

[26] W. D. Howells, 'Henry James, Jr', *Century Magazine*, 25 (Nov. 1882), 25–9, p. 26; in *W. D. Howells as Critic* (The Routledge Critics Ser.), ed. Edwin H. Cady, London, 1973, 64–72, at p. 66.

8

The Values of *The Aspern Papers*

i. The Past in the Light of the Present

These hours of backward clearness come to all men and women, once at least, when they read the past in the light of the present, with the reasons of things, like unobserved finger-posts, protruding where they never saw them before. The journey behind them is mapped out and figured, with its false steps, its wrong observations, all its infatuated, deluded geography (*The Bostonians*).[1]

The first-person narrator of *The Aspern Papers*, when he has suffered the grievous humiliation of an unexpected proposal from the spinster in possession of the papers, rushes to his gondola and gives instructions to the gondolier. In the version of 1888

He rowed me away and I sat there prostrate, groaning softly to myself, with my hat pulled over my face (*1888*, i. 226).

In the *NYE* revision (sent to Scribners in February 1908) this changes very slightly.

He rowed me away and I sat there prostrate, groaning softly to myself, my hat pulled over my brow (*NYE* xii. 135–6).

'Brow' prevents a repetition of 'face' six lines later, but also brings the phrasing into line with an eloquent speech from *Macbeth* to which James often looks when thinking about the relief of grief that can be found in telling it—that of Malcolm, addressed to the bereaved Macduff:

> Merciful heaven!—
> What, man, ne'er pull your hat upon your brows.
> Give sorrow words. The grief that does not speak
> Whispers the o'erfraught heart and bids it break. (IV. iii. 208–11)

What the allusion brings up is the question of *why* the narrator of *The Aspern Papers* tells his story and, consequently, how our reading of it is framed. I want to suggest that if the narrator behaves badly in the

---

[1] *The Bostonians*, 3 vols., London, 1886, iii. 171.

action of the tale his conduct in the telling of it is a different matter
and that the meanings in this allusion (if we choose to take it) are not
beyond the range of his narration. Seen in this light, the story becomes
the utterance of a persistent grief (a well-merited one) as much as what
many critics consider it, the narrator's self-exonerating gloss. The
revisions of the story have been used by Wayne C. Booth to argue for
the unreliability of the narrator, that is, the untruthfulness of his telling
as well as the immorality of the actions he narrates. Such ideas (carried
to an extreme in Susanne Kappeler's *Writing and Reading in Henry
James*[2]) follow from a misinterpretation of the nature of the narration,
and an examination of the revisions forces and helps us to think about
whose intentions—so far as the reader is concerned—give rise to the
nuanced prose of the story.

The *Macbeth* allusion brings up the question of the narrator's heart
and of what he is giving words to, but some readers may be reluctant
to treat a single verbal reminiscence as convincing proof of an intention
on his part rather than on James's. Another Shakespeare allusion
brought in by the *NYE* revisions serves as further evidence on this
matter. If with Wayne C. Booth we believe the narrator to be unreliable
(*as* a narrator), it seems to follow that James's intention in this respect
will manifest itself in signals to the reader behind the narrator's back;
we have to notice as we read meanings which the narrator inadvertently
overlooks in writing. In Booth's words, 'There can be little doubt that
James has deliberately planted clues here to make us see that the
narrator is rationalizing his conduct.'[3] He introduces quotations from
the narrator with 'Observe how he betrays himself';[4] while Susanne
Kappeler finds Freudian slips set up by James in the narrator's discourse

---

[2] Susanne Kappeler, *Writing and Reading in Henry James*, London, 1980. For Kappeler,
the narrator's purposes in telling his story are only self-exoneration and self-glorification,
and we are to assume a self-serving selection and distortion of incidents on his part. She
sees no authentic confessional motive in his retrospect. She argues that 'Henry James's
commentary on the narrator's tale resides in the wide space between the narrator's first-
person voice and the title and authorship of the novel' (*Writing and Reading*, p. 24),
but takes this as the only 'space of irony'. Her reading makes no allowance for what
she might call a second *lecture*, previous to that of James's attitude: the self-directed
irony of the narrator telling his story. Anything which shows the narrator in a good
light she makes an ironic signal about his vanity from Henry James to the 'detective-
reader' she imagines. The accusing moralism of such a view does not recognize the
value of a 'respect for the liberty of the subject', and makes the story elaborately
sterile.
[3] Wayne C. Booth, *The Rhetoric of Fiction*, Chicago, 1961, p. 360.
[4] *The Rhetoric of Fiction*, p. 358.

for our detection and analysis.[5] The question of how much of the story the narrator himself intends, therefore, comes to a head when in the *NYE* (and not in *1888*) we meet an evident allusion to *The Merchant of Venice*. The narrator, a literary man, confesses near the end that he failed to notice a change in Miss Tina because

I had been too full of stratagems and spoils to think of that (*NYE* xii. 141).

This comes from a famous context, Lorenzo's speech about 'the sweet power of music', which eloquently denounces those capable of 'stratagems and spoils' as unreliable.

> The man that hath no music in himself,
> Nor is not moved with concord of sweet sounds,
> Is fit for treasons, stratagems, and spoils.
> The motions of his spirit are dull as night,
> And his affections dark as Erebus.
> Let no such man be trusted.   (v. i. 83–8)

Is this a wink from James to the reader, a tip that the narrator is not to be trusted? An alternative to such a view has us imagine the narrator as capable of a retrospection at enough of a distance to denounce himself, to imply that he was not—then—to be trusted; capable of 'betraying himself' on purpose. Adrian Poole notes the echo, and is understandably non-committal. 'The lines are painfully pertinent— though whether the narrator is conscious of this and thereby obliquely passing a judgement on himself, it is impossible to say.'[6] If we are to believe, though, that this is a signal to us direct from the author—the narrator stupidly giving himself away by missing the rebuke to him in the Shakespearian context—it reports to us disturbingly on our sense of the moral processes of the work. Such a denial of consciousness to the narrator would hardly exemplify the 'respect for the liberty of the subject' James praises as the mark of the great novelist in 'The Lesson of Balzac'; he would be persecuting his own creation, shooting fish in a barrel. If, on the other hand, we take the verbal texture, the detailed implications of phrasing in the telling of the story, to have artistic

---

[5] *Writing and Reading*, p. 28.
[6] Adrian Poole, 'Notes', *The Aspern Papers and Other Stories*, Oxford, 1983, p. 202. 'Treasons' seems to suggest the allusion (from his sense of betraying Miss Tina), while 'spoils' thrice comes in to describe the eponymous objects in the *NYE*: 'the papers' (*1888*, i. 4) becomes 'my possible spoil' (*NYE* xii. 5); 'the papers' (*1888*, i. 16) becomes 'my spoils' (*NYE* xii. 11); 'extracting the papers from her' (*1888*, i. 45) becomes 'getting hold of my "spoils"' (*NYE* xii. 28).

significance, we are at least called on to take seriously as a constitutive part of our reading the relation between the narrator's present telling of and attitude to his actions, and the feelings he had about those actions as he did them. Our recognizing subtle intentions in the narration—like those in 'stratagems and spoils'—obliges us to think out the extent of the narrator's independent consciousness, to estimate the emotional and experiential depth of the temporal perspective that extends between his present act of looking back and his past actions. It will be objected that the story gives us too little of the present tense for us to judge or feel any such depth; but we *know* that the narrative, though in the past tense, is written from the present, and it would be naïve to set aside the medium through which the action is transmitted to us.

The Aspern Papers is written in a remarkable mode, a variation on the indirect free style where the present 'I' is a different *person* from the past 'I', and has a relation to the past 'I' like that of an impersonal narrator to his third-person subject. This grants the narrator an intelligence which allows shifts of tense to build out a comparative dimension to the play of attitudes and relations in the story—as is apparent in a revision about the papers where Miss Tina has remarked wonderingly 'How much you must want them!' and the narrator has replied 'Oh I do, passionately!' *1888* has 'I conceded, smiling' (*1888*, i. 185); the *NYE* vigorously turns this round to 'I grinned, I fear, to admit' (*NYE* xii. 112), where the comma after 'fear' holds on to the syntax and holds off a differently weighted, more fearful possibility: 'I grinned, I fear to admit'. Simultaneously in this revision 'I fear' gets pressed towards mere mock-penitence—and the clash of 'grinned' and 'fear' engenders a suspense about why he might be sorry now when he was not sorry then. We might compare a disconcerting slip of tenses in a sentence introduced early in the *NYE*:

I feel again my thrill at this close identification of Juliana; in spite of which, however, I kept my head (*NYE* xii. 20).

'In spite of *which*' refers back to the past thrill rather than to its being felt again in the present; but the syntax is hauntingly equivocal. This has a compacted force of undead emotion that emerges into the narration elsewhere. The difficult commerce between attitudes here dramatizes the gap between the narrator's present tense and the past tense in which the action is presented as a charged space of withheld comment, of possible change but also of compelling continuity.

Once we see that there is a distance in time between the narrator and his past self (which is compatible with the continuity we assume), we recognize that his present re-presentation of his past thoughts and actions may express different intentions and a new process of judgement. Wayne C. Booth does not allow for such a temporal distinction when he says that 'the New York revision moves in the direction of our sharper awareness of the narrator's immorality'.[7] He quotes in support of this the revision from 'I had never said it to Tita Bordereau' (*1888*, i. 227) to 'I had never said it to my victim' (*NYE* xii. 136) as evidence of the emphasis 'on the moral deterioration and ultimate baseness of James's narrator'.[8] In this case the narrator is giving an account of the defence he (rightly) thought out against the charge of his having deliberately made up to Miss Tina (her name in the *NYE*)—of having made her his 'victim'—so that the revision ironically takes up the terms of the possible accusation, realizing that his innocence is only partial and that his words have been appallingly open to misinterpretation. With the pained self-rebuke of a sadly won consciousness, at the same time, he is recognizing some measure of partial responsibility—that his minor indiscretions, as he sees them, expose him by their unintended effects to imputations of major and fully intended criminality (he has just mentioned his pain at thinking how 'I had been so much at fault, that I had unwittingly *but none the less deplorably* trifled' (*1888*, i. 227, my emphasis)). In neither of these respects does the use of the word 'victim' involve the narrator's (present) immorality, though it names his past one.

Another example quoted by Booth comes near the end of the story: the narrator pities Miss Tina as having been left by his neglect to the cruel conclusion that he has her in horror—'since I hadn't come back before night to contradict, even as a simple form, even as an act of common humanity, such an idea' (*NYE* xii. 142; 'even as an act of common humanity' is inserted in revision). It is inaccurate to cite this as evidence of *James's* 'condemnation of the narrator',[9] since it's the narrator's condemnation of his past self, something that may on the

---

[7] *The Rhetoric of Fiction*, p. 356. David Timms, in a powerfully argued essay called 'The Governess's Feelings and the Argument from Textual Revision of *The Turn of the Screw*', shows the shakiness of the grounds for a comparable interpretation of revisions as indicating a narrator's unreliability in that story (*Yearbook of English Studies*, 6 (1976), 194–201).

[8] *The Rhetoric of Fiction*, p. 358.

[9] *The Rhetoric of Fiction*, p. 363.

face of it be virtuously candid. We can just as reasonably *admire* as disapprove of people, that is, for having the courage to admit their faults (especially their unintended ones): in the 1886 *Kidnapped*, for instance, by James's friend Stevenson, we admire the first-person narrator David Balfour the more for the manner in which he retrospectively rebukes himself for his behaviour during the quarrel with his friend Alan Breck (in a chapter which James singled out for praise).[10] Thus: 'He seemed disconcerted; at which I was meanly pleased.'[11] 'Meanly' comes as a harsh judgement of the past action; but our sense of it is complex—its disinterested harshness inclines us by reflection to trust in and sympathize with the present narration. The narrator's self-accusations in *The Aspern Papers* need in the same way to be seen as a perspective, his before James's, within the story— though he is a more sophisticated narrator than Alan Breck, more manipulative and slippery. This is to say that he struggles to become his own impersonal author; he knows enough (from the events of the crisis) to be able to tell his story with a degree of dramatic irony, following over the successive states of mind and knowledge that led him to his mistakes—the false steps, the wrong observations, the infatuated, deluded geography—without overtly thrusting on us the hindsight which would disturb the sequence, and incidentally noting his failure to grasp the situation (in words and phrases about others' acts and speeches like 'unexpected', 'irrelevant', 'taking for granted'). When a revision heightens and emphasizes his 'immorality', therefore, we have to read it strictly according to the conditions of his narration; it increases our sense of how badly he behaved, certainly, but also accentuates our interest in how he is behaving now in recalling that behaviour, whether candidly or with special pleading. To read in this way is complex, but considerably more interesting than the show-trial reading, for it involves us as readers in a sympathetic and ironic relation to the centre of consciousness rather than a hostile and rampantly distrustful work of detection.

The difference made by the action in the attitudes of the narrator, the change which interposes a significant distance between his past point of view and his present re-presentation of it, is registered in the story through his attention to questions of value. It is in the layering of the narration, in other words, that we find reproduced the emotional

[10] See 'Robert Louis Stevenson', *LC* i. 1254.
[11] Robert Louis Stevenson, *Kidnapped*, London, 1886, ch. XXIV, p. 237.

readjustment, the learning process, which is so often James's subject—though its end in this case is in even more than the usual doubt. From hyperbolically thinking of the Aspern papers as worth *anything*, the narrator has undergone, by the time he writes his account, a comic and serious conversion which convinces him they are at least not worth one particular human cost (that of marrying Tina Bordereau). The *NYE* revisions frequently engage the relation between different ideas of value, of price and measure; a relation which is the dramatic substance of the story.

ii.   *The Precious Papers*

James recorded in a notebook on 12 January 1887 the anecdote about the Byronist Captain Silsbee on which he was to base *The Aspern Papers*; and then stated

It strikes me much. The interest would be in some price that the man has to pay—that the old woman—or the survivor—sets upon the papers. His hesitations—his struggle—for he really would give almost anything (*Nks.*, p. 34).

This interest is paid out in full by the story's development, an account of the expenses incurred: when 'the survivor' has proposed to him, the narrator explicitly realizes that 'that was the price—that was the price!' (*1888*, i. 226); he feels that 'it went without saying that I could not pay the price' (*1888*, i. 228); and then just before the end for a delusive moment 'It seemed to me I *could* pay the price' (*NYE* xii. 142). These prices are both financial and human; the narrator's obsessive reluctance to think of the papers as anything but priceless (worth more than any price)—his 'passionate appreciation' (*1888*, i. 234) of them—is the ironic *donnée* of the action. 'The only way to get hold of the papers' (*1888*, i. 235) becomes in the *NYE*, with a turn on what holds *him*, 'the only way to become possessed' (*NYE* xii. 141). There is a comedy of disproportionate desire about this, and the story translates into literal cash terms his metaphorical language of limitless expenditure, so that (of the portrait) 'I said that I would give anything to possess it, yet that I had not a thousand pounds' (*1888*, i. 171). More accurately, as James says in the Notebook, he would give 'almost' anything.

Later in the story his other metaphorical language about the papers, that of high sexual passion (jocularly applied by him to his editorial yearning), rebounds on him even more disconcertingly in Tina's mis-construction of his ironic words: he tells her that

> I expected her now to settle my fate.
> 'Your fate?' said Miss Tita, giving me a queer look (*1888*, i. 211).

He himself sets no limit on the value of the papers: 'Oh I've never in my life made a bargain' (*NYE* xii. 70), as he puts it. A revision notes his 'resolve to be genial from the threshold at any price' (*NYE* xii. 15). Only the experience of the inflationary demands made of him in Venice—both financially and personally—imposes a sense of actual limits on him before the 'total exhaustion of matter' otherwise imagined by James (in an 1872 Hawthorne review (*LC* i. 307)) as the only restraint on the age's biographical curiosity. This external compulsion brings him to regret his measureless obsession:

> As the day went on I grew to wish that I had never heard of Aspern's relics, and I cursed the extravagant curiosity that had put John Cumnor on the scent of them. We had more than enough material without them and my predicament was the just punishment of that most fatal of human follies, our not having known when to stop (*1888*, i. 229).

'Extravagant' refers both to the editors' indiscreet breaking of bounds and more practically to the *cost* of such transgressions, the recklessness which has brought the narrator to his humiliating punishment. Both in *1888* and the *NYE*, the word rings up throughout the story that he is living beyond his means. When at the start he shows Mrs Prest his specially engraved visiting card, with 'a name that was not my own' (*1888*, i. 19; revised for the French urbanity of 'a well-chosen *nom de guerre*' (*NYE* xii. 13)), she responds 'You are very extravagant'. This is poised between the money and moral senses; in the *NYE* she adds archly, spanning the two, that '—it adds to your immorality'. This, another of Booth's list of examples, gives him the word 'immorality' to use of the narrator; but Mrs Prest makes the mock accusation with a flirtatious insincerity that prevents our extending it directly into our judgement. Later the narrator calls the offer of his gondola to Juliana 'somewhat extravagant' (*1888*, i. 42); and Miss Tina seems after his acceptance of the lodging to 'wish to remind me that if I had been extravagant I was not really foolishly singular' (*1888*, i. 52)—both using the money sense. Meditating on Juliana's motives in making him spend too much, he recalls that 'my almost extravagant comedy on the subject of the garden had presented me irresistibly in the light of a victim' (*1888*, i. 145), where the word makes him both a punishable encroacher on territories and otherwise a recklessly big spender (Tina announces to him that she told Juliana 'I thought you were rich' because of 'the way you talked' (*1888*, i. 52)). The commerce between the personal, moral, and economic senses of 'extravagance' in the story helps to realize the questions of value by the metaphor of price, to represent the whole outlay of his yearning.

'Price' yields a word with a connected range of meanings in the story—'precious': a complex word which, especially in the revisions, likewise constructs an ironic dimension—a set of relations—concerning notions of value. Its first *OED* sense is monetary: 'Of great price; having a high value; costly'. Its second is beyond money: 'Of great moral, spiritual, or non-material worth; held in high esteem'. But it can descend to the colloquial and ironic (4b): 'Of little worth, worthless, good-for-nothing'. The special aptness of 'precious' for the narrator's story comes then with the dictional slides it offers: from indefinite high valuations, expressed in cash or reverence, to the slangy disrespect which pushes it towards the Bertie Woosterish sense 'in fact over-rated'. This possible plunge into irony makes the word work richly for a narrator writing about his past excessive estimate of things. Thus, for instance, he 'not only spent time, but (hang it! as I said) spent precious money' (*NYE* xii. 44; 'precious' comes in as a revision); which playfully avoids tautology by distinguishing price from value. When he takes Tina out for the evening and she admits Juliana has 'everything', her 'words caused all my pulses to throb, for I regarded them as precious evidence' (*1888*, i. 129). (Just below Tina answeringly lingers at shop-windows 'asking what I thought of things, theorising about prices'.) Juliana reveals that the portrait of Aspern was painted by her father, and 'That makes the picture indeed precious!' (*1888*, i. 159) the narrator exclaims, again using it as a synonym for 'admirable'. The other, slangy, usage hanging about the word and the story is taken up by Mrs Prest when at the start she exclaims, at the schemes of the editors, 'Well, you're a precious pair!' (*1888*, i. 20.) Used in this way it comes with the force of, say, 'precious rascal'; a revision replaces 'venerable woman' (*1888*, i. 152) with the more overtly ironic 'precious personage' at a stage where the narrator's financial extravagance is starting to reach actual limits:

I was willing to pay the precious personage with whom my pecuniary dealings were such a discord twice as much as any other *padrona di casa* would have asked, but I wasn't willing to pay her twenty times as much. (*NYE* xii. 92.)

'Precious' here looks both to the value Juliana embodies for him (as Aspern's ex-mistress and custodian of the papers), and to her not estimable conduct in the pecuniary dealings about the rent; it contains, that is, an ambivalence about his involved relation with her, the slangy sense serving as a defence against his discomfort at the way his obsession commits him to a prickly dependence. Such an ambivalence recurs in the revised final sentence, about the portrait which hangs above his writing-table (at which presumably he has written the account we are reading): in *1888*,

When I look at it my chagrin at the loss of the letters becomes almost intolerable (*1888*, i. 239).

The *NYE* makes this (with another alliteration)

When I look at it I can scarcely bear my loss—I mean of the precious papers (*NYE* xii. 143).

The comic wobble of embarrassment whereby we might understand his 'loss' as that of Tina rather than the papers is corrected by him, but leaves us with the ambivalence in 'precious', the sense 'not priceless' having been brought home by his embarrassing predicament. His crisis has turned the papers (Juliana's 'treasure' (*1888*, i. 70, 143, and additionally *NYE* xii. 69, 93)) into a 'bundle of tattered papers' (*1888*, i. 228), or 'crumpled scraps' (*1888*, i. 230); and it has become impossible for him to value them any more as supremely important. The pleasure of this metaphorical way of talking has been taken from him by events. The slangy sense here is a gauge of his return on himself; he is left at the end of the story to live with—live over in memory—a disappointed ambition he can no longer even respect.

    1888 repeatedly resorts to a related word and idea, that of 'measure'; and the *NYE* amplifies our sense of its significance for the story. The network in *1888* is already extensive. Trying to persuade Miss Tina of the justice of his cause, the narrator claims:

It is simply that they would be of such immense interest to the public, such immeasurable importance as a contribution to Jeffrey Aspern's history (*1888*, i. 136).

'Immense' and 'immeasurable' are synonymous; the language of infinite value is always on the narrator's lips and pen, a stylistic extrava-

gance to be chastened by an action that establishes at least one thing
the papers aren't worth.

The narrator, as the outcome shows, fails in the action to measure
what is going on. The measurements he makes at first take for granted
his possession of an adequate rule but soon have their work cut out
as *he* comes under examination: he takes the 'magnificent measure'
(*1888*, i. 52) of the sala, and after six weeks 'I had made no measureable
advance' (*1888*, i. 61); but when he is called in to see the suspicious
Juliana 'I stood there to be measured' (*1888*, i. 113). The narrator has
during the action his absolute standard (the justifying requirements of
Aspern studies), but can perceive even before the dénouement the
oddity of a niece's peaceably accepting his searching inquiries about
Juliana's reputation:

> It was strange enough, as I afterwards thought, that she had not the least air
> of resenting my want of consideration for her aunt's character, which would
> have been in the worst possible taste if anything less vital (from my point of
> view) had been at stake. I don't think she really measured it (*1888*, i. 135).

The conditional is defensive about whether 'taste' *can* be only relative
in this way, and the parenthesis '(from my point of view)' measures
the distance you would expect between their measures of the situation;
while the present tense of 'I don't think' advances from the intermediate
retrospect of 'as I afterwards thought' to a rueful, unabated wonder.

If the papers would be of 'immeasureable importance as a contribution to Jeffrey Aspern's history', the intense veiled argument of
the narrator with Juliana over the need for biographical truths about
writers shows him as believing the importance one *of* measure:

> 'We are terribly in the dark, I know,' I admitted; 'but if we give up
> trying what becomes of all the fine things? What becomes of the work I just
> mentioned, that of the great philosophers and poets? It is all vain words if
> there is nothing to measure it by.'
> 'You talk as if you were a tailor', said Miss Bordereau, whimsically ...'
> (*1888*, i. 149).

Juliana's joke is a proper put-down, classes the narrator's idea of the
importance of measure as vulgarly inappropriate; and a few speeches
earlier a revision has evoked a corresponding tremor of unease about
the narrator's measure of the human situation, a sudden realization
that he has gone too far. Asked what he says about the great writers,
he playfully announces that 'I say they sometimes attached themselves

to very clever women!' In *1888* these words are followed by

I answered, laughing. I spoke with great deliberation, but as my words fell upon the air they struck me as imprudent (*1888*, i. 148).

In the *NYE*, with an alertness to the moment's risk that recalls the revisions of Newman's conversation with Claire de Cintré in *The American*,

I replied as for pleasantness. I had measured, as I thought, my risk, but as my words fell upon the air they were to strike me as imprudent (*NYE* xii. 90).

The more complex relation of the tenses here—with the breathtakingly suspended prospective 'were to strike' catching the moment of alarm between intention and effect—yields a rich temporal perspective on the measures taken by the narrator, the way he keeps having to pay for his words.

In his first meeting with Juliana she tells him he can have rooms for 'a good deal of money' (*1888*, i. 44): he mistakenly thinks her idea of a large sum will not be his and as a result lets himself in for great expenses. In *1888*

I hesitated but for a single instant, long enough to ask myself what she meant in particular by this condition.

In the *NYE*

I hesitated but an instant, long enough to measure what she meant in particular by this condition (*NYE* xii. 28).

'Measure' here ironically suggests he has got the sum right—the truth it phrases is to his *idea* that he has made a successful estimate (according to the indirect free style of his *dramatic* recollection)—so that the figure then actually named by Juliana comes as a shock to his sense of proportions. After the first climax of his discovery by Juliana the word comes in to render another misunderstanding: the self-excited narrator imagines Tina as disgusted by his apparent villainy, not suspecting the attitude in her which produces the second climax. In *1888*,

It struck me there was a kind of scorn in Miss Tita's silence (little disdainful as she had ever been), so that I was uncomfortable and sore (*1888*, i. 200).

In the *NYE* he asks

Couldn't I measure the scorn of Miss Tina's silence—little disdainful as she had ever been? Really the soreness pressed; . . . (*NYE* xii. 120).

It isn't scorn, though—as he is to find out. Shortly afterwards, on his return to Venice, she refuses to let him see the papers and he makes an unfortunately personal appeal—before realizing her design on him—in a voice of 'infinite remonstrance' (*1888*, i. 213). The *NYE* again introduces 'measure' to gauge his grasp of the wrong end of the stick.

She coloured and the tears came back to her eyes; I measured the anguish it cost her to take such a stand, which a dreadful sense of duty had imposed on her (*NYE* xii. 128).

The real 'anguish' is her embarrassment at a stand not exactly of duty; as these examples suggest, each time a revision brings in the word 'measure' (here replacing 'I saw that it cost her a kind of anguish'), the narrator's past errors of judgement are dramatically rendered as assured comprehensions.[12] By the significant frequency of terms of measurement and comparison and degree (for instance 'almost', 'so much', and 'marked') the story tacitly develops its argument about value, about the narrator's increasing embarrassment in the action; an embarrassment which culminates in the submerged distress of his present narrating, at the discovery of upsetting limits on his relation to the things he has unquestioningly thought of as immeasurably precious.[13]

---

[12] Here again we could note that since the narrator knows all too well by experience the true nature of Miss Tina's 'stand', the ironic opacity to hindsight of his use of the past tense—'saw' and 'measured' rather than 'thought I saw' or 'thought I measured'—makes clear the equivalence of his narration to the indirect free style, a deliberate choice on his part.

[13] Related to the business of measure as part of the narrator's dramatic account of his past misreading of things, and more closely involved in incident, are the repeated turns on his expectations. Miss Tina's appearance at their last meeting disconcertingly includes 'something which had not been in my forecast' (*1888*, i. 236), something that turns out to be a sign of her destruction of the papers. Making forecasts and theories with a certain liberty has been one of his editorial pleasures; the satisfaction of being confirmed is early on rendered by a revision: '"Orpheus and the Maenads!" had been of course my foreseen judgement when first I turned over his correspondence' (*NYE* xii. 7)—where the pleased knowingness of the superfluous 'foreseen' makes it doubly 'of course' that events should show him right. His spinning of theories (*1888*, i. 79) has the splendid casualness of expertise: 'It was a part of my idea that the young lady had had a foreign lover—and say an unedifying tragical rupture—before her meeting with Jeffrey Aspern' (*NYE* xii. 48). (That blasé dictatorial 'say' comes in with the *NYE*.) So that he has a professional pride in correct predictions to be gradually worn down by his failure to seize what goes on in the action. The phrase 'taking for granted' is frequent (*1888*, i. 28, 48, 52, 124, 177); when he finds her in the garden at night, she speaks, and: 'At first I took for granted that the words she uttered expressed discomfiture at my arrival; but as she repeated them—I had not caught them clearly—I had the surprise of hearing her say, "Oh, dear, I'm so very glad you've come!"' She and her aunt had in common

iii.   His Sense of Things

In the *NYE* the narrator tells Mrs Prest early on of the deceit he means
to practise, in another of the revisions cited by Booth:

Hypocrisy, duplicity are my only chance. I'm sorry for it, but there's no
baseness I wouldn't commit for Jeffrey Aspern's sake (*NYE* xii. 12).

In *1888* this last phrase was just, comparatively, 'but for Jeffrey
Aspern's sake I would do worse still' (*1888*, i. 16): the revision specifies
superlatively that he pretends to feel no limit to the justification his
end affords to his means. This way of talking is irresponsible, but
not literally meant, being rather the humorous inflation of a minor
misdemeanour to fit an ironically assumed attitude of mock-grandeur.
Such a trick of speech swaggeringly makes light of the act it takes off
from. This kind of flippancy, a sense of not needing to take responsibility for his acts, informs the narrator's speech and thoughts during
the action of the story; we can recognize it as a Byronic habit, that of
ironically exaggerating the case against himself in order to be forgiven
(and to forgive himself), so that his conduct shouldn't be measured.

This (highly coercive) emphatic jocularity in the revisions extends
a habit he has in *1888* to cover his encroachments: intruding on the
Bordereaux he becomes the lovable rogue and says to Tina 'I'm afraid
you'll think me odiously intrusive, but you know I *must* have a garden'
(*1888*, i. 26; and he admits 'that I had intruded' again to Juliana soon
after (*1888*, i. 39)). He imagines at one point that Juliana is going to
call him 'such a monster of indiscretion' (*1888*, i. 44)—when he is
indeed acting as such a one. Several times in the *NYE* he refers to
himself, with the ne'er-do-well's disarming candour, as an invader:
violent 'invasion' (*NYE* xii. 53) replaces sinister 'creeping' in the garden
(*1888*, i. 87); 'invasion and research' (*NYE* xii. 61) inflates the threat
in 'the interviewer' (*1888*, i. 100); and when Tina is left alone on the
piano nobile he feels different about 'the invasion of it' (*NYE* xii. 125),

the property of unexpected speeches' (*1888*, i. 87). Again and again he notes their
unexpectedness: at his first meeting with Juliana 'the remark she made was exactly the
most unexpected' (*1888*, i. 38; and our attention reaches into the next chapter for her
actual words); Tina has 'unexpected serenities' (*1888*, i. 111) or speaks 'without any
immediate relevance' (*1888*, i. 186); Juliana behaves with 'unexpected rudeness' (*1888*,
i. 160); Tina speaks with 'a strange, unexpected emotion' (*1888*, i. 183), and proposing
achieves an 'unexpected, persuasive volubility' (*1888*, i. 224). Revisions tell of surprise:
'I quite gasped' (*NYE* xii. 77), 'I gasped as it passed into my hand' (*NYE* xii. 130), and
slow-wittedly, like Amerigo with his '"Two—?"' (*GB*, p. 424), for the confounding
proposal, 'I wondered. "If I were a relation—?"' (*NYE* xii. 133).

not simply about 'visiting her there' (*1888*, i. 208). When Mrs Prest
says in the *NYE* that his extravagance in having the false cards
engraved 'adds to your immorality' (*NYE* xii. 13), she is wittily joining
in this sociable irony rather than deeply disapproving. The assumption
behind all this is that his misrepresentations are relatively trivial and
justified by his editorial function; they are also exceptional: 'I did what
I disliked myself for doing (reflecting that it was only once in a way)'
(*1888*, i. 65).

His hyperbolically embattled actions thus offer him the irresponsible
pleasure of play-acting, a holiday—only an apparent one—from
himself (one revision brings in Goldoni (*NYE* xii. 60), and in the
beautiful paragraph about the city near the end he compares Venice
to a theatre (*1888*, i. 233)). The scheming and rivalry with Juliana
strike him as a game, and his playfully competitive spirit is much
enlivened in the revisions, where grievances are gleefully collected and
ill intentions melodramatically harboured. Cumnor's enquiring letters
become 'his respectfully writing' (*NYE* xii. 12) (from 'when he wrote'
(*1888*, i. 16)); and in the *NYE* he becomes answeringly 'their snubbed
correspondent' (*NYE* xii. 13). Juliana concentrates these adversarial
feelings in him: for instance in conversation 'Miss Bordereau inquired'
(*1888*, i. 147) becomes 'implacably pursued' (*NYE* xii. 89), her 'fine
tranquillity' (*1888*, i. 149) becomes 'hard complacency' (*NYE* xii. 90),
and 'with a cynical little sigh' (*1888*, i. 161) becomes more blatantly
'with a crudity of cynicism' (*NYE* xii. 97). The *NYE* narrator gladly
takes these notes as justifying his campaign, whose countervailing
refusal to give quarter he vividly evokes. When he first sees her, her
great age impresses him and he crows that 'She would die next week,
she would die to-morrow—then I could seize her papers' (*1888*, i. 37);
the *NYE* has 'then I could pounce on her possessions and ransack
her drawers' (*NYE* xii. 24), alliteratively representing (not actually
deploring) a self-consciously callous keenness. This is another of
Booth's instances of immorality; it shows the past thought as having
been deplorable; but the absence of present comment gives no foothold
for the belief that the narration is unreliable. It seems more appropriate
to identify the moral confusion, or at least curiosity, produced in the
reader when a character whom we have no firm reason to suppose
reformed describes his past conduct in such lurid terms.

In the *NYE* the titular letters (usually 'the papers' in *1888*) are
described in remarkably various terms reflecting the vicissitudes of the
desire whose history the narration traces: 'obtain the documents' (*1888*,

i. 16) comes bluntly to the point as 'get what I wanted' (*NYE* xii. 11), and 'the documents' on the same page become cherished as 'her relics and tokens'.[14] 'Her papers' (*1888*, i. 113, 234) twice become with the force of his and her desire her 'treasure' (*NYE* xii. 69, 140)—on the first occasion producing an analogy with that of Byron's *Sardanapalus* (who burns his). 'Annihilated the papers' (*1888*, i. 153) becomes 'sacrificed her treasure' (*NYE* xii. 93). The portrait which has been 'her treasure' in *1888*, (i. 158) becomes 'her prize' (*NYE* xii. 95)—perhaps for loving Aspern so well—as against the prize it would be for the narrator. 'To think that I was nearer the documents I coveted' (*1888*, i. 164) realizes itself as 'to feel myself so close to the objects I coveted' (*NYE* xii. 99), a vivid translation of thought to sensation. 'The tormenting treasure' (*1888*, i. 192) inflates to 'the source of my hopes' (*NYE* xii. 116) punning on his usual biographical 'sources' and with an ambiguous 'of' for an intense reciprocity of relation. Before the proposal scene where the narrator gloomily imagines he'll soon learn 'that the papers had been reduced to ashes' (*1888*, i. 210), the *NYE*, with a leap into metaphor that suggests where he *should* have laid up his treasure, turns 'the papers' to 'my dream' (*NYE* xii. 126).

These revisions greatly extend the existing play of descriptions in *1888*, a play of valuations which sometimes resembles the crashing and booming of a stock exchange. When marriage to Miss Tina is suddenly the asking price, the value of Aspern's letters dramatically plunges to that of 'a bundle of tattered papers' (*1888*, i. 228), or 'Miss Bordereau's crumpled scraps' (*1888*, i. 230), before returning again to the level of 'the papers' for the rest of the story. In the *NYE* the variations of name more closely articulate the narrator's changing complex of feeling about his quest, building up to the revised last words, words which ironically contain the plot of his shift of attitude to 'the precious papers' (*NYE* xii. 143).

The sensuous language of attraction, touch and grasp (as where above he feels himself 'so close to ... objects') strongly renders in *1888* the impulsion of a curiosity about Aspern and about the past that wishes 'to feel a transmitted contact in any aged hand that his had touched' (*1888*, i. 10), that has 'an irresistible desire to hold in my own for a moment the hand that Jeffrey Aspern had pressed' (*1888*, i. 49). (This is echoed in James's own image in the Preface to the story of

[14] 'Relics' is frequent in *1888*: i. 18, 36 (where Juliana is one), 70, 165, 208, 229; and in the *NYE* xii. 94, 125.

touching the not-too-distant past 'as by making a long arm' at the table (*LC* ii. 1177).) Juliana won't let him shake hands—as he dauntedly puts it she's 'too venerable to touch' (*1888*, i. 113)—and in the story as a whole he finds that keeping his hands off is his only possible course under the hard-pressing necessity which keeps him forever at arm's length from the 'tangible objects' (*NYE* xii. 12) he yearns for. The embarrassing posture in which he's discovered by Juliana, bending down to examine a 'secretary', intimately relates to his feelings about these matters and his absurdly wishful expectations. With a Venetian schemer's 'super-subtle inference' (*NYE* xii. 117; recalling *Othello* I. iii. 357), he suspects Tina may have unlocked the desk for him:

the lid would probably move if I touched the button. This possibility pressed me hard and I bent very close to judge. I didn't propose to do anything, not even—not in the least—to let down the lid; I only wanted to test my theory, to see if the cover *would* move. I touched the button with my hand—a mere touch would tell me; and as I did so—it is embarrassing for me to relate it— I looked over my shoulder (*NYE* xii. 117–18).[15]

Earlier he has worried about the survival of the papers and decided to 'put the case to the very touch of my own senses' (*NYE* xii. 87; revising the more scrupulous 'judge so far as was possible with my own senses', *1888*, i. 143). Here he is 'pressed' by his desire to touch, to get physical confirmation of his theory; and the violently disconcerting sequence of tenses at the climax keeps us from knowing what a 'mere touch would tell'. 'I touched' seems a past historic, a simple act; then as an afterthought we get the conditional we'd have expected *before* ('*would* tell me'); next the action, whose result we now expect, turns back into an imperfect ('as I did so'); we leap into the present of the narrator's sense of this embarrassed past ('it is embarrassing'); and then another simple action moves us away from the desk, never to discover the truth of the touch ('I looked over my shoulder'). We may wonder whether he is here sparing Tina the revelation of an abject treachery towards her aunt, or himself the revelation of the fatuity of his hopes. At any rate, he is left with the physical yearning on his hands that has so violently manifested itself (on his hands) when Juliana passes him the miniature portrait of Aspern to value; a revision gives the physiological measure of his excessive sense of it. In *1888*

---

[15] 'This possibility pressed me hard' is the only verbal change from *1888* in this passage, except the contraction.

I possessed myself of it with a hand of which I could only hope that she did not perceive the tremor (*1888*, i. 155).

In the NYE

I possessed myself of it with fingers of which I could only hope that they didn't betray the intensity of their clutch (*NYE* xii. 93–4).

Where the 'tremor' suggested reverence just as much, an 'intensity' of 'clutch'—and one that may be apparent—implies a barely controlled acquisitiveness—which is ironically met and transformed in the climactic proposal scene, where another revision apprises the narrator of an unforeseen truth about his reach. The freely enterprising Tina continues to sketch their future

with her unexpected persuasive volubility. 'You could see the things—you could use them.' She stopped, seeing I grasped the sense of her conditional (*NYE* xii. 134).

'The things' and 'grasped' are revisions from 'them' and 'that I perceived' (*1888*, i. 224): the way he 'grasps' in the NYE not 'the things' but an abstraction, an abstract truth, evokes the narrator's baffled apprehension that he can't get the purchase he wants on his choice objects, that their price—Tina's 'conditional'—is too much for him.

One revision in particular conveys through the beauty of its detail the pleasure which he imagines in possession and of which he is left with only the imagination. Miss Tina reports that Juliana said Aspern was a god. She does it in a flat tone,

But it stirred me deeply as she dropped the words into the summer night; their sound might have been the light rustle of an old unfolded love-letter (*NYE* xii. 64).

(In *1888* the clause after the semicolon is 'it seemed such a direct testimony' (i. 105).) The enactive echoes of delicate internal rhyme— 'stirred' and 'words', 'night', 'might', and 'light', and specially the folding of 'old' into 'unfolded'—intricately suggest a lyrical continuity with the poetic past, a desired contact conceived even up to the vibrant aural sensitivity recorded here. By so passionate and sensuous an expression of editorial desire James allows us to measure—with the necessary comic distance—the narrator's loss.

iv. Jokes and Consequences

The final price of the papers themselves—marrying Miss Tina—is too high, but the narrator also pays a price for his desire to obtain them, and not only in the cash of his rent and the spending of his time. The story comes to a double crisis, his successive embarrassing confrontations by Juliana and Miss Tina, each of whom gives him a particular look. When Juliana finds him apparently trying to force her secretary, she finally uncovers her eyes, and the *NYE* (in a revision which is another of Booth's examples) introduces a simile that gives—only as a simile—the force of what she *supposes* him to be doing:

> for the first, the last, the only time I beheld her extraordinary eyes. They glared at me; they were like the sudden drench, for a caught burglar, of a flood of gaslight; they made me horribly ashamed. I never shall forget her strange little bent white tottering figure (*NYE* xii. 118).[16]

We should give some heed to the narrator's assurance just before that 'I did not propose to do anything' (*1888*, i. 194), since otherwise he would be readable as entirely the 'publishing scoundrel' (*1888*, i. 195) Juliana declares him. He claims, we must note, to have 'candidly narrated' (*1888*, i. 190), 'frankly stated' (*NYE* xii. 115) the 'importunities, the indelicacies' of which his desire has made him capable. If we assume he is lying about the 'extenuating circumstances', we miss one serious point of his punishment for extravagant curiosity—that he fatuously exposes himself to the imputation of criminal intentions which he has irresponsibly played with but never seriously entertained. This is not to deny that his lack of serious knowledge of his own motives is part of what is deplorable in him, and that *had* he found the papers in the drawer the temptation might have been too strong for his principles, such as they are.

The simile of the 'flood of gaslight' does not exactly say that he *is* 'a caught burglar', rather that his situation is like that of one and that

---

[16] There is a strange collocation of possible Marvell echoes in the story—first Juliana's eyeshade, several times referred to as a 'green shade', which, in a story where a garden is important, recalls 'The Garden' with its 'To a green thought in a green shade' (Andrew Marvell, *The Complete Poems*, ed. Elizabeth Story Donno, Harmondsworth, 1972, p. 101). Juliana is the name of the lady in the 'Mower' poems, whose eyes have harmful power: 'Damon the Mower' includes the reflection that 'Only for him no cure is found,|Whom Juliana's eyes do wound' (*The Complete Poems*, p. 108). The ironic relation of the narrator's horrible shame to the quite different pains of love in this love-poem would suggest in *The Aspern Papers* the persistence of Juliana's ocular power to compel.

he feels like one. It is ludicrous but not exactly mendacious of him to attempt in writing to Miss Tina afterwards to 'account for the posture in which I had been discovered' (this comes in with the *NYE* xii. 119). 'It rankled for me that I had been called a publishing scoundrel', he says, 'since certainly I did publish and no less certainly hadn't been very delicate' (*NYE* xii. 120): the humiliation of shame (which 'I shall never forget') and the discomfort of bad faith more than the remorse of one actually guilty of intending burglary and seduction fuel and drive his retrospection. His editorial passion blinds him to the moral claims—to be treated as ends in themselves—of people associated with the papers, and he finds himself seeming to act in blatant contravention of the social and ethical codes he would in other contexts recognize as his own. His guilt is real but relatively minor; it appears greater because of his failure of moral intelligence—which is galling for him. When Tina cannot bring herself to agree to further searches while her aunt lies there ill, he assents: 'No, it isn't decent';

And the words, on my lips, were not hypocritical, for I felt reprimanded and shamed (*1888*, i. 183).

Soon after feeling reprimanded here he finds reason to feel it again, when he lets slip his facile assumption that Tina has agreed to *give* him the papers once she has found out whether they survive; she takes this up:

'Ah nothing', I answered rather foolishly, being ashamed to tell her what had been implied in my acceptance of delay—the idea that she would perhaps do more for me than merely find out (*NYE* xii. 114).

'Ah' replaces 'Oh' (*1888*, i. 188) for a blanker misgiving; and 'perhaps' and 'for me' arrive with the *NYE* (which also cunningly makes the end of this sentence the end of an awkward isolated paragraph). 'For me' assumingly catches his blandly egoistic idea of Miss Tina's disinterested desire to please *him*, while events show that her realization of just how much he expected of her strikes her not with the sting of insult but as further proof of affectionate intimacy and trust.

These points show how unsatisfying is Booth's account: 'The story, then, consists simply of this unscrupulous man's quest for the Aspern papers, his discovery that the best way to get to them is to make love to the owner's unattractive niece, Tina ...'.[17] 'Discovery' turns an off-

---

[17] *The Rhetoric of Fiction*, p. 358.

colour joke of his into an experimentally evolved strategy; and her proposal, when it comes, supremely disconcerts him because although unforeseen it incongruously matches that early joke of his plan 'to make love to the niece' (*1888*, i. 21). Once she has proposed, he asks 'Did she think I had made love to her, even to get the papers?' (*1888*, i. 226),[18] and later insists to himself:

But I hadn't given her cause—distinctly I hadn't. I had said to Mrs Prest that I would make love to her; but it had been a joke without consequences and I had never said it to my victim (*NYE* xii. 136).

'Without consequences' refers only to the intention of making love as such, not to the idea of being sociable to Miss Tina and winning her confidence (a difference between American and old-world *mœurs* is operative here), and when he's accepted as a lodger he records that 'my plan was from this moment to spend as much of my time as possible in her society' (*1888*, i. 51). This 'plan' begins with an insinuatingly personal remark, introduced in *1888* by 'I only observed at the end of a minute: . . .' immediately after the 'plan' has been announced, and in the *NYE* by more of a retrospective sense of its significance: 'a minute indeed elapsed before I committed myself' (*NYE* xii. 32).

The 'consequences' exceed his intentions, then, with a logic of which his narration is the retracing, and make her as the revision realizes his 'victim' (in *1888* she was 'Tita Bordereau', i. 227). He fails, that is (as an American dealing with a Europeanized sense of sexual propriety) to measure the legitimacy of Miss Tina's response, though her desperate situation and perhaps Juliana's urging anyway make her go further than he could expect; so that he holds back all too comically late when, for instance, he responds, on her saying she doesn't understand him:

'That is just the sort of occasion to have faith.' I could not say more, though I should have liked to, as I saw that I only mystified her; for I had no wish to have it on my conscience that I might pass for having made love to her (*1888*, i. 101–2).

The sexual language he has used to himself as a playful metaphor for interestedly winning her over to his side (recalling 'the example of Verona' (*1888*, i. 86), or being 'sure of her full surrender' (*NYE* xii.

[18] It is small wonder Booth finds the narrator 'unreliable' and the story unsatisfactory ('Good as it is, "The Aspern Papers" is not as good as James might have made it' (*The Rhetoric of Fiction*, pp. 363–4))—if he 'simply', as here, refuses to credit the narrator's statements of his intentions.

76)) rebounds on him with humiliating literalness. Yet his constant free handling of her as a 'piece of middle-aged female helplessness' (*1888*, i. 210), 'a perfectly artless and a considerably witless woman' (*NYE* xii. 62), is only half of an ambivalence, does not prevent painful recognition of the pity of her miserable confinement and her wasted youth[19]—a recognition which points his predicament with the intense desire not to wound and a sharp sense of his importance for her. If he did not like and respect her and feel for her plight the proposal scene would not so appal him, bringing as it does the poignant knowledge that he has misread the meaning both of his own actions and of the action as a whole (Emma Woodhouse, for instance, is *less* horrified by Mr Elton's proposal, in so far as Mr Elton is a deeply unsympathetic individual). The very title of the story construes the action from the editorial point of view, indeed as his plot, to the neglect of the human considerations active in other points of view (like Tina's); and the climactic scenes represent the convergence of the two actions, the story of the irresponsible literary quest and the story of the responsive human relation, as a ghastly discovery of mutual misconstruction.

v. Still Running

The revisions I have dealt with commonly put an accent on or give a personal turn to the expressions of *1888*, only to increase our consciousness of what we can regard as the authorial inscrutability of the story. We might compare the way in which the revisions of *Daisy Miller* heighten Winterbourne's affective responses to the action of that story and yet by placing them *as* Winterbourne's recall us to a sense of the other responses constituting the whole action. We cannot generally see life steadily and whole in our immediate experience; so that for a work of fiction to see lives steadily and whole takes a comprehensive effort to include partiality and unsteadiness, a technique able to mediate between people's experience and the larger life of which it is a part (the life that fiction makes into action). Where *Daisy Miller* achieves this meeting of nearness and distance in the third person, through the indirect free style, *The Aspern Papers* finds a parallel process within its first-person narration; the function of the

---

[19] Juliana is for instance her 'yoke-fellow of long years' (*NYE* xii. 97), and she repeatedly figures as 'the poor lady' (*1888*, i. 106), 'the poor woman' (*1888*, i. 212–13 and *NYE* xii. 130), or 'this sad personage' (*NYE* xii. 57).

omniscient narrator, by *1888* seldom evident in James's fiction, is taken over by the remembering self, who passes the action through a process of distancing and irony like that elsewhere in James's *œuvre*. (James himself is present as arranging author behind this narrating character.) In this case the process works by the substantial restriction of the narration to a dramatization of past consciousness, the present narrator being as excluded as if he were another person; the thoughts and sentiments expressed are presumptively those of the time in the action. Yet the expression of them comes from a later source, a containing, if limited, intelligence.

As Flaubert says, the impersonal narrator in the indirect free style, nowhere seen, may be felt everywhere: the fact of narration, of a retrospection dramatically rendering his past consciousness—in so far as this is the mode of the story—both speaks with potent suggestiveness, taken as characterization, about the story's narrator in the present, and actually *tells* us nothing of his attitude to his past acts except that he has an intention—or motive, or compulsion—in reflectingly reliving them. What the revisions vividly bring home to us is an equivocal passion in this dramatizing retrospection, whose expression of the past has the ambiguity of our not knowing if, for instance, 'I thought it more decent not to show greed again so soon after the catastrophe' (*NYE* xii. 124–5; from 'not to betray my anxiety so soon', *1888*, i. 207) represents indirect (inner) speech, a self-conscious joke from that juncture in the action, or a present inflection, a liberty of paraphrase, incorporating a present judgement in the description, perhaps with the hope of anticipating and pre-empting the reader's disapproval. These possibilities are not even mutually exclusive, since much of the narration realizes the grim substance in what were originally jokes. The impersonal wit of James's story appears in the way the flow of the narrator's impersonal narration is repeatedly broken by reference to his present personal sense of the events, finally coming up to date with himself writing in the present tense (the portrait, in the penultimate sentence, 'hangs above my writing-table' (*1888*, i. 239)). If his original in the anecdote which was the germ of the story, the Bostonian Captain Silsbee, '*court encore*'—is still running (*Nks.*, p. 33)—the narrator too is still in flight from the scene of his discomfiture, though only in the shiftiness of his telling. The story demonstrates his punishment for extravagant curiosity; the mode of its telling is thematically continuous with the action.

James may have recognized the conceit of *The Aspern Papers* in the

Silsbee anecdote because it matches one of his attitudes (distrust of the excesses of biographical curiosity about writers), but in the working-out of that conceit he uses other attitudes (including his love of Venice and his own biographical curiosity); so we can apply to *The Aspern Papers* his ironic words to Howells of 1904, about ' "hates" and loves':

I seem to feel, about myself, that I proceed but scantly, in these chill years, by those particular categories and rebounds; in short that, somehow, such fine primitive passions *lose* themselves for me in the act of contemplation, or at any rate in the act of reproduction (*LHJ* ii. 9).

The project of making a perfect work of fiction, that is, one whose form is finished but whose meanings are satisfyingly in motion, requires for James fidelity to a truth about the relation of points of view, involves an imaginative grasp of the articulations of a drama in such a way that the conditions of life still inhere, to the extent that values circulate and no single point of view gets an automatic passage to authority. This is one of the formal truths taught by the medium (which conventionally didactic works and critics ignore at their peril). 'The act of reproduction' deflects and refracts the 'fine primitive passions', candidly submits them to a measure of experience, loses its generalizations in the pressing imagination of the particular case; and in *The Aspern Papers* this process takes sad, comic, vivid possession of a consciousness returning upon itself, living with an unspent and expensive passion, recalling harm done to itself and to others.

9

A Decent Perfection: The Lesson of the Master

i. His Present Experiment

Stories of literary and sexual passion intersect and threaten to frustrate each other in *The Lesson of the Master* (1888; first book publication 1892), whose hero Paul Overt, an aspiring young writer, seems at the end to consummate his professional aspirations by writing a probably great novel, but to forfeit his personal ones by not proposing to the woman he loves. In so choosing, and most of all in seeing the two questions *as* a choice, Overt is greatly influenced by the title's 'Master', an older novelist called Henry St George, who confesses in a dramatic scene to having wasted his early promise and attributes his comparative failure to the constraints of non-bohemian marriage, which he represents as incompatible with the discipline and purity of a true artistic career. Yet St George himself, left a widower by his philistine first wife during Overt's subsequent productive absence on the Continent, becomes engaged to marry the young woman Overt admires—announcing, as if to be consistent with his earlier 'lesson', that he has given up the life of writing altogether.[1]

It is James's achievement in the tale to represent an action susceptible of two opposing interpretations, between which the reader is unable rationally to decide, without sacrificing emotional intensity or seriousness in the relations between the characters. Shlomith Rimmon has elegantly detailed, in *The Concept of Ambiguity—the Example of James*, the co-presence in the work of the story where St George

---

[1] Matthiessen and Murdock comment in their edition of the *Notebooks* that this final marriage 'adds an ironic twist to the story and makes a neatly finished plot, but possibly blurs the main point by raising an ambiguity, and distracting the reader into conjectures about how far St George's advice to Overt was sincere and how far it was dictated by his selfish wish to drive away a rival in love' (p. 87). 'Possibly' equivocates, but, as Shlomith Rimmon argues in *The Concept of Ambiguity—the Example of James* (Chicago, 1977), this 'ambiguity' is a constitutive part of Paul Overt's experience; and the reader's sympathy with Paul's profound doubts about St George's motives is pivotally functional, 'the main point', not a distraction.

sinisterly schemes to rid himself of an impressionable young rival for the favours of Marian Fancourt, and of another story where St George 'saves' Overt from the artistic deterioration marriage would bring by stepping into the breach himself. As she points out, we have no real reason to think St George a cruel manipulator of Overt for his own ends until we learn near the conclusion that he is to marry Marian Fancourt; and even when this information becomes available it is not unequivocal evidence about his motives. Leon Edel is therefore wrong to say that 'the Master does not follow his own counsel'[2] in marrying again, for St George's 'counsel' is that good writing and marriage will not mix, and he has, or says he has, 'stopped writing' (*1892*, p. 79). The twist by which the sense of the story may seem to be inverted needn't logically *be* a twist: 'the supplanting reading is fully balanced by the interpretation which it is supposed to supplant, and perpetual oscillation is imposed upon the reader'.[3] Such full balance makes the plot a mechanism that will keep our minds in perpetual motion: an unsettlement in us which corresponds to that of poor Paul Overt, who can in the nature of things never be quite sure whether his work will be good enough to justify his sacrifice of Marian Fancourt, whether even if it *is* good its goodness would have been impaired by marriage, and whether St George's eloquent sermon on 'the doctrine of renunciation' (*1892*, p. 68) was in good faith—which may be a different question from the other two.

The story echoes *Roderick Hudson*, of thirteen years before, in its concern with the vicissitudes of genius and the choices confronting the young artist. The relation between Roderick and the well-established sculptor Gloriani is rethought and rhetorically recharged in that between Paul Overt and St George. Gloriani has spent his fortune by the age of twenty-six and 'found himself obliged to make capital of his talent' (*1883*, i. 80); fifteen years later he is advising Roderick that the artist 'must learn to do without the Muse!' (*1883*, i. 94.) The scornful young American reacts in *1883* with 'Gloriani's an ass!' (i. 111), and in the *NYE*, more 'fiercely', by judging him 'a murderous mountebank! ... He has got a bag of tricks and he comes with it to his studio as a conjurer comes for twenty francs to a children's party' (*NYE* i. 148). The more sympathetic St George claims to despise his own tricks and confesses that 'As an artist, you know, I've married

---

[2] Leon Edel, *Henry James: The Middle Years 1884–1894*, London, 1963, p. 177.
[3] *The Concept of Ambiguity*, p. 83.

for money ... I refer to the mercenary muse whom I led to the altar of literature' (*1892*, p. 55); the major difference from Gloriani being his adverse judgement on his own career, his compromised consciousness (which matches Overt's private estimate and thus seems unlikely to be mere pretence) of his failure to do his best. His advice to Overt is thus based on his own experience of working for money, as is Gloriani's, but it is advice to do otherwise, not likewise.

The 'regularity' of work which is a feature of the career of Roderick's more respectable colleague Singleton, in whom it is voluntary, recurs in St George under the regime of the demanding wife, with results we know to be some way below the high level of perfection: he is politely asked about his 'flowers' and replies that 'I produce mine between ten and one every morning; I bloom with a regularity!' (*1892*, p. 35). St George's self-deprecating irony here, reducing the organic process to a mechanical rotor, has more truth in the tale than that of mere social amenity, for his quantitative productivity goes with qualitative adulteration. When converting Paul to 'the doctrine of renunciation', St George in his workplace, 'a good big cage' he says was invented by his wife, describes himself as 'walled in to my trade' (*1892*, p. 52); but once she is dead he writes puzzlingly to his young disciple, revising his phrase into a tribute to her helpfulness: 'She carried on our life with the greatest art, the rarest devotion, and I was free, as few men can have been, to drive my pen, to shut myself up with my trade' (*1892*, p. 68). Constraint is rewritten here as freedom, as if St George's 'trade' hadn't squandered its claims to be art (the bereavement makes such an adjusted perspective understandable). The image of the author hacking to support a family recalls James's outbreak to Howells in 1909 that 'authors can't to advantage be worked like ice-cream freezers or mowing-machines', though there is a serious question about *whose* advantage. At any rate, 'regularity' in this case does not save St George from mediocrity—even if his hours of work are James's own.

The young artist in *Roderick Hudson* is seen at a distance, from the point of view of his anxious mentor Rowland Mallet; Paul Overt in *The Lesson of the Master* is the story's centre of consciousness, and his mentor, St George, therefore only appears to us at a distance. With Paul Overt's more equable temperament and the fact that he shares James's vocation of novelist, this more direct involvement gives us a less Romantic but no less touching account of how momentous the beginning of an artistic career can be, of the crises of faith involved and the gamble on one's unpredictable capacity. The comparison of

Paul Overt's position with James's own has a bearing, though without simple equivalence; as is suggested by the notebook entry for 11 March 1888, the first after that in which James sketched the 'germ' of *The Lesson of the Master*:

Here I sit: impatient to work: only wanting to concentrate myself, to keep at it: full of ideas, full of ambition, full of capacity—as I believe. Sometimes the discouragements, however, seem greater than anything else—the delays, the interruptions, the *éparpillement*, etc. But courage, courage, and forward, forward. If one must generalise, that is the only generalisation. There is an immensity to be done, and, without vain presumption—I shall at the worst do a part of it. But all one's manhood must be at one's side. x x x x x (*Nks.*, p. 44).

Approaching forty-five, and suffering from the comparative failures of *The Bostonians* and *The Princess Casamassima*, as well as the delays of the magazines in publishing many shorter things, James eggs himself on despite 'the discouragements' to a stoical self-sufficiency, a confidence 'without vain presumption' that he is 'full of capacity' (he is not 'vain' in the sense of hollow, but, paradoxically, replete with capaciousness: able to take in and handle material).

The Lesson of the Master represents a similar moment of self-doubt and self-rededication during Paul Overt's Swiss exile, when he learns of Mrs St George's death and is discouraged by the widower's tone of unqualified regret about her, a tone inconsistent with 'the doctrine of renunciation': his resolve is tested, but he looks again at 'the first chapters of his new book', the one started under the influence of St George's lesson. His scene of rereading, anticipating the sadder reperusals of the dying Dencombe in 'The Middle Years' five years later, reminds him of what is 'to be done':

This led to his catching a glimpse of some pages he had not looked at for months, and that accident, in turn, to his being struck with the high promise they contained—a rare result of such retrospections, which it was his habit to avoid as much as possible. They usually made him feel that the glow of composition might be a purely subjective and a very barren emotion. On this occasion a certain belief in himself disengaged itself whimsically from the serried erasures of his first draft, making him think it best after all to carry out his present experiment to the end (*1892*, pp. 68–9).

The renewed vision of the opening of his book leads to the qualified confidence of 'a certain belief in himself', 'disengaging itself whimsically from the serried erasures' as if the sight of the traces of correction and improvement suggested for *him* a motion 'forward, forward', as James has it. 'Whimsically' takes heed of the gamble in this: the possibility that the 'glow' of rereading as well as of composition 'might be a purely subjective and a very barren emotion'.

Overt's situation as a writer uncertainly committing himself to celibacy for the sake of his art dramatizes James's position in the 1880s as we can trace it in his letters: in his assurance to Lizzie Boott in December 1883 that *'non mi sposarò mai—mai!'* (*HJL* iii. 17–18), or in his fuller account to Grace Norton in November 1884 of the reasons why he will 'to a dead certainty never change my free unhoused condition'.[4] He tells his old friend 'that since definitely and *positively* (from a merely negative state) making up my mind not to marry, I feel that I have advanced in happiness and power to *do* something in the world' (*HJL* iii. 54). In the summer of 1891, writing in good humour to his heavily committed brother William, who was *en pleine famille* at rustic Chocorua, he referred by way of contrast to his own 'wifeless, childless, houseless, classless, mother- and sister-in-lawless, horseless, cowless, and useless existence' (*HJL* iii. 350), an ironic negative cata- logue reversing the usual direction of Anglo-American comparisons. Such resolution is not according to the letters a matter of sexual preference, but of reluctance to take on a responsibility (to wife and children) which would impose serious financial demands and thus compromise artistic independence. The financial consideration sur- faces in the memorial essay of January 1884 on Turgenev:

It is not out of place to allude to the fact that he possessed considerable fortune; this is too important in the life of a man of letters. It had been of great value to Turgénieff, and I think that much of the fine quality of his work is owing to it. He could write according to his taste and his mood; he was never pressed nor checked (putting the Russian censorship aside) by considerations foreign to his plan, and never was in danger of becoming a hack (*LC* ii. 1019).

In the context of the questions of marriage and children and keeping up social comforts, James's own 'fortune' must be regarded as *in*con- siderable, though useful enough in tight corners, giving him a certain margin 'to write according to his taste and his mood'. The risk to 'the fine quality of his work' from the 'danger of becoming a hack'

---

[4] Unlike Othello, who uses the words in declaring that he *will* marry: 'But that I love the gentle Desdemona, | I would not my unhoused free condition | Put into cir- cumscription and confine | For the sea's worth' (I. ii. 25–8).

continued to preoccupy him, partly no doubt because of his lack of success in the theatre. It surfaces, for example, with wry turns, in *The Next Time* of 1895, where the married and badly off Ray Limbert, a variation on Gissing's Edwin Reardon in *New Grub Street* (1891), is desperate to exploit his sensibility for cash, and tries to become a hack, but can't sufficiently coarsen his grain.

That the 1888 story's lesson is given by *Henry* St George, and that Henry James himself was later known as 'the Master', has led many to read that lesson as essentially James's own. Logan Pearsall Smith, though, was to recall more than thirty years after the event an occasion during the 1890s when James warned him of the emotional cost of the literary profession, presenting the other side of St George's coin:

'There is one word—let me impress upon you—which you must inscribe upon your banner, and that,' he added after an impressive pause, 'that word is *Loneliness*.'[5]

This sounds authentic enough, though anecdotes of James are not always to be taken straight; at any rate *'Loneliness'* doesn't quite tally with the 'advance in happiness' announced to Grace Norton in 1884. The anxiety and sense of loss dramatized in Paul Overt are not feelings from which James himself is exempt, and in 1903 we find him writing to the paterfamilias Gosse that

I often fancy I am gleeful at not having *bambini*; then I think how rich & mellow it must be to have them like yours, & I feel then that I have failed of the true life.[6]

We could set on the same side of the slate the melancholy and despair of the fruitlessly unmarried John Marcher in *The Beast in the Jungle* (1903), where two lives are ruined through his vain assumption that he has a vocation requiring celibacy. To be able to imagine what James calls in his essay on 'Browning in Westminster Abbey' 'the special relation between man and woman' (*LC* i. 790), for a novelist whose work centres (however unusually) on love and marriage, is necessary for creative success; so that the capacity to feel celibacy as a real sacrifice—as the renunciation of something valued rather than the codification of a distaste—is vital if the sacrifice is to be worth making, if the resulting career is to be a success.

The Lesson of the Master, then, incorporates many tensions with

---

[5] Quoted in Simon Nowell-Smith, *The Legend of the Master*, London, 1947, p. 126.
[6] *Selected Letters of Henry James to Edmund Gosse*, p. 205.

bearing on James's own life; but this in no way makes it a 'confessional' work, for it is a fiction created by a writer who has himself undertaken the 'experiment' of a pursuit of high artistic standards—which includes the creation of fictional worlds separate from himself. The story itself can be read as an example of the kind of 'decent perfection' the revised St George pleads for (xv. 75). We have seen for instance how from *Roderick Hudson* and the stories preceding it to *The Portrait of a Lady* six years later James refined confessions by his characters and integrated them more plausibly into the action; the subsequent technical advances are richly illuminated by the use of St George's great 'confession' in this tale, where an apparently frank avowal of artistic failure takes on dramatic roundness through its quite possibly being used with manipulative cunning to further a morally dubious sexual success. The ambiguity of St George's motive for his over-determined utterance, in other words, is the crux of the story; which could not be said of the Cavaliere's outburst to Rowland in the early texts of *Roderick Hudson*. And the ambiguity here functions not simply as a formalistic trick or philosophical gesture; it is an aspect of the work's appropriately tragi-comic meaning, rendering Paul Overt's mixed sense of the action. Near the end Paul, like an unhappy schoolboy,

felt as if some of the elements of a hard sum had been given him and the others were wanting: he couldn't do his sum till he was in possession of them all (*1892*, p. 73).

But the up-to-the-minute ending, like those of *The Bostonians* and *A London Life*, leaves some elements still wanting; 'it is too soon to say' (*1892*, p. 80), and the completion of the sum here is endlessly deferred. The reader will be able to derive satisfaction from this crafted uncertainty only by recognizing that, in a measure no omnisciently informative narration with a long view could, it imitates the testing life of an author, who has to bank on possibly delusive powers and pass up other chances in the world. Such satisfaction on our part, moreover, serves indirectly to confirm at least the wisdom of James's own wager, *his* devotion to the life of writing.

ii. Frames of Reference

Part of what takes Paul Overt's fancy in Marion Fancourt is her sympathy with the aspirations of the artist; in their most intimate *tête-à-tête* they are to be found 'discussing, with extreme seriousness, the

high theme of perfection' (*1892*, p. 44), and more precisely 'the perfection ... of which the valid work of art is susceptible' (*1892*, pp. 44–
5). Miss Fancourt is shocked at, and seems unlikely to lapse into, the
philistinism of Mrs St George, who boasts of having got her husband
to 'burn up a bad book' (*1892*, p. 8) and speaks of his writing 'a few'
(*1892*, p. 9) with desolating casualness. Paul Overt's response to these
remarks is to ask himself: 'Didn't she, as the wife of a rare artist, know
what it was to produce *one* perfect work of art?' The one thing St
George has reportedly said of his wife to Miss Fancourt is 'that she
didn't care for perfection'; whereas the younger woman exclaims 'Ah,
perfection, perfection—how one ought to go in for it!' (*1892*, p. 44).

This contrast forcibly suggests that *The Lesson of the Master* is far
from presenting its women as uniform, and raises doubts about the
general applicability of the law St George enunciates, 'that one's
children interfere with perfection. One's wife interferes. Marriage
interferes' (*1892*, p. 58).[7] In an essay on 'Edmond Rostand' in 1901
James sketches a comparable ironic general law about artistic quality—
that the great popular success will never be the distinguished work of
art—only to qualify it with some germane warnings.

The insidious part of the perplexity is that acclamation may swell to its
maximum, and the production acclaimed, the novel, the poem, the play, none
the less truly *be* the real thing and not the make-believe. It is so often the
make-believe that we are all but driven comfortably to generalise—so great
is the convenience of a simple law. The law, however, ceases to be simple
from the moment even one book in five hundred does appeal, distinguishably,
to a critical sense. The case, though of the rarest, occurs, and it thereby
deprives the conscientious student we have postulated of the luxury of a hard-
and-fast rule.[8]

If St George's 'hard-and-fast rule' is to be broken, we might think,
surely so exceptional a woman as Marian Fancourt will be a likely
candidate to do it. Paul indeed asks St George, 'Isn't there even *one*
who sees further?', but is assured by the authority: 'Of course I know
the one you mean. But not even Miss Fancourt' (*1892*, p. 62). For Paul

---

[7] As Christopher Ricks points out, there is a striking echo of *The Lesson of the Master*
in Tennyson's sentimental 'Romney's Remorse', written the following year (1889) and
taking the side of marriage against art. Romney, who left his wife because Reynolds
and others said 'marriage spoilt an artist', repents the desertion on his death-bed: 'My
curse upon the Master's apothegm, | That wife and children drag an artist down!' (*The
Poems of Tennyson*, iii. 212.)

[8] *The Scenic Art*, p. 304.

at this point his elder speaks with the disinterested voice of experience, and the Master makes enough allowance for Marian Fancourt's uniqueness to save the law from ludicrous rigidity; yet the reader is unlikely to be convinced by this alone that she is necessarily ruled out by St George's grim regulation. What may be more relevant is the treatment of the young woman elsewhere, the possible presence of hints that she is superficial; and as Shlomith Rimmon points out every clue we have may point in *either* direction. If we are to hold it against her that she is so keen on St George, since he hasn't achieved the highest perfection, why can't we hold the same thing against Paul Overt, who is equally thrilled to receive the Master's attention? If it seems shallow of her to marry St George and not to 'wait for' Paul Overt, how could she be expected to do otherwise when Overt has not told her of his love and has left the country, without telling her, for a two-year absence?

Such insidious questions surround *The Lesson of the Master* with a perplexing hinterland of missing elements, realistic puzzles vividly recreating the conditions under which major personal decisions usually have to be made; or, as James puts it in 'The Art of Fiction', 'Catching the very note and trick, the strange irregular rhythm of life' (*LC* i. 58). For this particular story we might say that the achievement of an engaging but irresoluble knotting of impulses around the central action—of the sort that the insidious questions conjure up—constitutes in itself 'a decent perfection', as the *NYE* revision calls the McGuffin of this artistic tale (xv. 75). James himself, in this light, would have attained 'the great thing', as St George eloquently defines it:

The sense of having done the best—the sense, which is the real life of the artist and the absence of which is his death, of having drawn from his intellectual instrument the finest music that nature had hidden in it, of having played it as it should be played (*1892*, p. 57).

James's *NYE* revisions, moreover, sent to Scribners in July 1908, exactly twenty years after the story began to appear in the *Universal Review*, indicate in their measure that unlike St George James has not undergone 'any decline' (*1892*, p. 29), or as they more precisely phrase it, 'any decline of talent or of care' (*NYE* xv. 35). The 'care', as the conditions of fiction make it, is both a care for the details of the text *and* a care for the feelings and situation of the characters which the text enshrines. Since the work is an ambiguous secular parable of the talents, moreover, such care in this case will involve *imagining* those talents convincingly—a task difficult, as James points out in the Preface, discussing his invention of great writers, 'from the moment ... that one worked out at all their greatness; from the moment one didn't simply give it to be taken on trust' (*LC* ii. 1231). St George benefits from such a working-out in the story's final scene, where as Marian Fancourt's fiancé he is confronted by an accusing Paul Overt, and with supreme urbanity does his best to see the young man's point of view: he

went on, as if, now that the subject had been broached, he was, as a man of imagination and tact, perfectly ready to give every satisfaction—being able to enter fully into everything another might feel (*1892*, p. 77).

The gift of sympathetic imagination he seems granted here ('perfectly' hovering between sociable alacrity and deep human acuity) is a prime requirement of the novelist, *is* together with his powers of expression the talent he has wasted; and the *NYE* registers this thematic connection by reworking the working-out: 'being both by his genius and his method so able to enter into everything another might feel' (*NYE* xv. 93). For Paul, bewildered and anxious and feeling betrayed, such a confident application of St George's 'genius and his method' is all too bitter, for it may be interpreted as the mark of a possible artistic regeneration not stifled but enabled by marriage to Marian Fancourt. We may say that if St George, after giving such advice to Paul Overt, does not feel that marrying Miss Fancourt puts him in a false position, he is singularly insensitive. Great writers, on the other hand, have been known to behave in cruel and stupid ways.

The sympathetic imagining of another person's situation and sensations, here attempted by St George with doubtful success, is eloquently discussed by James in the Preface to *The American*, where he considers the treatment of Newman in terms which recall to us that the reference to the Master's 'genius and his method' is not James speaking, but renders Paul Overt's point of view on St George:

the interest of everything is all that it is *his* vision, *his* conception, *his* interpretation: at the window of his wide, quite sufficiently wide, consciousness we are seated, from that admirable position we 'assist'. He therefore supremely matters; all the rest matters only as he feels it, treats it, meets it. A beautiful infatuation this, always, I think, the intensity of the creative effort to get into the skin of the creature; the act of personal possession of one being by another at its completest—and with the high enhancement, ever, that it is, by the same stroke, the effort of the artist to preserve for his subject that unity, and for his use of it (in other words for the interest he desires to excite) that effect of a *centre*, which most economise its value (*LC* ii. 1067–8).

The intensity of this creative effort is also the intensity that directs James's attention in revision, and not just in the case of *The American*. The *NYE* persistently personalizes earlier descriptions, referring them back to their *'centre'* with inventive precision. The force of James's emphatically reiterated *'his'* lies in the recognition that the particularities of a character and situation—the things peculiarly 'his'—will be necessary conditions of the general truth and interest of any given story, since a relation to intensely particular circumstances is part of the predicament of each of us. Thus the initial idea of a story (like the 'simple law' produced by St George) is subjected to a creative development which makes it not the whole, but the compositional focus, of a character's experience; it is as fully as possible dramatized, surrounded with an involving mesh of details and doubts, subordinated to the unifying vision which one person, 'the creature', has of it. The 'law', the governing idea, makes for form; the character whose experience of it is to be central, since 'Experience is never limited, and it is never complete' (*LC* i. 52), makes for an expansive tendency which we might call life. A case for preferring *The Lesson of the Master* to the witty allegory of *The Private Life,* say, where the conceit of a split between the public and private selves of the artist is forced on the reader as if a law of nature, might rest on the generosity with which Paul Overt's experience is allowed to question and corrode the story's apparent premiss, a premiss which is rendered vulnerable to irony by being explicitly put forward in the action. The perpetual motion this questioning sets up could represent one kind of perfection in the rendering of experience.

iii.   Humblest Questions

The *NYE* revisions of *The Lesson of the Master* operate on an 'economy' we might call centripetal: seeking to refer the story's events as fully as possible to the centre of consciousness, they work to point for us Paul Overt's double sense of the action, his living participation in two points of view, two sets of desires, neither of which he is keen to relinquish. Where *The Aspern Papers* progressively brings the editorial view of the narrator and the marital one of Miss Tina to a comic and poignant meeting, tracing till then a mutual unconsciousness of motive in its two main characters, *The Lesson of the Master,* with its more intelligent and sympathetic centre, freights Paul Overt during the action with a finely tuned consciousness of the twofold nature of the events he undergoes, the conflict between their meanings for his heart and for his art. His two sets of desires focus on St George and Marian Fancourt; and James's particular realization of his general law works through an intimate registration of the nuances of relation and inclination between his triangle of figures.

Seymour Chatman, in *The Later Style of Henry James*, comments on the way in which James's developed manner refers to its filtering centre of consciousness mainly by the pronoun alone, often in cases where the traditional nineteenth-century novel (including James's own earlier works) would resort to a name, a title, or a redescription: the casual and frequent use of the pronoun, by tacitly *assuming* that we are seeing the action through the eyes of the one person, manœuvres us into a more intimate relation with the character than we may be used to.[9] *The Lesson of the Master* is certainly a case where this insight applies, for the NYE revision, by the cumulative effect of more intimate reference, both intensifies our sense that Paul Overt's is the crucial sensibility in the story and, because there is less formal distancing of him, makes our relation to him freer and easier. This is not out of keeping with the *1892* frame of reference: the very first word in the tale, characteristically for mature James, is a 'He' only subsequently to be given a local habitation and a name. He is thus further established in the NYE as a sympathetic centre of consciousness by a subtle adjustment in the story's interpersonal formulas.

The story of the names and pronouns and descriptive noun-phrases cannot be told by simply telling up the figures, but statistics give stimulating hints about the general picture. In *1892* the hero is called 'Paul Overt' 108 times, 'Paul' 57, and 'Overt' 46; in the NYE there is a significant shift, with 'Paul Overt' 45 times, 'Paul' 93 times, and 'Overt' 25 times. The effect of these revisions is to put the reader most often on first-name terms with the hero. The NYE uses a proper name on 48 fewer occasions than *1892*, a reduction of about a quarter, treating proper names as if they were less necessary for our identification of the character whose experiences are being narrated. The style, then, *assumes* more in the NYE that it is transmitting Paul's point of view, amiably diminishing its own distance and ours from the reflector of attention. The gesture whereby the character's full name

---

[9] *The Later Style of Henry James*, p. 58.

is uttered to recall us to the larger view, the frame in which we are reading the experiences of 'Paul Overt', is severely cut down to less than half its original frequency in the *NYE*; though some of the 45 occurrences that James keeps (one actually introduced in the *NYE*, xv. 60) may serve to remind us of the way an author's name appears on the cover of his books, of the household name 'Paul Overt' may possibly become.

The totals of statistics may mislead, though, in this as in other cases; for they conceal finer gradations and are prompted by more precise determinants than are allowed for in the notion of cumulative effect. There are three cases, for example, in which *1892*'s 'Paul Overt' is revised not to 'Paul' (as happens 35 times), nor to the pronoun or a noun-phrase (as happens 25 times), but to 'Overt' (*1892*, pp. 32, 40, 53; *NYE* xv. 39, 49, 64). On each of these occasions the young writer is with 'the Master', and we might take as a clue to understanding this seeming anomaly the remark during the great persuasion-scene (*1892*, pp. 49–65, where the *NYE* brings in 'the Master'—with a capital letter for authority—seven times (xv. 60–79)) that Paul feels partly 'like a happy little boy when the schoolmaster is gay' (*1892*, p. 54). The surname may well, like 'Jennings' or 'Molesworth', make Paul again into a docile pupil, a less than senior member of a male structure of authority (some Oxbridge colleges have 'Masters').

The statistical totals here may permit another misconception: that kinds of change are evenly spread across the work. But they are carefully distributed by James already in *1892*, where of the 46 uses of 'Overt' 40 occur in the first half of the story. The *NYE* keeps to the same proportions, with 21 of its 24 uses of 'Overt' occurring in the first half. We can bring together this striking deviation from what the totals might nudge us to believe and a related one: that in the first chapter of the story, in both *1892* and the *NYE*, 'Paul' occurs only once, while 'Overt' occurs 15 times in *1892* and 12 times in the *NYE*. The single 'Paul' in *1892* comes on page 8 with his 'irrepressible laugh' at Mrs St George's debonair philistinism, and is revised to 'our young friend' in the *NYE* (xv. 11); the first chapter of the *NYE* saves *its* 'Paul' for the last paragraph, replacing 'Paul Overt' (*1892*, p. 11; *NYE* xv. 15)—as if to announce an intimacy to come, now that introductions are out of the way. In Chapter II of the *NYE* text, this first-name term is multiplied, so that 'Paul' occurs 9 times and 'Overt' only 3; reversing the proportions in *1892*'s second chapter, where 'Paul' comes 3 times and 'Overt' 14.

James seems in the *NYE* consciously to be speeding up the process of our getting to know, or getting to *feel* we know, 'Paul'—perhaps because in the second chapter the young man is meeting the very attractive Marian Fancourt. Sterne in *Tristram Shandy* varies the sex of the reader he addresses according to context, 'Madam' almost exclusively when he is provoking prudish objection through sexual innuendo, 'Sir' when trying on some learned bluff. James, addressing his reader on the subject of his character, calls on 'Paul' and 'Overt' to evoke different roles and worlds: the surname belongs mostly to the masculine world of professional men (including writers; James is 'James', after all); while the first name carries a charge of private intimacy, associable with the address of a loved one, and not impossibly with the feminine world of love. In the following chapter, where the hero meets St George for a real talk in the smoking-room at Summersoft, an exclusively male domain, the *NYE* has 'Overt' six times, twice as often as it does in Chapter II.

To look into James's exhaustive and intricate rehandling of such minute but vitally indicative details may well persuade us that there has been in *him* no 'decline of talent or'—certainly—'of care'. His 'care' for us, the readers, is not neglected either: he attends, as he says in the Preface to *The Golden Bowl*, 'to my and your "fun"—if we but allow the term its full extension; to the production of which no humblest question involved ... is not richly pertinent' (*LC* ii. 1338). 'We' ourselves, and especially our possessives, play a greater part in the *NYE* than in *1892*—in a measure which corresponds to our coming more on to first-name terms with 'our hero', as Paul becomes on five occasions (*NYE* xv. 32, 38, 44, 64, 82). He becomes 'our youth' (*NYE* xv. 16) and 'our young man' (*NYE* xv. 60, 74, 93); and as relayer of the action for us 'our beholder' (*NYE* xv. 12) and 'our listener' (*NYE* xv. 87). Most of all he is 'our friend' or 'our young friend', twelve times in the revisions, a member of the community in which 'we', the readers, are rhetorically included.

This community has three main triangulation points within the action, three corners articulating the dramatic space; and while the *NYE* makes Paul 'our' particular 'friend' and contact (not extending this cordiality to Henry St George or Marian Fancourt), it also increasingly attaches him, via the possessives which establish relations and their claims, to the two people who embody his dearest aspirations.

Both the possessives with which the *NYE* prefaces so many nouns, and the nouns themselves, contribute to the drawing-in of Paul's 'related state'. By contrast with the names they replace—which weakly yield evidence for the nature of the particular relation only in the degree that 'Miss Fancourt' or 'St. George' may be Paul's mental form of reference to them—possessives suggest a positive bond of one person to another; while the nouns used precisely convey two-way relations: 'host', 'hostess', 'visitor', 'acquaintance', 'companion', or 'friend'. This form of reference to characters has its own nuances and 'rich pertinences': the two contenders for the hand of Marian Fancourt both, when the three are together, receive the doubtful benefit of being singled out as an odd adjunct to the couple made up by the other two. First 'Paul Overt' (*1892*, p. 39), being jocularly treated by St George who is speaking to Marian Fancourt, becomes, ominously, 'their companion' (*NYE* xv. 48). And then soon after James balances the books: he grammatically couples Paul and his loved one by turning a reference to St George as 'her companion' (*1892*, p. 41) to make him 'their friend' (*NYE* xv. 49). The tension between exclusion from a group in 'their' and inclusion in it in 'companion' and 'friend' surreptitiously plays, at the level of linguistic detail, with the possibilities dramatized in the story as a whole. At the end of the scene in which these revisions try out the two pairings-off, Marian Fancourt goes to Hyde Park to 'look at types' (*1892*, p. 40) with St George, and Paul's uneasy status is realized in his isolation 'as he took his way on foot alone' (*1892*, p. 41), prefiguring his final '*Loneliness*'.

iv. Tremendous Talk

One of the finest musics nature had hidden in James's intellectual instrument is that which informs his dialogue: as in *The American* and *Daisy Miller*, the dramatic interchanges of speech, with their possibilities of tonal range and emotional truth, come closer with the *NYE* to being played as they should be played—that is, to carrying and extending the tale's emotional and intellectual argument. In the second chapter, where Paul talks with Marian Fancourt, the *NYE* works to promote and sharpen the patterned movements of *1892* from first meeting through flirtatious give-and-take towards (on his side) profound admiration. The scene traces from speech to speech his sense of her natural charm, the amusing tone of their sympathetic exchange; and the revisions of it, less 'serried erasures' than complements and amplifications, allow us further insight into the ties the tiny nuances of such conversations may form, putting expression on faces that were blank in *1892* or into voices that were not particularly inflected. Seated with him on a sofa in the Summersoft picture-gallery, Marian Fancourt surprisingly declares herself 'so glad to have a chance to thank you' (*1892*, p. 15). Paul's reply in *1892* is functionally presented: 'To thank me?'; but in the *NYE* many more functions are performed: ' "To thank me—?" He had to wonder' (xv. 19). This registers his blankness, which makes him confess to incomprehension when he might prefer to take social command; and suggests pleasurable bemusement at this unexpectedly personal overture from a pretty girl. Her behaviour, as this revision more pointedly shows, is exceptional, on account of the easy tone, the 'charming serenity' (*NYE* xv. 22) she derives from her colonial upbringing, and while *1892* goes to some lengths to mark Paul's special enjoyment of such unusual freedom of talk with a woman in society, the *NYE* takes the denotation of this comic flirting some way further.

Paul manages to take mock-offence at an innocent remark of hers about his novels (by inferring that she means his characters all talk alike):

> She thought a moment, not a bit disconcerted. 'Well, it must be so difficult. Mr. St. George tells me it *is*—terribly. I've tried too—and I find it so. I've tried to write a novel.'
> 'Mr. St. George oughtn't to discourage you,' Paul went so far as to say.
> 'You do much more—when you wear that expression' (*NYE* xv. 21).

Before the *NYE* the only words other than direct speech in this passage were a 'said Paul Overt' (*1892*, p. 17): the *NYE* retimes the exchange to convey the playful comedy of upset and restoration Paul and Miss Fancourt are inventing. 'She thought a moment, not a bit disconcerted' puts in a pause for her not being embarrassed when she should be, in order to set off, as funnily even more embarrassing, her next remark (which doesn't retract the original gaffe, but blunders into an unconsoling extenuation). 'Paul went so far as to say' indicates his teasing vocal irony and his sense of extravagance, his sense that she lets him make unconventional advances; it neatly anticipates 'You do much more', the sequence suggesting that his being 'so far' personal has been recognized and then sanctioned in a joke. The joke incidentally illustrates that Marian Fancourt is intelligent and responsive, qualities which make a necessary balance for her entertaining and likeable good faith. 'When you wear that expression' in the *NYE* satisfyingly matches the expression in Paul's voice with a signalled expression of assumed dismay on his face; and the expressions worn by the exchange in the revised version give the reader clear access to a delicately staged pantomime of friendly ironies and recognitions that establishes the relation between these two young people as valuable and sympathetic. James's own characters, here at least, are unlikely to be accused of speaking too alike—though the point of the scene is their discovery that they speak the same language.

As in the dialogue of *Daisy Miller* (which also moves—though in a different spirit and with a different seriousness—from chatting-up to renunciation), the NYE revision traces the responses of the young man and young woman to each other by inserting, before or after the speeches of *1892*, sentences which give Paul's sense of her effect on him, and his sense of his effect on her. Thus:

The way she talked of Asia somehow enchanted him (*NYE* xv. 22).

It was as if she didn't care even *should* he amuse himself at her cost (*NYE* xv. 22).

It fairly stirred in him the sacred chord (*NYE* xv. 22).

She took this in with interest (*NYE* xv. 24).

—she was all sweet wonder (*NYE* xv. 25).

He is 'somehow enchanted' and 'stirred', she is charmingly happy to be joshed by him, she gives out 'interest' and 'sweet wonder': the rhythms of intimacy are freshly established. Yet even within this formation of personal bonds, Marian Fancourt's feelings about Henry St George (which help to make her attractively literary) emerge as somewhat in conflict with her interest in Paul. The younger writer ventures, not without encouragement, on to familiar ground with her, only to discover a reservation, an area on which his mild freedoms are a little checked.

Paul's aroused attention notes that Marian Fancourt is especially sensitive about her relation to St George. Much of her appeal in the scene with Paul seems to flow from her pleasure at the chance to talk of him; and when Paul makes a jocose remark about the Master's infatuation with her, a compliment responding to her kindly interest in his dead mother, she perceptibly bristles. It starts when Paul is impressed by her generous candour:

He could at first, on this, only gaze at her. 'What right things you say! If you say them to St George I don't wonder he's in bondage.'

It pulled her up for a moment. 'I don't know what you mean. He doesn't make speeches and professions at all—he isn't ridiculous.'

'I'm afraid you consider then that I am.'

'No, I don't'—she spoke it rather shortly. And then she added: 'He under-stands—understands everything' (*NYE* xv. 25).

The revised text differs slightly but considerably from *1892* in this passage, where the first sentence quoted was originally a report of an action—'Overt looked at her a moment' (p. 20)—rather than, like 'He had to wonder', a further expression of amazement at her benign unconventionality. Part of the rhythmic function of 'He could at first ... only gaze' in this context is that it says he is *speechless*; when he does utter his exclamation it reveals that the period of dumbness has come to an end (as promised in 'at first'). In *1892* 'It pulled her up ...' had no counterpart; the *NYE* thus introduces a symmetrical moment in which she is speechless—as if Paul is the first to put the idea of St George's charmed state explicitly before her, and she needs a delay before she can digest it and reply. The metaphor of onward motion in 'It pulled her up', moreover, makes clear James's dynamic conception of the scene, as if the talk of these two described a movement in space as well as in time. Her first utterance in defence of St George is only proper in respect of his reputation, as well as only proper for her own modesty—though we might notice the hyperbolic nature of the love-making being denied—making 'speeches and professions', being 'ridic-ulous'. Paul's aestheticizing response to her 'right things', in fact her unguarded kindnesses, could into the bargain be regarded as something of a provoking rudeness. But her second utterance, after Paul has gone too far by flirtatiously putting himself forward as a rival to St George ('I'm afraid you consider then that *I* am'), volunteers more about her relations with St George, goes from dismissing Paul's flippancy to a hyperbolic *praise* of the older man. In *1892* her last speech ran: ' "No, I don't", the girl replied, rather shortly. "He understands everything" '; and the revision makes the first words more snappingly detached ('—she spoke it rather shortly'), putting the stress on *how* she says it more than on *what* good manners anyhow oblige her to say; which it follows by more momentously giving her tribute to St George's sym-pathy first a dramatic introduction ('And then she added') and after that a gushier, more expansive tribute ('He understands—understands every-thing'). These transformations bring a telling equivalent to the tricks, the embarrassed pauses and defensive resumptions, of speech: they substantially furnish our conception of Paul's peculiar, torn situation.

'Is she in love with him?' (*1892*, p. 21), Paul's observation soon makes him wonder. *1892* has just before this had her thrilled at St George's approach: '"He is going to speak to us!" she exclaimed, almost breathlessly' (p. 21), the grand Master taking—'almost'—her breath away. The *NYE* wittily reverses this for a more erotically inspired excitement: 'she fondly breathed' (xv. 26). Later on, at the private view in Chapter IV, she again reaches a high pitch of enthusiasm in a way which promises well for Paul but turns rapidly to disappointment. James produces a highly compressed sequence of expectation and displacement which prefigures the terrible jealousy and sense of exclusion Paul suffers before the end. He sees her across the room, and

> had a freshness of pleasure in seeing that she did not pretend to await his arrival with composure. She smiled as radiantly as if she wished to make him hurry, and as soon as he came within earshot she said to him, in her voice of joy: 'He's here—he's here—he's coming back in a moment!' (*1892*, p. 37).

The shocking turn for the worse of her apparently auspicious unrestraint, the unsettling sameness-but-difference for us of 'his . . . him . . . he . . . him' (Paul) from the real occasion of her radiance, 'he . . . he . . . he' (St George); this desolating transposition of persons is prepared in the *NYE* by a phrase connoting irrepressible excitement: 'said to him' becomes 'broke out' (xv. 46). Her lack of 'composure' receives a retrospective reinterpretation: 'as radiantly as if . . .' comes to sound as if her eagerness *wasn't* for Paul, and '*and* as soon' rather than '*but* as soon' makes the sentence run into its reversal without any application of brakes. Paul fortunately thinks at first—or defensively pretends to—that she is referring here to her father; but at the end of Chapter IV, when Paul pays a second Sunday afternoon call on her, the tone of her allusions to St George is less easy for Paul to interpret optimistically. The elder man has declared that he won't visit her again, she reports, and Paul makes a startled enquiry: '"I don't know what he means", the girl replied, smiling. "He won't, at any rate, see me here"' (*1892*, p. 49). 'Smiling' here *could* represent insouciance: the *NYE* makes this 'the girl bravely smiled' (xv. 59), the adverb poignantly giving her credit for a courage her very need of which requires in turn courage from the probably less-valued Paul Overt.

The story's fifth chapter contains its greatest scene, that in which Paul is asked by the Master to stay on after the other dinner-guests in Ennismore Gardens and, in the writer's windowless study, given the 'lesson' of his lifetime. St George, developing remarks dropped earlier in the smoking-room at Summersoft, brings together in an exposition which is indeed masterly the two facts about himself of which Paul has been most conscious—his literary decline and his worldly success— and alleges a causal relation between them, pressing on Paul the necessity of choosing. It is an unforeseen necessity, which Paul struggles to resist, since one half or other of his envisaged future is at stake.

James's ironically alert imagination sees that the perfect way of 'working out' the 'greatness' of a Master whose actual writing has suffered a decline is to give him an overmastering personal eloquence; his genius, like that of the Coleridge figure in *The Coxon Fund*, is shown as having gone into his talk. In the smoking-room at Summersoft Paul has asked what St George means by 'false gods', and a revision prefaces the reply ('The idols of the market' (*1892*, p. 30)) with a suggestive comment: 'His companion had no difficulty whatever in saying' (*NYE* xv.36). Once on his own territory, launched on his argument, St George exercises his facility to the full, and by the strange though convincing paradox which gives the tale its title, draws on his authority *as* a 'Master' authoritatively to demolish his right to that title, making the example of his own imperfect success the basis of his appeal to Paul. The twists and turns of his explanations and unexpected reactions to Paul's recalcitrant objections make him, as a *NYE* revision phrases it, 'the more and more interesting Master' (xv. 63); and in the *NYE* James does indeed, detailing the twists and turns, make him 'more and more interesting' to Paul and us than in *1892*.

In this scene the revisions newly register the magisterial weight of St George's discourse: as where 'the Master pursued' (*NYE* xv. 69), 'the Master said' and 'the Master wound up' (*NYE* xv. 72). The older writer's false position—or if he is a manipulative faker his clever rhetorical abuse of his false position—makes him intriguingly unpredictable: the division in him between the dictates of his family responsibilities and his writerly dejection produces a bewildering range of apparently perverse responses to Paul's natural objections to 'the doctrine of renunciation' as it unfolds. Paul's double-takes and failures of understanding provoke a series of new, sarcastically knowing looks and sounds: 'It produced on the Master's part a laugh of odd acrimony' (*NYE* xv. 66); 'St George smiled as for the candour of his question' (*NYE* xv. 69); 'St George's eyes had a cold fine light' (*NYE* xv. 71); 'he pulled up—from the restless motion that had come upon him; his fine smile a generous glare' (*NYE* xv. 74); 'St George wonderfully grinned' (*NYE* xv. 78). Such expressive accents suggest the histrionic power and confidence of the performance (which need not impugn its sincerity); and when a distressed Paul cries 'The artist—the artist! Isn't he a man all the same?', St George's reply is representatively revised to highlight theatrical bravura.

St George hesitated. 'Sometimes I really think not' (*1892*, p. 63).

St George had a grand grimace. 'I mostly think not' (*NYE* xv. 76).

We might recall a similar scene of calculated dramatic exposition, that by the Countess Gemini in *The Portrait of a Lady*, where the villainy of Osmond and Madame Merle is revealed. There, though, Isabel fails to respond to the melodramatic revelations in the expected operatic manner. The comparison enforces St George's mastery not only in terms of results—his appeal comes off and the worked-up Paul leaves the country—but also in those of technique, the trick of creating an impression in words. His bitter, friendly smiles convey to Paul and the reader that, as Marian Fancourt says, 'He understands—understands everything.'

Paul Overt, on the other hand, experiences in this scene great difficulty in understanding what St George is getting at; he becomes an enthralled, thoroughly mastered, spectator or reader, subject to the manipulations of this powerful author who dazzlingly denies his own worth. The revisions copiously fill in this dimension of the scene, driving home its implications for the career and the life of the young man and his lively response to the urgency of the address: notations of affect arrive at every paradoxical turn. 'Our hero watched him, wondering and deeply touched' (*NYE* xv. 67), for instance; 'Paul was struck, and gaped' (*NYE* xv. 68); 'Paul kept echoing' (*NYE* xv. 69). The technique by which the *NYE* revisions register Paul's growing attraction in the dialogue in Chapter II recurs here to amplify Paul's suspense (and our own) about what St George means by his odd remarks. Speeches presented by themselves in *1892* are in the *NYE* prefaced by sentences with the force of oblique stage directions, like:

The young man then could but have the greater tribute of questions to pay (*NYE* xv. 70).

Paul turned it over: it took, from eyes he had never felt open so wide, so much looking at (*NYE* xv. 71).

Paul continued all gravely to glow (*NYE* xv. 71).

Paul frankly wondered (*NYE* xv. 75).

The young man had a strained smile (*NYE* xv. 77).

Moving Paul to such a spectrum of overt emotion—compelled curiosity, dazed wonder, serious enthusiasm, and, when the proposal is clarified, courageously borne anxiety—the *NYE* points the personal, and not just polite, motive for Paul's defence of the value of St George's worldly success.

The 'simple law' St George has invented or discovered is not a literal object, but an abstract situation, yet like the complex propositions of James's later fiction it has to be, metaphorically speaking, focused; as Paul finds, 'it took ... so much looking at'. The difficulty for Paul of *seeing* this possible truth he had not envisaged is rendered in what we can think of as an inwardly directed scrutiny, an abstracted vision. St George asks Paul: 'Are you in love with her?'

> 'Yes', said Paul Overt.
> 'Well, then, give it up.'
> Paul stared. 'Give up my love?'
> 'Bless me, no; your idea.'
> 'My idea?'
> 'The one you talked with her about. The idea of perfection' (*1892*, p. 62).

The changes in the *NYE* here seem slight, but give a more vivid dynamic to the exchange, signalling a profounder puzzlement for Paul. The same question is asked:

> 'Yes', Paul Overt presently said.
> 'Well then give it up.'
> Paul stared. 'Give up my "love"?'
> 'Bless me, no. Your idea.' And then as our hero but still gazed: 'The one you talked with her about. The idea of a decent perfection' (*NYE* xv. 75).

'Presently' delivers a new and anxious delay for Paul's avowal of his love; and St George's newly comma-less imperative 'Well then give it up' comes unhesitatingly out as an immediate response to it. 'It' has no clear referent, so Paul's puzzlement is understandable: ' "love" ' goes into inverted commas both to query the referent of St George's enigmatic command and to convey an evasive reluctance to expose his intimate feelings to the rigour of the Master's law. Paul's second echo from *1892*—'My idea?'—is simply suppressed in the *NYE*, creating a second silence (like that noted in 'presently'): so that Paul may here already have understood and be sightlessly 'gazing' at the enormity of what is being put to him, a demand for heroism which 'our hero' ruefully absorbs. '*Decent* perfection' actually echoes not Paul's account of his talk with Marian Fancourt, but St George's own question nine pages before in the *NYE*: 'What I mean is have you it in your heart to go in for some sort of decent perfection?' (*NYE* xv. 66); in *1892* it had read 'some sort of little perfection' (p. 54). St George's putting of his own words into Paul's mouth—with the special coerciveness of 'decent'—may be alerting us to the possibility that his rhetorical art is delusive in its ends, and that Paul is being duped.

The timing and vividness of this conversation as it impinges on Paul Overt, 'as he feels it, treats it, meets it', are greatly sharpened, then, in the *NYE*'s dramatic rethinking of the attitudes of the speakers, of the rhythm in and between utterances, of the argumentative structure of the occasion. This modification of the rate of exchange shows exemplarily in a tiny revision which gives us a violent subliminal effect to correspond to the effect on Paul of St George's remarkable self-denunciation. In *1892*:

'You know as well as you sit there that you would put a pistol-ball into your brain if you had written my books!'
It appeared to Paul Overt that the tremendous talk promised by the master at Summersoft had indeed come off (p. 60).

The revising James spots here an opening for a subtle metaphorical refinement of the young man's extreme impressionability: 'It appeared to Paul Overt' becomes 'It struck his listener' (*NYE* xv. 72). The revision flickeringly reverts to the image of the pistol-ball in the brain for the start of the new paragraph, as if *that* 'It', going off, were what 'struck' the listening Paul Overt, before the sentence shifts its axis—on 'that'—to specify another subject (one already given the force of a ricochet by this glancing connection of the bullet with Paul's 'brain'). James takes trouble here to find a metaphorical effect like a shot, as with the moment in the revised *American* where Noémie Nioche looks forward to the boost a duel—'a meeting and a big noise'—will give her career as a courtesan, 'clapping with a soft thud her little pearl-coloured hands'. This trouble shows James thinking it best to carry out his experiment, his projected fiction, 'to the end', even after first publication, to the 'decent perfection' where most readers will scarcely be aware of the intricacy of the verbal devices working on their passage from word to word.

v. Endowments for Expression

Just before he begins to urge his young admirer to sacrifice the prospect of marriage for the life of art, St George becomes distracted, looking over 'the sheets of his new book', and Paul has a moment to reflect enviously on the favouring isolation of the Master's study, which has no windows, only a large skylight. In the *NYE* version:

> The outer world, the world of accident and ugliness, was so successfully excluded, and within the rich protecting square, beneath the patronising sky, the dream-figures, the summoned company, could hold their particular revel (*NYE* xv. 64).

'Revel' recalls the imaginative power of another summoner of companies, another Master of potent art: Shakespeare's Prospero. 'Our revels now are ended', he announces in IV. i. 148, bringing to a premature end the Masque of Iris, Ceres, and Juno which was to have entertained Ferdinand and Miranda; 'the outer world, the world of accident and ugliness' has not in *The Tempest* been altogether 'successfully excluded', for there is a conspiracy by Caliban and his confederates to kill Ariel's 'potent master' (IV. i. 34) and usurp his power. James seems to be thinking of Prospero's speech as a source for meditation on the threatened status of the creative imagination—as he does with the 'melting' and 'fading' of imaginative objects when the American scene is becoming less vivid to him in 1905—and the one verbal revision in this sentence extends the reference: 'the dream-figures, the summoned company' is in the *1892* text, less poetically, 'the figures projected for an artistic purpose' (p. 53). Prospero's announcement of the end of the revels turns, famously, to a statement that human life has little more staying-power than artistic illusion, that 'We are such stuff | As dreams are made on' (IV. i. 156–7).

Both 'our revels now are ended' and 'We are such stuff | As dreams are made on' express a loss of power, confess to human weakness; there is thus an ironic undertow of unsuccessful association to Paul's cheerful current of thought about the Master's art, a suggestion of failure that is to be fully realized, as the scene in Ennismore Gardens develops, with St George's denial of his own magisterial standing. James's 'Master' achieves, like Prospero, the rhetorical potency of an immensely impressive relinquishment of his art: first metaphorically, by declaring himself only 'a successful charlatan' (*1892*, p. 56); and at the end literally (if we are to believe him) by telling Paul he has 'stopped writing' (*1892*, p. 79). The dramatic cogency of such self-demotion is the way in which it makes a compellingly unstable spectacle while broadcasting the drop of any pretension to compel; Prospero and St George simultaneously exercise exceptional dominance and win sympathetic wonder by a generously adopted humility. We have seen how the *NYE* alerts us to the tonal control and argumentative mastery of St George's representations of his own shortcomings.

The Tempest itself has often been taken as just such a masterly farewell to mastery. In his preface of 1907 to the play, thinking about this, James writes of 'its complexity and its perfection together', and compares it to all other 'examples of literary art':

The felicity enjoyed is enjoyed longer and more intensely, and the art involved, completely revealed, as I suggest, to the master, holds the securest revel (*LC* i. 1208–9).

The 'holding' of a 'revel' here, with the presence of 'the master', brings to mind Paul's appreciation of St George's escape from 'accident and ugliness'. For James in the *Tempest* essay, Shakespeare's romance presents us with a baffling biographical mystery, that of the dramatist's unimaginable motives for retiring from the stage after producing so consummate a work. St George's basis for giving up—his final self-consciousness of 'decline' and charlatanism—would not apply, though, as James points out with a punning twist, to Shakespeare: 'His powers declined, that is—but declined merely to obey the spring we should have supposed inherent in them' (*LC* i. 1207). The line of speculation James considers here is that which parallels Prospero's abdication of his 'rough magic' (v. i. 50), his declarations that 'I'll drown my book' (in v. i. 57) and 'Now my charms are all o'erthrown' (in the Epilogue), with Shakespeare's own situation. For James, passionately committed to his creative vocation, the idea is intolerable that after such an achievement Shakespeare, in full possession of the human maximum of imaginative power, could complacently settle into the existence of a Stratford burgher, without wishing again to write and draw on his unequalled 'endowment for Expression' (*LC* i. 1211).

As much as Henry St George, the irascible master of *The Tempest* has been subjected, and quite properly, to inquiry concerning the manipulativeness of his art, his 'project' as he calls it in v. i. 1. In both works the creation of an illusion, the magic produced in a magician's cell, has a declared purifying purpose as regards those on whom it is enforced; the question to be asked in either case is whether the magician can be so exempt from human self-interest as to be sure of acting—of seriously intervening—with due respect for the liberty of the subject. The lesson of the Master may be what St George says, that the sincere pursuit of perfection (which is not to say the attainment of it) is possible only to the artist with no family to support by his creations; but it may also be the lesson his case constitutes, that of the compromised and corrupted waster of talents who cannot bear to see a young rival supplant him in both art *and* love, so practises a further 'successful charlatanism' by concocting a minatory didactic tale of the causes of his decline. Even if he *is* insincere, though, it doesn't follow that his theory must be false, just as his sincerity would not prove the theory true: the relation between general rule and particular case is as tricky as James's subtle intelligence usually discerns it to be.

Prospero and St George drown their books, reabsorbed into the system of social responsibilities; so, mystifyingly, does Shakespeare; Paul Overt and Henry James push ahead with '*Loneliness*' inscribed on their banner, solaced only by an asexual act of union, that of the creative imagination, 'the act of personal possession of one being by another at its completest'. The superlative in 'completest' offers an ideal to aim at, but doesn't expect completeness or perfection: James's story of Paul Overt just directs itself towards a presentation of the action as Paul experiences it. The *NYE* revision recognizably aspires to 'a decent perfection' in the creation of Paul's experience, making it like the action of *The Portrait of a Lady* 'complete in itself'; and for James as for Shakespeare in *The Tempest* 'It is by his expression of it exactly as the expression stands that the particular thing is created' (*LC* i. 1212). In *The Lesson of the Master*, however, 'the particular thing', the 'particular revel', is far from excluding 'the world of accident and ugliness' in which Paul's striving might be in vain or his sacrifice unnecessary: the ambiguity of the narrative holds these possibilities, with all the emotional damage they connote, even while it holds open also the chance that St George is 'saving' Paul for his true vocation, sustains the possible value of a life lived for art. James's own career, a momentous gamble on the value of artistic dedication, puts us the same question, with a similar ambiguity. Except that Paul Overt's works are not available for our inspection and judgement, whereas James's *Lesson of the Master*, one result of *his* career, is; a particular created thing, an experience constituted, as the *NYE* revisions remind us, 'by his expression of it exactly as the expression stands'.

Last Words

James was intrigued and baffled by Prospero and Shakespeare in their seeming capacity to release their masterly hold on inspired art before exhaling their last gasp of life. In James's own creation of Henry St George, this kind of enigma recurs—only with the strong suggestion that the master is in any case unworthy of his mastery, so that the abdication is not exactly his choice. We are presented with no such mysterious election of silence at the end of James's career: only with the different mystery of his continuing to exercise his gifts to the very last, acting as if living and writing had become for him inseparable.

After the *NYE* James did not abandon revision. In 1910, as he wrote to Mrs William Darwin, he sent off the revised *Italian Hours*, 'Tricked out in their abandoned ancientry, and their great out-of-printness, to make—or to seek—some sort of fresh little fortune' (*HJL* iv. 550). And in 1911 he began to review his own life, and those of the rest of his family, in his autobiographies, controversially rewriting old texts as part of the process of creating new ones. November 1911 saw him at work on this project, writing to Edith Wharton of his doings at his Chelsea workplace: 'In said *repaire* I propose to crouch and *me blottir* (in the English shade of the word, for so intensely revising an animal, as well), for many more weeks' (*HJL* iv. 592). Huddling in a retreat and forever blotting your lines (unlike Shakespeare) are here brought together by a farcical Anglo-French pun to characterize James's fixity and concentrated industry. He blots *himself*, also, partly because the work under his hand is his autobiography.

It was not only himself, though, that James revised in *Notes of a Son and Brother*, the second volume of the work. Alfred Habegger has found himself distressed at 'Henry James's Rewriting of Minny Temple's Letters' as a result of collating with the versions in the autobiography newly discovered longhand copies of the letters made by James's sister-in-law and niece. James's revisions of his cousin's words, according to Habegger, 'raise some disturbing questions about his use of historical documentation and his general accuracy and truthfulness'.[1] The most serious offence Habegger alleges on James's part is a 'small pious fraud', an act not of collaborative refinement as in the other cases but of solo creativity: he seems 'to insert a passage of his own composition'.[2] The evidence for this particular transgression of good editorial practice is of a negative order, though, since the claim rests on the absence from the longhand copies of the letters of a passage present in *Notes of a Son and Brother*, and one ought to be reluctant to put too much weight on such a lack; but there is no doubt that James heavily rewords and repoints his cousin's texts.

Minny Temple, in the longhand copy of the original, writes to her friend John Gray about her dancing-partner at a ball, and then turns wittily on herself.

I don't know why I have tried your patience by writing about an individual that you have never seen. This is merely to show you that I have not retired irrevocably from the world, the flesh & the devil. I am conscious of a very faint Charm about it still, when taken in small doses.

James turns this into a single sentence, whose control on the logical turns brings it closer to his own habitual power to make the improvised seem premeditated and the premeditated improvised.

I don't know why I have tried your patience by writing so about a person you have never seen; unless it's to show you that I haven't irrevocably given up the world, the flesh and the devil, but am conscious of a faint charm about them still when taken in small doses.[3]

What is going on here? Whereas in works like *The Portrait of a Lady* and *The Wings of the Dove* James revised Minny Temple into new forms with the traditional sanction of the novelist, this shows him lightly transmuting her very words into entertaining fluency when the apparently factual nature of the undertaking—as we understand such undertakings now—seems to forbid it. James may have been led too far astray here by the instinct he had previously described as applying only to fiction: 'If a work of imagination, of fiction, interests me at all … I always want to write it over in my own way' (*LHJ* i. 396).

---

[1] Alfred Habegger, 'Henry James's Rewriting of Minny Temple's Letters', *American Literature*, 4/2 (May 1986), 159–80, pp. 159–60.
[2] 'Henry James's Rewriting of Minny Temple's Letters', pp. 167, 166. See also Habegger's *Henry James and the 'Woman Business'*, p. 165.
[3] These passages come from one (that on p. 169) of the four letters given in parallel text form by Habegger.

Habegger is not the first to note James's possession and recon-
ditioning of others' letters in *Notes of a Son and Brother*, nor the most
forceful in his recriminations. In 1914 James's book quoted William
James writing to their sister Alice in September 1863, having returned
to his lodgings at Cambridge, Massachusetts, and found the cost of
board raised too high.

> I then with that fine economical instinct which distinguishes me resolved to
> take breakfast and tea, of my own finding and making, in my room, and only
> pay Miss Upham for dinners. Miss U. is now holding forth at Swampscott,
> so I asked to see her sister Mrs. Wood and learn the cost of the 7 dinners a
> week. She with true motherly instinct said that I should only make a slop with
> my self-made meals in my room, and that she would rather let me keep on
> for 4.50, seeing it was me (*Autobiog.*, pp. 328–9).

In 1920 *The Letters of William James* appeared with a text of the same
letter different in wording and punctuation.

> I then, with that fine economical instinct which distinguishes me, resolved to
> take a tea and breakfast of bread and milk in my room and only pay Miss
> Upham for dinners. Miss U. is at Swampscott. So I asked to see [her sister]
> Mrs. Wood, to learn the cost of seven dinners. She, with true motherly instinct,
> said that I should only make a slop in my room, and that she would rather
> let me keep on for $4.50, seeing it was me.[4]

The letters were edited by Henry James's nephew Henry, who had
made pained and painful objection in 1913 to his uncle's tamperings
with his father's correspondence. In a long, confessional but defensive
letter of 15–18 November 1913, the rebuked uncle had written to say
he was grieved to learn of 'the effect on you of the *cumulative*
impression you get from individual retouchings often repeated' (*HJL*
iv. 800).

Henry James III was to understand from this letter that in his
uncle's view the proprieties in such cases were not absolute, but varied
between the kinds. To include a letter or extract in an artistic work
aiming at '*atmosphere*' (*HJL* iv. 801), like *Notes of a Son and Brother*,
was to incur a lesser responsibility for textual accuracy than to make
it part of an edition like the one which eventually appeared in 1920.
The modern scholar's horror at James's freedoms with the words of
others may be comforted by this recognition of the validity of 'the
high standard of *rigid* editing' in cases where editing as such is in

[4] *The Letters of William James*, i. 50.

question. To include old letters in the autobiographies, for James, required something more like copy-editing. The 'attitude and state of feeling' he had worked under was, he emphasized,

one so distinct, by its whole 'ethic' and aesthetic (and indeed its aesthetic, however discredited to you in fact, *was* simply its ethic) from what I should have felt my function in handling my material as an instalment merely of the great correspondence itself, just a contribution, an initial one, to the long continuity of *that*. Then the case would have been for me absolutely of the plainest—my own ethic, with no aesthetic whatever concerned in the matter, would have been the ideal of documentary exactitude, verbatim, *literatim et punctuatim*—free of all living back imaginatively, or of any of the effects of this (*HJL* iv. 800).

The difference for the uncle's use of the texts was that of their 'related state to innumerable *other* things, the things I was to do my book *for*' (*HJL* iv. 800). He imagines the stern nephew calling the revisions he made as he read out the letters for typed transcription 'dictating liberties' (*HJL* iv. 801). But for James they were not 'liberties' in that sense; rather, they were attempts at fidelity to this 'related state'.

James goes on to expound with painstaking fullness his sense of the purpose of his book—'to be a reflection of all the amenity and felicity of our young life of that time at the highest pitch that was consistent with perfect truth—to show us all at our best for characteristic expression' (*HJL* iv. 802). Minny Temple and his brother have enshrined the spirit of the past in their letters; he is their future restorer. 'Perfect truth' seems for him here to include *his* later perfecting of it; and William's 'characteristic expression' is sometimes best rendered by his, Henry's, imaginative revision of it:

when I laid hands upon the letters to use as so many touches and tones in the picture I frankly confess I seemed to see them in a better, or at all events in another light, here and there, than those rough and rather illiterate copies I had from you showed at their face value (*HJL* iv. 802).

In writing about his brother James was moved to 'a passion of tenderness for doing the best thing by him that the material allowed', and seemed to hear William's ghostly presence pleading for revision:

'Oh but you're not going to give me away, to hand me over, in my raggedness and my poor accidents, quite unhelped, unfriended, you're going to do the very best for me you *can*, aren't you, and since you appear to be making such claims for me you're going to let me seem to justify them as much as I possibly may?' (*HJL* iv. 802).

To revise someone's words becomes rather a duty to them than a disservice or an imposition of self. The essential is not the text of the letter but its intention and context, its value as one of 'so many touches and tones in the picture'; and thus the transcripts James uses become 'rough and illiterate copies'—deprived of their presumably immediate relation to the originals—and have a low 'face value' that can be raised by the application of the reviser's pen. In conforming to William's intuited plea, James did not regard himself as transgressing:

These were small things, the very smallest, they appeared to me all along to be, tiny amendments in orders of words, degrees of emphasis etc., to the end that he should be more easily and engagingly readable and thereby more tasted and liked—from the moment there was no excess of these *soins* and no violence done to his real identity (*HJL* iv. 802–3).

He may have been wrong, he now admits, to arrogate such power: 'I daresay I did instinctively regard it at last as all *my* truth, to do what I would with.' But he maintains that the alternative attitude would have been of the 'absolutely hands-off kind', and that in such a case the letters would have simply been omitted. Confessing his probable error to his nephew, of having failed to anticipate the extent of his compulsion to rewrite, James resites the proper place of revision—in one's own work.

That really will have been my mistake, I feel—there it will have begun; in thinking that with so literary, so compositional, an obsession as my whole bookmaking impulse is governed by, any mere merciless transcript might have been possible to me. I have to the last point the instinct and the sense for fusions and interrelations, for framing and encircling (as I think I have already called it) every part of my stuff in every other—and that makes a danger when the frame and circle play over too much upon the image. Never again shall I stray from my proper work—the one in which that danger is the reverse of one and becomes a rightness and a beauty (*HJL* iv. 803).

James manages a noble turn, then—saying, for instance, 'the sad thing is I think you're right in being offended' (*HJL* iv. 804)—but can't help defending the aesthetic instincts towards the construction of coherence and the establishment of meaning which his career as a novelist has taught him.

The nephew's qualms about his uncle's revisions have in this case self-evidently firm grounds. But three years after the writer's death, on 5 July 1919, Henry James III wrote to Pinker from Belgrade in Serbia, where he was part of the 'American Commission to Negotiate Peace' and the 'Reparative Commission', with what seems a deep reservation about his uncle's revisions even in a case where they were to be 'a rightness and a beauty'. The letter concerns the planned 'cheap' edition of all James's fiction to be published by Macmillan, and shortly wishes it to suppress as far as possible its connection with the *NYE*.

I take it that this edition will not include the prefaces. In view of the popular prejudice against the revised text, I would suggest that this edition be made up in such a way as not to call attention to the fact that the revised text is used, by any more conspicuous announcement than may be required under the Copyright Act.[5]

This slightly chilling note, however, did not inhibit Percy Lubbock, who supervised the eventual 1921 'cheap' edition. The advertisement at the back of each volume braves 'popular prejudice' by declaring that 'The text used in this issue is that of the "New York" edition, and the critical prefaces written for that series are retained in the volumes to which they refer.'

The care for the last comma stayed with James to the last, even when the shock of the Great War staggered his manner of proceeding. He picked himself up and took up his past works, preparing a Uniform Edition of his tales for Martin Secker. On 11 February 1915 he wrote:

Dear Martin Secker,
Please find enclosed within my revised copy for the volume of *Glasses*. It ought to present no difficulty at all to your compositors—the little emendations are so clear & careful; but I think I should nevertheless like to see a proof—just to make sure that everything, especially in the way of punctuation, is absolutely right.

Yours very truly
Henry James[6]

'Especially in the way of punctuation' is an inserted afterthought, which looks back to the characteristic condition for the volumes he had asked Pinker to pass on to Secker on 11 September 1914, as war was starting. He had insisted that Secker 'conform literatim and punctuatim to the [*NYE*] text. It is vital that he adhere to that authentic punctuation—to the last comma or rather, more essentially, no-

[5] Henry James III to J. B. Pinker, 5 July 1919 (Yale MS).
[6] HJ to Martin Secker, 11 Feb. 1915 (Yale MS).

comma'.[7] In wartime James came to see exact punctuation as a symbolic mark of the complex civilization which was being defended. Martin Secker himself valued James's care, and showed the fact by requesting the manuscript of the *Glasses* revision—a recent piece of work, since the story had at the last moment been excluded from the *NYE* and had thus still to be revised. James sent it to him on 15 March 1915: 'This unlovely relic you are indeed very welcome to keep, and I only wish it were *more* curious and more culinary.'[8]

Nine days later James wrote to Brander Matthews, who had asked to use James's 1887 essay on the actor Coquelin, sending it back 'as much "done over" as was absolutely inevitable' (*HJL* iv. 744). The passage of twenty-eight years had brought a consciousness of negligence, of neglected duties towards offspring.

I have, as you will see, so very much re-expressed the sense of it as to have had to have recourse to a new text, that is a new pen and new paper, altogether; and I must ask you to be so good as to take it in this way or not to take it at all. It has been really dreadful to me to be reminded of how filthily (yes, *je maintiens le mot*) I could at one time write, how imperfectly I could leave my intention expressed. This paper, as the *Century* printed it (without so much as a proof sent me in common decency) simply bristles with those intentions baffled and abandoned; and nothing could have induced me, from the moment of owning any relation to them again, not pityingly to refather them, not decently to feed and clothe them, not, in short, to pop them into the hideous gaps that have so long and so disgracefully awaited them (*HJL* iv. 744).

James maintains the *'mot'*—'filthily'—that perfectly expresses his imperfect expression in the past, his reason for not maintaining so many others; he echoes, in his solicitude to 'feed and clothe' his younger intentions, the Preface to *The Golden Bowl*, where they are an 'uncanny brood' (*LC* ii. 1331) in need of tidying up before they are presentable in public. He goes on to ask Matthews to attach a footnote stating that ' "The substance of this paper appeared in the *Century Magazine* for" such and such a date' (*HJL* iv. 744). It is the set of intentions and not the exact phrasing which thus makes up the 'substance' of the piece of writing; the comparative materiality of the actual language used, with its particular histories and nuances, is by this formulation

---

[7] Quoted in Leon Edel and Dan H. Laurence, *A Bibliography of Henry James*, 3rd edn., revised with the assistance of James Rambeau, Oxford, 1982, p. 155.

[8] HJ to Martin Secker, 15 Mar. 1915 (Yale TS).

made not unimportant but secondary to the authorial process of which it is the result.

Here, in March 1915, we find James a potent and tenderly responsible conceiver and reconceiver of intentions, 'refathering' them to re-establish a strong paternal relation. On 3 November, not long before his final collapse, we find him making a wry response to Rhoda Broughton's praise of one of his old books, again looking for a relationship to his work, but this time relegated from fatherhood.

I greatly appreciate meanwhile your fidelity and your explicit response to old perpetrations on the part of this fairly extinct literary volcano—your generous allusion to one of whose ancient masterpieces gives me, I assure you, the liveliest pleasure. I think of it, the masterpiece in question, as the work of quite another person than myself, at this date—that of a rich (so much rather than a poor) relation, say, who hasn't cast me off in my trouble, but suffers me still to claim a shy fourth cousinship.[9]

Like Keats, only after a much longer span, or like his own Roderick Hudson looking on one of his works as if it were someone else's, James in this ironic excess of modesty no longer claims a direct attachment. His 'shy fourth cousinship' presumably gives him a remotely avuncular rather than a powerfully parental relationship to the work itself, allows him access on sufferance rather than by right. James flirts here with the 'disconnexion' from his works of which he speaks at the end of the Preface to *The Golden Bowl*, but without altogether relinquishing his powers. '*Fairly* extinct literary volcano' equivocates between a proper and a partial extinction.

Such appreciation as Rhoda Broughton's compensated James for the sense that his expenditure of care had not met with due recognition. Three months before writing to her, and six before his death, James had sent to Edmund Gosse, on 25 August, the letter already quoted grimly comparing the public neglect of the *NYE* to the oblivion so memorably evoked in Shelley's 'Ozymandias'. The interest of his revisions—as his nephew was to confirm—had not been generally felt. The cost of revision had been great, and its returns small. James's faith in the life of writing, and in the life of his writing, was not fully repaid in this world; he was too often left with his confidence on his hands.

When James collapsed from a stroke in December 1915, one way in which he struggled to hold on to life was by recourse to the imaginative

[9] H J to Rhoda Broughton, 3 Nov. 1915 (Lubbock T S, Harvard).

grasp he had retained over the texts he retouched. In his delirium he gave a series of last dictations—and as well as, notoriously, imagining himself endowed with Napoleonic power, perhaps for a fiction, he imagined himself one last time exercising his now-failing literary powers. On 11 December he declared it

Wondrous enough certainly to have a finger in such a concert and to feel ourselves touch the large old phrase into the right amplitude. It had shrunken and we add to its line—all we can scarce say how, save that we couldn't have left it (*HJL* iv. 809–10).

'Wondrous ... to feel ourselves touch' makes contact with the old James's awed consciousness of the continuance of his faculties; but the sense lurches, desolatingly, with the missing of some step in 'all we can scarce say how', which has puzzlingly lost the grip of the large old phrase. The pointless lacuna sadly brings home to roost the brave humour of a letter to T. S. Perry of the year before, where a slip of the pen received a witty comment: '(how I do, in *gaga* fashion, leave out words!)'[10]

In the last, undated dictations, James's flow of eloquence visibly dwindles; his arching syntax crumbles into grammatical fragments. Some of the concerns I have considered seem to reappear in a touchingly broken paragraph which ends with an indisputable and indisputably complete short sentence.

across the border
all the pieces
Individual souls, great ... of [word lost] on which great perfections are If one does ... in the fulfilment with the neat and pure and perfect—to the success or as he or she moves through life, following admiration unfailing [word lost] in the highway—Problems are very sordid (*HJL* iv. 812).

Problems *are* sordid, impeding the 'great perfections' for which James strove. In the face of the greatest problem of all for the works of man, death, James recognized a truth running counter to the one on which we have seen him act hitherto: 'it all better too much left than too much done', he goes on. 'Doing' rather than 'leaving' had been his preference over the preceding half-century. His ultimate recorded words seem to have been *meant* to be recorded, and may speak to us

[10] Letter to T. S. Perry, 13 Apr. 1914, in Virginia Harlow, *Thomas Sergeant Perry: A Biography*, Durham, NC, 1950, p. 345.

of their own lastness (he has just spoken of the dictation as 'these final and faded remarks').

I never dreamed of such duties as laid upon me. This sore throaty condition is the last I ever invoked for the purpose (*HJL* iv. 812).

For James the life of writing had indeed laid unforeseeable duties upon him, duties like those of a parent to take responsibility for his progeny until death. We may understand the last sentence as meaning that he will never again call on his sore throat to dictate: it is a farewell to prose, and its flickering transition from present 'is' to past 'invoked' leaps forward into an unimaginable future from which the author can look back and close his book.

The final dictations were not James's actual last words. On 2 February 1916, twenty-six days before his death, the nephew who had taken so amiss the revision of William James's letters wrote with emotion to T. S. Perry, reporting of the invalid that 'His fragmentary speech abounds in amplified courteousnesses—sometimes more ample than ever.'[11] And as Leon Edel tells us, only the end of life could entirely extinguish James's impulse to keep writing, even after he lapsed into a coma: 'Occasionally Mrs. William James observed his hand moving across his bedcover as if he were writing' (*HJL* iv. 809). He died on 28 February 1916.

It would probably have mortified James to have known his 'Last Dictation' would be published, a set of fragments he had never consciously checked and which shows his consciousness beginning to weaken. A truer testament to his lifelong literary endeavour was the posthumous appearance, in September 1916, of Martin Secker's Uniform edition of *Glasses*. It contained a note, which reads:

'Glasses' is not included in the Definitive Edition: it first appeared in the volume 'Embarrassments', published by Mr William Heinemann in 1897. The text was revised by the author for this edition very shortly before his death.

[11] Henry James III to T. S. Perry, in *Thomas Sergeant Perry*, p. 349.

Appendix

A Chronology: James during the Period of the New York Edition

The following selective chronology, which where possible takes the form of quotation from letters, is offered as a source of information relevant to the main text of this book. In it, using over 200 letters mainly from Princeton's holdings of Scribner material in the Firestone Library and James's correspondence with his agent J. B. Pinker in the Beinecke Library at Yale, I have attempted to lay out in clear sequence the complicated story of James's writing life in the period of the New York Edition. James's letters are from Lamb House unless otherwise stated. I hope the abbreviations will help readers to follow through the histories of single projects (the dates in brackets are of first book publication); and for convenience I give also a list of the contents of each of the published volumes of the Edition.

ABBREVIATIONS

AS	*The American Scene* (1907)
CEN	'An American Art-Scholar: Charles Eliot Norton' (1909)
Chap.	*The Chaperon* (play)
EH	*English Hours* (1905)
FMC	Projected essay on F. Marion Crawford
GB	*The Golden Bowl* (1904)
GD'A	'Gabriele D'Annunzio' (1914)
HB	*The High Bid* (play)
IH	*Italian Hours* (1909)
ITALAD?	'Is There a Life After Death?' (1910)
L	Projected book on London
LB	'The Lesson of Balzac' (1905)
N	Projected novels
NYE	*The New York Edition of the Novels and Tales* (1907–9)
OH	*The Other House* (play)
Out.	*The Outcry* (play)
QS	'The Question of Our Speech' (1905)
S & M	'The Speech and Manners of American Women' (1960)
Sal.	*The Saloon* (play)
T	Various tales
Temp.	'The Tempest' (1907)
TP	Unfinished article on 'The Turning Point of my Life'

V & R   *Views and Reviews* (1908)

WF   *The Whole Family: A Novel by Twelve Authors* (1908)

FINAL CONTENTS OF NYE VOLUMES

i   *Roderick Hudson*

ii   *The American*

iii & iv   *The Portrait of a Lady*

v & vi   *The Princess Casamassima*

vii & viii   *The Tragic Muse*

ix   *The Awkward Age*

x   *The Spoils of Poynton; A London Life; The Chaperon*

xi   *What Maisie Knew; In the Cage; The Pupil*

xii   *The Aspern Papers; The Turn of the Screw; The Liar; The Two Faces*

xiii   *The Reverberator; Madame de Mauves; A Passionate Pilgrim; The Madonna of the Future; Louisa Pallant*

xiv   *Lady Barbarina; The Siege of London; An International Episode; The Pension Beaurepas; A Bundle of Letters*

xv   *The Lesson of the Master; The Death of the Lion; The Next Time; The Figure in the Carpet; The Coxon Fund*

xvi   *The Author of 'Beltraffio'; 'The Middle Years'; Greville Fane; Broken Wings; The Tree of Knowledge; The Abasement of the Northmores; The Great Good Place; Four Meetings; Paste; 'Europe'; Miss Gunton of Poughkeepsie; Fordham Castle*

xvii   *The Altar of the Dead; The Beast in the Jungle; The Birthplace; The Private Life; Owen Wingrave; The Friends of the Friends; Sir Edmund Orme; The Real Right Thing; The Jolly Corner; Julia Bride*

xviii   *Daisy Miller; Pandora; The Patagonia; The Marriages; The Real Thing; Brooksmith; The Beldonald Holbein; The Story in It; Flickerbridge; Mrs Medwin*

xix & xx   *The Wings of the Dove*

xxi & xxii   *The Ambassadors*

xxiii & xxiv   *The Golden Bowl*

1900

2 Apr.   (NYE) Scribners to Pinker (telegram): 'Would You Care on any terms to arrange for Collected Edition Henry James | Burlingame' [Pinker reply: 'Disposed Consider James'] (Princeton MS).

1903

22 June   (L) HJ encloses agreement for *London Town* to Mac-
                 millans (*HJL* iv. 278).

8 Sept.   (*GB*) HJ to Pinker: about *The Golden Bowl*, 'which I am
                 getting on with steadily for Methuen' (Yale TS).

25 Oct.   (*GB* & GD'A) HJ to Pinker: 'I have not been unmindful
                 that I promised Copy for "The Golden Bowl" to Methuen
                 for the end of November—if humanly possible ... I have
                 in good order, "highly finished" and copied, some 110,000
                 of the (about) 170,000 words of which it is my plan that
                 the Book shall consist.' Can deliver three-quarters at the
                 end of Nov. Has had for last ten days to do D'Annunzio
                 article for *Quarterly* (Yale TS; also *HJL* iv. 285, wrongly
                 called 'MS').

1 Nov.   (*GB* & N) HJ to Pinker: 'If I have delayed two or three
                 days to answer your note conveying Mr. Methuen's offer
                 of a delay of some three or four months for the publication
                 of *The Golden Bowl*, it has been in order to take full
                 counsel with myself on the matter. The result is that I
                 accept the offer with thanks, as on the whole it will ease
                 me off and contribute to the higher perfection, so to speak,
                 of the book.' Publication date now to be Aug. 1904; will
                 send the whole copy in 'some 10 or 12 weeks from now—
                 & the second book by the moment *The Golden Bowl* is
                 published' (Yale MS).

1 Dec.   (*GB*) HJ to Pinker (from Reform Club): has been trying
                 to finish a book—'(which I've after all but *almost* fin-
                 ished)'—before quitting the country for town (Yale MS).

11 Dec.   (N) HJ to Howells: would like 'to write another
                 (another!!) American novel or two' (Harvard MS).

1904

19 Jan.   (N & *AS*) HJ to Mrs WJ: Harper's want another novel
                 of the length of *The Ambassadors*, to be serialized in the
                 North American Review, which if contracted for would
                 be the next job after American book (*AS*) for McClure
                 (Harvard MS).

Apr.   (GD'A) 'Gabriele D'Annunzio' pub. in *Quarterly Review*.

14 Apr.   (L) HJ to Hueffer (from Reform Club): London book
                 'relegated to dim futurity': FMH to go ahead with his
                 (*Selected Letters* (1956), pp. 185–6).

20 May   (*GB*) HJ to Pinker: 'I will indeed let you have the whole
                 of my M.S. on the very first possible day, now not far off;

but I have still, absolutely, to finish, and to finish right, and Methuen's importunity does meanwhile, I confess, distress me. I have been working on the book with unremitting intensity the whole of every blessed morning since I began it, some thirteen months ago, and I am at present within but some twelve or fifteen thousand words of Finis ... I have written, in perfection, *200,000* words of the G.B.—with the rarest perfection!—and you can imagine how much of that, which has taken time, has had to come out' (Yale TS; also *LHJ* ii. 15–16, with an omission).

11 June 1904   (*GB*) HJ to Pinker: 'I am much obliged to you for your suggestion of the possibility of postponing my novel till the spring ...'. But 'It is so all *but* finished that I can promise you the whole, I think, by the 1ˢᵗ July.' Has had interruptions (Yale MS).

28 June   (*GB*) HJ to Pinker: 'I have but one more chapter of my interminable ["task" crossed out] book to write ... I am really close to my Finis' (Yale TS).

29 June   (*GB*) HJ to Pinker: glad at the possibility of serializing *The Golden Bowl*; but it was unforeseen, so divisions difficult (Yale MS).

30 June   (*GB*) HJ to Pinker: sends 11 parts of *The Golden Bowl*; 'The twelfth and last shall follow on the wings of the hardest-blowing wind I can raise.' Has taken out 'three priceless gems of chapters' for serialization (Yale TS).

10 July   (*GB*) HJ to Pinker: awaiting news about serialization; will bring him Part Twelfth, 'which is finished, praise to the Highest!' (Yale TS).

27 July   (*GB*) HJ to Pinker: American news of non-serialization 'rather a blow'; but maybe decision is because serialization was not planned for (Yale MS).

2 Aug.   (*GB & T*) HJ to Pinker: sends the three cut chapters to be restored; has been doing 'polishing-off and winding-up of the short tale for Harper' ('Fordham Castle') (Yale TS).

5 Aug.   (*GB*) HJ to Pinker (from Reform Club, London): thanks for £450 paid in for *The Golden Bowl* from Methuen and Scribner, minus Pinker's 10% commission (Yale MS).

30 Aug.   HJ arrives in New York (*HJL* iv. 319).

14 Sept.   (*NYE*) HJ to Pinker (from Chocorua, NH): no urgency about coming over to negotiate; *The American Scene* gives him plenty to do. Collective Edition can wait till spring (Yale MS; also *HJL* iv. 321–3).

17 Sept. 1904	(*GB*) HJ to Scribners (from Cambridge, Mass.): returns first galley proofs of *The Golden Bowl* (Nos. 1–6). 'It is distinctly the most *done* of my productions' (Princeton MS).
26 Sept.	(*GB*) HJ to Scribners (from Cambridge): returns proofs of *The Golden Bowl* galleys 7–77; has received up to Galley 137—nearly the End (Princeton MS).
1 Oct.	(*GB*) HJ to Pinker (from Cambridge): today sent all *The Golden Bowl* to Methuen [duplicate corrected proof from Scribners edition] (Yale MS).
8 Oct.	(*GB*) HJ to Scribners (from Cambridge): looking over 2 packets of paged Revise for *The Golden Bowl* (Princeton MS).
21 Oct.	(*GB*) HJ to Scribners (from Lenox, Mass.): they have received revised proofs from him up to vol. ii, p. 259 of *The Golden Bowl*; the rest should now have arrived. Sorry for delays; has been staying with friends [the Whartons]. Has sent Methuen the second set of paged proofs of vol. ii (Princeton MS).
22 Oct.	(*AS*) HJ to Pinker (from Lenox): planning a preliminary 'New England' (Yale MS).
10 Nov.	(*GB*) *The Golden Bowl* pub. in New York by Scribners.
16 Nov.	(*GB*) HJ to Scribners (from Cambridge): thanks for half-dozen copies of *The Golden Bowl*; 'I rejoice in the charming appearance of the book' (Princeton MS).
Dec.	(*T*) 'Fordham Castle' pub. in *Harper's Magazine*.
6 Dec.	(*AS*) HJ to Pinker (from Boston): has 'two Instalments of my Book almost ready' ['New England: An Autumn Impression': HJ to Pinker (from Cambridge), 2 Mar. 1905: 'I had written it for but two, but ... I am cutting it into three' (Yale TS)] (Yale MS).

1905

10 Feb.	(*GB*) *The Golden Bowl* pub. in London by Methuen.
Apr.–June	(*AS*) 'New England: An Autumn Impression' pub. in *North American Review*.
11 May	(*NYE*) HJ to Pinker (from New York): urges him to come over; 'I shall feel some regret, I think, if I shall have left the country without the question of my collective Edition having in any degree been started, or the ground sounded for it'; already sure it should be 'a very wise & full *selection*' (Yale MS).
c. 6 June	(*NYE*) Pinker arrives in New York to negotiate *NYE*.

25 June 1905	(*NYE*) HJ to Pinker (from Cambridge): sends thanks in his wake (Pinker *en voyage* for England). Sorry for 'the up-hill moments, in New York, that you found yourself again condemned to' (Yale TS).
4 July	(*NYE*) HJ sails home in SS *Ivernia*; not sticking closely to revision of *Roderick Hudson,* according to Elizabeth Robins (*Theatre and Friendship,* p. 251).
30 July	(*NYE*) HJ to Scribners: copious memorandum about plans for *NYE*; proposes 'The New York Edition' as title; mentions that revision of *Roderick Hudson* and *The American* is demanding 'extreme (and very interesting) deliberation'; promises revised copy of *Roderick Hudson* and *The American* with Prefaces by 25 Sept. (*HJL* iv. 366–8).
Aug.	(*QS*) 'The Question of Our Speech' pub. in *Appleton's Booklovers' Magazine.*
Aug.	(*LB*) 'The Lesson of Balzac' pub. in *Atlantic Monthly.*
7 Aug.	(*NYE*) HJ to Pinker (from Lamb House): thanks for having *Roderick Hudson* pages 'so beautifully put into condition for revision for me. This is a brilliant piece of work which will greatly help me & for which I am exceedingly obliged to you' (Yale MS).
1 Sept.	(*NYE & AS*) HJ to Pinker: thanks for 'the beautiful, beautiful last job of pasting-up work done, which has put the book into a form it is a joy for me to work upon'. Constable as possible publishers of *NYE* in England. Is sending three 'New York' papers promised to Duneka for *Harper's Magazine* [probably the three-part 'New York Revisited'] (Yale TS).
15 Sept.	(*AS*) HJ to Munro: sends 'New York and the Hudson: A Spring Impression' for *North American Review* (Yale TS).
19 Sept.	(*NYE*) Houghton, Mifflin to Scribners: state 'our conditions' for use in *NYE* of material published by them: that their Riverside Press make plates and do printing and binding of those volumes, and that they receive 5% royalty on retail price. No wish to be obstructive, but 'a fundamental principle'—the right of the original publisher to make plates (Princeton TS).
26 Sept.	(*AS*) HJ to Munro: promised chapters for *North American Review* include 'The Middle West: an Impression'; 'California and the Pacific Coast'; 'The Universities and Colleges: an Impression (not elsewhere workable-in)'; 'Manners: an Impression (not workable-in elsewhere!') [none of these written] (Yale TS).

29 Sept. 1905	(*NYE*) HJ to Pinker: is 'without impatience' about Scribners delay; glad of 'The margin for revision meanwhile accruing' (Yale TS).
7 Oct.	(*QS* & *LB*) *The Question of Our Speech: The Lesson of Balzac: Two Lectures* pub. in Boston by Houghton, Mifflin.
9 Oct.	(*AS*) HJ to Munro: has just sent 'New York: Social Notes' for *North American Review* (Yale MS).
18 Oct.	(*EH*) *English Hours* pub. in London by Heinemann.
25 Oct.	(*NYE*) Houghton, Mifflin to Scribners: decline Scribners offer (of 19 Oct.) to take over publication of *NYE*; 'we do not ourselves care to go into such an enterprise'. Want to co-operate (Princeton TS).
28 Oct.	(*EH*) *English Hours* pub. in Boston by Houghton, Mifflin.
31 Oct.	(*NYE*) Scribners tell Pinker of problem with Houghton, Mifflin (see Pinker to Scribners, 9 Nov. 1905, Princeton TS).
3 Nov.	(*NYE* & *AS* & L) HJ to niece: has spent time writing *The American Scene*, revising for the *NYE*, and in last weeks doing reading about London to assuage nerves about delay of London book (*LHJ* ii. 36–7).
7 Nov.	(*AS*) HJ to Munro: sends 'Boston' for *North American Review* (Yale TS). HJ to Pinker: plans for second volume of American impressions (Yale TS).
9 Nov.	(*NYE*) Pinker to Scribners: is reluctant to disappoint HJ (Princeton TS).
10 Nov.	(*NYE*) Pinker writes to Houghton, Mifflin (see 24 Nov.).
23 Nov.	(*NYE*) George H. Mifflin to Charles Scribner: is delighted at frank letter; 'our suggestions (hardly intended for you as "conditions")' were reasonable but can be adjusted; will only keep plates for three years (Princeton MS).
24 Nov.	(*NYE*) George H. Mifflin to Pinker (replying to letter of 10 Nov.): had misunderstood situation; 'we did not intend to name any conditions, but we made rather suggestions'. Relations with HJ and Scribners too valuable and of too long standing to allow rigidness (Princeton TS).
24 Nov.	(*NYE*) Scribners to Pinker: problems are being solved (see 6 Dec. 1905).
24 Nov.	(*AS*) HJ to Duneka: sends 'The Bowery and Thereabouts' and 'Salem and Concord' [later 'Concord and Salem'] for *Harper's Magazine*; has done 'The Sense of Newport', but keeps it back (Yale TS).

25 Nov. 1905	(*NYE*) George H. Mifflin to Charles Scribner: encloses draft agreement for *NYE*; to keep plates only for three years (Yale TS & MS).
Dec.	(*AS*) 'New York and the Hudson: A Spring Impression' pub. in *North American Review*.
5 Dec.	(*AS*) HJ to Pinker: just sending 'Philadelphia' to Munro for *North American Review*; may call second volume *The Sense of the West*; Harper's delays in serialization hold up book publication (Yale TS).
6 Dec.	(*NYE*) Pinker to Scribners (replying to letter of 24 Nov.): pleased to hear news about Houghton, Mifflin agreement. Will make no agreement with an English publisher yet; one will probably take sheets or plates from Scribners (Princeton TS).
21 Dec.	(*AS*) HJ to Duneka: sends 'The Sense of Newport' for *Harper's Magazine* (Yale TS).
30 Dec.	(*NYE*) Herbert S. Stone (Publishers, Chicago) to Scribners: about to sell his list; claims Pinker is wrong and that he still possesses *What Maisie Knew* and *In the Cage* (Princeton TS).

1906

Jan.	(*AS*) 'New York: Social Notes. I' pub. in *North American Review*.
8 Jan.	(*NYE*) HJ to Pinker: 'I am sending you instantly those revision-riddled pages of The American' (Yale TS).
9 Jan.	(*AS*) HJ to Munro: sends 'Washington' for *North American Review* (Yale TS).
Feb.	(*AS*) 'New York: Social Notes. II' pub. in *North American Review*.
Feb.–Mar.; May	(*AS*) 'New York Revisited' pub. in *Harper's Magazine*.
7 Feb.	(*NYE*) Pinker to Scribner: returns draft contract for *NYE*; 'In a few days I shall send the first volume revised, as Mr. James has practically completed it' (Princeton TS).
19 Feb.	(*NYE*) Pinker to Scribners: hopes to send 'corrected copy for the first volume very shortly, as Mr. James tells me that it is nearly ready' (Princeton TS).
Mar.	(*AS*) 'Boston' pub. in *North American Review*.
8 Mar.	(*NYE*) Pinker to Scribners: sends revised copy of *Roderick Hudson*, pp. 1–161. Constable will write about English publication of *NYE*. Please to send back original copy with proofs (Princeton TS).
9 Mar.	(*NYE & AS*) HJ to Pinker: 'I thank you for the packet

of transferred revisions of *The American*—carefully &
excellently done & a great help & blessing to me.' Sends
tonight end of revised copy of *Roderick Hudson*; 'I am
pleased to gather (now that I see the retouches of the
American clearly exhibited) that they are required on a
smaller scale than those of R.H. & therefore will take less
time to do. If you send R.H. now to New York I will
follow it with its new Preface as soon as possible, but am
afraid I may, for nervousness' sake, have to do another
paper for Munro before I can write it' (Yale MS).

12 Mar. 1906	(*NYE*) Pinker to Scribner: sends balance of revised copy of *Roderick Hudson*; Preface 'shall follow as soon as Mr. James can get it to his satisfaction' (Princeton TS).
14 Mar.	(*NYE*) Constable to Scribners: ask for specimen pages and prices; 'The selling of these two editions is not going to be an easy matter here'; will only order 10 and 25 sets at a time (Princeton TS).
26 Mar.	(*NYE*) Pinker to Scribners: encloses copy of *NYE* contract signed by HJ. About Stone's claim, the English publishers say 'he quite understood that there was a time limit on the rights, and it is curious that he can produce no contract' (Princeton TS).
Apr.	(*AS*) 'Philadelphia' pub. in *North American Review*.
5 Apr.	(*NYE*) Houghton, Mifflin to Scribners: now enclose draft agreement for *NYE* (Princeton TS).
7 Apr.	(*NYE & AS*) HJ to Pinker: disconcerted yet not deeply surprised to hear of compositors' difficulty with revised copy of *Roderick Hudson*; Pinker to write 'asking that the Copy be sent back to be typed & revised *here*, & please say that they shall receive it in as perfect form as that of the Golden Bowl' [on 27 Mar. 1906 Scribners have suggested—'and indeed it seems to us as if this were the only solution of the difficulty—that typewritten "copy" be furnished us' (Yale TS)]. Has 'a very good Typist whom I have employed for 20 years ... She does difficult things' [HJ to Pinker, 30 Apr. 1906, gives address: 'Miss Gregory|6 Lithos Road|South Hampstead|N.W.' (Yale MS)]. Expects to make *The Portrait of a Lady* first in series. Has a 'Baltimore' ready to send Courtney [of the English *Fortnightly Review*]; and only awaits a clean copy of 'Richmond' to send Munro for *North American Review* (Yale MS).
9 Apr.	(*NYE*) Pinker to Scribner: has received their letter about

compositors' difficulties with revised copy of *Roderick Hudson*; HJ wants copy back to be typewritten and revised, 'so that you may receive a copy in as perfect a form as that of "The Golden Bowl". Mr. James will follow this system all through' (Princeton TS).

27 Apr. 1906   (*NYE*) Scribners to HJ: enclose specimen page and memorandum about number of words in each novel—six of them divided into two volumes; thus 'the total number of volumes will be 23. This is in excess of what was proposed and we think it will be better not to consider at present the including of THE BOSTONIANS.' Retyping the copy of *Roderick Hudson* too much trouble; but hope 'future volumes will not be so difficult in this respect' (Princeton TS).

May–June   (*AS*) 'Washington' pub. in *North American Review*.

9 May   (*NYE*) HJ to Scribners: regrets *Roderick Hudson* copy not sent back; 'I shall send you the *American* completely re-typed ... And I shall send you *The Portrait of a Lady* with all the worst pages (I mean the most amended ones) re-copied.' Will send *The Portrait of a Lady* before *The American,* and plans for it to appear second. Is on point of returning to Lamb House after three months of London—'whence I shall very quickly send you the Preface of *R.H.*—sending that of the *Portrait* with the copy'. Likes specimen page; happy with 23 volumes for *NYE*. About volumes of Tales; 'should you consider 150,000 for these volumes excessive?'; is prepared to come down to 120,000 or even 100,000 words. Relieved to postpone question of *The Bostonians* for the present. Was photographed the other day by Alvin Langdon Coburn (Princeton MS; also in *HJL* iv. 402–4).

12 May   (*NYE*) HJ to Scribners: wants to see *Roderick Hudson* proof—'for the full security of the text. This will not be to *work over* the latter in any degree ... but to ensure that absolutely supreme impeccability that such an Edition must have & that the Author's eye alone can finally contribute to ... I beg the compositors to *adhere irremovably* to my punctuation and *never* to insert death-dealing commas' (Princeton MS).

12 May   (*NYE*) HJ to Pinker: 'You will see that they are *not* returning Copy of *Roderick Hudson* to be typed here, but setting up straight from my amended pages. I shall send them the *American* all already typed (it is being done), &

The Portrait of a Lady with the most intricate pages about (half the whole perhaps), [*sic*] typed; & the latter will reach them first' (Yale MS).

22 May 1906   (L) HJ to Violet Hunt: London book not to be written for an eternity (Harvard: Lubbock TS transcript).

1 June   (*NYE*) Scribners to HJ: will do as he asked on 12 May. Question of illustrations. 'We should, we confess, regard 150,000 words for each of these volumes [of short novels and tales] as an excessive maximum, and should be inclined to adopt your suggestion of 120,000 as the limit which it would not be well to exceed.' Trust such necessities 'will not compel the rejection of material which if you desired to include it in an ideal edition, you could hardly desire more earnestly than ourselves' (Princeton TS).

8 June   (*NYE*) Scribners to HJ: send proofs pp. 1–84 of *Roderick Hudson*; printers now setting at rate of over 200 pages per week (Princeton TS).

10 June   (*NYE*) HJ to Pinker: has had 'to have a great deal more of the revised *Portrait* typed than I expected (to spare their compositors) & that & the whole thing, the close nature of the work, have taken time. I shall have hugely *improved* the book—& I mean not only for myself, but for the public: this is beyond question ... The revised *American* all typed [*sic*], is proceeding *pari passu*—& I want to repeat for them (the Scribners), that once these first 3 difficult books are cleared away there will be no obstacle at all to the going very fast of the rest of the business' (Yale MS).

12 June   (*NYE*) HJ to Scribners: assents to 120,000 word limit on volumes of 'Shorter Fictions'—with a few qualms. Finds question of illustrations 'formidable'; wants photographs rather than drawings. Revision has proved 'slower (as well as really more beneficent) work than I fondly dreamed ... it will be *all* in type that you will receive the revised American'. After first three volumes it will be faster and easier (Princeton TS; also in *HJL* iv. 407–8).

12 June   (*NYE*) HJ to Pinker: 'I have engaged to keep down the 8 vols of the shorter fictions to 120,000 words. This will necessitate marked and invidious omissions, but it is inevitable' (Yale TS).

14 June   (*NYE*) HJ to Pinker: relieved at idea of handing over illustrations to Scribners—happy to make suggestions. 'I only recoil in terror from undertaking *too much*' (Yale TS; also in *HJL* iv. 409–10, wrongly called 'MS').

15 June 1906   (NYE) Pinker to Scribners: sends pp. 1–312 of revised copy of *The Portrait of a Lady*. 'The revision of *The American* is proceeding'; it is being 'typed as it leaves Mr. James' hands'. Charles Scribner when in London was anxious about revision, 'lest Mr. James should so transform his early books that those who had known and delighted in them for years should feel disappointed with the new edition, owing to loss of freshness'. But HJ declares 'that he has greatly improved the books, not only for himself but for the public' (Princeton TS).

25 June   (NYE & AS) [but note discrepancy with Pinker to Scribners, 15 June 1906] HJ to Pinker: 'I sent you on Saturday the rather ponderous packet of 300 revised pages of *The Portrait of a Lady*' to be sent to Scribners. 'I am doing as fast as I can the rest of the book & also doing Scribners' now almost complete proofs of *Roderick Hudson*.' Sent the other day 'Charleston' to Munro for *North American Review* (Yale MS).

27 June   (NYE) HJ to Pinker: 'I have returned one vol. of corrected proof of R.H. to the Scribners—but they send a special statement that they desire the revised *Copy* also back with the proof. So I am embarrassed to give it to you. What I *can* do will be to give you with pleasure as a curiosity of literature (at least of *my* literature), the revised Copy of the *American,* which is to be *all* typed for transmission to N.Y.; so that I shall preserve the original revised sheets & let you have them' (Yale MS).

27 June   (S & M) HJ to Elizabeth Jordan: agreeing to do *Speech and Manners of American Women,* as many 3,000-word papers as she wants, for *Harper's Bazar* (*Bazar Letters*).

28 June   (NYE) HJ to Scribners: sends back 'the greater part of the proofs of Roderick Hudson yet received'. Doesn't want the copy sent back. Apologizes for state of copy; 'I revised the text, prepared the copy, for this book in very embarrassing & contracted conditions of space, often— & that has led to my having still to make a few more retouches &c on these proofs than I expected. But the case will be different for the next two books, practically all *typed* (or almost all), first, *from* my muddled copy. The greater part of *The P. of a L.* has already gone to you' [presumably James's 'embarrassing & contracted conditions of space' were those on the pasted-up pages of *Roderick Hudson*, which may have had insufficient

margins, not the working conditions in Lamb House]
(Harvard MS).

3 July 1906   (*NYE*) Coburn visits Lamb House to photograph it and
HJ.

13 July   (*NYE*) Pinker to Scribner: encloses Coburn portrait of
HJ, a view of London for *The Princess Casamassima,* and
four views of Lamb House. HJ is keen Coburn should
do as much for *NYE* as possible, for example a Paris
photograph for *The American*. Pinker will look after
Coburn's interest (Princeton TS).

17 July   (S & M) HJ to Elizabeth Jordan: sends first 'Speech' paper
(*Bazar Letters*).

20 July   (S & M) HJ to Elizabeth Jordan: sends second 'Speech'
paper; third will follow a day or two later (*Bazar Letters*).

27 July   (S & M) HJ to Elizabeth Jordan: sends fourth and last
'Speech' paper (*Bazar Letters*).

31 July   (*NYE* & T) HJ to Pinker: 'I send you today all the End
of the Revised Copy of *The Portrait of a Lady* to send to
New York, if you will kindly do so'; suggests [wrongly]
it be sent directly to Riverside Press. 'Some few months
ago' Duneka asked a tale of him for *Harper's Magazine*
(Yale MS).

Aug.   (*AS*) 'The Sense of Newport' pub. in *Harper's Magazine*.

Aug.   (*AS*) 'Baltimore' pub. in *North American Review*.

1 Aug.   (*NYE*) Pinker to Scribner: sends balance of revised copy
of *The Portrait of a Lady* (Princeton TS).

17 Aug.   (*NYE*) HJ to Scribner: returns last batch of corrected
Portrait proof and sends copy for the Prefaces to *Portrait*
and *Roderick Hudson*. 'I find them very interesting to do,
and promise you good ones for all the other books ... a
certain inevitable delay in getting off to you Copy for
"The American" shall now imminently cease' (Princeton
TS).

28 Aug.   (*NYE*) Scribners to HJ: cannot refrain from expressing
'absolute delight' with Prefaces. Had hoped to issue first
four volumes this autumn; still just possible. Worry about
having illustrations for these volumes in time (Princeton
TS).

28 Aug.   (T) HJ to Duneka: sends 'The Second House' for *Harper's
Magazine* (Yale TS).

1 Sept.   (*AS* & T) HJ to Pinker: 'Florida' not yet finished; waiting
till second Harper fiction finished ('Julia Bride') (Yale
TS).

7 Sept. 1906   (*NYE*) HJ to Pinker: Scribner's letter 'brings to a point
                    ... the rather important question of date', complicated
                    by question of illustrations. Assenting 'with a pang' to
                    'the postponement of publication (of the first Book) till
                    the nearest possible moment *after* the autumn: which
                    would mean, I suppose, a couple of months, at the soonest,
                    after Christmas'. Sees the advantages in delay. Busy
                    summer has impeded 'my adequate revision of the rest of
                    The American; my evenings, on which I mainly depend for
                    attention to this, have gone to pieces, and I am regrettably
                    backward. However, I should be able to make this up
                    (with regard to the American) in a very short time—by
                    taking a precious fortnight of mornings, in other words
                    of *all-days,* to the job, if it didn't seem that the accursed
                    picture business must still, for the start, be allowed more
                    of a margin' (Yale TS).

12 Sept.   (*NYE*) HJ to Pinker: Pinker's letter decides HJ to write
                    to Scribners postponing 'to (about) February ... I can
                    promise them several things all ready and in hand by that
                    time—five or six revised Books, with Prefaces, plates and
                    everything' (Yale TS).

14 Sept.   (*NYE*) HJ to Scribners: has with regret to delay beginning
                    of publication 'to the earliest possible date after the New
                    Year'. Hopes Feb. 1907 will not be too early. Has been
                    this summer subject to much interruption. Promises 'four
                    or five additional Books, finished as to revision, with their
                    Prefaces and plate-subjects, for your definite Start ... You
                    shall now positively receive The American at the very
                    earliest date' (Princeton TS).

14 Sept.   (T) HJ to Duneka: sends for *Harper's Magazine* 'Julia
                    Bride', which 'ought to knock "Daisy Miller" into a
                    cocked hat'. It is as long as the tale before [4 Oct. HJ to
                    Pinker, both stories 'so remarkably rejected' (Yale TS);
                    15 Oct. HJ to Pinker, has changed title of first ['The
                    Second House' to 'The Jolly Corner'] (Yale TS)] (Yale TS).

27 Sept.   (*AS & NYE*) HJ to Pinker: 'Florida' (last paper) ready to
                    send off to Munro for *North American Review*; 'had on
                    Tuesday a really successful couple of hours with Coburn
                    in St. John's Wood' [Coburn: 'It was a lovely afternoon,
                    I remember, and H.J. was in his most festive mood' (*Alvin
                    Langdon Coburn: Photographer*, p. 58)]; plate made for
                    one volume of *The Tragic Muse*. Coburn 'is to do me the

picture for the other within a week or two in Paris'
[Coburn makes six illustrations for *NYE* during Paris visit
in early October (*Alvin Langdon Coburn: Photographer*,
p. 52)] (Yale TS).

16 Oct. 1906   (*WF*) HJ to Elizabeth Jordan: is considering contributing
               to *The Whole Family* (*Bazar Letters*).

31 Oct.   (S & M) HJ to Elizabeth Jordan: sends first 'Manners'
               paper (*Bazar Letters*).

Nov.   (*AS*) 'Richmond, Virginia' pub. in *Fortnightly Review*
               (London).

Nov.–Dec.   (S & M) 'The Speech of American Women' pub. in *Har-*
Jan.–Feb. 1907 *per's Bazar.*

16 Nov.   (NYE) Pinker to Scribners: sends today revised copy of
               vol. i of *The American* (Princeton TS).

18 Nov.   (*NYE*) HJ to Pinker: forgot to write 'a word to accompany
               the 1st vol. of *The American* sent you to be transmitted
               to the Scribners, three days back' (Yale MS).

27 Nov.   (*WF* & S & M) HJ to Elizabeth Jordan: will contribute
               to *The Whole Family* as 'The Married Son' when he
               receives Edith Wyatt's Chapter VII; sends second 'Man-
               ners' paper (*Bazar Letters*).

30 Nov.   (S & M) HJ to Elizabeth Jordan: sends third 'Manners'
               paper (*Bazar Letters*).

Dec.   (NYE) Coburn making plates in Rome and Venice.

17 Dec.   (NYE) HJ to Pinker: Hueffer says Pinker knows '(in
               Norfolk St?) an excellent & trustworthy type-copyist';
               HJ's typist has lately become too ill, '& I have my remain-
               der of the *revised "American"* on my hands. I am having
               it *all* typed over—as I had had the 1st Half, which you
               sometime since kindly forwarded for me to the Scribners,
               & if you can have it—I mean this rest—competently
               & properly done for me (& my marginally revised &
               interpolated sheets require care), I shall be extremely
               obliged to you.' Sends third quarter of the whole; 'there
               remain a little more than a 100 pages more to follow, &
               which will now follow very soon ... Of course I shall like
               the *copy* of all this back—& you are welcome to *keep* the
               original (revised sheets) as a monument of my deviltry.'
               He will retrieve first half from unwell typist (Yale MS).

18 Dec.   (S & M) HJ to Elizabeth Jordan: sends fourth and last
               'Manners' paper (*Bazar Letters*).

1907

2 Jan.   (*WF*) HJ to Elizabeth Jordan: will go ahead with 'The Married Son' disregarding Edith Wyatt's feeble Chapter VII (*Bazar Letters*).

11 Jan.   (*WF*) HJ to Elizabeth Jordan: is in *The Whole Family* 'up to my neck' (*Bazar Letters*).

25 Jan.   (*WF*) HJ to Elizabeth Jordan: 'The Married Son' goes by this mail for *Harper's Bazar* (*Bazar Letters*).

30 Jan.   (*AS*) *The American Scene* pub. in London by Chapman and Hall.

c. 5–13 Feb.   (*NYE*) HJ to Pinker (from Reform Club): has been in town 'for some days' [since 2 Feb.]; has 'hoped each day to be able to bring you the whole of Vol. II of the Revised *American* to send for me to the Scribners ... But I have only *just* (this hour) been able to bestow on the at last achieved clear type-copy (the whole book so done) the last rectifying touch.' Brings it 'tomorrow, Thursday' (Yale MS).

7 Feb.   (*AS*) *The American Scene* pub. in New York by Harper's.

14 Feb.   (*NYE*) Pinker to Scribners: sends second half of *The American*; the Preface to follow 'in a few days' (Princeton TS).

15 Feb.   (*NYE*) HJ to Scribners (from Lamb House): 'The whole of the Second Half of the minutely-revised "American", (in complete type-copy) is forwarded you this week ... & I am to-day mailing you the Preface to accompany it. Please pardon my long delay—which must have been discouraging to you—over *The American*; it has all been the fruit of the intrinsic difficulty of happy & right & *intimate* revision—which defied considerations of time: the process has had to be so extremely deliberate ... I shall quickly send you the Princess C., the Tragic Muse & the Awkward Age.' Coburn goes to New York 'a week hence' with *all* the illustrations, save one or two to be taken in the US (Princeton MS).

24 Feb.   (*NYE & OH*) HJ to Pinker: about 'Nelson's proposal to bring out some early fiction of mine at sevenpence'; there is little left out of 'the Scribner–Constable edition'; would want to revise any work, and has not the time. 'The one thing I *can* think of is "The Other House", which I don't put into the N.Y., & yet *should* be willing, decidedly, to present afresh. (I have been looking it over).' But there would be complications with 'the fell Heinemann'. Going

to Paris about 5 March, will come back to matter on return (Yale MS).

26 Feb. 1907   (NYE) Scribners to Pinker: vol. ii of revised copy of *The American* and the Preface received and forwarded to printers (Princeton TS).

Mar.   (Temp.) HJ Introduction to *The Tempest* pub. in the US.

5 Mar.   (NYE) HJ to Pinker (from Lamb House): about to leave for Paris tomorrow or Thursday. 'I am just sending the Scribners copy for the 1st half of the revised Princess Casamassima. The Revision goes much faster now' (Yale MS).

5 Mar.   (AS & S & M) HJ to Elizabeth Jordan: would like to amplify her proposed book of *The Speech and Manners of American Women* with further Western sketches; but not till he gets back from the Continent (*Bazar Letters*).

6 Mar.   HJ to Pinker: goes abroad 'an hour or two from this' (Yale MS).

19 Mar.   (NYE) HJ to Scribners (from Paris): sends pp. 1–304 revised copy of *The Princess Casamassima* (Princeton MS).

Apr.–July   (S & M) 'The Manners of American Women' pub. in *Harper's Bazar*.

23 Apr.   (NYE) HJ to Scribners (from Paris): acknowledges error in *Portrait* revisions, pointed out in letter of 9 Apr.; and returns proof of *The American,* pp. 49–419. 'All the rest follows 2 days hence' (Princeton MS).

3 May   (NYE) HJ to Scribners (from Paris): returns corrected proof of *The Princess Casamassima*, pp. 1–122 (Princeton MS).

3 May   (AS & S & M) HJ to Elizabeth Jordan (from Paris): she has told him sketches must be addressed to women; and he *will* try ... (*Bazar Letters*; also *HJL* iv. 445–7).

10 May   (NYE) HJ to Scribners (from Paris): sends revised copy of *The Princess Casamassima*, pp. 304–402 (Princeton MS).

16 May   (NYE) HJ to Scribners (from Turin): sends revised copy of *The Princess Casamassima*, pp. 403–544. Will send the rest 'in three or four days, from Rome' (Princeton MS).

22 May   (NYE) HJ to Scribners (from Rome): sends last pages of revised copy of *The Princess Casamassima* (Princeton MS).

23 June   (NYE) HJ to Scribners (from Venice): soon to leave for England. 'From the 1st days of next month I shall be back at Lamb House Rye for a long time to come, & then

everything will be *really* (this time!) more prompt & swift' (Princeton MS).

26 June 1907 (*NYE*) HJ to Scribners (from Venice): thanks for pointing out errors of date in the revised *American*; has sorted them out in the accompanying revise (Princeton MS).

10 July (*NYE*) HJ to Scribners (from Lamb House): sends vol. i of revised copy of *The Tragic Muse*, pp. 1–408 (Princeton MS).

6 Aug. (*NYE*) HJ to Scribners: sends final quarter of revised copy for *The Tragic Muse*; 'the second half of Vol. II—from p. 691 to Finis'. Sent preceding quarter, '1st half of Vol. II—some fortnight, or a little more, ago' (Princeton MS).

22 Aug. (*NYE*) HJ to Scribners: is 'greatly pleased' with front matter for the *NYE*—'all except *Stories,* to which I should prefer *Tales*' (Princeton MS).

22, 23, 24 Aug. (L) HJ makes notes on the spot for London book (*Nks.,* pp. 273–7).

28 Aug. (*NYE*) HJ to Scribners: sends Preface to *The Princess Casamassima* and first half of revised copy of *The Awkward Age*; 'I shall now immediately send you, with the second half of the latter, the Prefaces for this book & for "The Tragic Muse"' (Princeton MS).

6 Sept. (*NYE*) Scribners to HJ: 'We are experimenting with some kind of a small decorative cartouche for the page.' Printers write 'apropos of your note regarding commas', guaranteeing fidelity to copy (Princeton TS).

8 Sept. (*NYE & N*) HJ to Pinker: 'I have looked up the copy of *The American* for you, & it's quite at your disposal'; but part is missing [which Pinker already has, HJ hears next day (Yale MS)]. Harvey has apologized for Harper's rudeness over *The American Scene* &c.; HJ *will* do novel for them (Yale MS).

9 Sept. (*NYE*) HJ to Scribners: sends second half of revised copy of *The Awkward Age* (Princeton MS).

5 Oct. (*NYE*) HJ to Scribners: sends 'about a third of the copy for Vol. X' of NYE: pp. 1–144 of *The Spoils of Poynton,* 'there being 286 pages ... in all'. When done by copyist Preface to *The Tragic Muse* goes to them (Princeton MS).

7 Oct. (*NYE*) HJ to Scribners: sends 'Second Half of revised Copy for *The Spoils of Poynton*—making two thirds, about', of vol. x (Princeton MS).

8 Oct. (L) HJ makes notes on the spot for London book (*Nks.,* pp. 277–8).

9 Oct. 1907	(*HB*) HJ asks Elizabeth Robins for copy of *Summersoft* (play prototype of *Covering End*) back for conversion into *The High Bid* (*The Complete Plays*, p. 549).
14 Oct.	(*HB*) HJ to Pinker: is charmed at idea of doing *The High Bid* for Sir Johnston Forbes-Robertson (Yale MS).
15 Oct.	(*NYE*) HJ to Scribners: 'I now, settled here for the winter, am ready to go so straight & so steadily, that I am quite yearning for proofs of the rest of *The Tragic Muse*' (Princeton MS).
16 Oct.	(*NYE*) HJ to Scribners: sends Preface to *The Tragic Muse* (Princeton MS).
23 Oct.	(*HB*) HJ starts dictating *The High Bid* (*The Complete Plays*, p. 549).
24 Oct.	(*HB*) HJ to Pinker: is doing Forbes-Robertson job 'with immense & valuable improvements! It's very interesting!' (Yale MS).
25 Oct.	(*NYE*) HJ to Scribners: sends Preface to *The Awkward Age* (Princeton MS).
Nov.	(Temp.) HJ Introduction to *The Tempest* pub. in England.
12 Nov.	(*NYE*) HJ to Scribners: sends revised copy of *A London Life* and *The Chaperon*, completing vol. x. 'The Preface for this volume will go in a week or two' (Princeton MS).
14 Nov.	(*Chap.*) HJ abandons work on scenario for play of *The Chaperon* in favour of *The Saloon* (*The Complete Plays*, p. 641).
1 Dec.	(*Sal.*) HJ starts by dictating sketch for *The Saloon* [based on *Owen Wingrave*], then works on it by hand in evenings (*The Complete Plays*, p. 641).
12 Dec.	(*NYE*) HJ to Scribners: sends Preface to *The Spoils of Poynton* volume (Princeton MS).
14 Dec.	(*NYE*) Scribners publish first two volumes of NYE, *Roderick Hudson* and *The American*.
17 Dec.	(*NYE*) Scribners to HJ: 'we take pleasure in sending you by book post, with our compliments, one copy of the first and second volumes of the new edition of your Novels and Tales, the publication of which we are beginning this month' [volumes also sent to Pinker on same day, with quotation of prices of sheets for English publishers (Princeton TS)] (Princeton TS).
22 Dec.	(*Sal.*) HJ starts dictating *The Saloon* from his MS (*The Complete Plays*, p. 641).
31 Dec.	(*NYE*) HJ to Scribners: 'I am delighted with the appear-

ance, beauty and dignity of the Book—am in short almost ridiculously proud of it'; is [mis]led by their [erroneous] Prospectus into thinking later long novels 'publishable directly after The Awkward Age'. Will send Preface and text of *What Maisie Knew* volume [xi] 'because I have them all but ready'; then will go on to revise *The Wings of the Dove* and its two successors. Asks for copies of their two-volume editions of *The Wings of the Dove* and *The Golden Bowl*—'the one-volume English edition is in each case much less convenient for revision' (Princeton TS; also *HJL* iv. 484–5).

31 Dec. 1907   (*NYE*) HJ to Pinker: 'I rejoice that you are in as punctual possession as I am of the two beautiful volumes (for beautiful I hold them to be), in which I quite agree with you that we may take pleasure & pride. They are in every way felicitous, they do every one concerned all honour, & the enterprise has now only to march majestically on. I have but to glance over the books to feel, I rejoice to say, how I have been a thousand times right to revise & retouch them exactly in the manner & in the degree in which I proposed to myself to do it.' Wonders when Constable will take action on *NYE*. 'P.S. I don't think I've said with half due emphasis how much the 2 purple volumes make me value all that ingenious effort & patience & temper of yours, 3 years ago &c., without which they would be so far, at this hour, from reposing gloriously on on [*sic*] our tables!' (Yale MS)

1908

Jan.   (*Sal.*) HJ shows *The Saloon* to Granville-Barker (*The Complete Plays*, p. 642).

2 Jan.   (HB) HJ to Edith Wharton: has just finished *The High Bid* (*HJL* iv. 485–7).

3 Jan.   (*NYE*) HJ to Scribners: wants his 5 complimentary copies sent to: (1) WJ; (2) Mrs Wharton; (3) Howells; (4) Kipling; (5) Bourget (Princeton TS).

18 Jan.   (*NYE*) HJ to Scribner: sends revised copy of *What Maisie Knew*. 'The other two stories (for same volume) [*In the Cage* and *The Pupil*] are ready; but I think it better to keep them over to the next mail; when I will despatch them with the Preface' (Princeton MS).

22 Jan.   (*NYE*) HJ to Scribners: sends revised copy of *In the Cage* and *The Pupil*; and Preface for that volume [xi]. Will soon

have revised copy of *The Wings of the Dove* ready; 'The Preface to "The Wings of the Dove" has already gone to the copyist.' Please cancel despatch of *NYE* to HJ [one of his sets], Howells, and Mrs Wharton; send instead to Owen Wister, Mrs Cadwalader Jones, and Miss Evelyn Smalley (Princeton MS).

27 Jan. 1908 (*NYE*) HJ to Scribners: sends first volume of revised copy of *The Wings of the Dove*. Has received today first volumes of 'the dazzling special series of the Edition— splendid & monumental & of which I am very proud' (Princeton MS).

29 Jan. (*NYE*) Scribners to HJ: glad he likes volumes; have sent their editions of *The Wings of the Dove* and *The Golden Bowl* as requested; on the question of order, 'we must confess with chagrin to an error on the last page of the circular for which we can hardly account'; hope he will return to the original order, and that the *NYE* order will be as chronological as possible (Princeton TS).

30 Jan. (*NYE*) HJ to Scribners: sends Preface to *The Wings of the Dove*; second volume of revised copy of *The Wings of the Dove* 'goes a few days hence' (Princeton MS).

31 Jan. (*NYE*) HJ to Scribners: sends 'Revised Copy of the first Half of the Second Volume of *The Wings of the Dove*' (Princeton MS).

12 Feb. (*NYE*) HJ to Scribners (from the Athenaeum): has theirs of 29 Jan.—will revert to original order and next send revised copy for third volume of group of Shorter Novels and Tales. Is in London 'a few days, but return to the country tomorrow & will then as quickly as possible despatch you The Aspern Papers and the 3 things that go with it' (Princeton MS).

19–20 Feb. (*HB*) HJ makes more revisions in *The High Bid* (*The Complete Plays*, p. 550).

26 Feb. (*NYE*) HJ to Scribners (from Lamb House): sends remainder of revised copy ('The Liar' and 'The Two Faces') for vol. xii, 'the bulk of which I despatched to you three days ago in the form of two registered packets containing respectively "The Aspern Papers" and "The Turn of the Screw" ... the whole making up almost exactly 150,000 words' [a mistaken sum: on 20 July HJ sees 'with anguish that I might well have made the latter Volume a little more substantial—by the addition of two or three short things that I should have been glad to get into it'

(Princeton TS)]. Gives proposed list of volume contents [See '*Friction with the Market*', pp. 156–60]. 'Let me also note here that the composition of each of these Volumes of different pieces has been very difficult to arrive at neatly and right; since I have had as much as possible to take account of precedence by *length,* of congruity of subject and tone, that is of classification, and also in a general way of chronology, ... and yet make, above all, these combinations of things square and fit with the appointed number of words (for each volume)' (Princeton TS).

27–8 Feb. 1908   (*NYE*) John Murray to Scribners: 'We should not want to take more than 25 sets to start with—I hope that we may sell more than this, but as we are not very confident, we do not want to risk more than this' (Princeton MS).

28 Feb.   (*NYE*) Scribners to HJ: Mrs Wharton *is* expecting to receive presentation copies of the *NYE* as they come out (Princeton TS).

Mar.–Apr.   (T) 'Julia Bride' pub. in *Harper's Magazine*.

10 Mar.   (*NYE*) HJ to Scribners: specifies details of inscriptions on spines (Princeton TS).

13 Mar.   (*NYE*) HJ to Scribners: sends Preface to *The Aspern Papers* volume [xii]; also revised copy of 'first volume of original London issue' of *The Reverberator*, which begins vol. xiii (Princeton MS).

18 Mar.   (*NYE*) HJ to Scribner (from Reform Club): sends second half of revised copy of *The Reverberator*; but keeps back Preface to the volume 'as I find it will require some rewriting of last few pages in consequence of a table of contents altered as to its last item (or 2 items)'. Volume now to terminate with 'The Author of "Beltraffio"' and 'Louisa Pallant' (Princeton MS).

18 Mar.   (*NYE*) HJ to Theodora Bosanquet (from Reform Club): asks her to look out 'Louisa Pallant' in green room and send it to 'Midland Hotel | Manchester' (Harvard MS).

21 Mar.   (*HB*) HJ joins company at Manchester for final rehearsals (*The Complete Plays*, p. 550).

24 Mar.   (*NYE*) Scribners to Pinker: 'We were disappointed at the smallness of Mr. Murray's order' and therefore have to decline: 'we have incurred a very heavy expense in the preparation of this edition' (Berg TS).

26 Mar.   (*HB*) First night of *The High Bid* at Edinburgh; HJ present (*The Complete Plays*, p. 550).

5 Apr.   (N & L) HJ to Macmillan (from Lamb House): has to

finish *NYE* and a contracted-for novel before he can do London book (*Letters to Macmillan*, pp. 172–3).

6 Apr. 1908   (*HB*) HJ to EG: has hopes that London performances of 'comedy-rot' [*The High Bid*] will yield 'sordid coin' (*HJ to Edmund Gosse*, pp. 236–7).

16 Apr.   (*Sal.*) HJ tries to improve *The Saloon* by amplifying it; but it is not wanted by Forbes-Robertson and is laid aside (*The Complete Plays*, p. 642).

23 Apr.   (*NYE*) HJ to Scribners: sends 'Madame de Mauves' and the greater part of 'A Passionate Pilgrim' for vol. xiii. 'The second half of the latter, with "The Madonna of the Future" & "Louisa Pallant" immediately follow.' Preface to vol. xiii also goes today (Princeton MS).

24 Apr.   (*NYE*) Scribners to HJ: have been anxiously awaiting Preface to vol. xiii and remaining text of it—announced by HJ on 18 Mar. as forthcoming. Remind HJ that last quarter of revised copy of *The Wings of the Dove* (from vol. ii, p. 205) still not sent (Princeton TS).

May   (*V & R*) *Views and Reviews* by HJ, collected and introduced by Le Roy Phillips, pub. in Boston by The Ball Publishing Company.

20 May   (*NYE*) HJ to Scribners (from Reform Club): posts the greater part of revised copy for 'Lady Barbarina' for vol. xiv, also Preface to this volume; the whole of the rest will go 'within the next few days'. Has, safe, the last portion of revised copy of *The Wings of the Dove*, which will follow. 'You shall be subjected to *no* further delay or inconvenience whatever' [they have recently had a delay in setting up] (Princeton MS).

23 May   (*NYE*) HJ to Scribners (from Lamb House): posts further revised copy for vol. xiv (Princeton MS).

27 May   (*NYE*) HJ to Scribners: posts further copy for vol. xiv, '*Madame de Mauves*—the end of which goes to you by the next post' [but cf. 23 Apr.] (Princeton MS).

June   (*WF*) HJ's chapter of *The Whole Family*, 'The Married Son', pub. in *Harper's Bazar*.

5 June   (*NYE*) Scribners to HJ: last received is further revised copy of *The Siege of London*; right to think 'The Author of "Beltraffio"' left out of vol. xiii? [HJ telegram, no date: 'Beltraffio different volume' (Princeton MS)] (Princeton TS).

6 June   (*NYE*) HJ to Scribners (from Reform Club): posts further revised copy for vol. xiv (Princeton MS).

12 June 1908	(*NYE*) HJ to Pinker (from Stratford-upon-Avon): is glad Macmillans 'express themselves so favourably to the idea of undertaking the London issue of the Edition' (Yale MS).
20 June	(*NYE*) HJ to Scribners (from Lamb House): 'The Author of "Beltraffio"' better in vol. xv; detail about copyright on stories. Posts as on 17 June further copy for vol. xiv, which begins with 'Lady Barbarina' (Princeton MS).
23 June	(*NYE*) Scribners to Pinker: glad to hear Macmillan agreed to buy 100 sets (Princeton TS).
26 June	(*NYE*) HJ to Scribners: mails (as on 24 June) further revised copy of 'The Pension Beaurepas' for vol. xiv (Princeton MS).
July	(*OH*) HJ picks up *The Other House* again to turn it into a play (the form he had originally intended for it) (*The Complete Plays,* p. 678).
10 July	(*NYE*) HJ to Scribners: mails 'the whole Revised Copy of "The Point of View", which terminates Vol. Fourteenth' [must by now have sent revised copy of 'An International Episode' and 'A Bundle of Letters'] (Princeton MS).
14 July	(*NYE*) HJ to Scribners: sends pp. 1–46 of revised copy of 'The Lesson of the Master' for vol. xv (Princeton MS).
15 July	(*NYE*) HJ to Pinker: encloses his reply to Heinemann about English rights &c.; Heinemann has 'definitely named the sum by which he is to the bad. What I want to do is to make up that sum to him, as from myself, in the shortest and quickest way—and then have done with him, so far as possible, for ever!' Also returns signed Macmillans agreement (Yale TS).
17 July	(*NYE*) HJ to Scribners: sends pages from 47 to end of revised copy of 'The Lesson of the Master' and the whole of 'The Death of the Lion' for vol. xv (Princeton MS).
20 July	(*NYE*) HJ to Scribners: sends the whole of revised copy of 'The Next Time' and 'The Figure in the Carpet' and 'the greater part of "The Coxon Fund"' [this crossed out: but see 24 July (Princeton MS)]. Would like 'Miss Gunton of Poughkeepsie' and 'Fordham Castle' at the end of already-long vol. xiv [letter later in the day wants 'Miss Gunton of Poughkeepsie' and '"Europe"' instead (Princeton MS)]. 'My inevitable exclusions and omissions, from the whole array, are already costing me some few pangs' (Princeton TS).
24 July	(*NYE*) HJ to Scribners: mails today 'the remainder (end) of

"The Coxon Fund"—the earlier part of which went to you the other day in the same envelope as "The Next Time"—& also nearly the first half of "The Author of 'Beltraffio' " ' (Princeton MS).

28 July 1908   (*NYE*) HJ to Scribners: mails conclusion of 'The Author of "Beltraffio" ' for vol. xv (Princeton MS).

30 July   (*NYE*) Scribners to HJ: answering his letters of 20 July and deciding to exclude extra stories on grounds of economy and symmetry between volumes (Princeton TS).

4 Aug.   (*NYE*) HJ to Scribners: mails whole of rest of vol. xv— 'a batch of revised copy that begins with "The Middle Years" and ends with "The Great Good Place" ' [*if* still list of 14 July, then this is 'The Middle Years', 'Greville Fane', 'Broken Wings', 'The Abasement of the North-mores' and 'The Great Good Place'; but some doubt; see Scribners to HJ, 2 Dec. 1908 (Princeton TS)]. Also mails today Preface to vol. xv (Princeton TS).

6 Aug.   (*NYE*) HJ to Scribners: wants to put 'Brooksmith' in vol. xvii—but first page of it is also last page sent as copy for 'The Pupil'; would like it back if they keep copy (Princeton TS).

11 Aug.   (*NYE*) HJ to Scribners: 'cheerfully resigned' to theirs of 30 July. Mails the greater part of revised copy of vol. xvi; they will already have 'The Altar of the Dead', 'The Beast in the Jungle', and 'The Birthplace'; is now sending 'The Private Life', 'Owen Wingrave', and 'The Friends of the Friends' [HJ in some confusion here about batches]. 'There will be thus still to go to you immediately "Sir Edmund Orme", "The Real Right Thing", "The Jolly Corner", "Four Meetings" and "Mrs. Medwin".' Keeps back Preface to the volume (Princeton TS).

14 Aug.   (*NYE*) HJ to Scribners: sends for vol. xvi revised copy of 'Sir Edmund Orme', 'The Jolly Corner', 'The Real Right Thing', and Preface to volume. This leaves 'Four Meetings' and 'Mrs. Medwin', which 'now immediately follow' (Princeton TS).

17 Aug.   (*NYE*) Scribners to HJ: have no Preface for vol. xiv; wanting last page of revised copy of 'The Great Good Place'; can supply first page of 'Brooksmith' because all copy is being kept (Princeton TS).

17 Aug.   (*NYE & IH*) HJ to Howells: much about Prefaces, omissions, and revisions; is to do titivations for *Italian Hours* (for money) 'on a meagre understanding with Houghton

and Mifflin, re-attenuated by the involvement of Pennell' [illustrator] (Harvard: Lubbock TS transcript; also *LHJ* ii. 98–104, which omits the quoted matter).

25 Aug. 1908   (*NYE*) HJ to Scribners: encloses last page of 'The Great Good Place'. May have misnumbered Preface to vol. xiv. Mails rest of revised copy for vol. xvi—'Four Meetings' and 'Mrs. Medwin'. The Preface went 'a few days ago'. PS 'on second thoughts' keeps over 'Four Meetings' and 'Mrs. Medwin' to next steamer (Princeton TS).

1 Sept.   (*NYE*) HJ to Scribners: glad they have Preface to 'The Lesson of the Master' volume. Sends 'Four Meetings' and 'Mrs. Medwin' (Princeton TS).

3–5 Sept.   (*OH*) HJ dictates new scenario from *The Other House* volume; then works on it for rest of month (*The Complete Plays*, p. 678).

15 Sept.   (*HB*) HJ to Pinker: upset by Forbes-Robertson's '(practical) perfidy' about producing *The High Bid*; HJ had built on the prospect of money from London performances of the play in Sept. and Oct. (Yale MS).

16 Sept.   (*NYE*) Pinker to Scribners: HJ's work on *NYE* 'means that I have received practically nothing for him for the last twelve months, and if I could pay something into his account I should like very much to do it ... Mr. James does not know I am writing to you as he is sensitive on these matters' (Princeton TS).

16 Sept.   (*OH*) HJ to Pinker: is doing good work for a magnificent four-act play (Yale MS).

25 Sept.   (*NYE*) HJ to Scribners: sends 'Complete Copy for "Daisy Miller", the first item in Volume Seventeenth'; and the Preface to the same volume. Worried about length of Preface (Princeton TS).

Oct.   (*WF*) Book of *The Whole Family* pub. by Harper's.

6 Oct.   (*NYE*) Scribners to Pinker: 'I wish very much that the sale of the New York Edition of Mr. James's books justified a substantial remittance.' Payment made to Macmillan for use of books exceeds credit due to author (Princeton TS).

9 Oct.   (*NYE*) Scribners to HJ: Preface length not excessive. Printers have not had proof back of vol. xiv, pp. 520–41, or vol. xv, pp. 22–5 (Princeton TS).

10 Oct.   (*NYE*) HJ to Scribners: mails for vol. xvii revised copy of 'The Marriages'. Sent earlier in week 'Pandora' and 'The Patagonia' for same volume (Princeton TS).

13 Oct. 1908	(*NYE*) HJ to Scribners: mails further revised copy for vol. xvii—'The Real Thing' and 'Brooksmith' (Princeton MS).
16 Oct.	(*NYE*) HJ to Scribner: mails further revised copy for vol. xvii—'Flickerbridge', 'The Beldonald Holbein', 'The Story in It', and 'Paste'. Whole of remainder of volume goes by next mail (Princeton MS).
20 Oct.	(*NYE*) HJ to Pinker: 'I return you the Scribner's documents—which have knocked me rather flat—a greater disappointment than I have been prepared for; & after my long & devoted labour a great, I confess, & a bitter grief. I hadn't built *high* hopes—had done everything to keep them down; but feel as if comparatively I have been living in a fool's paradise. Is there *anything* for me at all?' (Yale MS)
23 Oct.	(*NYE*) HJ to Pinker: has picked himself up considerably since Tuesday morning, 'the hour of the shock'. 'In the absence of special warning, I found myself concluding in the sense of some probable fair return.' Hoped for compensation after the 'so disconcerting failure to get anything from the Forbes-Robertsons'. Keen to get back to 'out-&-out "creative" work' (Yale MS; also *HJL* iv. 497–9).
23 Oct.	(*NYE*) HJ to Scribners: mails two last items of revised copy for vol. xvii—'Julia Bride' and 'Fordham Castle'. '"Europe"' and 'Miss Gunton of Poughkeepsie' also go by this post (Princeton MS).
27 Oct.	(*NYE*) HJ to Scribners: mails remainder of revised copy of *The Wings of the Dove*. Revised copy of the whole of *The Ambassadors* and Preface to same will follow 'a very few days hence'. Wants edition sent to Howells after all, at HJ's own expense (Princeton TS).
6 Nov.	(N) Harper's to Pinker: glad to hear HJ hoping to have contracted-for American novel ready by June 1909 (Berg TS).
Dec.	(T) 'The Jolly Corner' pub. in Hueffer's *The English Review*.
2 Dec.	(*NYE*) Scribners to HJ: 'serious complication'; 'the volumes of tales reach proportions destructive of almost all expectation of profitable publication'; there is a need for an additional volume, 'the set thus numbering twenty-four instead of the determined twenty-three'. Sending copy in instalments disguised quantities. 'The value, interest and importance of the present grouping' are

appreciated. Propose that vol. xv be kept down to first five items, and the others put in a new vol. xvi, making 274 pages; making in all, with 200 pages from the present vol. xvii, a volume of about 470 pages; 'Daisy Miller' thus leads the new vol. xviii. Hope Prefaces can be adjusted (Princeton TS).

3 Dec. 1908   (T) HJ to Pinker: H. M. Alden of Harper's has lately written to ask for a tale in 5,000 words (Yale MS).

4 Dec.   (T) HJ to Pinker: sends 'The Top of the Tree' (later 'The Velvet Glove') maybe for Hueffer's *The English Review*; hopes within a week to have 'the small abomination' ready for Alden (Yale TS; also in *HJL* iv. 504–5, wrongly called 'MS').

14–15 Dec.   (*NYE*) HJ to Scribners: the complication is 'a good deal of a shock; but I brace myself powerfully'. Assents to most of their proposals. 'The mechanical can now be our only law.' To get Coburn, now in New York, to do a 'Julia Bride' illustration for the extra volume. Feels at last 'rather completely *spent*!' Will do what is possible 'in respect to the two or three compromised Prefaces'. [Next day]. Encloses new Tables of Contents for vol. xvi, xvii, and xviii (Princeton TS).

1909

Jan.   (CEN) 'An American Art-Scholar: Charles Eliot Norton' pub. in *Burlington Magazine*.

3 Jan.   (T) HJ to Pinker: has been 'trying to produce 5000 words of fiction—detestable number!', and has 'one consequent thing of *10,000* finished, another of about 8,000 almost finished & two others started which, or one of which, *will* be a true 5000' (Yale MS).

5 Jan.   (*NYE*) HJ to Scribners: mails rearranged Prefaces; 'the majestic coherency, so to speak, of these introductions, has not a little, I fear, lost itself'. Sends revised copy for Books IX and X of *The Ambassadors*, and also Preface to it. 'Books One to Seven you will some time since have received' (Princeton TS).

5 Jan.   (T) HJ to Pinker: sending today to Alden one of the longer things mentioned, 'of about 12,000 words', intended to be 'a (very American) thing he will like' [probably 'Crapy Cornelia'] (Yale TS).

12 Jan.   (*NYE*) Scribners to HJ: thanks for much-appreciated letter of 14 Dec. 'We have followed your rearrangement

implicitly.' Coburn illustration for 'Julia Bride' already made and sent to HJ for caption. When they receive reordered Prefaces they will print the books (Princeton TS).

17 Jan. 1909   (*Sal.*) G. B. Shaw to HJ: writes refusing *The Saloon* on behalf of the Incorporated Stage Society, to whom it had been submitted at the instigation of St John Hankin late in 1908 (*The Complete Plays*, p. 642).

18 Jan.   (*NYE*) Scribners to HJ: have Books One to Ten of *The Ambassadors* and Preface to it. Want to put 'Daisy Miller' at head of its volume (xviii), so return Preface for final adjustment (Princeton TS).

19 Jan.   (*T*) HJ to Pinker: has been 'rather sharply unwell'; has done '3 masterpieces "for" Alden' (Yale MS).

22 Jan.   (*NYE*) HJ to Scribners: they will by now have the redone Prefaces; perhaps not perfect—'but at any rate let matters stand as they are, please, in spite of any such small irregularity' (Princeton TS).

26 Jan.   (*NYE*) HJ to Scribners: mails pp. 1–292 of vol. i of revised copy of *The Golden Bowl* (Princeton MS card).

1 Feb.   (*NYE*) Scribners to HJ: his letter of 22 Jan. received with the last of the revised copy of *The Ambassadors*. They have divided book into two volumes at end of Book Six (Princeton TS).

2 Feb.   (*NYE*) HJ to Scribners: sends back Preface adjusted for moving 'Julia Bride' to new volume [xvii instead of xviii]. 'This seems to exhaust the rectifications' (Princeton TS).

18 Feb.   (*HB*) First of several matinées of *The High Bid* at His Majesty's Theatre; not paired, as HJ had hoped, with *The Saloon* (*The Complete Plays*, p. 552); on 10 Mar. HJ thanks Pinker for £56 4s. 4d. received from Forbes-Robertson (Yale MS).

26 Feb.   (*NYE*) HJ to Scribners: mails the complete conclusion (pp. 293–412) of vol. i of revised copy of *The Golden Bowl* (Princeton MS).

Mar.   (*T*) 'The Velvet Glove' pub. in *The English Review*.

1 Mar.   (*NYE*) HJ to Scribners: mails pp. 1–126 of revised copy of vol. ii of *The Golden Bowl* (Princeton MS).

7 Mar.   (*NYE*) HJ to Scribners: mails all remaining revised copy for *The Golden Bowl* except the last 72 pages (Princeton MS card).

8 Mar.   (*NYE*) HJ to Scribners: mails 'my last instalment—for the Edition—of revised copy—that for the end of The Golden

	Bowl'. Preface kept back; 'It has been written these many weeks, but I am making an alteration in it' (Princeton MS card).
12 Mar. 1909	(N) HJ to Pinker: in his interest 'to produce a "short novel" of 70 or 80 thousand words as immediately as possible'; has 'a very excellent American subject' (Yale MS).
16 Mar.	(*NYE*) Scribners to Pinker: £9 0s. 0d. is the balance due to HJ on the *NYE* (Princeton TS).
17 Mar.	(*NYE*) HJ to Pinker: is a little surprised at Nelsons' choice of *The American*; will give them the revised text but not the Preface—and 'they won't *want* it' (Yale MS).
19 Mar.	(T) HJ to Pinker: has previously sent 'The Bench of Desolation' to him and another tale to be forwarded to Harper's [probably 'A Round of Visits'; see 13 May 1909 (Yale MS)]; suggests 'The Bench of Desolation' for *Putnam's Magazine* in three parts (Yale MS).
28 Mar.	(*NYE*) HJ to Pinker: returns signed agreement with the Nelsons (Yale MS).
1 Apr.	(*NYE*) HJ to Pinker: thanks for his cheque for £7 14s. 2d.—the first Scribners remittance on *NYE*, minus commission. 'This first instalment of a "serialization" on that exhausting enterprise is very agreeable—as a sign of a probable More—to yours, in his destitution, very truly|Henry James' (Yale MS).
13 Apr.	(T & FMC) HJ to Pinker: posts with this 'Mora Montravers' for Hueffer's *The English Review*; and proposes also for Hueffer an article on his old friend F. Marion Crawford (Yale MS).
18 Apr.	HJ to Pinker: 'I have been rather tiresomely unwell for three or four—or five—days, & partly in bed'; menace of jaundice, but passing (Yale MS).
27 Apr.	(FMC) HJ to Pinker: can't do article on Crawford's novels; had forgotten the 'systematic cheapness of—well, of everything' (Yale TS).
3 May	(*IH*) HJ to Howells: has been putting together, 'under the name of "Italian Hours", various old scraps from the faraway Atlantic and Nation of our prime (but all previously re-printed) and re-touching and re-titivating them as much as possible; in fact, not a little re-writing them, with expansions and additions to trick the book out further' (Harvard MS).
13 May	(T) HJ to Pinker: Alden has taken 'Crapy Cornelia', but

	'shuffled out of taking' the other tale offered ['A Round of Visits'] (Yale MS).
14 May 1909	(*NYE*) HJ to Scribners (telegram): 'Still wanting pages 178 to 193 proof second golden bowl' (Princeton MS).
19 May	(*NYE*) HJ to Pinker: sends 'my very brilliant friend's article on an Unworthy Subject', W. Morton Fullerton on HJ; to be placed by Pinker—with Hueffer's *English Review* if possible (Yale MS).
June	(*OH*) HJ begins to convert scenario of *The Other House* into a play for Herbert Trench repertory season at the Haymarket (*The Complete Plays*, p. 679).
22 June	(*NYE*) HJ to Scribners (from Reform Club): their cable has had him get corrected but unsent proof of *The Golden Bowl* Preface looked out and sent off from Lamb House; blames his 'wretched absent-mindedness (which alas *grows*!)' (Princeton MS).
26 June	(*OH*) HJ to Pinker: gets £90 from Trench for work on *The Other House* (Yale MS).
18 July	(L) HJ to WJ: coming to point of doing London book; hopes for high sales to tourists; but the theatre knocks (Harvard MS).
19 July	(*OH & Out.*) HJ to Lucy Clifford: making painful cuts in *The Other House* [Trench's repertory collapses in due course before play produced]; difficulty of *The Outcry* fascinates (*LHJ* ii. 129–31).
21 July	(T) HJ to Pinker: problems with placing tales such that 'clearly I have written the last short story of my life' (Yale MS).
29 July	(ITALAD?) HJ to Elizabeth Jordan: is posting her overdue article, 'Is There a Life after Death?' for *Harper's Bazar* symposium; was difficult to do, and HJ has taken 'exquisite pains'; is longer than was agreed (*Bazar Letters*).
31 July	(*NYE*) Scribners publish last two volumes of *NYE* (*The Golden Bowl*) in New York.
Aug.–Sept.	(T) 'Mora Montravers' pub. in *The English Review*.
17 Aug.	(*Out.*) HJ to Pinker: 'deep in my theatrical jobs—deeper & more interested, & really with more horizon, I think, than ever in anything!' (Yale MS).
21 Sept.	(L) HJ makes notes on the spot for London book (*Nks.*, p. 278).
23 Sept.	(T) *Julia Bride* pub. as separate volume in New York by Harper's.
Oct.	(T) 'Crapy Cornelia' pub. in *Harper's Magazine*.

Oct.–Dec. 1909	(T) 'The Bench of Desolation' pub. in *Putnam's Magazine*.
1 Oct.	(L) HJ makes notes on the spot for London book (*Nks.*, pp. 279–80).
4 Oct.	(*NYE*) Scribners to Pinker: $596. 71 due to HJ on *NYE* in Dec. (Princeton TS).
14 Oct.	(*NYE & Out.*) HJ to Pinker: 'I am delighted at last with your news of something substantial from the Scribners & rejoice to know, at once, that I may count on it for December, even though that means more waiting—in a year of such long waitings.' Is working on *The Outcry*, 'very ardent and interested'; slow work is necessary for *rightness* [16 Oct. to Granville-Barker: will need more weeks (*The Complete Plays*, p. 763)] (Yale MS).
28 Oct.	(*IH*) *Italian Hours* pub. in London by Heinemann.
14 Nov.	(*TP*) HJ to Elizabeth Jordan: will *try* to write article for series on 'The Turning Point of my Life' [produces only a fragment] (*Bazar Letters*).
20 Nov.	(*IH*) *Italian Hours* pub. in Boston by Houghton, Mifflin.
Dec.	(*Out.*) HJ stays at Reform Club, sending great batches of MS back to Lamb House for typing by Theodora Bosanquet (*The Complete Plays*, p. 763).
17 Dec.	(*Out.*) HJ completes the play (*The Complete Plays*, p. 763).
1910	
Jan.–Feb.	(ITALAD?) 'Is There a Life after Death?' pub. in *Harper's Bazar*.
12 Jan.	(*Out.*) HJ revises Act I of play; but is ill (*The Complete Plays*, p. 763).
16 Jan.	(N) HJ to Pinker: the ill-health to which Duneka alludes 'refers to my explanation to him of *why* last winter, my "Edition" at last done, I didn't tackle the job of a serial for them on the basis we had some time previously settled. I had a troublesome, though superficial, heart-ailment, which has wholly subsided, & it made me nervous and anxious about undertaking a *long winded* thing' (Yale MS).
2 Feb.	(*TP*) HJ to Pinker: has been ill, and is 'but a lame duck yet'. Has not yet written *Bazar* paper (Yale MS).
10 Feb.	(ITALAD?) 'Is There a Life after Death?' pub. by Harper's in *In After Days*.
11 Feb.	HJ to Pinker: has had 'another beastly little *drop* or collapse, of convalescence' (Yale MS).

22 Feb. 1910	HJ to Pinker: 'I am very sorry to say that I have had a bad set-back again' (Yale MS).
Apr.–May	(T) 'A Round of Visits' pub. in *The English Review*.
24 Apr.	(*Out.*) HJ to Pinker: getting better slowly, and WJ and wife are with him; is too ill to consider coming up to London for rehearsals; regrets 'my long illness & almost heart-breaking interruption of work' (Yale MS).
6 May	(*Out.*) Death of Edward VII closes theatres and prevents production; HJ paid a forfeit of £200 by Frohman (*The Complete Plays*, p. 765). In next year converts *The Outcry* into a novel [25 Oct. 1911 HJ to Edith Wharton comments on how well novel is doing (*HJL* iv. 587–8)].
3 June	(*NYE*) Scribners to Pinker: send £127. 4s. 2d. for HJ on the *NYE* as rendered 1 Feb. (Princeton TS).
9 July	HJ to Pinker (from Geneva): returning to England with WJ, who is only the worse for 'the drastic Nauheim'; and then back to US with him on 12 Aug. (Yale MS).
26 Aug.	Death of WJ at Chocorua NH; HJ present.
23 Sept.	(*NYE*) Scribners to Pinker: $432. 78 due to HJ on *NYE* [paid 2 Dec.: £89. 0s. 7d. (Princeton TS)].
6 Oct.	(T) *The Finer Grain* pub. in New York by Scribners.
13 Oct.	(T) *The Finer Grain* pub. in London by Methuen.
15 Nov.	(*Sal.*) HJ posts *The Saloon* to Pinker; Gertrude Kingston produces it [badly] on 17 Jan. 1911 (*The Complete Plays*, pp. 647–9).
1912	
8 Jan.	(*NYE*) HJ to Miss Beatrix Chapman: 'There are gradually to be a few more volumes of the Edition, and then the "Papers" will come, and three or four—or perhaps half a dozen—other postponed things; that you have missed which is a great encouragement to yours very truly	Henry James' (Harvard: Lubbock TS transcript).

Bibliography

What follows is in the case of James a list only of works referred to in this book, and in other cases a list only of works with a special bearing on the book's subject.

1. WORKS BY HENRY JAMES

I give these works as far as possible in chronological order of publication. For ease of use I have attached to each its number in Leon Edel and Dan H. Laurence, *A Bibliography of Henry James* (The Soho Bibliographies, viii), 3rd edn., revised with the assistance of James Rambeau, Oxford, 1982.

Transatlantic Sketches, Boston, 1875 (A2a).

Roderick Hudson, Boston, 1876 (A3a); 3 vols., London, 1879 (A3b); 2 vols., London, 1883 (A20 vols. 4 and 5).

The American, Boston, 1877 (A4a); 2 vols., London, 1883 (A20 vols. 6 and 7).

Daisy Miller: A Study, An International Episode, Four Meetings, 2 vols., London, 1879 (A8b); *Daisy Miller: A Study, Four Meetings, Longstaff's Marriage, Benvolio*, London, 1883 (A20 vol. 13).

Confidence, 2 vols., London, 1880 (A11a).

Washington Square, The Pension Beaurepas, A Bundle of Letters, 2 vols., London, 1881 (A15b).

The Portrait of a Lady, 3 vols., London, 1881 (A16a); 1 vol., London, 1882 (A16c).

The Siege of London; Madame de Mauves, London, 1883 (A20 vol. 11).

Portraits of Places, London, 1883 (A21a).

Stories Revived, 3 vols., London, 1885 (A27a).

The Bostonians, 3 vols., London, 1886 (A28a).

The Princess Casamassima, 3 vols., London, 1886 (A29a).

The Reverberator, 2 vols., London, 1888 (A31a).

The Aspern Papers, Louisa Pallant, The Modern Warning, 2 vols., London, 1888 (A32a).

A London Life, The Patagonia, The Liar, Mrs. Temperley, 2 vols., London, 1889 (A33a).

The Tragic Muse, 3 vols., London, 1890 (A34b).

Alphonse Daudet, *Port Tarascon: The Last Adventures of the Illustrious Tartarin*, trans. Henry James, New York, 1891 (B6).

The Lesson of the Master, The Marriages, The Pupil, Brooksmith, The Solution, Sir Edmund Orme, London, 1892 (A36b).

Terminations, London, 1895 (A45a).

Embarrassments, London, 1896 (A46a).

The Spoils of Poynton, London, 1897 (A48a).

What Maisie Knew, London, 1897 (A49a).

The Two Magics: The Turn of the Screw, Covering End, London, 1898 (A52a).

The Awkward Age, London, 1899 (A53a).

The Soft Side, London, 1900 (A54a).

The Sacred Fount, London, 1901 (A55b).

The Wings of the Dove, London, 1902 (A56b).

The Better Sort, London, 1903 (A57a).

The Ambassadors, London, 1903 (A58a).

William Wetmore Story and His Friends, 2 vols., London, 1903 (A59a).

The Golden Bowl, London, 1905 (A60b).

The Question of Our Speech, The Lesson of Balzac: Two Lectures, Boston, 1905 (A61a).

English Hours, Boston, 1905 (A62a).

The American Scene, London, 1907 (A63a).

The New York Edition of the Novels and Tales of Henry James, 24 vols., New York and London, 1907–9 (A64a and A64c).

The Whole Family: A Novel by Twelve Authors (William Dean Howells, Mary E. Wilkins Freeman, Mary Heaton Vorse, Mary Stewart Cutting, Elizabeth Jordan, John Kendrick Bangs, Henry James, Elizabeth Stuart Phelps, Edith Wyatt, Mary R. Shipman Andrews, Alice Brown, Henry Van Dyke), New York, 1908 (B27a); repr. New York, 1986, introduced by Alfred Bendixen.

Italian Hours, London, 1909 (A67a).

A Small Boy and Others, London, 1913 (A71b).

Notes of a Son and Brother, London, 1914 (A72b).

Glasses, London, 1916 (A74a).

The Ivory Tower, London, 1917 (A77a).

The Sense of the Past, London, 1917 (A78a).

The Letters of Henry James, ed. Percy Lubbock, 2 vols., New York, 1920 (C4b).

Letters to A. C. Benson and Auguste Monod, ed. E. F. Benson, London, 1930 (C9).

Theatre and Friendship: Some Henry James Letters with a Commentary by Elizabeth Robins, New York, 1932 (C10b).

The Art of the Novel (collected Prefaces to the New York Edition), ed. R. P. Blackmur, New York, 1934 (A89a).

The Notebooks of Henry James, ed. F. O. Matthiessen and Kenneth B. Murdock, New York, 1947 (A92a).

The Scenic Art: Notes on Acting and the Drama 1872–1901, ed. Allan Wade, London, 1949 (A93b).

The Complete Plays of Henry James, ed. Leon Edel, London, 1949 (95b).

Virginia Harlow, *Thomas Sergeant Perry: A Biography, and letters to Perry from William, Henry and Garth Wilkinson James*, Durham, NC, 1950 (C69).

Selected Letters of Henry James, ed. Leon Edel, London, 1956 (C11b).

Autobiography: A Small Boy and Others, Notes of a Son and Brother, The Middle Years, ed. Frederick W. Dupee, New York, 1956.

The Painter's Eye: Notes and Essays on the Pictorial Arts, ed. John L. Sweeney, London, 1956 (A100a).

'Henry James and the *Bazar* Letters', ed. Leon Edel and Lyall H. Powers, in *Howells and James: a Double Billing* (repr. from the *Bulletin* of the New York Public Library), New York, 1958, pp. 27–55.

Parisian Sketches: Letters to the New York Tribune 1875–1876, ed. Leon Edel and Ilse Dusoir Lind, London, 1958 (A101b).

Letters to Macmillan, selected and edited by Simon Nowell-Smith, London, 1967.

The Tales of Henry James, ed. Maqbool Aziz, 3 vols. of projected 8, Oxford, 1973 to date (1973, 1978, 1984).

Henry James Letters, ed. Leon Edel, 4 vols., Cambridge, Mass., 1974–84 (1974, 1975, 1980, 1984) (C175).

'*The American*': the version of 1877 revised in autograph and typescript for the New York Edition of 1907, reproduced in facsimile from the original in the Houghton Library, Harvard University*, with an introduction by Rodney G. Dennis, London, 1976 (A106).

Henry James: Novels 1871–1880 (Library of America), ed. William T. Stafford, New York, 1983.

Henry James: Literary Criticism (Library of America), ed. Leon Edel and Mark Wilson, 2 vols., New York and Cambridge, 1984.

The Complete Notebooks of Henry James: the Authoritative and Definitive Edition, edited with introductions and notes by Leon Edel and Lyall H. Powers, New York and Oxford, 1987.

Selected Letters of Henry James to Edmund Gosse, 1882–1915: A Literary Friendship, ed. Rayburn S. Moore, Baton Rouge and London, 1988.

II. Other Works

ANESKO, MICHAEL, '*Friction with the Market': Henry James and the Profession of Authorship*, Oxford, 1986.

AZIZ, MAQBOOL, '"Four Meetings": A Caveat for James Critics', *Essays in Criticism*, 18/3 (July 1968), 258–74.

—— 'Revisiting "The Pension Beaurepas": The Tale and its Texts', *Essays in Criticism*, 23/3 (July 1973), 268–82.

BALZAC, HONORÉ DE, *Œuvres Complètes de Honoré de Balzac: La*

Comédie Humaine: Études Philosophiques, ii, texte révisé et annoté par Marcel Bouteron et Henri Longnon, Paris, 1925.

BANTA, MARTHA, *New Essays on 'The American'*, Cambridge, 1987.

BAZZANELLA, DOMINIC J., 'The Conclusion to "The Portrait of a Lady" Re-examined', *American Literature*, 41/1 (Mar. 1969), 53–63.

BELL, MILLICENT, *Edith Wharton and Henry James: The Story of their Friendship*, London, 1966.

BERCOVITCH, SACVAN, 'The Revision of Rowland Mallet', *Nineteenth Century Fiction*, 24/2 (Sept. 1969), 210–21.

BERRYMAN, JOHN, 'The World of Henry James' (1945), *The Freedom of the Poet*, New York, 1976, pp. 161–7.

BEWLEY, MARIUS, *The Complex Fate: Hawthorne, Henry James and Some Other American Writers*, New York, 1954.

BLACKMUR, R. P., *Studies in Henry James*, ed. Veronica A. Makowsky, New York, 1983.

BOOTH, WAYNE C., *The Rhetoric of Fiction*, Chicago, 1961.

BOSANQUET, THEODORA, *Henry James at Work* (The Hogarth Essays), London, 1924.

—— 'The Revised Version', *The Little Review*, 5 (Aug. 1918), 56–62.

BRADBURY, NICOLA, *An Annotated Critical Bibliography of Henry James*, Brighton, 1987.

—— *Henry James: The Later Novels*, Oxford, 1979.

BUITENHUIS, PETER, *The Grasping Imagination: The American Writings of Henry James*, Toronto, 1970.

CARGILL, OSCAR, '"The First International Novel"', *PMLA* 73 (Sept. 1958), 418–25.

CHATMAN, SEYMOUR, *The Later Style of Henry James* (Language and Style Series), Oxford, 1972.

COBURN, ALVIN LANGDON, *Alvin Langdon Coburn, Photographer: An Autobiography*, ed. Helmut and Alison Gernsheim, New York, 1966; Dover ed. New York, 1978.

DAUDET, ALPHONSE, *Port-Tarascon: Dernières Aventures de l'Illustre Tartarin*, Paris, 1890. .

DAVIE, DONALD, *The Language of Science and the Language of Literature, 1700–1740*, London, 1963.

DON VANN, J., (ed.), *Critics on Henry James: Readings in Literary Criticism*, Miami, 1972; London, 1974.

DRYDEN, JOHN, *Essays of John Dryden*, selected and edited by W. P. Ker, 2 vols., Oxford, 1926.

DUNBAR, VIOLA R., 'The Revision of "Daisy Miller"', *Modern Language Notes*, 65/5 (May 1950), 311–17.

—— 'A Source for "Roderick Hudson"', *Modern Language Notes*, 63/5 (May 1948), 303–10.

DUPEE, F. W., (ed.), *The Question of Henry James: A Collection of Critical Essays*, New York, 1945.

DURKIN, MARY BRIAN, 'Henry James's Revisions of the Style of "The Reverberator"', *American Literature*, 33/3 (Nov. 1961), 330–49.

EDEL, LEON, 'The Architecture of James's "New York Edition"', *New England Quarterly*, 24/2 (June 1951), 169–78.

—— *The Life of Henry James*, 5 vols., London, 1953, 1962, 1963, 1969, and 1972; revised ed. in 2 vols., Harmondsworth, 1977; further rewritten as *Henry James: A Life*, London, 1987.

—— and TINTNER, ADELINE (eds.), 'The Library of Henry James, From Inventory, Catalogues, and Library Lists', *The Henry James Review*, 4/3 (Spring 1983), 158–90.

ELIOT, T. S., 'Andrew Marvell', *Selected Essays*, London, 1951.

—— 'Donne in Our Time', in *A Garland for John Donne 1631–1931*, ed. Theodore Spencer, Cambridge, Mass., 1931, pp. 1–19.

—— 'From Poe to Valéry' (1948), *To Criticise the Critic and Other Writings*, London, 1965; repr. 1978, pp. 27–42.

—— 'Introduction', to Paul Valéry, *The Art of Poetry*, trans. Denise Folliot, New York, 1961, pp. vii–xxiv.

—— Review of *The Education of Henry Adams*, *Athenaeum*, 4647, 23 May 1919.

EMPSON, WILLIAM, *The Structure of Complex Words* (1951), 3rd edn., London, 1977.

FLOWER, DEAN, *Henry James in Northampton: Visions and Revisions*, Northampton, Mass., 1971.

FOWLER, VIRGINIA C., *Henry James's American Girl: The Embroidery on the Canvas*, Madison, 1984.

FREUD, SIGMUND, 'The Relation of the Poet to Day-Dreaming' (1908), *On Creativity and the Unconscious: Papers on the Psychology of Art, Literature, Love, Religion*, ed. Benjamin Nelson, New York, 1958, pp. 44–54.

GALE, ROBERT L., *The Caught Image: Figurative Language in the Fiction of Henry James*, Chapel Hill, 1964.

GARD, ROGER (ed.), *Henry James: The Critical Heritage*, London, 1968.

GARDNER, HELEN, *The Composition of 'Four Quartets'*, London, 1978.

GEGENHEIMER, ALBERT FRANK, 'Early and Late Revisions in Henry James's "A Passionate Pilgrim"', *American Literature*, 16/4 (Jan. 1945), 279–95.

GETTMAN, ROYAL A., 'Henry James's Revision of "The American"', *American Literature*, 16/4 (Jan. 1945), 279–95.

GOODE, JOHN (ed.), *The Air of Reality: New Essays on Henry James*, London, 1972.

GOODER, JEAN, 'Introduction', *Daisy Miller and Other Stories*, Oxford, 1985, pp. vii–xxviii.

GOODER, RICHARD, 'Introduction', *The Bostonians*, Oxford, 1984, pp. vii–xxxiii.

GRAHAM, KENNETH, *Henry James: The Drama of Fulfilment: An Approach to the Novels*, Oxford, 1975.

GREENE, JUDITH, *Thinking and Language*, London, 1975.

HABEGGER, ALFRED, *Henry James and the 'Woman Business'*, Cambridge, 1989.

—— 'Henry James's Rewriting of Minny Temple's Letters', *American Literature*, 4/2 (May 1986), 159–80.

HARVITT, HÉLÈNE, 'How Henry James Revised "Roderick Hudson": A Study in Style', *PMLA* 39 (1924), 203–27.

HAVENS, RAYMOND D., 'The Revision of "Roderick Hudson"', *PMLA* 40 (1925), 433–4.

HAWTHORNE, NATHANIEL, *The Blithedale Romance*, Centenary Edition, general editors William Charvat, Roy Harvey Pearce, Claude M. Simpson, 14 vols., Ohio, 1962–80: iii, 1964.

—— *The Marble Faun: Or, The Romance of Monte Beni*, Centenary Edition, 14 vols., Ohio, 1962–80, iv, 1968, ed. Claude M. Simpson and Fredson Bowers.

—— *Mosses from an Old Manse*, Centenary Edition, x, Ohio, 1974.

HAZLITT, WILLIAM, 'Whether Genius Is Conscious of Its Powers?' (1823), *The Complete Works of William Hazlitt*, ed. P. P. Howe after the edition of A. R. Waller and Arnold Glover, 21 vols., London, 1931, xii.

HEATH, STEPHEN, *The Sexual Fix*, London, 1982.

HERRICK, ROBERT, 'A Visit to Henry James', *Yale Review*, NS 12/4 (July 1923), 724–41; 13/1 (Oct. 1923), 206–8.

HIGGINS, CHARLES, 'Photographic Aperture: Coburn's Frontispieces to James's New York Edition', *American Literature*, 53/4 (Jan. 1982), 661–75.

HOCKS, RICHARD A., *Henry James and Pragmatistic Thought: A Study in the Relationship between the Philosophy of William and the Literary Art of Henry James*, Chapel Hill, 1974.

HOPKINS, VIOLA, 'Gloriani and the Tides of Taste', *Nineteenth Century Fiction*, 18/1 (June 1963), 65–71.

HORNE, PHILIP, 'Henry James and the Poetry of Association' (Le Bas Prize Essay, 1982), copy deposited in Cambridge University Library.

—— 'Independent Beauty', *Journal of American Studies*, 21/1 (1987), 87–93.

—— 'Introduction' and 'Variant Readings', *A London Life and The Reverberator*, Oxford, 1989, pp. vii–xxxiv, 369–90.

—— 'Relations will stop at nothing' (review-essay on *The Whole Family*), *London Review of Books*, 9/5 (5 Mar. 1987), 14–16.

—— 'Writing and Rewriting in Henry James', *Journal of American Studies*, 23/3 (Dec. 1989), 357–74.

W. D. Howells as Critic (The Routledge Critics Series), ed. Edwin H. Cady, London, 1973.

HUMPHRIES, S. M., 'Henry James's Revisions for "The Ambassadors"', *Notes and Queries*, NS 1 (Sept. 1954), 397–9.

JAMES, ALICE, *The Death and Letters of Alice James*, ed. Ruth Bernard Yeazell, Berkeley, 1981.

—— *The Diary of Alice James*, ed. Leon Edel, London, 1965.

JAMES, WILLIAM, *Human Immortality*, Boston, 1898.

—— *The Letters of William James*, edited by his son Henry James, 2 vols., London, 1920.

—— *The Varieties of Religious Experience: A Study in Human Nature* (1902), ed. Arthur Darby Nock, London, 1960.

—— *William James: A Selection from his Writings on Psychology*, ed. Margaret Knight, Harmondsworth, 1950.

JOYCE, JAMES, *Ulysses: the corrected text*, ed. Hans Walter Gabler with Wolfhard Steppe and Claus Melchior, New York, 1986.

KAPPELER, SUSANNE, *Writing and Reading in Henry James*, with a foreword by Tony Tanner, London, 1980.

KELLEY, CORNELIA PULSIFER, *The Early Development of Henry James*, Urbana, Ill., 1930; rev. ed., introduced by Lyon N. Richardson, Urbana, Ill., 1965.

KRAUSE, SYDNEY J., 'James's Revisions of the Style of "The Portrait of a Lady"', *American Literature*, 30/1 (Mar. 1958), 67–88.

LEAVIS, F. R., 'The Appreciation of Henry James' (review of F. O. Matthiessen, *Henry James: The Major Phase*), *Scrutiny*, 14/3 (Spring 1947), 229–37.

—— *The Great Tradition*, London, 1948.

—— 'Henry James's First Novel', *Scrutiny*, 14/3 (Spring 1947), 295–301.

LEITCH, THOMAS M., 'The Editor as Hero: Henry James and the New York Edition', *The Henry James Review* (Fall 1981), 24–32.

LEWIS, R. W. B., 'The Names of Action: Henry James in the Early 1870s', *Nineteenth Century Fiction*, 38/4 (Mar. 1984), 467–91.

—— *The Little Review* (Henry James Number), 5 (Aug. 1918).

LONG, ROBERT EMMET, *The Great Succession: Henry James and the Legacy of Hawthorne*, Pittsburgh, 1979.

McCOLGAN, KRISTIN PRUITT, *Henry James 1917–1959: A Reference Guide*, Boston, 1979.

MARVELL, ANDREW, *The Complete Poems*. ed. Elizabeth Story Donno, Harmondsworth, 1972.

MATTHIESSEN, F. O., *Henry James: The Major Phase*, Oxford, 1944.

—— *The James Family: A Group Biography*, New York, 1947; reissued New York, 1980.

MAZZELLA, ANTHONY J., 'The New Isabel', *The Portrait of a Lady* (Norton Critical Edition), ed. Robert D. Bamberg, New York, 1975, pp. 597–619.

MELCHIORI, GIORGIO, 'Locksley Hall Revisited: Tennyson and Henry James', *Review of English Literature*, 6 (Oct. 1965), 9–25.

MÉRIMÉE, PROSPER, 'La Vénus d'Ille' (1837), *Lokis et autres contes*, ed. George Faugeron, Paris, 1964.

MILTON, JOHN, *Paradise Lost* (1667), ed. Alastair Fowler, London, 1971.

MOORMAN, MARY, *William Wordsworth: A Biography: The Early Years 1770–1803*, Oxford, 1968.

—— *William Wordsworth: A Biography: The Later Years 1803–1850*, Oxford, 1968.

NEWBERRY, FREDERICK, 'A Note on the Horror in James's Revision of *Daisy Miller*', *The Henry James Review*, 3/3 (Spring 1982), 229–32.

NORRMAN, RALF, *The Insecure World of Henry James's Fiction: Intensity and Ambiguity*, London, 1982.

NOWELL-SMITH, SIMON (ed.), *The Legend of the Master*, London, 1947.

—— Editorial Note, *The Reverberator*, New York, 1957, pp. v–x.

OHMANN, CAROL, ' "Daisy Miller": A Study of Changing Intentions', *American Literature*, 36/1 (Mar. 1964), 1–11.

PARKER, HERSCHEL, 'Henry James "In the Wood": Sequence and Significances of his Literary Labors, 1905–1907', *Nineteenth Century Fiction*, 38/4 (Mar. 1984), 492–513.

POIRIER, RICHARD, *The Comic Sense of Henry James: A Study of the Early Novels*, London, 1960.

POOLE, ADRIAN, 'Introduction', 'Notes' and 'Variant Readings', *The Aspern Papers and Other Stories*, Oxford, 1983, pp. vii–xxiv, 197–204, 205–12.

POPE, ALEXANDER, *The Poems of Alexander Pope: a one-volume edition of the Twickenham text with selected annotations*, ed. John Butt, London, 1977.

—— *The Rape of the Lock*, ed. Geoffrey Tillotson, London, 1941; repr. 1981.

PUTT, S. GORLEY, *The Fiction of Henry James: A Reader's Guide*, London, 1966; repr. Harmondsworth, 1968.

REYNOLDS, LARRY J., 'Henry James's New Christopher Newman', *Studies in the Novel* (North Texas), 5/4 (Winter 1973), 457–68.

RICHARDS, BERNARD, 'Introduction' and 'Variant Readings', *The Spoils of Poynton*, Oxford, 1982, pp. vii–xxxiii, 193–201.

RICKS, BEATRICE, *Henry James: A Bibliography of Secondary Works* (The Scarecrow Author Bibliographies, No. 24), Metuchen, NJ, 1975.

RICKS, CHRISTOPHER, and SHANNON, EDGAR F., Jr., ' "The Charge of the Light Brigade": The Creation of a Poem', *Studies in Bibliography*, 38 (1985), 1–44.

RIDLEY, M. R., *Keats' Craftsmanship: A Study in Poetic Development*, Oxford, 1933; repr. London, 1965.

RIMMON, SHLOMITH, *The Concept of Ambiguity—the Example of James*, Chicago, 1977.

ROLLINS, HYDER EDWARD (ed.), *The Keats Circle: Letters and Papers and More Letters and Poems of the Keats Circle*, 2nd edn., 2 vols., Harvard, 1965.

SCHULZ, MAX F., 'The Bellegardes' Feud with Christopher Newman: A Study of Henry James's Revision of "The American"', *American Literature*, 27/1 (Mar. 1955), 42–55.

SCURA, DOROTHY McINNIS, *Henry James 1960–1974: A Reference Guide*, Boston, 1979.

SEGAL, ORA, *The Lucid Reflector: The Observer in Henry James's Fiction*, New Haven, 1969.

SELTZER, MARK, *Henry James and the Art of Power*, Ithaca and London, 1984.

SHANNON, EDGAR F., JR., and RICKS, CHRISTOPHER, '"The Charge of the Light Brigade": The Creation of a Poem', *Studies in Bibliography*, 38 (1985), 1–44.

SHELLEY, PERCY BYSSHE, *The Complete Poetical Works of Shelley*, edited with textual notes by Thomas Hutchinson, Oxford, 1904.

SHUMSKY, ALLISON, 'James Again: the New York Edition', *Sewanee Review*, 70/3 (Summer 1962), 522–5.

SNOW, LOTUS, '"The Prose and the Modesty of the Matter": James's Imagery for the Artist in "Roderick Hudson" and "The Tragic Muse"', *Modern Fiction Studies*, 12/1 (Spring 1966), 61–82.

STAFFORD, WILLIAM T., 'The Ending of James's "The American": A Defense of the Early Version', *Nineteenth Century Fiction*, 18/1 (June 1963), 86–9.

—— (ed.), *James's 'Daisy Miller': The Story, The Play, The Critics* (Scribner Research Anthologies), New York, 1963.

STEVENSON, ROBERT LOUIS, *Kidnapped*, London, 1886.

STROUSE, JEAN, *Alice James: A Biography*, Boston, 1980.

TANNER, TONY (ed.), *Henry James: Modern Judgements*, London, 1968.

—— *Henry James: The Writer and His Work*, Amherst, Mass., 1985.

—— 'Introduction', *Roderick Hudson*, Oxford, 1980, pp. ix–xxxviii.

—— *The Reign of Wonder: Naivety and Reality in American Literature*, Cambridge, 1965.

TARTELLA, VINCENT, 'James's "Four Meetings": Two Texts Compared', *Nineteenth Century Fiction*, 15/1 (June 1960), 17–28.

TENNYSON, ALFRED, LORD, *The Letters of Alfred Lord Tennyson*, ed. Cecil Y. Lang and Edgar F. Shannon, Jr., 2 vols. to date, Oxford, 1981, 1987.

—— *The Poems of Tennyson*, ed. Christopher Ricks, 3 vols., London, 1987.

TENNYSON, HALLAM, *Alfred Lord Tennyson: A Memoir*, 2 vols., London, 1897.

TILLEY, WESLEY H., *The Background of 'The Princess Casamassima'* (University of Florida Monographs, Humanities, No. 5), Gainesville, 1961.

TIMMS, DAVID, 'The Governess's Feelings and the Argument from Textual Revision of *The Turn of the Screw*', *Yearbook of English Studies*, 6 (1976), 194–201.

TINTNER, ADELINE, and EDEL, LEON (eds.), 'The Library of Henry James, From Inventory, Catalogues, and Library Lists', *The Henry James Review*, 4/3 (Spring 1983), 158–90.

TRASCHEN, ISADORE, 'An American in Paris', *American Literature*, 26/1 (Mar. 1954), 67–77.

—— 'Henry James and the Art of Revision', *Philological Quarterly* (Iowa City), 35/1 (Jan. 1956), 39–47.

—— 'James's Revisions of the Love Affair in "The American"', *New England Quarterly*, 29/1 (Mar. 1956), 43–62.

TURGENEV, IVAN S., *A Nest of Gentlefolk* (1859), trans. W. R. S. Ralston as *Liza*, 1869; introduced by Nikolay Andreyev, London, 1975.

—— *On the Eve* (1860), trans. Gilbert Gardiner, Harmondsworth, 1950.

VALÉRY, PAUL, 'Au Sujet du "Cimetière Marin"' (1933), *Variété*, iii, Paris, 1936, pp. 57–74.

—— 'Concerning "Le Cimetière Marin"', *The Art of Poetry*, trans. Denise Folliott, New York, 1961, pp. 140–52.

WARD, Mrs HUMPHRY, *A Writer's Recollections (1856–1900)*, London, 1919.

WATKINS, FLOYD C., 'Christopher Newman's Final Instinct', *Nineteenth Century Fiction*, 12/2 (Sept. 1957), 85–8.

WITTGENSTEIN, LUDWIG, *On Certainty*, ed. G. E. M. Anscombe and G. H. Von Wright, trans. D. Paul and G. E. M. Anscombe, Oxford, 1969.

WORDSWORTH, WILLIAM, *'Benjamin the Waggoner' by William Wordsworth*, ed. Paul F. Betz, Ithaca and Brighton, 1984.

—— *'Poems in Two Volumes', and Other Poems 1800–1807 by William Wordsworth*, ed. Jared Curtis, Ithaca, 1983.

—— *The Prelude: 1799, 1805, 1850: Authoritative Texts: Context and Reception: Recent Critical Essays* (Norton Critical Edition), ed. Jonathan Wordsworth, M. H. Abrams, Stephen Gill, New York, 1979.

—— *The Salisbury Plain Poems of William Wordsworth*, ed. Stephen Gill, Ithaca and Hassocks, 1975.

—— *William Wordsworth, Poems*, ed. John O. Hayden, 2 vols., Harmondsworth, 1977.

—— and COLERIDGE, S. T., *Lyrical Ballads*, ed. R. L. Brett and A. R. Jones, London, 1981.

YEAZELL, RUTH BERNARD, *Language and Knowledge in the Late Novels of Henry James*, Chicago, 1976.

Index